George J. (George John) Stevenson

The Methodist hymn-book and its associations

George J. (George John) Stevenson

The Methodist hymn-book and its associations

ISBN/EAN: 9783742840783

Manufactured in Europe, USA, Canada, Australia, Japa

Cover: Foto ©Thomas Meinert / pixelio.de

Manufactured and distributed by brebook publishing software
(www.brebook.com)

George J. (George John) Stevenson

The Methodist hymn-book and its associations

THE

METHODIST HYMN-BOOK

AND

ITS ASSOCIATIONS.

PRINTED BY BALLANTYNE AND COMPANY
EDINBURGH AND LONDON

THE

METHODIST HYMN-BOOK

AND

ITS ASSOCIATIONS.

BY

GEORGE J. STEVENSON.

WITH

*A CHRONOLOGICAL CATALOGUE OF THE POETICAL
WORKS OF JOHN AND CHARLES WESLEY.*

LONDON:

HAMILTON, ADAMS, & CO.

SOLD ALSO AT 66 PATERNOSTER ROW.

NEW YORK: PHILIP PHILLIPS.

1872.

PREFACE.

THE Founders of Methodism were well aware of the importance of hymns and psalms as aids to a religious life. John Wesley published a small volume for this purpose, before the first Society was formed; and during the year 1739 he published a much larger volume, containing selections from various authors, with many of his brother Charles's original hymns. This book reached a third edition the same year. The number of Charles Wesley's hymns, written and published up to about ten years before his death, was not less than six thousand. Nearly all these poetical tracts were in extensive demand, some of them were often reprinted, and large editions were sold both in England and Ireland.

From the very beginning of Methodism, these hymns have been made an abundant blessing to the thousands of readers into whose hands they have fallen, sometimes as helps to devotion for individual Christians, or in the service of song—at the out-door preaching as well as in the more social means of grace. They have been largely used in the work of conversion, in relieving daily toil, and especially in times of suffering, bereavement, and death. More than five hundred instances of their usefulness are recorded in this volume, and above twice that number of incidents could have been given if the plan of the work had permitted. In these the advantages of early devotion to the service of God, and of attachment to the Methodist class and prayer meetings, will be seen to be a marked feature. The Index will direct the reader to the pages of the *Methodist Magazine*, where fuller biographical details will be found respecting each person, and these may serve to illustrate another advantage arising from religion—the tendency which it has to prolong life, a large proportion of those whose names are there recorded having lived to threescore years and ten, while not a few have reached fourscore, and some have even passed through the whole course of a century.

From a conviction that the historical, biographical, and explanatory information which the work contains will be found useful, not only to Methodists, but to the religious public generally, and that the book will be especially welcome for Sunday reading, and as a suitable work for presentation, the author commends it to all lovers of Wesley's Hymns, in the hope that it may be deemed in some respects a not unworthy companion to those invaluable compositions.

The author acknowledges his obligations to the Rev. Elijah Hoole, D.D., the Rev. William Butters, and other friends, for contributions which have added considerably to the interest of the volume. To Mr David Creamer, of Baltimore, he cheerfully offers sincere thanks for permission to make extracts from his valuable "Hymnology," written to illustrate the American edition of Wesley's Hymns.

PREFACE TO THE SECOND EDITION.

THE kind reception which has been given to the first edition of this work, not only by Methodists and lovers of Wesley's Hymns, but by the religious public generally, demands and has a grateful acknowledgment from the author. He would especially record his appreciation of the universal welcome, and high commendation, given to his labours by the conductors of the religious press in England, Ireland, France, and Australia.

The author is desirous of finding incidents connected with those hymns which at present have no such illustrations. Any such information the author will gratefully acknowledge if forwarded to his address.

It has been a source of encouragement as well as thankfulness to the author to learn that, as a book for Sunday reading, this volume has afforded much interest and instruction to many families, and that it has proved acceptable alike to old and young.

More than two thousand copies of the book were sold in

eighteen months, at the price of six shillings. In issuing
this new edition, considerably reduced in price, but not
abridged in size, the author cannot but pray that it may
be made an abundant blessing to the thousands of our
Israel.

54 PATERNOSTER ROW, LONDON,
October 20, 1871.

In Memoriam

CHARLES WESLEY, HYMNOLOGIST.

"Thou sealest up the sum, full of wisdom, and perfect in beauty. . . . Thou
wast upon the holy mountain of God ; thou hast walked up and down in the
midst of the stones of fire."—EZEK. xxviii. 12 and 14.

BARD ! inspired by love divine,
Hallowing influence benign,
Ever vital, ever rife,
Throbbing warm with inner life ;
Holy unction, quenchless fire,
All concentre in thy lyre ;
Wreathe the laurel round thy brow,
Israel's sweetest singer thou.

Who in like majestic lays
Ever voiced Jehovah's praise?
Earth is choral with thy songs,
From her countless million-tongues;
Girdling the great world around,
Wheresoever man is found,
Hearts are melted, harps are strung,
And thy jubilates sung.

Who beside has hymn'd like thee
Jesu's death and agony,
Jesus on the altar bound,
Jesus crucified and crown'd ;
He of loving, tender heart,
Meekly bearing sorrow's smart,
He, omnipotent to save,
Conqueror, rising from the grave ?

Thou hast sounded an alarm,
Broken Satan's hellish charm ;
Sinners, starting from their sleep,
Thou hast woo'd to pray and weep ;
Spoken gentle words which prove
Winning as a mother's love ;
Softest sympathy is thine,
Pouring in the oil and wine.

Tenderest pathos, comfort sweet,
Blending in concretion meet ;
Quickening power and life diviue
Here mysteriously conjoin ;
Joy unspeakable, and peace,
Flow together and increase ;
Streams of mercy, deep and broad
As the "plenitude of God."

Words with wondrous thought combined,
All euphonious, all refined,
Pure and exquisitely bright,
As a diamond's flash of light ;
Nature's everlasting rhyme,
Welcome as the evening-chime,
More divine to listening ears
Than the music of the spheres.

Faith and courage, at thy word,
Fight the battles of the Lord,
Burnish'd shields and swords of flame
Clash in war for Jesu's name ;
Onward in the glorious strife !
Onward ! grasp the crown of life !
Battle-hymns are heard around,
And the victor-warriors crown'd.

O'er affliction's waste of woe,
Where the weeds of sorrow grow,
Come thy angel-hymns of love
Like soft whisperings from above ;
Gladsome songs and bliss are given,
Grand rehearsals, hymns of heaven,
While on Pisgah's top we stand
Gazing o'er the promised land.

At the death-bed, o'er the grave,
Where the sable banners wave,
Thou hast struck the chord of peace,
Sung the dirge cf sweet release :
Changed the slow funereal knell
Into a triumphant swell,
Until gloomy death grows bright
In the resurrection's light.

As we pass the surging flood
" Hanging on the arm of God,"
Songs of victory, bursts of joy,
Still our raptured tongues employ ;
Songs for life, and songs for death,
Shout we with our latest breath,
Burning words of victory given,
Last on earth and first in heaven.

Bard of bards ! in peerless light
On the empyrean height,
All surpassing, all above,
In thy canticles of love,
Joining hands with those who dwell
Where eternal anthems swell,
Now we wreathe thy deathless brow,
Israel's sweetest singer thou.

BENJAMIN GOUGE.

MOUNTFIELD, FAVERSHAM,
October 1894.

THE

METHODIST HYMN-BOOK

AND ITS ASSOCIATIONS.

METHODIST societies and congregations have always been impressed and influenced greatly by the power of sacred song. This was a part of divine worship in which both John and Charles Wesley took a lively interest from the commencement of their evangelistic labours; and as they both possessed the gift and spirit of sacred poetry, they applied themselves to the composition of hymns adapted to the use and edification of those who united with them in the worship of God. Charles Wesley will ever be considered to be the poet of Methodism. In the early years of his public life he was almost daily exercised in the composition of hymns. His thoughts flowed in numbers, and his deep feelings of joy, confidence, and zeal could find no adequate expression but in verse. His hymns were not the productions of a lively imagination, suggested by the beauties of nature; nor were they the fruits of hard mental toil. They were the spontaneous effusions of his heart, prompted by love and gratitude to God, and they testify to his joyous confidence in the divine truth and mercy, and to his yearning affection for the souls of redeemed men everywhere. Their wide-spread and enduring popularity is chiefly due to their eminently experimental and scriptural character, and the distinctness in their statement of doctrine.

No merely human compositions can compare with them for the universality of their use, and for their variety and adaptability to all the wants and circumstances of life. Both John and

A

Charles Wesley wrote freely on important subjects previously
to their conversion, but nearly all their hymns date their origin
to incidents which followed the great spiritual change in their
minds. Is it their purpose to state the utter depravity of human
nature ? or the freeness and fulness of the gospel plan of salvation ? or a sense of grateful obligation to the Giver of all good
for countless mercies received ?—they express themselves in
verse, with a simplicity, purity, and power, which have never
been surpassed by any uninspired writer. Apart from the many
beauties of sentiment and diction which abound in the sacred
compositions of the Wesleys, they contain many historical
allusions and biographical references, which, when intelligently
explained, greatly increase the interest which is felt in writings
so widely known and so extensively used. The design of these
notes is to try and make the Hymn-book more instructive and
more conducive to general edification.

The addition of several hundred illustrative incidents of the
practical use of the hymns, will greatly enhance the value of
these compositions.

HYMN I.*—"Oh for a thousand tongues to sing."—*For the Anniversary Day of One's Conversion.*—TUNE, Birstal, 1761.

This hymn was written in May 1739, and was first published
in "Hymns and Sacred Poems," 1740. The interest which
attaches to this hymn, and the happy circumstance which it
commemorates, may justify a statement of the particulars.
Charles Wesley, at the time of his conversion, Sunday, May 21,
1738, was confined by a severe attack of pleurisy to his room in
the house of Mr Bray, brazier, in Little Britain. In his journal
he writes,—

"*Friday, May* 19, 1738.—At five this morning the pain and

---

* The original title of each hymn will be given throughout, after the
first line, as far as it can be ascertained ; those in the supplement will
be taken from that work, when not found with the originals. The
tunes named after the titles are those chosen by Mr Wesley, and printed
in the "Sacred Melody," 1761, or the "Sacred Harmony," 1781.
The last named work is sometimes designated, though incorrectly, as
"Lampe's Tunes to the Great Festival Hymns." The "Sacred Harmony" was republished in 1789, without the words of the hymns, and
in a much smaller form. Tunes of subsequent date are such as were
chosen by the editors of the Hymn-Book, after Mr Wesley's death in
1791.

difficulty in breathing returned. The surgeon was sent for, but I fell asleep before he could bleed me a second time. At seven Mrs Turner came, and told me I should not rise from that bed till I believed. I believed her saying, and asked, ' Has God, then, bestowed faith upon you?' ' Yes, He has.' Feeling an anticipation of joy upon her account, and thanking Christ as I could, I looked for Him all night with prayers and sighs, and unceasing desires.

"*Saturday, May* 20.—I waked much disappointed, and continued all day in great dejection, which the Sacrament did not in the least abate. Nevertheless God would not suffer me to doubt the truth of His promises." He then opened a Testament, and read the first words that presented, Matt. ix. 1 : "And He entered into a ship," &c. It was a long while before he could read this through for tears of joy.

THE DAY OF PENTECOST.—"*Sunday, May* 21, 1738.—I waked in hope and expectation of His coming. At nine my brother and some friends came and sang a hymn to the Holy Ghost. My comfort and hope were hereby increased. In about half an hour they went. I betook myself to prayer ; the substance as follows :—' O Jesus, Thou hast said, " I will come unto you ;" Thou hast said, " I will send the Comforter unto you ;" Thou hast said, " My Father and I will come unto you, and make our abode with you." Thou art God, who canst not lie ; I wholly rely upon Thy most true promise ; accomplish it in Thy time and manner.' Having said this, I was composing myself to sleep in quietness and peace, when I heard one come in and say, ' In the name of Jesus of Nazareth, arise, and believe, and thou shalt be healed of all thy infirmities.' The words struck me to the heart. I lay musing and trembling. With a strange palpitation of heart, I said, yet feared to say, ' I believe, I believe !'" Mr Bray told Mr Wesley that his sister had been ordered by Christ to say those words to him. By degrees the darkness of his unbelief was cleared away ; and immediately he was thoroughly convinced, he fell to intercession. Looking into the Scriptures, he read, "And now, Lord, what is my hope? Truly my hope is even in Thee." And again, "He hath put a new song in my mouth, even a thanksgiving unto our God." Mr Wesley adds, "I now found myself at peace with God, and rejoiced in hope of loving Christ."

On the first anniversary of this happy event the hymn was

written which is now placed first in the "Methodist Hymn-Book." It is the first also in the collections used by other sections of the Methodist family.

The original hymn extends to eighteen verses, the first of which commences thus :—

> "Glory to God, and praise, and love
> Be ever, ever given ;"

and the author proceeds to say, " on that glad day the glorious Sun of Righteousness arose" on his benighted soul, "and filled it with repose." The doctrine of present and instant salvation is plainly stated, and was fully demonstrated in his subsequent life. The first six stanzas of the original hymn, and the fifteenth and sixteenth, were omitted by John Wesley when he selected the hymn with which he commenced his collection. The fact of its being the first hymn in the book has caused it to be as widely known as any hymn which was ever written. It forms an appropriate introductory hymn ; and it occupies a prominent place in other collections besides Mr Wesley's.

The whole composition reads like a sketch of the Christian career of a new-born soul ; it is full of Christ, and glowing with the desire to commend His love to sinners. When the poet consulted Peter Böhler about praising Christ, Böhler replied, " Had I a thousand tongues, I would praise Him with them all." This memorable utterance of the pious Moravian, Charles Wesley has enshrined in this glorious hymn ; and the same sentiment is embodied in some German hymns, as well as in one by the Rev. H. F. Lyte. In this hymn, as also in most of the other instances in which Mr John Wesley abridged his brother's compositions, we observe, once for all, that the best verses are selected.

Mr Alexander Mather, who was sent out by Mr Wesley to travel at the Conference of 1757, during the same year visited a poor condemned malefactor in Nottingham Gaol, who had been so hardened that he was resolved to be a devil. Mr Mather was himself a young convert, and his zeal in trying to rescue this poor criminal was signally owned of God. On the morning of execution he accompanied the wretched man to the scaffold, erected at the outskirts of the town, " where," writes Mr Mather, " we sung part of a hymn—

> ' Oh for a thousand tongues to sing,'

During the first three verses he seemed lifted up, but when he came to the words in the fourth verse—

> 'His blood can make the foulest clean,
> His blood avail'd for me,'

then he rejoiced with joy unspeakable and full of glory."

In the year 1837 Mr John Lawson, a devout local preacher in the Leeds Circuit, was conducting the Sabbath morning service. Soon after entering the pulpit he became unwell, and called on a friend to give out a hymn. Some delay arose, during which Mr Lawson called out, "The first hymn—

> 'Oh for a thousand tongues to sing.' "

Before the last verse was sung the dying Christian soldier fell in the pulpit, and in doing so he cried out, "Sing, John, sing!" and an hour afterwards he entered Paradise.

We read in the *Wesleyan Methodist Magazine* for 1862 of a North American Indian chief in the wilds of the Hudson's Bay Territory, who only a few moments before his spirit fled to heaven was exceedingly happy whilst singing a free translation of the hymn commencing—

> "Oh for a thousand tongues to sing,"

and, having finished the hymn, he immediately expired.

Mrs Green, of Southport, formerly of Bolton, was a member of the Methodist Society fifty-three years, and she remembered with lively gratitude the good she received under a sermon preached by the Rev. John Wesley, in Bolton. During the protracted affliction which preceded her death, she frequently prayed, "Come, Lord Jesus; come quickly." On the day previous to her departure she repeated with peculiar delight the verse—

> "Oh for a thousand tongues to sing," &c.

Mrs Clarkson, of Cheetham Hill, wife of James Clarkson, Esq., was a member of the Methodist Society more than forty years, but owing to the extreme weakness of her faith was unable to realise a clear sense of her acceptance with God till within a few hours of her death. When she obtained the blessing, she called on all around her bed to join her in celebrating redeeming love in the verse commencing—

> "Oh for a thousand tongues to sing," &c.

Her end was peace.

Mrs Collier, of Leicester, was the daughter of godly Method-

ists, and the wife of a local preacher. She was convinced of
sin at the age of fourteen, by reading the life of Miss Bingham.
She joined her mother's class, and became an exemplary
Christian. During her last illness, the fear of death distressed
her; but ere the end came, joy succeeded fear, and her happiness was abounding. Amongst her last words were, "I rest
sweetly in the arms of Jesus. I have done with the world: I
am going home: I shall see Jesus as He is. Glory, glory be to
God!" And then with surprising energy she repeated the
verse, commencing—

"Jesus, the name to sinners dear," &c.

On the morning of her death her peace seemed to flow like a
river. As the end approached, she twice raised her hand,
faintly breathing out, "Praise the Lord;" and so she fell asleep
in Jesus.

Mrs Mary Day, of Whitefield Street, London North Circuit,
feared the Lord from her youth. She bore a long affliction
with patient resignation. As the closing scene drew nigh, her
faith and hope increased, and with emphasis she repeated the
lines—

"Jesus, the name that charms our fears.
That bids our sorrows cease," &c.

Her last words were, "Jesus is precious."

Anthony Triffit, of Stillingfleet, near York, was convinced of
sin whilst hearing a local preacher declare the truth as it is in
Jesus. At a love-feast held in York, soon afterwards, he found
peace with God, whilst the congregation was singing the lines—

"He breaks the power of cancell'd sin,
He sets the prisoner free," &c.

He became a useful local preacher, and was transferred into the
separated ministry, in which he laboured with acceptance for
fifty years. Among his last words were "Blessed Jesus."

Thomas Molineux was born in 1789. Having a pious
mother, he was early taught the way to heaven, and at the age
of ten years enjoyed a clear sense of the pardon of sin. As a
youth he was appointed to lead a class, and at that time regularly attended, at Madeley, Mrs Fletcher's Sunday morning
meeting, and at her request made his first attempt to preach
the gospel in 1815. He was an earnest, industrious, godly
man; meeting in class every Sunday at five o'clock in the

morning. Throughout life, and in death, he manifested entire
submission to the will of God. On the verge of mortality, he
said to a friend, who asked how he felt, " Free from grief ; free
from care ; free from sin." To one of his daughters, shortly
before his exit, he replied—

> " His blood can make the foulest clean,
> His blood avails for me.'

With a countenance beaming with hope and joy he fell asleep
in Jesus.

Peter Bentley was born at Helmsley, February 25, 1786. He
was blest with godly parents, who early led him to associate
with the Methodists, and to meet in class. Whilst attending
this blessed means of grace, and the lines were being sung,

> " He breaks the power of cancell'd sin,
> He sets the prisoner free," &c.,

his chains fell off, and he broke forth in prayer and praise. As
an exciseman, he lived in the fear of God, and peacefully changed
mortality for life, at Baldersly, near Thirsk, April 24, 1859.

HYMN 2.—"Come, sinners, to the gospel feast."—*The Great
Supper* (Luke xiv. 16–24).—TUNE, Invitation, 1761.

This is one of Charles Wesley's finest compositions, offering
to all a free and full salvation. It was first published in
1747, and forms No. 50 of " Hymns for those that seek and
those that have Redemption in the blood of Jesus Christ ; " a
tract of sixty-eight pages, containing fifty-two hymns. The
original has twenty-four stanzas, only nine of which Mr Wesley
has selected, and of these he has made various alterations in
four of the verses, some of which are undoubtedly improvements. Mr James Nichols printed an edition of this hymn,
with notes from the author's MS., in 1842. The first edition of
the Redemption Hymns appeared in 1747 ; the fourth edition
in 1755 ; the 7th edition in 1763. The hymn which immediately follows this in the original tract is the well-known
Pilgrim's Hymn, " How Happy is the Pilgrim's lot ! " The
tune here affixed is that used in the " Great Festival Hymns "
by Lampe.

Sarah Baker, of Culmstock, Tiverton, lived more than forty
years ignorant of God and unconcerned about her soul's salvation. In the year 1799, she was going one Sabbath afternoon

to church. Mr Rouse, a local preacher, was preaching in a
house on her way; from curiosity, she stayed to listen at the
window, and it pleased the Lord to apply the word preached
with power to her heart, and to give her to feel the need of a
Saviour. As the preacher was giving out the words of the hymn—

> "This is the time, no more delay," &c.,

she resolved to accept the offered mercy : she sought the Lord,
and found Him, to the joy of her heart. She never lost her
confidence in God; and, though poor in this world's goods,
she was rich in faith, giving glory to God. In great peace she
fell asleep in Jesus, in a good old age.

HYMN 3.—" O all that pass by, To Jesus draw near."—*On God's
Everlasting Love.*—TUNE, Tallis, 1761.

This hymn was first published in Charles Wesley's tract of
"Hymns on God's Everlasting Love," 1741, in which it is the
third. It is copied entire, with only the alteration of one word ;
"and" is printed for "of" in the fourth line of the fifth stanza.
This was a favourite subject in Charles Wesley's early sermons,
and the hymn was often sung by the first Methodist converts.

HYMN 4.—" Ho ! every one that thirsts, draw nigh."—*The
Fifty-Fifth Chapter of Isaiah.*—TUNE, Angel's Hymn, 1761.

The original of this fine and dignified paraphrase consists
of thirty-one stanzas, and appeared first in 1740, in Charles
Wesley's " Hymns and Sacred Poems," where it is the first
hymn in the third part of the book. The entire chapter is paraphrased ; but John Wesley selected only the first nine verses,
and these are printed as the fourth hymn in his collection, with
the substitution of "ye" for "you" in the sixth verse.

HYMN 5.—"Thy faithfulness, Lord, Each moment we find."—
On God's Everlasting Love.—TUNE, Newcastle, 1761.

This forms the second in Charles Wesley's "Hymns on
God's Everlasting Love," 1741. The first verse of the original
is omitted; the word "foulest" is changed for "vilest" in the
first stanza ; and in the third, "If sin is your burden," "is" is
changed into "be."

Mrs Ellen Ince, of Lowton, Lancashire, mother of Mr
William Ince, late of Southampton Street, London, was born in

1769, and in early life was convinced of sin, chiefly by means
of the Liturgy of the Church of England. In reply to her inquiry after the way of salvation, she was taken to a Methodist
chapel, where she soon found peace through believing in Jesus.
She walked in the fear of the Lord for sixty-seven years. Of
her thirteen children, nine preceded her to heaven. The
death of her last surviving son affected her much. A few days
before her death, she said of her son, "What a glorious state he
is in, free from his weak and suffering body, in the presence of
his Lord! We shall not be parted long." On the morning of
the day of the first anniversary of her son's interment, she read
the Scriptures for two hours, chiefly in Isaiah ; and on closing
the book, she exclaimed to her daughter, "Glory be to God in
the highest for His great love in dying for sinners!" Later in
the day, having read her hymn-book for some time, she repeated
the lines—

> " We all are forgiven for Jesus's sake,
> Our title to heaven, His merits we take ; "

and then she added, "Now let me rest. I think I can go to
sleep." And in a few minutes she sweetly fell alseep in Jesus,
without even a sigh.

HYMN 6.—" Sinners, turn, why will ye die?"
   „   7.—" Let the beasts their breath resign."
   „   8.—" What could your Redeemer do."
" *Why will ye die, O house of Israel ?* " (Ezek. xviii. 31.)
TUNE, Hotham, 1761.

Charles Wesley's "Hymns on God's Everlasting Love" appeared first in 1741, the second edition in 1756, the third in
1770, the fourth in 1792. The tract consists of two parts, of
thirty-six pages and forty-eight pages, respectively. To the first
was originally added a singular poem entitled, "The Cry of a
Reprobate." This will be found reprinted in the first volume of
Jackson's Life of Charles Wesley. That which forms No. 13
in the second part, is reprinted in Wesley's Collection as three
separate hymns. It forms a long, comprehensive, and affecting
inquiry, based on the prophet Ezekiel's words, "Why will ye
die, O house of Israel?" Four out of the sixteen stanzas of the
original are omitted. There are only three words altered, excepting that in several instances "you" and "ye" are interchanged
by John Wesley, in order to give greater emphasis to his

brother's words. Mr Bunting suggests that, as the seventh hymn is both "prolix and prosaic, it would be better left out."

HYMN 9.—"Sinners, obey the gospel word."—"*Come, for all things are now ready.*"—TUNE, The Invitation, 1761.

The original forms hymn 155 in the first volume of "Hymns and Sacred Poems," 1749, by C. Wesley. It is an exact reprint. A present salvation for every penitent sinner is the poet's theme, and he represents the whole three Persons in the Trinity as waiting to welcome sinners to the Saviour. There is a detailed pathos and simplicity in the hymn which give much beauty to the poetry. Mr Bunting suggests that this hymn would be improved by dividing it at the fifth verse.

Speaking of these early volumes of the Wesley poetry, and of John Wesley in particular, the Rev. Samuel Bradburn once observed, "John Wesley had a fine taste for poetry, and composed, himself, many of our hymns; but he told me that he and his brother Charles agreed not to distinguish their hymns from each other's." This rule was observed by them for just ten years; but in 1749, Charles Wesley published, on his own account, the two volumes from which the ninth hymn is chosen. This work contains a large number of the hymns in the collection of 1780, now in use throughout the connexion. In John Wesley's "Plain Account of Christian Perfection" the author makes the following statement :—"In the year 1749, my brother printed two volumes of 'Hymns and Sacred Poems.' As I did not see these before they were published, there were some things in them which I did not approve of. But I quite approved of the main of the hymns on this head—'Present Salvation and Perfect Love.'" It is important that these two testimonies should be recorded. This hymn is the first which is extracted from those volumes.

HYMN 10.—" Ye thirsty for God, to Jesus give ear."— John vii. 37.—TUNE, Newcastle, 1761.

The original forms No. 432 in Charles Wesley's "Short Scripture Hymns," vol. 2, which first appeared in 1762. The work was considerably altered, and in that form it was republished in two volumes in 1794, six years after the author's death. The only alteration made is in the fourth line, which reads thus— " The sense of salvation accepting through grace."

HYMN 11.—" God, the offended God Most High."—"*Now then we are ambassadors for Christ,*" *&c.* (2 Cor. v. 20.)—TUNE, Canon, 1761.

The original forms No. 20 in Charles Wesley's " Hymns on the Trinity," first published in 1767. The only alteration made is in the last line of the third verse, where "goodness" in the original is changed to "mercy."

HYMN 12.—" Come, ye that love the Lord."—*Heavenly joy on earth.*—TUNE, Lampe's, 1746.

This hymn was written by Dr Watts, and first published in July 1707. It forms No. 30 in the author's second book. Mr Wesley has made judicious alterations in eleven lines, and the original is two verses longer. It is placed as the first hymn in the second section of Mr Wesley's collection, under the head of "Describing the Pleasantness of Religion." The hymn has always been a favourite ; the simplicity of its language and its natural imagery have greatly aided its popularity. Every verse of it has been used as dying testimony.

Bartholomew Calvin, a converted Stockbridge Indian, died in his eightieth year, saying, " My trust is in the merits of the Lord Jesus Christ. Sing at my funeral—

> ' Come, ye that love the Lord,
> And let your joys be known,' " &c.

He continued to pray whilst speech remained, and gently sunk into the arms of death without a struggle.

Mr James Martin, of Liverpool, was convinced of sin under a sermon preached by the Rev. V. Ward, and soon afterwards he found peace with God. He was appointed a leader in 1811, and held that office for forty-five years. In 1831, he was a passenger in the *Rothsay Castle* when she was wrecked between Liverpool and Beaumaris, when ninety-three persons perished, and only twenty-one were saved. When he was floating on a plank from off which several had been washed, as the waves were breaking over him, he exclaimed,

> " The God that rules on high,
> That all the earth surveys,
> That rides upon the stormy sky,
> And calms the roaring seas," &c.

After he was rescued, his life was afresh dedicated to God. He became a leader of three classes, and worked with untiring energy in the cause of God. In his last hours of consciousness he said, "I know nothing about doubts and fears." Thus calmly resting on the everlasting arms, he entered into life.

Thomas Hazlehurst, of Runcorn, was born in 1779. At the early age of seven years he was convinced of sin by means of a conversation with the schoolmistress who taught him the first elements of learning. At the age of twenty-seven he obtained peace with God through faith in Jesus Christ. Both he and his wife joined the Methodist Society, and remained faithful witnesses for Christ to the end of life, and they entered Paradise separated only by a few weeks. Mr Hazlehurst had several favourite hymns, which he often repeated with strong feeling. One of these was the 12th, and especially the third verse, commencing,

> " There we shall see His face,
> And never, never sin," &c.

He died quite suddenly,. but fully prepared for the change, February 17, 1842.

Mrs Topham was early converted to God by a sermon preached from the words, "I know that my Redeemer liveth," &c. In 1832, she joined the Methodist Society, and remained a consistent member to the end of her days. She set a particular value on the class-meeting. A long and painful affliction preceded her death, during which her mind was sweetly stayed upon God, and she was truly happy. Shortly before the last struggle, fierce temptation assailed her, but she came off more than conqueror, repeating " All is well now," and then added—

> " There we shall see His face,
> And never, never sin, " &c.

Shortly after, without a struggle, she fell asleep in Jesus.

The quiet village of Wicken, Soham, near Mildenhall, was formerly the residence of Henry, son of Oliver Cromwell, and the birthplace of the well-known Andrew Fuller. Methodism has flourished there for half a century—one of its oldest members being John Docking. He was a Churchman in early life, but under the preaching of the Methodists he was convinced of sin, and with them he cast in his lot. After obtaining a clear sense of pardon, he threw all his energies into the service of God, and

through his efforts a new chapel was erected in the village.
During a long life, he was always "abounding in the work of
the Lord." For eighty years he scarcely knew a day's illness.
He was a man of one book, and searched the Scriptures often
many times in 'a day. Shortly before his death, he said to a
friend, " We shall soon meet in heaven."

> " There we shall see His face,
> And never, never sin," &c.

He died exhorting all around his bed to trust in Christ.

Methodism in Canterbury owes much of its stability and success to the labours of the venerable Vincent Perronet and his
son Charles. The latter was for some years an inmate under
the roof of Mrs Bissaker, and in the *Arminian Magazine* for
1785 is the copy of a remarkable " Memorial to Miss Nancy
Bissaker, in her seventh year." This was intended by the
estimable writer to be a guide to his young friend in after-life.
Mrs Bissaker was one of Mr Wesley's hearers in that ancient
city, at the very beginning of Methodism. Her daughter Ann
had her mind greatly moulded by Mr C. Perronet, of whom she
says, "he taught me the fear of God, abhorrence of lying, a love
for the poor, contempt for finery, a strong attachment to the
Bible, and a high veneration for my mother." She found a
sense of pardon whilst Mr Bramwell was meeting her mother's
class in 1786, and joined the Methodist Society in January 1787.
In 1788, she was married to Mr Parnell, and entered upon the
busy duties of life, discharging them for fourscore years with
godly sincerity and fidelity. She suffered much in her last
days, and during an interview with the Rev. Samuel Hope the
conversation turned on the happiness of heaven, when Mr Hope
observed,

> " The thoughts of such amazing bliss
> Should constant joys create."

"Yes," said the sufferer, "constant joys! constant joys!!"
These words were her last testimony; unconsciousness immediately followed, and shortly afterwards she peacefully passed
away to the skies.

Elizabeth Jackson was awakened to a sense of her sinful condition at the age of fifteen, and soon afterwards found pardon
through faith in Jesus. She served God faithfully during a long
life. She was a member of the Methodist Society at Thirsk for

sixty-two years, and a witness to the doctrine of Christian perfection fifty-three years.   Attending the means of grace to the
end of her days, she started for her class one day, but a distressing asthma compelled her to halt at a friend's house on
the way, where, in the state of acute suffering, she patiently
said, " ' Jesus is mine, and I am His.'

> ' The men of grace have found
> Glory begun below,' &c.

I never could have thought that I could have been made so
happy as I am now.   Oh, what happiness !   Oh, what glory !
It is too sweet for dying."   After a short period she added, " All
is right ; all is well," and peacefully expired.

George Bottomley was brought to God when about eighteen
years of age.   His consistency of character was maintained
throughout life, and as a class-leader he was greatly beloved.
He dwelt much on the promises of God ; and his last words,
half an hour before he died, were—

> " We 're marching through Immanuel's ground,
> To fairer worlds on high."

HYMN 13.—" Happy soul, that, free from harms."—*Waiting
for full Redemption.*—TUNE, Arne, 1781.

The original forms No. 106 in Charles Wesley's "Hymns and
Sacred Poems," 1749, vol. ii.   Eight lines in the original are left
out ; the first line is altered from " Happy soul, that, safe from
harms," to " Happy soul, that, free from harms," and in the
second line, fourth verse, " Perfect in " is altered to " Perfect
through."

HYMN 14.—" Happy the man that finds the grace."—Proverbs
iii. 13, &c.—TUNE, Stanton, 1761.

This was written by Charles Wesley as one of his Redemption
Hymns, 1747.   The original is three verses longer.   In the first
line "that" is substituted for " who."

HYMN 15.—" Happy the souls to Jesus join'd."—*The Sacrament
a pledge of Heaven.*—TUNE, Spitalfields, 1761.

The original forms No. 96 in Charles Wesley's "Hymns on
the Lord's Supper," 1745.   The third and fourth lines read thus
as first written :—

" Walking in all thy ways, we find
Our heaven on earth begun."

Thomas Ross was brought up a Roman Catholic ; but on his coming of age, he read the Scriptures for himself, saw the errors of his past life, began to attend the ministry of the Methodists in 1797, and was admitted a member of Society by the Rev. Samuel Bradburn. He was for some years a steward, trustee, and class-leader, and faithfully served in each office. His last illness was short, but his mind enjoyed much peace. The night before his departure he repeated his favourite hymn, which spoke the language of his heart :—

" Happy the souls to Jesus joined,
And saved by grace alone," &c.

In this delightful frame, his spirit returned to God who gave it.

HYMN 16.—"Happy the souls that first believed."
    „   17.—"Jesus, from whom all blessings flow."—
Primitive Christianity.—TUNE, Athlone, 1781.

This appears as one hymn in Charles Wesley's " Hymns and Sacred Poems," 1749, vol. ii., and forms No. 246. The original has thirty stanzas ; and John Wesley has printed twenty-two verses in making the two hymns. In the last line of verse six, in the second part, " may" is altered from " might," but this change was made after Mr Wesley's death.

The poetry of this composition is smooth and harmonious. It describes the Church as composed of living stones, and the conversion of sinners as the result of the preaching of the gospel. The allusion in the ninth verse, " Draw by the music of thy name," seems to have been suggested by the fable of Orpheus, who by the charms of his lyre subdued the wildness of savage beasts, and held mountains, rivers, and trees in subjection to the power of his music—" And charm into a beauteous frame." This hymn appeared first in 1744, and was printed by John Wesley at the end of his " Appeal to Men of Reason and Religion," and separately as one of Mr Wesley's halfpenny tracts. Mr Benson records the fact that this hymn was long a favourite with Mr Fletcher, Vicar of Madeley, who after dinner spent some time in devotional services, and generally selected verses from " Primitive Christianity," particularly this :—

" Oh that my Lord would count me meet
To wash His dear disciples' feet!"

He has been known to read this hymn till tears of joy and
gratitude streamed down his face, that he had been made a
partaker of that Christianity.

Joseph Mood, Wesleyan minister, was born near Bedal, in
1818. In early youth, he was dedicated by a pious mother to
the service of God ; and one Sunday morning before breakfast,
at the prayer-meeting, he found peace through believing. Converted himself, he soon began to preach the gospel by which
he had been saved, and after five years' labours as a local
preacher, in 1843 he took a circuit. His ministry was attractive, acceptable, and useful, and he won many of the young to
Christ. His last illness was brief, but he was prepared for its
issues. The morning on which he died, he repeated the seventeenth hymn throughout. Shortly after he said, " Sing! get your
hymn-book and sing ;" and whilst his friends were trying to meet
his wishes, his countenance was lighted with a heavenly smile,
which remained for some minutes. He then said, " I shall live
for ever," and almost instantly his spirit escaped to immortality.

HYMN 18.—" Maker, Saviour of mankind."—*For Children.*—
TUNE, Amsterdam, 1761.

This is an exact reprint of No. 15 of Charles Wesley's " Hymns
for Children," the first edition of which appeared in 1763, the
second in 1768, and the third in 1778.

The estimation in which these compositions were held is
indicated in a letter written by Mr Thomas Pearse, of Camel-
ford, Cornwall. To his daughter, at school, he writes :—" Buy
of Mr Evans Mr Wesley's 'Hymns for Children,' and get them
by heart : I will pay for the book and give you a penny for each
hymn [you learn], which, I believe, will amount to nearly four
shillings. Those hymns afforded much comfort to your sister
Peggy, who is now in heaven." This volume contains just
one hundred hymns ; and a considerable number of them are
favourites with the young. In verse three, line six, Mr Bunting
alters " when " to " till."

HYMN 19.—" Rejoice evermore with angels above."—*For those
that have found Redemption.*—TUNE, Tallis, 1761.

This forms No. 3 in Charles Wesley's " Redemption Hymns,"
1747.

HYMN 20.—" Weary souls, that wander wide."—*The Invitation.*
—TUNE, Dedication, 1781.

The original is No. 4 of Charles Wesley's " Redemption Hymns." The first line in the original reads thus, " Weary souls, *who* wonder wide," and the fourth line of the third verse reads, " Live on earth," instead of " Find on earth the life of heaven." There is an earnest and loving spirit of exhortation to sinners pervading the whole, and some striking contrasts are exhibited throughout.

HYMN 21.—" Ye simple souls that stray."—*For those that have found Redemption.*—TUNE, Olney, 1761.

This hymn forms No. 16 of the " Redemption Hymns," but whether written by John or Charles Wesley seems hardly to be decided. Dr Whitehead claims the hymn for Charles, and Mr Henry Moore says it is John Wesley's. The internal evidence, the purity, strength, and sobriety of the language suggest that it was written by John. It was published first in 1747. The original is eight lines longer, and there are alterations made in every verse. In the fifth verse the ministration of angels is admirably stated. The fact that so many alterations are made throughout would indicate Charles Wesley to be the author and John the corrector.

HYMN 22.—" Behold the Saviour of mankind."—*On the Crucifixion.*—TUNE, Fetter Lane, 1761.

The author of this hymn was the Rev. Samuel Wesley, rector of Epworth, who died in the year 1735. The hymn was first published by his sons in 1739, in their first collected volume of " Hymns and Sacred Poems." In the collection, as it appeared in 1780, it has the first place amongst the hymns under the title " Describing the goodness of God." And certainly never was goodness more strongly manifested than in the gift of Christ to save a lost world, and in His dying to redeem man. The internal structure of the hymn shows how fully the writer appeared to realise the infinite importance of the event he so touchingly and effectively describes. But there is a short and touching history of this hymn which should not pass without notice. It was probably written a short time before the Rectory at Epworth was burnt down in 1709 ; for immediately after the fire the

B

original manuscript, blown by the wind out of the Rectory window, was found partly burnt in the Rectory garden. Thus when many more valuable things were consumed, a gentle breeze carried this lately finished manuscript off the study table into a place of safety. The hymn has music adapted to it, probably by Henry Purcell or Dr Blow. It is the only hymn by the rector of Epworth in the Methodist collection. Two verses are left out, one after the first, and one after the fourth, as they appear in the hymn-book. We shall be pardoned for inserting here the omitted verses :—

> " Though far unequal our low praise
> To Thy vast sufferings prove,
> O Lamb of God, thus all our days,
> Thus will we grieve and love.

> " Thy loss our ruins did repair,
> Death, by Thy death is slain ;
> Thou wilt at length exalt us where
> Thou dost in glory reign."

The hymn would not be much improved by the addition of these verses. It was at this fire, and on this occasion, that John Wesley himself was saved, but only by being lifted out of his bedroom window, by one man standing on the shoulders of others, just before the burning roof of the parsonage fell in, when everything else was consumed, including the rector's library, furniture, and all his manuscripts, his sermons, and a work on Hebrew poetry, which was an English poetical rendering of the Psalms and other Hebrew hymns in the Bible.

Of the author himself, the father of the Wesleys, it is scarcely possible to speak too highly. He was born at Winterburn-Whitchurch, in 1662 ; educated at Dorchester, and Newington Green, London, and Exeter College, Oxford, where he wrote and published " Maggots " to obtain the means of living. He was ordained in 1688, made a priest in St Andrew's Church, Holborn, in 1689, and became a curate on £28 a year. During the same year he was married to Susanna Annesley, and nineteen children were afterwards added to their family circle. Such privations, sufferings, and hardships seldom fall to the lot of any household, as became the lot and inheritance of the Wesley family ; and yet no other family since the days of the Apostles did more for the spread of pure religion, and for the glory of

God. The venerable rector was author of the " Life of Christ,"
an heroic poem ; the " History of the Old and New Testament"
in verse, in 3 vols. ; the " History of Job," in Latin, and other
books ; and died, after being rector of Epworth forty years, April
25, 1735, aged 72.

This hymn has been instrumental in the hands of God of
pointing sinners to their only Saviour. The Rev. Owen Davis,
born at Wrexham, North Wales, in 1752, was influenced by the
example of godly Methodists, through whom he was led to their
preaching, and once there one asked him if he had " a desire to
flee from the wrath to come ?" Another one invited him to a
class-meeting, and through meeting with the people of God
light soon rose on his dark mind. After meeting in class nine
months, at a love-feast, while one was giving out the hymn
commencing—

> " Behold the Saviour of mankind
> Nail'd to the shameful tree !"

he was enabled to see that Christ bore his sins in His own body,
and that His blood was a sufficient atonement for the sins of the
whole world. The change wrought in his life was manifest to
all. He became one of the Community preachers in London,
and by Benjamin Rhodes, for whom he preached at five o'clock
one morning in City Road Chapel, he was recommended to Mr
Wesley, and afterwards accepted as a preacher. A long life of
useful labour as an earnest minister of the gospel was the best
evidence of his change of heart ; and he died as he had lived,
honouring the gospel and the grace of God.

We commemorate the dying of our blessed Lord on the day
we call Good Friday. On that day, in 1840, a truly good man,
Mr H. Wight, a class-leader, and a man of upright character, attended divine worship in the Wesleyan Chapel at Plymouth in the early part of the day, in his usual health. In the
afternoon he walked with his wife to the prayer-meeting, and
went up to the desk. Opening the hymn-book, he announced
the 22d hymn, and read,—

> " Behold the Saviour of mankind
> Nail'd to the shameful tree !"

Scarcely had he uttered the last word when he fell ; pulsation
and breathing appeared to cease in a moment ; his spirit had
passed, without a moment's notice of illness, to the beatific

vision amongst the redeemed, and he saw Jesus for himself without a cloud between. Few die so suddenly—none more safely ;
his was a translation ; he knew not death or dying, but by one
step he passed direct from blissful service on earth to eternal
rest in heaven.

Another example is worthy of record of the words of this
hymn having been made use of by the Holy Spirit to lead a
penitent into the enjoyment of the liberty which pardon brings.
The mother of the Rev. Dr Jobson has left the impress of her
transparent piety on the heart of her son, and in return that
son has embalmed the memory of his sainted mother in a
memoir which exhibits much of heavenly wisdom. In early
life, that mother had partaken of the sacred emblems of our
Lord's passion, and with a bruised spirit she returned home to
seek a personal interest in the atonement. On repeating the
hymn commencing—

"Behold the Saviour of mankind," &c.,

she was enabled to appropriate by faith, to her own case, the
merits of the death of Christ ; and then, while uttering the
verse—

"But soon He'll break death's envious chain," &c.,

her soul burst into the clear sunlight and liberty of the children
of God. The bright example of a life of more than fifty years
was the best evidence of the certainty of the change which
divine grace had wrought.   -

HYMN 23.—"Extended on a cursed tree."—"*They shall look
on Me whom they have pierced*" (Zech. xii. 12).—TUNE,
Pudsey, 1761.

John Wesley was very successful in his translations of Ger-
man hymns. The original of this one was written by Paul
Gerhardt, in 1659 ; it forms No. 104 in the Hernhutt Collection,
and in its English dress, prepared by John Wesley, first
appeared in "Hymns and Sacred Poems," 1740, on page 34.
It is reprinted in the first volume of Charles Wesley's "Poetical
Works," 1868. There are twenty-four of John Wesley's translations in the hymn-book, of which this is the first. Paul
Gerhardt was born at Graefenhaenichen, in Saxony, in 1606.
He suffered much during the thirty years' war. He first became
a village pastor, when he married ; and in 1657 was called to

St Nicholas Church in Berlin, and soon became known and esteemed through his beautiful hymns.   He published the first collection of his hymns in 1666, and in the same year he was deposed from his spiritual office because he would not belong to either the Lutheran or the Reformed party in the Church. He was deposed, then reinstated, then altogether removed from office in the Church, and had to depend on the alms of his friends to save him from want.   During the period of his non-employment in the Church he wrote some of his best hymns. He died, weary and aged, June 7, 1676, giving a beautiful dying charge to his only son, urging him to remain steadfast in the faith.   His portrait, in the church at Lübben, bears the inscription, "A divine sifted in Satan's sieve."   He left one hundred and twenty-three hymns, of which more than thirty are patterns of hymns for all time. . Next to Luther, Paul Gerhardt was the greatest and most popular hymn-writer in Germany, and emphatically the people's poet.   No other German writer has had so many of his hymns translated into English.

> HYMN 24.—" Ye that pass by, behold the Man ;"
>   „   25.—" O Thou dear suffering Son of God."—
>   *A Passion Hymn.*--TUNE, Dresden, 1761.

In Charles Wesley's "Hymns and Sacred Poems," 1742, and in the early editions of the Hymn-book, these two hymns are found as one, but extended to eighteen verses, of which three are omitted.   The fourth line of the third verse of the second part reads thus, " And bow with Jesus crucified," which is altered to "And die," &c.

Objection has been taken to verse 2 of the second part, commencing "Give me to feel Thy agonies."   " In the great work of atoning for sin Jesus Christ stood alone ; none to help, none to bear any part of His burden, nor to drink one drop of His sad cup.   The work of atonement was performed solely and exclusively by the Lord Jesus."   Some Christians may be said to suffer with Christ, but He had to tread the wine-press alone, and with Him there was none to help.   The fourth verse Mr Bunting suggests the omission of, which many would think to be an improvement.

In the fifth verse of the second part occurs this line, " O *rent* with thy expiring groan," which is altered in the hymn to "rend."   The use of that word is made the subject of a long and interesting article, by the Rev. Thomas Jackson, in the *Wesleyan Magazine*, 1854, page 778, *et seq.* The whole article is a defence of the language used by the Wesleys against some of the minor critics who have presumed to turn " correctors."

HYMN 26.—" I thirst, Thou wounded Lamb of God."—
A Prayer to Christ.—TUNE, Complaint, 1761.

The original of this hymn was written in German by Count Zinzendorf and John and Anna Nitzchman. It was translated by John Wesley, and published in " Hymns and Sacred Poems," 1740.

Like many of the German hymns, this combines scriptural truth, poetical fervour, and deep religious experience. It has been long a favourite with new converts, and will always find admirers amongst those who are beginning to know something of the boundless love of Christ, and who are desiring conformity to His mind and will.

John Tasker, late of Skipton, sought the Lord in early life. He was convinced of sin under the preaching of Dr Bunting and Dr Newton, and much encouraged in his religious life by the Rev. John Crosse, vicar of Bradford. When he gave his heart to God, he gave all his powers to be used in His service, and during a long life he faithfully served the Lord. When failing health indicated the approach of death, he said with resignation—

> " I thirst, Thou wounded Lamb of God,
> To wash me in Thy cleansing blood ;
> To dwell within Thy wounds : then pain
> Is sweet, and life or death is gain."

He died as he had lived, at peace with God.

During many years of suffering, Mary Pritchard testified by patient endurance, and loving obedience to the will of God, that she had passed from death unto life. The Methodist Society at Tintern Abbey was adorned by her godly example, and when death was before her, she called her husband to join her in singing her favourite hymn, commencing—

> " I thirst, Thou wounded Lamb of God," &c.

At its close she exclaimed, " I nothing have ; I nothing am Jesus ! Jesus ! " and with these words she fell on sleep.

A venerable man was William Walton, of Wakefield. After a

life of more than fourscore years, during which he enjoyed constant communion with God, at its close, with tranquillity, he faintly articulated, " Jesus is all the world to me !" and his last utterance before entering paradise was—

> "Take my poor heart, and let it be
> For ever closed to all but Thee !"

He calmly entered heaven.

James Isitt, of Bedford, was called at an early age to exchange mortality for life. But he left behind him a godly example and influence which is seen in the career of his son Francis, who has just dedicated his life to the service of God in the Wesleyan ministry. Important are the words of one who is just detaching himself from earth. Shortly before his departure to heaven, Mr Isitt repeated the verse commencing—   .

> " I thirst, Thou wounded Lamb of God," &c.

Then adding the next verse, "Take my poor heart," &c., he exclaimed with deep pathos, "Take it now, Lord ; I need not wait till I am better." His latest expressions indicated the serenity of undisturbed peace.

In the furnace of affliction, William Goodacre, of Long Sutton, Nottingham, found the consolations of the gospel more than equal to his sufferings. Rendered by disease incapable of bearing any excitement, he would yet often say—

> " How can it be, Thou heavenly King,
> That Thou shouldst me to glory bring?"

Nature at length yielded in the struggle, and triumph crowned the end.

There is a benignity and tenderness in the character of the Rev. William Entwisle, which his sainted father has placed on record. In the very prime of a most useful ministerial life, the Master saw fit to call him home ; and the blessed influence which attended his interviews with the preachers, indicates more of heavenly than of earthly manifestations. After partaking of the memorials of the Lord's death, he said—

> " How can it be, Thou heavenly King,
> That Thou shouldst me to glory bring ?

I am a poor sinner ; the chief of sinners ; but Jesus died for me. Free grace for ever, free grace !" Rejoicing with such hope he entered heaven.

HYMN 27.—"Saviour, the world's and mine."—*A Hymn to Christ.*—TUNE, West Street, 1761.

This is one of the earliest of Charles Wesley's compositions, and is found first in his "Hymns and Sacred Poems," 1739. This is an exact reprint, and was probably written a short time before his conversion.

HYMN 28.—"O love Divine ! what hast thou done ! "—*Desiring to Love.*—TUNE, 112th Psalm, 1761.

This hymn first appeared in Charles Wesley's "Hymns and Sacred Poems," 1742. It is a sweet and touching composition. Rev. Dr Thomas Summers, of America, supposes that the refrain of this hymn, "My Lord, my love, is crucified," is taken from Ignatius, martyr in the Primitive Church. The same line is found in J. Mason's "Songs of Praise," which appeared in 1683 It is also used by other sacred poets.

HYMN 29.—"Come, ye weary sinners, come."—*For those that seek Redemption.*—TUNE, Foundry, 1761.

This forms No. 10 in Charles Wesley's "Redemption Hymns," 1747. The latter half of the second and the first half of the third verse in the original are omitted. The second line is altered from "All who groan to bear your load," to "All who groan beneath," &c. ; and the fourteenth line is altered from "Cast on Thee our sin and care," to "Cast on Thee our every care."

Testimony to the value of class-meetings in Methodism is not wanting. Joshua Thorley, of Macclesfield, was taken to the house of prayer when a child, by a beloved sister. Under the ministry of Methodism, he became convinced of sin. He accepted an invitation to a class-meeting, in which he earnestly sought salvation by faith in Christ. While he was at that means of grace one day, and while the members were singing the verse—

> " Come, ye weary sinners, come,
> All who groan beneath your load,
> Jesus calls His wanderers home :
> Hasten to your pardoning God,"

he was enabled to believe on Jesus as his Saviour. Light and love sprang up in his heart, he rested on the promises, and returned home a happy man. From this time to the end of his earthly pilgrimage, he went on his way rejoicing in God as his reconciled Father ; and he gave to the Church of his choice forty years of consistent piety and devoted service.

The same hymn which had been used as the means of leading a sinner to Christ was also found equally useful and consoling to a dear departing one, at the end of her earthly journey. Matilda, daughter of the Rev. William Dalby, was in early life serious and thoughtful, and in riper years the comfort and joy of her parents. Seven of her sisters preceded her to heaven, her watchful care of whom, and especially over her suffering mother, impaired her own health. After Mrs Dalby's death, the health of her only surviving daughter rapidly declined ; but she knew in whom she had believed. During her last affliction, she delighted in hearing the Word of God read to her by her father. The following verse of the 29th hymn she often repeated—

> " Fain I would on Thee rely,
> Cast on Thee my every care,
> To Thine arms of mercy fly,
> Find my lasting quiet there,"

saying to her father, " That is just my place." She also delighted in the other verses. Shortly before her departure she sung with evident rapture, " There is a land of pure delight," &c., and then, after a brief rest, quietly fell asleep in Jesus.

HYMN 30.—" Where shall my wondering soul begin ?"—*Christ the friend of sinners.*—TUNE, Frankfort, 1761.

The original appears in the second part of Charles Wesley's " Hymns and Sacred Poems," 1739.

Very few are aware of the interest which belongs to this hymn. It was written in May 1738, by Charles Wesley, with another of like character, No. 201 in the Hymn-book, which commences, "And can it be that I should gain," &c. What the author of this hymn has written concerning it is so full of interest, we cannot refrain from quoting it. After the spiritual guidance which the brothers Wesley had received from Peter Bohler, they were separated, and Charles Wesley went to reside with a poor brazier named Bray, in Little Britain, " who knew nothing but Christ," who had to supply Bohler's place in explaining the way of salvation by faith. On May 21, 1738, Charles Wesley was enabled to say, " I believe, I believe ! " What follows is from his " Journal," under date of May 23. "At nine I began a hymn on my conversion, but was persuaded to break off for fear of pride. Mr Bray coming, encouraged me to proceed in spite of Satan. I prayed Christ to stand by me, and finished the hymn. Upon my afterwards showing it to Mr Bray, the devil threw in a fiery dart, suggesting that it was wrong, and I had displeased God. My heart sank within me ; when, casting my eyes upon a Prayer-book, I met with an answer for him : ' Why boastest thou thyself, thou tyrant, that thou must do mischief?' Upon this I clearly discerned that it was a device of the enemy to keep back glory from God. And it is not unusual with him to preach humility, when speaking will endanger his kingdom, or do honour to Christ. Least of all would he have us tell what things God has done for our souls ; so tenderly does he guard us from pride. But God has showed me He can defend me from it while speaking for Him." "There is," says the Rev. John Kirk, "a remarkable coincidence between the spirit and language of the ' Journal ' and that of the hymn. As soon as he begins to express his joy he is tempted to stay his pen. He resolves to perform his vows unto the Lord, of not hiding His righteousness within his heart. This harmonises exactly with the third and fourth verses, probably composed after the temptation to desist. He asks, ' And shall I slight my Father's love ? ' &c." Two days afterwards, John Wesley also was able to believe to the salvation of his soul. Happy in the pardoning love of God, John was accompanied by a number of his friends, shortly before ten at night, to Mr Bray's house in Little Britain, where Charles was confined by illness. The two brothers and their companions were overjoyed, and Charles records, "We sang the hymn with great joy, and parted with prayer."

HYMN 31.—" See, sinners, in the gospel glass ; "
   „   32.—" Sinners, believe the gospel word ; "
   „   33.—" Would Jesus have the sinner die ? "—
Jesus Christ, the Saviour of all men.—TUNES, Frankfort, Carey's, and Mourners, 1761.

The original forms hymn No. 10 in Charles Wesley's "Hymns on God's Everlasting Love," 1741, and it extends to twenty-eight stanzas, thirteen only of which are given in these three hymns. In two places "in" is changed for "through," as, for instance, " Pardon ye all in Him," is changed to "through Him," and as usual "dear" loving is altered to "thou" loving. in Hymn 33.

The widow of Thomas Smith, of Thurvaston, Derbyshire, after a long life of faithful service, was deprived of her husband, and herself laid prostrate, within a short period. The afternoon before her death she said to her children, "I have no abiding city here ; why should I wish to stay? My home is in heaven." During the night she repeated the hymn commencing—

"Would Jesus have the sinner die?" &c.,

and afterwards added, "What should I do now if I had religion to seek?" She exhorted those around her bed to give their hearts to the Lord : then with much solemnity and sweetness she exclaimed, "My Lord, and my God," and a few minutes later her redeemed spirit passed to the beatific vision.

During forty-four years James Stokoe served God and Methodism in his native county of Durham. He greatly loved the Scriptures and old Methodist preachers. As he drew near his end he enjoyed more than ever the preciousness of the Saviour, often repeating the verse in the 33d hymn, commencing—

"Oh, let me kiss Thy bleeding feet,
And bathe and wash them with my tears," &c.

and also another verse commencing,

"O love, thou bottomless abyss," &c.

He lived uprightly, and died happily.

Hymn 34.—"Let earth and heaven agree."—*On God's everlasting love.*—Tune, Trumpet, 1781.

This hymn forms No. 11 in Charles Wesley's "Hymns on God's Everlasting Love," 1741. Three verses are omitted, and in the sixth, "How swiftly" is changed from "How freely" in the original. Mr Wesley printed this hymn in the *Arminian Magazine*, vol. i., page 191.

Mrs Alice Carvosso, a Cornish lady of cultivated mind, good taste, and consistent piety, suffered in her last protracted illness the most intense agony of body ; but in the midst of her affliction she found great comfort in reading the Word of God, and in singing His praises as embodied in Wesley's hymns. Towards the close of her life she dwelt particularly on this admirable hymn,

"Let earth and heaven agree," &c.

This she thought was the most excellent in all Mr Wesley's

collection. Though her physical agony was intense, her mind was kept in peace, and just before her departure, her dying testimony was, " Precious Jesus ! "

A soul in deep distress will seek for relief, and next to the Bible no book has more aided the seeking penitent than Wesley's Hymns. The village schoolmaster of Walkeringham, Notts, William Morris, became concerned for the salvation of his soul. The verse of this hymn,

" Stung by the scorpion sin," &c.

so impressed his mind, that he gave God no rest till he found pardon, and in his after life, as a class-leader and local-preacher, he gave most gratifying evidence how entire was the change divine grace had wrought within him. Resting alone on the atonement, he fell asleep in Jesus.

The triumphs of divine grace are so often repeated, the recording angel alone can tell how great is the sum of blessing vouchsafed by God to man. Shortly before Mr Wesley's death, William Thompson, then a sailor, was induced to attend the Methodist preaching, and, becoming convinced of sin, in great distress of mind, whilst meditating on the verse,

" Stung by the scorpion sin," &c.,

he realised that inward comfort which constrained him to cry out, " O Lord, I will praise Thee ; for Thine anger is turned away," &c. From that period to the end of fourscore years he walked in the light of God's countenance, and died in holy composure.

Amongst many deeply afflicted followers of Jesus, Mrs Mary Jeffs, of Gloucester, was one who found abiding comfort and consolation through reading Wesley's Hymns. In her last illness she testified abundantly to the grace of God within her, and when very near her end she raised her voice, and joyfully exclaimed,

" Oh for a trumpet-voice, On all the world to call !
    To bid their hearts rejoice In Him who died for all ! " &c.

Shortly after, she said, " Jesus is increasingly precious ; " and after a change in her position in bed, she added, " Oh, how easy ! Praise the Lord," and, quietly reclining on her pillow, she peacefully fell asleep in Jesus.

One much younger in years experienced even greater ecstacy in death, and recorded her joyful experience in strains like a con-

queror's song. Miss Topham realised pardoning grace in early
life, at the sacrament of the Lord's Supper. She was early called
to exchange worlds ; and shortly before her death she exclaimed,
"Oh, what can this be? I never felt so happy before. Oh, tell
the servants and all to come and see how happy I am.

'Oh for a trumpet-voice, On all the world to call!'"

And again—

" 'The arms of love that compass me
Would all mankind embrace.' "

In this happy frame of mind she entered into rest.

HYMN 35.—" Jesus, Thou all-redeeming Lord ; "
    „   36.—" Lovers of pleasure more than God."—
Before preaching to the Colliers in Leicestershire.—TUNE,
Birstal, 1761.

The original will be found in vol. i., p. 316, of Charles Wesley's
"Hymns and Sacred Poems," 1749, as one hymn of eighteen
verses, six of which are omitted. In the fifth verse, " The hard-
ness" is changed from " The stony," " swearers " is substituted
for " railers," with a few other verbal alterations.

Mrs Paulina Wyvill was remarkable for high Christian attain-
ment, for unassuming benevolence, and for firmness of character.
From hearing a funeral sermon, at the age of twenty-one, she
became convinced of sin, began to meet in class, and soon found
pardon. Naturally fragile in body, she sought happiness in the
company of the righteous, and when called to leave this world
she found her chief delight in praising God. Shortly before her
death, she repeated the three verses commencing with

" Lovers of pleasure more than God."

Amongst her last counsels to her friends she said, " Pay strict
attention to the means of grace ; never forsake your class-meeting—those precious meetings ! what heavenly seasons have I
there enjoyed ! " A little later she whispered, " I want to be
filled with the presence of Jesus," and her request was granted ;
death was swallowed up in victory.

HYMN 37.—" Jesus, the Name high over all."—*After preaching
in a church.*—TUNE, Liverpool, 1761.

As originally written by Charles Wesley, this hymn extends
to twenty-two verses, only six of which are chosen. The first
line of the original is " Jesus, accept the grateful song ; " it is

found in "Hymns and Sacred Poems," 1749. The ninth verse of the original forms the first of Hymn 37.

This hymn has long been a great favourite with the Methodist people generally, and several well-authenticated instances are known of its having been used by godly persons to exorcise the devil. The facts which suggested the composition are recorded by Charles Wesley in his Journal under date of August 6, 1744. Having been preaching in the small church at Laneast, in Cornwall, and condemning the drunken revels of the people, whilst urging them to "repent and be converted," one in the congregation contradicted and blasphemed. Charles Wesley asked, " Who is he that pleads for the devil?" The reviler stood boldly forward, the preacher fearlessly exposed his iniquity, and showed the whole congregation their state by nature. Mr Wesley's withering exposure drove the man in disgrace out of the church. These circumstances are believed to have suggested the writing of the hymn.

In the Life of the Rev. Henry Ransom (*Wesleyan Magazine*, September 1857), an incident is related as having occurred in his presence, of an evil spirit being cast out after the singing of part of this hymn and prayer, at Darlaston.

Other spirits have been exorcised by the magic power of these verses, besides those indicated. Five of the six verses of this hymn have been quoted by happy saints departing to paradise.

Mrs Elizabeth Baker, of Banbury, was brought up without any sense of the fear of God resting upon her. At the age of nineteen she was married, and, becoming a mother, soon lost two beloved babes. This event the parents took as a visitation from God for their sins, especially that of trading on the Sabbath-day. They bought a Prayer-book to aid them in seeking mercy, but a revival breaking out in 1820 at Banbury, the mother attended the Methodist preaching, and found pardon through believing in Jesus. She maintained her confidence In God through a long course of domestic anxieties and afflictions. Just before she died, her family never having known her to sing, were surprised to hear her pour forth in clear, musical strains—

> " Jesus, the Name high over all,
> In hell, or earth, or sky :
> Angels and men before it fall,
> And devils fear and fly."

Her transparent, simple-hearted godliness was manifest in dying,—she literally slept in Jesus.

Robert Elliott, of Hutton-Rudby, Stockton, lived for twenty-eight years without religion, but was brought to a knowledge of sins forgiven through the preaching of the Methodists. For more than thirty years he was a faithful leader, and daily went about doing good. A worldly-minded professor once said of him, "I cannot but love Robert Elliott, but I hate to meet him." He was unflinching in reproving sin. On his death-bed, when visited by the preacher, he said to the friendly inquirer, "I am in great pain, but happy in God." Speaking of his confidence in Christ, he exclaimed, as in an ecstasy,

> "Jesus, the Name to sinners dear,
>   The name to sinners given ;
> It scatters all my guilty fear,
>   It turns my hell to heaven."

His last words were, "Happy, happy!" and without a struggle or sigh he ceased to breathe.

Miss Helen Hulse, niece of Mr Sykes, of Mansfield-Woodhouse, was called to endure severe affliction, which, however, was greatly alleviated by the recital of the hymns she had learned in youth. Not more than ten minutes before her departure, she spoke of all her blessings as coming through Jesus only, and repeated the lines —

> "Power into strengthless souls He speaks,
>   And life into the dead."

She asked her sister to read to the end of the hymn, earnestly joining in the last verse, commencing—

> "Happy, if with my latest breath
>   I may but gasp His name," &c.

Directly afterwards she sweetly fell asleep in Jesus.

Robert Voakes, in early life, was deprived of many religious advantages ; but Alleine's "Alarm," Nelson's "Journal," the "Pilgrim's Progress," and other similar works, convinced him that he was a sinner. He was for seven long years under the law. On removing into the Pocklington circuit, he joined a class, found mercy, and soon afterwards was made a leader. He laboured for God, through many severe trials, till he was eighty-five, when infirmity laid him aside. After a survey of his protracted life, he recorded much to the praise of God, and finished by writing, " Now my mind is relieved from the cares of the world,

> ' 'Tis all my business here below
> To cry, Behold the Lamb !'"

In his ninety-fourth year he entered into rest, having been a Methodist seventy-two years, and a class-leader more than seventy years.

On the lips of many of the Lord's people have the words of the last verse of this hymn faltered, just as they were entering paradise.   Four of the preachers we may name as examples :—

The Rev. Richard Robarts, after a brief but useful career in the Methodist ministry, closed his pilgrimage by repeating to a friend at his bedside the verse—

> ": Happy, if with my latest breath," &c.

His last words were, " Thank the Lord ! Now, Lord, come. Amen."

The Rev. James Needham appreciated the preciousness of many of Wesley's hymns, and quoted several of them to friends who visited him on his death-bed.   When strength was rapidly declining, and life fast ebbing out, one friend said to him, " You still preach Christ to us."   With much exertion, and difficulty of breathing, he exclaimed,

> " Happy, if with my latest breath
> I may but gasp His name," &c.

His last words were the following : " Glory, honour, might, majesty, and dominion, be ascribed to God and the Lamb for ever !"

After a brief ministry of only seven years, the Rev. Thomas Charles Rushforth exchanged mortality for life.   On the Saturday before his death, he desired a few friends to meet in his house for prayer ; and during that final service with the members of the Church militant he repeated with emphasis the verse commencing—

> " Happy, if with my latest breath
> I may but gasp His name," &c.

His last utterances were, " I shall soon be at rest,—my dear Redeemer."

Early conversion is a safe indication of a happy and useful

life. The Rev. Thomas Thompson began to preach before he came of age, and at twenty-two became a home missionary, faithfully and kindly fulfilling the duties of the Methodist ministry for twenty-nine years. During his last illness his mind was kept in perfect peace, and amongst his last earthly utterances were, " I am waiting for my change without desire of life or fear of death. I am an unworthy servant ; but all my trust is in the merits of Jesus Christ :

> " Happy if with my latest breath
> I may but gasp His name," &c.

He died trusting in the Lord.

HYMN 38.*—" O God, of good the unfathom'd Sea!"—*God's Love to Mankind.*

The original of this strikingly sublime hymn was written, in German, by John Angelus, or Angelus Silesius, or John Scheffler, a mystic, and member of the Roman Catholic Church, born in 1624, and who died in 1677. His hymns were published in Breslau in 1657, under the title of " Hoiy Delight of the Soul, or Spiritual Hymns of a Soul enraptured by Love to Jesus." Hymns of such a character were sure to attract the attention of John Wesley, who wrote a free translation of this one, which appeared in " Hymns and Sacred Poems," 1739. This hymn was added to the collection after Mr Wesley's death, as was also Hymn 39, which is indicated by the asterisk (*).

A mighty host will be found before the throne of God, gathered into the fold as the result of the ministry of the Rev. Robert Newton, and, amongst them, Benjamin Ward, of Oldham, who was so impressed by the manner of the preacher in giving out the verse commencing, " O God, of good the unfathom'd sea," &c., that he was enabled to give his heart to the Lord after the singing of that first verse. He joined the Methodist Society at the age of fifteen, and for forty years was actively employed as a class-leader, as leader of the congregational singing, and in the Sunday-school.

The Almighty God sometimes manifests Himself to His people in a manner so unusual that, like the Apostle Paul, they testify that, whether in the body or out of it, they know not. Mrs Marian Shipman, of Mansfield, was favoured, a short time before her death, with an extraordinary manifestation of the

C

Divine presence, and she gave utterance to her feelings in the language of the first verse of this hymn :—

> " O God, of good the unfathom'd Sea !
>   Who would not give his heart to Thee ?
>   Who would not love Thee with his might,
> O Jesu, lover of mankind ?
> Who would not his whole soul and mind,
>   With all his strength to Thee unite ?"

HYMN 39.*—" Father, whose everlasting love."—*On God's
Everlasting Love.*

This appeared in the first of Charles Wesley's "Tracts of Hymns," 1741, with the title just given. The original extends to twenty-seven verses. In the fourth verse, " a world " is altered to " the world."

The lay agency in Methodist preaching has, taking man for man, been more abundantly owned by the Holy Spirit in the saving of souls than the separated or priestly agency of the Established Church. John Johnson, of Gunnerside, Reeth, was brought to God under a sermon preached by Richard Buxton, a local preacher. Immediately he began to seek the souls of others, and became in turn a leader and local preacher himself, and was made a blessing to many. On the day of his death he had preached at Gayle, and, at tea with a friend at Hawes, spoke of being as happy as he could be. In the evening he opened the service at Hawes, and gave out the 42d hymn, the last two lines being—

> " Lift up the standard of Thy cross,
> And all shall own Thou died'st for all."

He commenced to pray, and had uttered a sentence of adoration, when he fell in the pulpit ; his spirit went straight to the paradise of God.

HYMN 40.—" Ye neighbours and friends, To Jesus draw near."—
After preaching to the Newcastle Colliers, December 4, 1746.
—TUNE, Triumph, 1761.

Under date of November 30, in his journal, Charles Wesley uses the same phraseology as he embodies in this spirited hymn. During that visit to the North, he preached several times in the streets of Newcastle to listening crowds, who forgot the sharpness of the frost while listening to the earnest, soul-stirring words of life from the man of God. The original appears in " Hymns and Sacred Poems," 1749, vol. i., p. 310, where it extends to twelve verses, five of which are omitted. John Wesley made a correct reprint of his brother's hymn, but some subsequent editor has sadly marred both the sense and the theology of the first line, which, in the original, reads thus—

> "Ye neighbours, and friends of Jesus, draw near,"

thus keeping the distinction between the world and the Church, sinners and saints, which is lost in the incorrect line now in the Hymn-book. "Praise" is also exchanged for "grace" at the end of the third verse. This hymn is correctly printed in John Wesley's first and subsequent editions issued during his lifetime ; but it is printed incorrectly in the penny edition of Wesley's hymns recently issued by the Book Committee.

HYMN 41.—" O God! our help in ages past."—*Man frail, and God eternal.*—TUNE, Bexley, 1761.

This much-admired composition is Dr Watts' paraphrase of one of David's Psalms. It was first published in 1719, and, after undergoing several corrections by John Wesley, was issued in Mr Wesley's first Hymn-book in 1738, in its altered form. In Watts', it commences "Our God, our help," &c.

William Kay, of Manchester, feared God from his youth, and was in communion with the Methodists for fifty-eight years. His confidence in God was unshaken ; and at the close of a life of more than fourscore years, when a member of his family repeated the lines—

> " O God, our help in ages past,
> Our hope for years to come ;
> Our shelter from the stormy blast,"——

Here the dying saint cheerfully added the last line—

> " And our eternal home."

Almost immediately after, his spirit returned to God.

HYMN 42.—" Thee we adore, eternal Name."—*Frail Life, and succeeding Eternity.*—TUNE, Chimes, 1761.

A hymn by Dr Watts, forming No. 55, Book II., in his collection. It was first published in 1709 ; and, with three of John Wesley's improvements, was inserted in his " Psalms and Hymns " (1738).

In the company of the redeemed in heaven, none will shine with brighter lustre than the devoted missionary of the cross, who wears out health and life in the work of proclaiming a free salvation for every man. The Rev. George Bellamy fell a victim to fever in Demerara. During his severe sufferings, whilst a coloured servant was bathing his head with vinegar, he solemnly exclaimed —

> " Thee we adore, Eternal Name,
>   And humbly own to Thee,
> How feeble is our mortal frame,
>   What dying worms we be."

The faith of the poor black servant was manifested in the reply, " Massa no 'fraid ; dis sickness for de glory of God." Brother Ames, another missionary residing near, was also ill, and about this time died ; but the sad event was concealed from his friend Bellamy by those around him. The spirit of the departed one must have appeared to him ; for, soon after, Mr Bellamy exclaimed, " Ames is gone ! I 'll go too." After this he changed for death, and at six next morning his spirit went to join his fellow-missionary in the land of the blessed.

HYMN 43.—" And am I born to die ? "—*For Children.*—TUNE, Lampe's, 1746.

This forms No. 59 of Charles Wesley's " Hymns for Children," 1763. " A land of deepest shade," is altered from " A world," &c., and " Shall " is exchanged for " Will angel bands convey." Of the one hundred hymns contained in this volume, the venerable Thomas Jackson remarks—" It would perhaps be difficult to mention any uninspired book that, in the same compass, contains so much evangelical sentiment. Charles Wesley's " Hymns for Children " are full of instruction, yet thoroughly devotional in their character. There is nothing puerile in them, either with respect to thought or expression. The language is simple, terse, pure, and strong. The topics which they embrace are the truths and facts of Christianity, especially in their bearing upon personal religion. In the hands of a Christian mother, these hymns would form a valuable help in the task of education. Most of the hymns, if committed to memory, would at once inform the memory and impress the heart. Some of the hymns are intended for the use of young children just beginning to speak and think, whilst others are adapted equally to the capacity and experience of adults. The design of the whole is to teach, to form the manners, and to discipline the understanding and conscience. The author leads the young mind to Christ as a sacrifice for sin, as the fountain of grace, as the great example of all excellence, and as the supreme Lord and Judge.

HYMN 44.—"And am I only born to die?"—*For Children.*—
TUNE, Snowsfields, 1761.

The original forms No. 64 in the same volume as the preceding. One incident out of many may be briefly alluded to, to show the power and influence of this hymn.

A young lady in America, of high position, and who had completed a thorough course of education, leaving school with certificates of the highest merit, had become the centre of a large and fashionable circle of friends. This gifted and accomplished young lady went one Sunday evening to hear a sermon preached by the venerable Bishop Asbury. The voice, manner, and earnest solicitude of the man of God fixed the truth so firmly on her mind that she sought and found pardon through faith in Jesus. She at once gave up her worldly companions and pursuits. Her fond parents used their utmost efforts to win back her affections to the world, but in vain. As a last resort, her father gave a large party to the most worldly and fashionable persons in the city. A more busy scene of pleasure-loving gaiety was never witnessed. During the evening it was arranged that their daughter should be invited to sing and play on the piano one of those fashionable airs to which they had so often listened with delight. Led by her father to the piano, she took her seat, and sang in a strain the most touching, because it came from the heart, and with a full, clear voice, that part of Charles Wesley's fine hymn which commences :—

> " No room for mirth or trifling here,
> For worldly hope, or worldly fear,
> If life so soon is gone."

She had not sung through one verse before her father, who stood by her side, drooped his head. Every whisper ceased, and the most intense feeling pervaded the entire company. Every word of the hymn was spoken distinctly, and heard by every one present ; each seemed an arrow from the Spirit's quiver, going

directly to the hearts of the hearers. Her father retired to his
room to weep for his own sinful folly with a deeply-stricken
heart. Mary had conquered. For many years she lived to
adorn her godly profession, and she passed away at last in
triumph to the skies.

A similar anecdote is related by Belcher, an American
author, of the daughter of an English nobleman, who, in like
manner, preferred to sing the same verses instead of her song
in turn with other young ladies present. The noble Lord
became converted, abandoned worldly company, joined the
people of God, and during his religious life distributed to promote the spread of the Gospel one hundred thousand pounds !

Methodism was established in the village of Rookly, in the
Isle of Wight, about 1783. In that society there was a youth
named Thomas Whitewood, whose devotedness to God, con-
stancy, fervour in the means of grace, and usefulness in prayer
meetings, public and social, had attracted general notice.
One morning while at work in his father's barn he was heard
singing that very solemn hymn of Charles Wesley's commencing—

> "And am I only born to die ?"

the last verse of which is as follows—

> " Jesus, vouchsafe a pitying ray ;
> Be Thou my guide, be Thou my way
> To glorious happiness !
> Ah, write the pardon on my heart,
> And whensoe'er I hence depart,
> Let me depart in peace ! "

Scarcely had he expressed the devout breathings of his heart to
God in this remarkable language, than he fell and expired.
This sudden death made a deep impression on many hearts,
and so aroused the conscience of one youth, named Robert
Bull, as to lead to his conversion to God.

Methodism was commenced at Haddenham in 1820, in a
barn ; and amongst the early worshippers in that primitive
place of worship was Priscilla Paine, then feeling the sorrows of
widowhood. Here the Lord was pleased to manifest Himself
to her in His saving power, and she soon identified herself with
the people of God, and opened her house for His servants. Her

convictions of sin were deepened by the minister giving out
the hymn commencing—

> "Lo, God is here, let us adore," &c.;

and at the closing scene, after a life of devoted service to the
Master's cause, she oft repeated the last verse of Hymn 44—

> "Jesus, vouchsafe a pitying ray," &c.,

adding, on one occasion after doing so, " Is not that sweet—
Jesus is precious. What He wills is best. My God is reconciled, and all is well. Come, Lord Jesus." She lay down in
peace, and her spirit returned to God who gave it.

HYMN 45. — "Shrinking from the cold hand of death."--
Genesis xlix. 33 ; and *Numbers* xx. 28.—TUNE, Palmis, 1761.

This hymn is made up of parts of two of Charles Wesley's
"Short Scripture Hymns," 1762. The third verse is based on
Numbers xx. 28, commencing—"O that without a lingering
groan," &c. This verse was generally given out by John
Wesley at the close of the society meetings he held after
evening preaching—a custom and a choice worthy of wider
extension. Illustrative examples of the use of this hymn are so
numerous, that every verse, and almost every line has its own
special interest.

Amongst the accidents which have hurried immortal souls
into eternity, none have been more fatal than those occurring in
collieries. Towards the class of people employed in mining,
Methodism has especially devoted its energies, and many
blessed results are on record as the reward of those labours.
John Jones, of Ashton-under-Lyne, was for some years a faithful
member of the Methodist Society. On the day of his death he
uttered a sentence in his family prayer which expressed a hope
that they might all meet in heaven, and said to a leader that he
would set out afresh to serve the Lord. At noon of the same
day he repeated to the members of his family the verse—

> "Shrinking from the cold hand of death,
>   I too shall gather up my feet,
> Shall soon resign my fleeting breath,
>   And die, my father's God to meet."

At one o'clock he entered the coal-mine, and wrought till ten
o'clock at night, when, being drawn to the surface of the earth,

the rope slipped, and he fell to the bottom of the pit a lifeless corpse. Many die as suddenly—would that all died as safely.

But few of the victims of that terrible scourge, consumption, have afforded to them opportunities for repentance during their rapid march into eternity. Mrs Fox, wife of the missionary, W. B. Fox, of Ceylon, was a happy believer in early life, and devoted to God her best energies. When her end was drawing near, she often repeated her favourite hymn, commencing—

"Shrinking from the cold hand of death," &c.

So partial was she to that hymn that she got an old Hymn-book bound and clasped with silver, because it contained the hymn (unabridged) with her favourite verse, as follows :—

" Walk with me through the dreadful shade,
    And, certified that Thou art mine,
My spirit, calm and undismayed,
    I shall into Thy hands resign."

The experience of James Thomas, a leader of three classes at Haverfordwest, and a man who walked with God, led him to repeat with animation and delight just before he died such hymns as " Rock of Ages" and

"Shrinking from the cold hand of death."

He died in the faith and hope of the Gospel.

Mrs Bullivant, mother of the Rev. W. J. Bullivant, was a careful student of God's Word, and of all the writings of the worthies of Methodism. She relied implicitly on the atonement of Christ for salvation, and often repeated this verse of her favourite hymn—

" O that without a lingering groan
    I may the welcome word receive;
My body with my charge lay down,
    And cease at once to work and live."

While in the act of rising from bed, her spirit fled to the paradise of God.

HYMN 46.—" The morning flowers display their sweets."—*On the Death of a Young Lady.* Isa. xl. 6, 8.—TUNE, Kettlesby, 1761.

This hymn was written by the Rev. Samuel Wesley, jun., in

the year 1735. It is an exquisitely fine composition. It was published first by John Wesley in " Hymns and Sacred Poems," enlarged edition, 1743.

Hymn 46.—" Come, let us anew Our journey pursue."—*For New Year's Day.*—Tune, New Year's Day, 1761.

Owing to editorial oversight, about the year 1807, when the Hymn-book underwent several alterations, there have been two hymns with this number. This is one of C. Wesley's Hymns for the New Year, 1750.

It is a fine lively composition, admirably adapted by its appropriate and weighty sentiments for the solemn service for which it is used. There is a peculiarity about the long and short syllables which gives ease to the rapid flow of the words, and testifies with what ease even difficult metres were composed by C. Wesley.

Grace and providence often co-operate. A little girl, belonging to the Scotch Church, was permitted by her father to go to the watch-night service of the Methodists in Aberdeen, on condition that she remembered the text, and repeated it on her return home. At the end of the service the accustomed hymn was sung,

" Come, let us anew Our journey pursue,
Roll round with the year," &c.

This was to her a novelty, and so fixed in the child's mind a love towards Methodism, that she ultimately became a member of the Society, and the wife of the Rev. John Shipman, Wesleyan minister. The text failed to influence her mind seriously, but the last hymn did so effectually.

Mrs Holy, of Sheffield, began to serve God in early life, and during a period of more than threescore years and ten took unceasing pleasure in helping forward the cause of God and Methodism. When laid aside by weakness and age, she delighted in repeating Wesley's hymns. The family not being able to attend the watch-night service, they were called together for a special service in the house, when she addressed some faithful and loving words to them, closing the service by singing the New Year's Hymn, in which she heartily joined. This was the last service she attended on earth. Extreme weakness set in ; but her confidence in God was unshaken, and her last words were, " I do feel Christ precious."

The death of one person is often the awakening to spiritual
life of many. Mrs Hobkinson, of Harrowgate, was called to part
with her son, an event which awakened her to a sense of her
lost state as a sinner. She sought and found redemption, and
to the end of life maintained her confidence in God. A little
before her departure she attempted to sing part of the New
Year's Hymn—

> " O that each in the day Of His coming may say,
>   I have fought my way through."

Adding with increased emphasis the last line—

> " I have finish'd the work Thou didst give me to do."

HYMN 47.—"Pass a few swiftly-fleeting years."—"*I am going the
way of all the earth*" (Joshua xxiii. 14).—TUNE, Purcell's,
1761.

This forms No. 387, vol. i., of Charles Wesley's " Short Scripture Hymns," 1762. Mr Wesley's volumes of Scripture Hymns are
too little known ; most of the hymns are concise, but some few
are lengthy. They are two thousand and thirty in number, and
are founded on particular texts throughout all the books of the
Bible. " Some of them," observes the Rev. Thomas Jackson,
" display a singular ingenuity, and nearly all breathe a spirit of
pure and fervent devotion. They prove the author to have been
a diligent, accurate, and critical student of the Sacred Books,
and often throw an interesting light upon important passages.
The metres are agreeably varied, and the entire work is perhaps
one of the best uninspired manuals for the closet of the Christian that was ever published in the English language." They
appeared in 1762, second edition in 1794-6.

The author, in his preface, remarks, " God having graciously
laid His hand upon my body, and disabled me for the principal
work of the ministry, has thereby given me an unexpected occasion of writing these hymns. Many of the thoughts are borrowed
from Mr Henry's Comment, Dr Gell on the Pentateuch, and
Bengelius on the New Testament. Several of the hymns are
intended to prove, and several to guard, the doctrine of Christian perfection. My desire is rightly to divide the word of
truth. But who is sufficient for these things ? Who can check
the self-confident without discouraging the self-diffident ?

Reader, if God ministers grace to thy soul through any of these hymns, offer up a prayer for the weak instrument, that, whenever I finish my course, I may depart in peace, having seen in Jesus Christ His great salvation."

How many thousands did offer up a prayer for the "weak instrument!" and how many thousands have been blessed as the result of those labours! What a glorious ending had their author! "My brother Charles fell asleep so quietly, that they who sat by him did not see when he died." So wrote John Wesley in a letter to Henry Moore, the original of which is now before the writer. Even the last utterances of that godly poet have been a source of comfort, hope, and consolation to hundreds since his death; and those glowing words of trust in Christ are the poet's last legacy to the Church. Charles Wesley, a few days before his death, composed his own epitaph. Having been silent and quiet for some time, he called Mrs Wesley to him, and bid her write as he dictated :—

> " In age and feebleness extreme,
> Who shall a sinful worm redeem!
> Jesus, my only hope Thou art,
> Strength of my failing flesh and heart ;
> O ! could I catch a smile from Thee,
> And drop into eternity ! "

"In age and feebleness extreme," has been used on hundreds of death-beds by devout followers of Christ in the Methodist Societies. *Vide* appendix at the end of the volume.

Two points of doctrine were introduced into the "Short Hymns" by Charles Wesley, in which he differs from his brother John. They were Spiritual Darkness and Christian Perfection. Many of the hymns in the collection are taken from this work, but not any in which the controverted points of doctrine are found. These two volumes were reprinted in an altered and abridged form after the author's death.

HYMN 48.—"Ah, lovely appearance of death !"—*On the Sight of a Corpse.*—TUNE, Funeral, 1761.

The original is one of Charles Wesley's " Funeral Hymns," a tract of twenty-four pages, first published in 1744, and of which nine editions appeared.

There have been differences of opinion as to the appropriateness of some of the language used in this hymn. The Rev. Richard Watson says that Charles Wesley's Funeral Hymns have too little of the softness of sorrow in them, but they are written in the fulness of faith which exclaims, even over the grave, " Thanks be to God, which giveth us the victory, through our Lord Jesus Christ." There is an interesting and appropriate illustration to this hymn in Mr Arthur's " Life of Mr Budgett," of Bristol, the octavo edition, 1852, in the death of Betty Coles (pages 89, 90), which is worth the reader's attention. Byron, in his " Giaour," records similar sentiments in describing death ; and Caroline Bowles, who became the wife of Robert Southey, poet-laureate, has written this passage :—

> " And is this death ? Dread thing !
> If such thy visiting,
> How beautiful thou art !

Mrs Hall, the poet's sister Martha, could not look at a corpse, because she said it was " beholding sin sitting on his throne." She objected strongly to the opening lines of this fine hymn—

> " Ah ! lovely appearance of death !
> No sight upon earth is so fair."

John Wesley altered the words " No sight " to " What sight," thus greatly modifying the strength of his brother's language by changing a harsh assertion into inquiry. A subsequent editor has altered a line in the fifth verse from " Sealed up in *eternal* repose " to " Sealed up in *their mortal* repose."

An extract or two from the journal of Charles Wesley will throw further light on this hymn.

Under date of Cardiff, August 12-14, 1744, Mr Charles Wesley relates having preached in the Castle-yard, and having visited two sick brethren. The next day he observes, " I was much revived by our dying brother, who is now ready to be offered up. I asked him whether he would rather die or live ? He answered, ' To depart, and be with Christ, is far better.' He is a pattern for all Christian graces, and was the first in Cardiff to receive the gospel of full salvation." The next day, Mr Wesley records, " we prayed last night with joy, full of glory for our departing brother, just while he gave up his spirit—as I pray God I may give up mine. This morning I expounded that last best triumph of faith. ' I have fought a good fight,' &c. The Lord administered strong consolation to those that love His appearing. We sung a song of victory for our deceased friend, then went to the house, and rejoiced, and gave thanks; and rejoiced again with singing over him. The spirit, at its departure, had left marks of its happiness on the clay. NO SIGHT UPON EARTH, IN MY EYES, IS HALF SO LOVELY."

John Wesley, in his journal, June 28, 1786, writes, "This morning Abigail Pilsworth, aged fourteen, was born into the world of spirits. I talked with her the evening before, and found her ready for the Bridegroom. A few hours after, she quietly fell asleep. When we went into the room where her remains lay we were surprised: a more BEAUTIFUL CORPSE I never saw. We all sung—

"' Ah, lovely appearance of death !'

All the company were in tears, but they were tears of joy." The Cardiff incident doubtless originated this hymn.

HYMN 49.—" Rejoice for a brother deceased."—*A Funeral Hymn.*—TUNE, Sion, 1761.

This forms the second of Charles Wesley's " Funeral Hymns," in the tract just named. Mrs Hall, the author's sister, commended this while she was unfavourable to the previous hymn. This was a great favourite with the author himself in the decline of life. Mr Henry Moore relates this anecdote of him when nearly eighty years of age :—" He rode every day (clothed as for winter even in summer) a little horse, grey with age. When he mounted, if a subject struck his mind, he proceeded to expand and put it in order. He would write a hymn thus given him on a card, with his pencil, in short-hand. Not unfrequently he has come to the house in the City-road, and having left his pony in the garden in front (the property was not then enclosed in wall and iron rails as it now is), he would enter crying out ' Pen and ink ! pen and ink.' These being supplied, he would write the hymn he had composed in his mind, and deposit it in his pocket-book." That same pocket-book, with two of Charles Wesley's manuscript hymns in its folds, is now in the possession of the writer of these notes. Mr Moore proceeds, " When this was done, he would look round on those present and salute them with much kindness, and thus put all in mind of eternity. He was fond of repeating the third stanza of this hymn on such occasions, which commences—

"There all the ship's company meet,
　Who sailed with the Saviour beneath," &c.

William Hindson, of Hegdale, Penrith, many years a local preacher and leader, maintained intimate, happy, and sanctifying communion with God during a long life, and closed it with calm assurance of heaven, leaving as his closing testimony the lines—

"There all the ship's company meet,
　Who sailed with the Saviour beneath."

Edward Maden, of the Burnley circuit, realised during his last illness an ecstacy of joy, and heavenly consolation ; and the full assurance of his heavenly inheritance he declared in the verse commencing—

"There all the ship's company meet ;"

adding, "I shall soon be one of them, and shall meet many whom I have known on earth who will welcome me home."

The honoured son of an honoured sire in the Wesleyan ministry, Nathaniel Francis Woolmer, of Gloucester, was a useful member and leader in Methodism ; and by a consistency of religious profession manifested his "walk with God." His delight in the services of the sanctuary, and in doing good to the bodies and souls of those around him, have made his memory precious. Often, when engaged in prayer, his face became radiant with joy, as well as when he spoke of the Saviour, or repeated portions of Scripture and of his favourite hymns. With remarkable feeling he quoted, as indicative of the hope that was in him at the end of his pilgrimage, the verse commencing—

"There all the ship's company meet," &c.

HYMN 50.—"Blessing, honour, thanks, and praise."—*A Funeral Hymn.*—TUNE, Love Feast, 1761.

This was first published in Charles Wesley's "Hymns and Sacred Poems," 1742. This, it is said, was the hymn sung by Mr Wesley and his sisters, immediately after the death of their mother in 1742.

HYMN 51.—"Hark ! a voice divides the sky."—*A Funeral Hymn.*—TUNE, Ascension, 1761.

This hymn is found in the same volume as the preceding. It is worthy of remark that the tunes affixed to this and the preceding hymn, indicate a much stronger leaning to the joys of the departed than the sorrows of the bereaved. Both these hymns are unaltered reprints.

The exultant tone which runs through this hymn has been caught by many a redeemed spirit on the border-land of both worlds, but was perhaps never more fully exhibited than in the closing scene of that devoted young missionary, the Rev. James H. Wayte. He had reached Freetown, Sierra Leone, and gladdened the hearts of the resident missionaries by his arrival. Rejoicing in the consciousness that Christ is able to cleanse from all sin, his desire to make known this great salvation was manifested by his intense zeal ; but Divine Providence cut short his earthly career. Suffering much from the time of his arrival in Africa, fever soon set in, and hastened him home to heaven. Ere the vital spark fled, Mr Dove, a brother missionary, visited him, and attempted to pray with him, but he was interrupted by the dying youth, who began to invoke the Divine blessing upon all his late brother students at Richmond. After a pause, he said, " O glory be to Jesus ! I feared I should depart without a shout for my Lord ; but He would not allow it ; bless His gracious name. I have preached Christ in life, though very unfaithfully ; and I will preach Him in death." Then raising his voice to a higher pitch, he added—

> " ' Mortals cry, A man is dead !
>   Angels shout, A child is born ! ' "

In this strain he continued for two hours. Soon afterwards he seemed to get a glimpse of the better land ; and just before he breathed out his spirit, he exclaimed, " Beautiful ! O how beautiful ! " and entered into rest.

HYMN 52.—" Again we lift our voice."—*On the Death of Samuel Hutchins.*—TUNE, Irene, 1761.

The original appears in Charles Wesley's " Hymns and Sacred Poems," 1749, vol. ii. Samuel Hutchins was a Cornish smith, one of the first race of Methodist preachers, who died at an early age. An account of his life, written by his father, was published by John Wesley in 1746.

William Parkin, of Hightown, was a zealous Yorkshire Methodist, who, yielding to the strivings of the Spirit of God, knelt down under a hedge, and, whilst praying there, entered into the liberty of the children of God. The testimony of his acceptance was clear and abiding, and abated nothing of its intensity in his latest hours. Shortly before death, he said, "My soul delights in God. Singing and praying never hurts me." To a brother local preacher, he said, his countenance radiant with a heavenly smile, "I am on the Rock, and feel it will bear me up." Expecting his end, he added, "before you take my body from the house, sing the verse—

> " 'Again we lift our voice,
>   And shout our solemn joys !
>   Cause of highest raptures this,
>   Raptures that shall never fail :
>   See a soul escaped to bliss,
>   Keep the Christian festival.' "

Whilst speaking to his wife of his intention to take an hour's drive out in the afternoon, he fell lifeless on the floor !

HYMN 53.—"Give glory to Jesus our Head."—*On the Death of a Widow.*—TUNE, Sion, 1761.

This hymn is No. 158 in the second volume of Charles Wesley's "Hymns and Sacred Poems," 1749. The original is eight lines longer, and two words are altered.

The poet has expressed an idea in the second verse which is worthy of remark ; it is—

> "Where glorified spirits, by sight,
>   Converse in their holy abode."

That intercourse should be carried on by sight, in the heavenly state, is certainly novel ; and yet the same thought is stated in a passage by Butler in his "Hudibras," which runs thus—

> "Or, who but lovers can converse
>   Like angels by the eye discourse?
>   Address and compliment by vision."

The parish of Madeley is classic ground ; and some of its memories are such as bring to mind those of Bethany. There John Wesley often preached ; and amongst his hearers was one Betsy Piggot, who, in 1785, the year in which John Fletcher died, was married to Thomas Milner. Convinced of sin under Mr Wesley, and led to Christ by the teaching of Mrs Fletcher, in whose class she was a member, her religious character was formed on the most God-like model. Becoming a widow in

1819, for forty years she was esteemed and loved for her work's sake, by both the Church and the world. For eighty-five years she enjoyed and used for the glory of God the blessing of health; and her trust in God was in no way abated when weakness and decay oppressed her. The day before her death, she said, "'Blessed are the dead which die in the Lord.' That is my case." Her last pœan was, "O Lord God, Rock of my salvation." Having sung this, she went straight to heaven. All business was suspended at the time of her funeral; and her remains were placed in the earth in front of Madeley Vicarage, and close to those of her endeared friends, John and Mary Fletcher, the funeral service being conducted by a grandson of the devout Hester Ann Rogers. While the vast crowd stood uncovered round the grave, the fifty-third -hymn was sung, which thus commences—

> "Give Glory to Jesus our Head,
>   With all that encompass His throne;
> A widow, a widow indeed,
>   A mother in Israel is gone!" &c.

HYMN 54.—"Hearken to the solemn voice."—*A Midnight Hymn.*—TUNE, Amsterdam, 1761.

Written by Charles Wesley, and published in "Hymns and Sacred Poems," 1742. The passage in St Luke xii. 35 seems to have suggested the third verse. This is the first hymn in the section "Describing Judgment."

HYMN 55.—"Thou Judge of quick and dead."—*For the Watchnight.*—TUNE, Olney, 1761.

First published in Charles Wesley's "Hymns and Sacred Poems," 1749, vol. ii. In the fourth verse, "*Our* lot" is changed to "A lot."

A venerable man was Richard Burdsall, of York; and his daughter, the mother of Richard and John Lyth, was scarcely less pious. When twelve years old, she gave herself to the Lord, and her piety grew with her growth. During her last days, her full heart overflowed in songs of praise, even in the night season. On being told that her end was approaching, she rejoiced greatly that she was going home. On the day before her death, she repeated—

> "O may I thus be found
>   Obedient to His word;

Attentive to the trumpet's sound,
And looking for my Lord."

Her last words were, "Praise, glory, my Father, my Redeemer."
Thus closed a life fragrant with holiness and peace.

HYMN 56.—"He comes! He comes! the Judge severe."—*Thy
Kingdom come.*—TUNE, Judgment, 1761.

This forms number 37 of Charles Wesley's "Hymns of Intercession for all Mankind," 1758. It is worthy of remark here, that
"neither the delight of social intercourse, nor the spiritual prosperity of his own people, could induce Charles Wesley to forget
the public welfare, and the cause of religion generally. England
was at war with several states on the Continent, domestic tranquillity was menaced, Protestant interests were in peril, the
clergy were asleep at the post of duty, and ungodliness and sin
everywhere prevailed at the time when Charles Wesley wrote
his 'Hymns of Intercession for all Mankind.'" So manifest
was the peril, that the principal Methodist societies had a
special meeting for prayer every Friday at noon, to intercede
with God on behalf of the Church, the nation, and the world.
To assist those services, and to fan the flame of Christian
patriotism, Mr Wesley published these hymns. From this
small work seven hymns in the Wesleyan collection are taken,
namely, hymns 56, 66, 441, 442, 443, 444, 451. There are forty
hymns in the tract; it appeared originally without author's
name or date, and this fact may help to account for the strange
and alien appropriation for so long a period of hymn 66, "Lo!
He comes with clouds descending," which is taken from its
pages.

HYMN 57.—"The great Archangel's trump shall sound."—
After Deliverance from Death by the fall of a House.—
TUNE, Canon, 1761.

The original forms number 174 in Charles Wesley's "Hymns
and Sacred Poems," 1749, vol. ii., and commences, "Glory and
thanks to God we give." The first five verses are omitted; this
hymn begins with the sixth verse of the original. The accident
which originated this fine composition is related in Charles
Wesley's journal. On his third visit to Leeds he met the society
in an old upper room, which was densely packed, and crowds
could not gain admission. He removed nearer the door that

those without might hear, and drew the people towards him. Instantly the rafters broke off short, close to the main beam, the floor sank, and more than one hundred people fell, amid dust and ruins, into the room below. One sister had her arm broken, and set immediately ; rejoicing with joy unspeakable. Another, strong in faith, was so crushed, that she expected instant death, but she was without fear, and only said, in calm faith, " Jesus, receive my spirit." A boy of eighteen, who had come to make a disturbance, who struck several women on entering, was taken up roaring, " I will be good !   I will be good !" They got his leg set, which was broken in two places. The preacher did not fall, but slid down softly, and lighted on his feet. His hand was bruised, and part of the skin rubbed off his head. He lost his senses, but recovered them in a moment, and was filled with power from above. He writes, " I lifted up my head and saw the people under me, heaps upon heaps. I cried out, ' Fear not : the Lord is with us ; our lives are all safe ;' and then gave out, ' Praise God, from whom all blessings flow.' " Several were seriously hurt, but none killed. After such a deliverance was this hymn written. It commences, " Glory and thanks to God we give ; " and after twenty lines, in which there are evident references to this remarkable escape from death, the sixth verse commences, " The great Archangel's trump shall sound," &c. This accident took place March 14, 1744.

Only the possession of mighty faith in God could give the calmness and composure of mind which are indicated in this sublime composition.

HYMN 58.—" Jesus, faithful to His word.—*A Funeral Hymn.*—
        TUNE, Hamilton's, 1781.

This hymn was first published in Charles Wesley's " Hymns and Sacred Poems," 1742. The original has six verses, the first three of which are omitted. It is based on 1 Thess. iv. 13. The first line reads thus : " Let the world lament their dead," &c.

HYMN 59.—" Thou God of glorious majesty."—*A Hymn for Seriousness.*—TUNE, Snowsfield's, 1761.

This hymn is found in Charles Wesley's " Hymns and Sacred Poems," 1749, vol. i. The Sheffield poet, Montgomery, says of this hymn : " It is a sublime contemplation, solemn, collected, unimpassioned thought, but thought occupied with that which is of everlasting import to a dying man, standing on the lapse of a moment between two eternities." Tradition states that this hymn was written by Charles Wesley after a visit to Land's End, Cornwall, in July 1743; but Mr Thomas Jackson, in "Mr Wesley's Life," says there is no proof thereof. There is at the Land's End a narrow neck of land betwixt two unbounded seas —the Bristol Channel to the north, and the English Channel to the south ; or, we may add, the Great Atlantic Ocean to the west, and the German Ocean to the east, all uniting at this point. The tradition is natural, and seems well supported ; it is given by Dr Adam Clarke in a manuscript letter before the writer, without doubt or hesitation ; Dr Clarke knew Charles Wesley personally, and the letter containing the tradition was written partly in pencil on the "narrow neck of land" itself, and finished at "the first inn in England," situated at the Land's End. Mr Thomas Taylor, a Methodist preacher, who visited the Land's End in 1761, records the words : "Here Mr Charles Wesley wrote, ' Lo! on a narrow neck of land,' &c."

In the third verse, Mr Wesley introduces an unusual word amongst Christians—"And tremble on the brink of fate." The word fate not only comes in to suit the rhyme, but is in this instance of its use a proper rescuing of the word from the claim of the infidel : fate, from *fatum*, what is spoken or decreed by Almighty power and goodness, and here it is applied to death.

Amongst the early friends of Methodism in Pilsley village, in the Peak of Derbyshire, Luke Bridge will be remembered with gratitude and affection. Once, in the Conference prayer-meeting at Sheffield, he asked the assembly to "help him to pray for poor Pilsley." For more than thirty years he ceased not to strive to bring his neighbours to God. At the end of his pilgrimage, protracted to more than fourscore years, he recorded his sentiments in the language of his favourite hymns, one of which was, "Thou God of glorious majesty," &c. He was eminent for his interceding power in prayer.

Mrs Ann Brown, the wife of the Rev. J. R. Brown, began to meet in class at the age of sixteen ; and from that time to the end of her life her uprightness of conduct and seriousness of demeanour secured for her the affectionate regard of a large circle of friends. At Whitby, her recovery from serious illness she attributed to the goodness of God in answer to the prayers of the people. An attack of typhus fever in Sunderland made short work with her ; and when told that medical skill could do no more for her, she replied, " The will of the Lord be done," and added—

> " Lo ! on a narrow neck of land,
> 'Twixt two unbounded seas I stand," &c.

Her mind was occupied with repeating portions of Scripture and hymns during her short stay on earth ; and she expired in peace.

HYMN 60.—" Righteous God ! whose vengeful phials."—*For the Year* 1756.—TUNE, Westminster, 1761.

This hymn forms number 15 of Charles Wesley's " Hymns for the year 1756," where it has six stanzas, the third and fourth being left out by John Wesley, as not suited for popular use.

The Government of the time appointed the 6th of February 1756 as a day of fasting and humiliation before God ; and to improve the occasion Charles Wesley wrote the seventeen hymns which form this tract. Hymns 60, 61, and 62 are selected from this tract, and three more sublime compositions have seldom been written. The fast was observed with deep solemnity ; the churches were all crowded, and a solemn seriousness sat on every face, " such as had not been seen," says John Wesley, " since the Restoration." The tract, possessing so much beauty and strength, and breathing so much fervent and elevated piety, quickly passed to a second edition, in the title of which the reference to the fast-day was omitted.

HYMN 61.— " Stand the omnipotent decree."— *For the year* 1756.—TUNE, Kingswood, 1761.

Charles Wesley's, written early in 1756 ; as fine a composition as ever came from an uninspired mind. " It is a strain more than human."

Mr Montgomery says—" It begins with a note abrupt and awakening, like the sound of the last trumpet. This is altogether one of the most daring and victorious flights of our author." Young's " Night Thoughts " doubtless suggested several of the sentiments and expressions in the hymn,—see Night vi.,—but in this, as in other instances, Young is greatly improved in sublimity and grandeur by Wesley. The first six

books of Young's "Night Thoughts" were published several
years before Charles Wesley wrote this grand hymn, and
whilst some of Young's conceptions are lofty and impressive,
Wesley's are much more so.   An interesting literary discus-
sion on this point is given in "Adam Clarke Portrayed," by
James Everett, vol. ii., 1844, page 339.

HYMN 62.—"How happy are the little flock."—*On the Over-
throw of Lisbon by an Earthquake.*—TUNE, Chapel, 1761.

Written by Charles Wesley in December 1755, on the occasion indicated by the title.   It forms the last of the seventeen
hymns in the tract of "Fast-day Hymns," published early in the
year 1756.   This composition exhibits the calm faith in the
divine love and protection which so eminently characterised
the early Methodists.   Besides the excitement caused by the
terrible earthquake, the English nation was daily expecting an
invasion by the French.

HYMN 63.—"Woe to the men on earth who dwell;"
  „   64.—"By faith we find the place above" (Rev. xvi. 16).
Occasioned by the Earthquake at Lisbon.—TUNE, Brockmer, 1761.

These two hymns form one of Charles Wesley's "Earthquake
Hymns," 1756, the second edition of a work which was first published in 1750.   The original is four verses longer.   In the third
line John Wesley has made an alteration.   "Lo, from their
roots" is changed to "Lo! from their seats," &c.

HYMN 65.—"Ye virgin souls, arise."—*For the Watchnight.*—
TUNE, Trumpet, 1761.

This is from Charles Wesley's "Hymns and Sacred Poems,"
1749, vol. ii.   The original is one verse longer.   It forms a fine
paraphrase of the parable of the ten virgins.

In the ranks of God's-heroes, no one will have a more prominent place than Samuel Hick, the "village blacksmith" of
Micklefield, Yorkshire.   He was a man of upright character,
untiring energy, deep piety, and singular usefulness.   Often he
said he had but one talent, but he was determined that it
should never be given to the man who had ten, for he would
use it up by hard trading.   When, after three-score years and
ten, he felt the tabernacle was being taken down, he exclaimed,
"Glory be to God; I have as much religion as will carry me to

heaven, but I have none to spare for either my wife or children."
His last words, distinctly uttered, were—" Peace, joy, and love !
peace, joy, and love !" His friends joined in singing the sixty-
fifth hymn, " Ye virgin souls, arise," &c. When they came to the
fifth verse—

> " The everlasting doors
> Shall soon the saints receive,
> Above yon angel powers
> In glorious joy to live ;
> Far from a world of grief and sin
> With God eternally shut in,"

here he lifted up his dying hand, and waved it round and
round, till it fell upon the bed ; then he lifted up his fore-finger,
and turned it round to show that he was going, as he had often
said he should like to go, "in full sail into the harbour." We
visited the house and room in which he died more than thirty
years after the event, and his memory was fragrant as ever
there ; and not a few were living who delighted to relate incidents of that good man's Christian heroism.

More gentle in disposition, and not less faithful in the service
of God, was Mrs Margaret Scott, of Newcastle. Like " Sammy
Hick," she never allowed sin to go unreproved. After a life of
scrupulous integrity and unspotted piety, on her death-bed she
felt her confidence in the merits of Christ to be unshaken.
Shortly before her death she sang twice, in a plaintive manner,
the verse—

> " He comes, He comes, to call
> The nations to His bar,
> And raise to glory all
> Who fit for glory are :
> Made ready for your full reward,
> Go forth with joy to meet your Lord."

She tried it a third time, and her voice failed her ; but she
added, "What a strange thing that I should gain a full reward !
a full reward ! " In this happy frame of mind she soon entered
on its enjoyment.

HYMN 66.*—" Lo ! He comes with clouds descending."—*Thy
Kingdom come.*—TUNE, Olivers (Helmsley), 1761.

The original of this grand hymn forms No. 29 in Charles
Wesley's " Hymns of Intercession for all Mankind," 1758. This
was not inserted in the collection till after Mr Wesley's death.

The notion that Thomas Olivers wrote this fine composition is entirely without evidence to support it. Olivers wrote the tune to it, and it appears in Mr Wesley's "Sacred Melody," 1761, with the proper words to the tune ; and as the tune is named after its author, Olivers, it has been supposed that both words and tune were produced by him. Investigation for years by many minds has now settled the dispute. Charles Wesley wrote the hymn as it now appears in the Wesleyan collection. The tune written by Olivers, and long known by his name, is now called "Helmsley." Both the hymn and tune are spirited compositions, and well adapted for either cheerful or solemn subjects.

"In death not divided," or but little, may be said of many family ties amongst the Lord's people. It was less than a year and a half since the Rev. William Pemberton had died in peace at Newcastle, that Mrs Pemberton, at Leeds, was called somewhat suddenly to rejoin the redeemed spirit of her husband. Seized with typhus fever, recovery was soon found to be hopeless ; but if her time was come, her work was done—she was ready, prepared to meet the Bridegroom. Just as the mortal conflict ended, with her latest breath she sang—

> " Lo ! He comes with clouds descending,
> Once for favour'd sinners slain," &c.,

when she calmly fell asleep in Jesus, leaving nine young orphan children to the care of God and His Church.

Enduring a long life of affliction, relieved only by the consolations of the gospel, Mrs Sarah Edwards, of Sccfton-Bach, Ludlow, realised a comforting assurance of her acceptance with God. The day before she died, her peace rose to triumphant joy, so that she exclaimed, "Conquering ! conquering ! glory ! glory !" she then sang the hymn commencing, "Lo ! He comes with clouds descending," &c., and fell asleep in Jesus.

This hymn, like many others, has been used by the Holy Spirit to carry conviction to the sinner's heart, as well as to afford consolation to the departing saint. Elizabeth Nuttall, of Rochdale, at the age of nineteen, was invited to a Methodist prayer-meeting, and while the hymn was being sung, commencing, "Lo ! He comes with clouds descending," &c., her mind was deeply convinced of sin, her distress became too much to be endured, and by faith she was enabled to believe to the salvation of her soul. She lived a consistent godly life, and died, saying,

"Praise the Lord"—"He is my God."

During the last illness of Mrs Sophia Charlotte Howes, she frequently said—"What a blessing it is that I found the Saviour when in health ; it could not be done now, I am too weak for that. Thank God ! I have now only to look to and trust in Jesus." As the end was approaching, she repeated some verses of the gospel by St John, after which she sang the third and fourth verses of the sixty-sixth hymn, commencing—

> " The dear tokens of His passion ;"

and—

> " Yea, Amen ! let all adore Thee," &c.

The powers of nature then rapidly declined, and she ceased to breathe, exclaiming, " God be merciful to me a sinner ! "

Hymn 67.—" How weak the thoughts, and vain."—*Written on the Earthquake in London.*—Tune, West Street, 1761.

This forms No. 9 of Charles Wesley's " Earthquake Hymns," 1750. This hymn is the first in the fifth section of the collection, with the title, " Describing Heaven." The original is in ten verses, only seven of which are given.

The circumstances which caused this hymn to be written were briefly these :—On February 8, 1750, there was a terrible earthquake in London, and many panic-stricken people rushed in hot haste to the Methodist chapels. In twenty-eight days God gave the people of London a second and far severer shock. Charles Wesley was preaching in the Foundry Chapel, just repeating his text, at a quarter past five A.M. The Foundry shook violently ; the alarmed people cried out ; the preacher changed his text and cried out, " Therefore will we not fear, though the earth be moved, and the hills be carried into the midst of the sea ; the God of Jacob is our refuge." God filled the preacher's heart with faith, and his mouth with suitable words, shaking the hearers' souls as well as their bodies. The excitement which spread over London baffles all description ; the people rushed in hot haste out of the city into Moorfields, Hyde Park, and other open spaces for safety. A mad dragoon intensified the wild excitement by declaring that all London would be swallowed up on April 4. The people believed the prediction, and at midnight Hyde Park was filled with people frantic with fear, to whom George Whitefield preached a sermon of masterly eloquence and power. Fear filled the Methodist preaching-house at midnight, and, observes Charles Wesley, "I preached my written sermon on the subject with great effect, and gave out several suitable hymns." It was a glorious night for the disciples of Jesus. The hymns composed for that occasion were nineteen in number, and they display all the highest qualities of the author's poetry.

Fearing God from her youth, and joining the Methodist society at the age of fourteen, Mrs Elizabeth Sims, of the Lincoln circuit, maintained her Christian integrity through life. During her last illness, she often called her family around her to join her in singing the praises of God. After a violent paroxysm of pain, she said, " My blessed Saviour! what should I have done without Thee now?" On her husband speaking of Jesus, she said, " 'Tis heaven below to know Jesus." Then exerting all her remaining energies, she sang, with great animation—

"How happy then are we,
Who build, O Lord, on Thee!" &c.

In the last note her voice faltered and died away, as her spirit returned to God.

HYMN 68.—" How happy is the pilgrim's lot!"—*The Pilgrim.*
—TUNE, Chapel, 1761.

The original was written by John Wesley, and forms No. 51 in "Hymns for those that seek and those that have Redemption," &c., 1747.

It was composed and published about five years before the author's marriage, and describes his own views and feelings on that question in terms of eloquent simplicity. It has been admired as a composition by multitudes who are not Methodists; and viewed in connexion with the unhappy marriage of its gifted and pious author, it will always possess, to the Methodists in particular, a special attraction. One verse is omitted between the third and fourth; and in the second verse " *low* design" is printed for " *self*-design " in the original.

This hymn has been a great favourite from the time of its first publication. The chief attraction of the poem clusters around the seventh verse, although the first and the last have had their special admirers. Mrs Bumby, of Thirsk, mother of the Rev. John Bumby, a woman of deep and sincere piety, benevolence, patience, humility, and affection, towards the end of life had her

affections weaned from all earthly things, and she delighted to
sing the first verse of this hymn, as indicating that she was
"Happy in her pilgrim's lot," but that "she only sojourned
here."

A cloud of witnesses cluster their affections around the following stanza—

> "There is my house and portion fair ;
> My treasure and my heart are there,
> And my abiding home ;
> For me my elder brethren stay,
> And angels beckon me away,
> And Jesus bids me come."

The sainted and truly holy, devoted, and loving Mary Fletcher,
of Madeley, after seventy-six years of toil, mourned because,
through great weakness, from exhausted nature, she could toil
no longer. Her sweet spirit said, " I am doing nothing ; neither
working nor reading, praying nor praising ; only sleeping."
Indeed, to her, doing nothing was very extraordinary. As the
end approached, she said, " I am drawing near to glory !" and
soon after—

> " There is my house and portion fair ;
> My treasure and my heart are there,
> And my abiding home."

Shortly afterwards she added, " He lifts His hand and shows
that I am graven there !"   Many more sweet words fell from
her gracious lips ere the spirit fled. The last time she lay down
she said to her beloved and attentive friend, Mary Tooth, " Now,
if I can rest, I will ; but let our hearts be united in prayer : and
the Lord bless both thee and me." She did rest, for shortly
after midnight all was silent ; she was " asleep in Jesus," and the
serenity of the face indicated the tranquillity of the heart.

The short but glorious career of the Rev. Daniel M'Allum,
M.D., was crowned with a triumphant end. When failing health
compelled him to cease his pulpit labours, he realised an inward
calmness and peace, varied only by so much of the gracious
presence of God as led him to cry out, " Lord, stay Thy hand,
lest the tabernacle break." On the last Sabbath he remained on
earth, knowing that his hours below were but few, he said to his
wife, with emphasis and sweetness—

> " There is my house and portion fair," &c.

The great and constant peace he enjoyed he believed to be in answer to the prayers of the Lord's people. His last words were, "I build only on the merit of my Saviour."

Mrs Horton, a beloved and useful class-leader, and the companion and helper of her husband, the Rev. W. Horton, during his missionary travels and labours, on reaching the end of her earthly pilgrimage, expressed her feelings by saying, "I am unspeakably happy; oh help me to praise the Lord." As she lay rapidly sinking, she said, "I have now nothing to do but to praise God to all eternity." Her last words, breathed in a faint whisper, just as she was departing, were those which form the seventh verse of hymn sixty-eight—

> "There is my house and portion fair," &c.

Venerable for her age, esteemed for her piety, and beloved for her godly example and Christian benevolence, Sarah Hall, of Bristol, wife of Mr John Hall, stands pre-eminent in the annals of Methodism. Joining her father's class at the age of thirteen, and receiving from John Wesley himself her first ticket, for more than seventy years she was a consistent member of the Methodist society, welcoming to her cheerful hospitality the leading worthies of the connexion—Coke, Pawson, Benson, Moore, Clarke, Reece, and others usually making her house their home. Till her eightieth year she was actively engaged in works of charity and benevolence. Her last letter, her last interview with her family, and the last entry in her journal, all tell of her Saviour's indwelling presence, whilst her dying words, uttered with brightened eye, uplifted hand, but tremulous voice, were—

> "*There* is my house and portion fair;
> My treasure and my heart are *there*,
> And my abiding home;"

after which the venerable saint departed "to be with Christ."

Service for God early in youth is usually followed by service for God during life. Maximilian Wilson gave his heart to God and the service of Methodism at the age of seventeen, and for sixty years and more he devoted his best energies in promoting its interests. During forty-five years he discharged the duties of the Wesleyan ministry, and as a supernumerary went about doing good. As the end drew nigh, his conversation was about things above. Frequently he was heard to say,

"Bless the Lord! I am going home; I shall soon be there. I live on the border of both worlds, and have fellowship with my departed friends in heaven." Then he would repeat the two closing verses of the Pilgrim's Hymn, commencing—

> "There is my house and portion fair," &c.

and when the end came, Christ smiled his peaceful spirit away to His own paradise, "where all the ship's company meet."

A somewhat novel adaptation of this favourite stanza was made by John G. Stevenson, of Chesterfield, a Methodist for half a century, whose wife, and six of his children had preceded him to heaven. The cares and anxieties of more than three-score years and ten had brought exhausted nature to the end of its pilgrimage, and, without any disease, the good man was patiently waiting the summons to depart, when, visited by the writer, he was found in an ecstasy of joy, ascribing all his happiness to Christ and His finished work; and then, as though holding communion with the redeemed spirits of his own family, he repeated, with surprising frequency—

> " For me my wife and children stay,
> And angels beckon me away,
> And Jesus bids me come."

HYMN 69.—" Thou, Lord, on whom I still depend."—*Revelation* ii. 10-12.—TUNE, Marienburn, 1761.

This hymn is formed of three of Charles Wesley's " Short Scripture Hymns," 1762, vol. ii., Nos. 831-833. One verse of the original is altered, and other verses are omitted.

There is a calm dignity in the manner in which the Christian is represented as going to meet death—

> " My soul the second death defies,
> And reigns eternal in the skies."

William Roach was one amongst the first Methodists in Shields, and had the privilege of hearing Mr Wesley preach in that locality. During a long life he was diligent in business, fervent in spirit, serving the Lord. On the Sunday previous to his death, exhausted nature having run its course, he desired his family to sing the hymn commencing—

> " Thou, Lord, on whom I still depend," &c.

It had often been sung by and for him before, but on this

occasion he thoroughly entered into the sentiment of this fine hymn ; and his joyous countenance reflected the gratitude his tongue could not express. He died in the full assurance of a blessed immortality.

The maxim, "Religion in youth, and religion for life," was verified in the case of Mrs Hannah Swindells, of Macclesfield. She strove to have every thought, word, and act conformed to the will of God. From a child she was a careful student of the Word, and a great admirer of Wesleyan poetry. During her last illness she was repeating almost continually verses of Scripture and hymns. Seated in her chair, shortly before her death, absorbed in thought, and adjusting her spiritual armour for the last conflict, she rose rather suddenly, and advancing towards the bed, she said, as she crossed the room—

> " Jesus, in Thy great Name I go
> To conquer death, my final foe !   ·
> And when I quit this cumbrous clay,
> And soar on angels' wings away,
> My soul the second death defies,
> And reigns eternal in the skies."

Then laying herself on the bed, like a warrior who had conquered, she instantly breathed out her soul into the hands of God.

HYMN 70.—"I long to behold Him array'd."—*Isaiah* xxxiii. 17, 23, 24.—TUNE, Thou Shepherd of Israel, 1761.

This hymn is made up of two of Charles Wesley's "Short Scripture Hymns," 1762, based on Isa. xxxiii. 17, 23, 24, of which passage it is a glowing and dignified paraphrase and amplification.

There is much grandeur in the expectant faith indicated throughout the hymn, and a glorious climax in

> " My fulness of rapture I find,
> My heaven of heavens, IN THEE."

Thus the author is represented as falling into, and reposing solely in, the arms of Jesus. The hymn is full of beauty.

The greater part of a life of threescore years and ten was spent by Mrs Atkinson, of Leeds, in the service of God and Methodism. The confidence of her faith and hope, at the end of her pilgrimage, often found expression in the words—

> " I long to behold Him array'd
> With glory and light from above," &c.

She peacefully breathed out her soul to God.

Good Mrs Henley, wife of the Rev. W. Henley, during a long and severe illness, preserved her confidence in God unshaken. Just before she breathed her last, she repeated her favourite verse—

> " I long to behold Him array'd, " &c.

Her departure was so peaceful, she seemed only to have fallen asleep.

At the age of seventy-two, George Cowley, a class-leader of Nottingham, was enabled to say, on his approach to the better world, " I owe so much to the Lord, that I am overwhelmed with gratitude." To the question, " Are you on the Rock?" he said, " Oh yes ; and I shall soon meet Jesus in heaven.

> " I long to behold Him array'd
> With glory and light from above,
> The King in His beauty display'd,
> His beauty of holiest love."

With these words on his lips, he fell asleep in Jesus.

A long course of unpretending but consistent piety marked the life of Bridget Daniell, wife of the Rev. Mark Daniell. Finding the end drawing nigh, she desired that nothing might be said of her if a funeral sermon was preached, adding, " I have been an unprofitable servant, but God accepts my imperfect service through the atonement of the blessed Jesus ; and "—her face becoming radiant with joy—

> " With Him I on Zion shall stand,
> For Jesus hath spoken the word."

In this spirit of calm resignation, she entered paradise.

HYMN 71.—" Leader of faithful souls, and Guide."—*The Traveller.*—TUNE, 112th Psalm, 1761.

This forms one of Charles Wesley's " Redemption Hymns," 1747, but two verses of the original are omitted.

A godly life dispels the fear of death. Mrs Catherine Pratt, wife of the Rev. J.-C. Pratt, died at Pettigo, very happy, having experienced the regenerating power of the Holy Ghost for many years. At the end of her pilgrimage, she testified of her confidence in God by exclaiming, " Victory, through the blood of the Lamb ! " adding the verse commencing—

> " Strangers and pilgrims here below," &c.

John Jottie began to serve God in early youth, and for nearly
fifty years he was a bright ornament of the Methodist society at
Walferden, near Colne. He was brought to a knowledge of the
truth in his eighth year, under a sermon preached by Mr Wesley at Southfield, who said in his sermon, " The best of us have
no grace to spare." These words carried conviction to his heart,
and he sought grace for himself, and found that which kept him
in perfect peace for nearly fourscore years. On the Thursday
before he died, while suffering severely, he was comforted by repeating the fourth verse of the " Traveller's Hymn "—

> " Patient the appointed race to run,
>   This weary world we cast behind ;
> From strength to strength we travel on,
>   The new Jerusalem to find :
> Our labour this, our only aim,
>   To find the New Jerusalem."

Here his strength failed him ; he lingered on a little longer,
triumphing in faith, till, on the Sunday afternoon, he exchanged
the earthly for the heavenly Sabbath.

HYMN 72.—" Saviour, on me the grace bestow."—*Him that
overcometh*, &c. (Rev. iii. 12).—TUNE, 112th Psalm, 1761.

Forms one of Charles Wesley's " Short Scripture Hymns,"
vol. ii., 1762.

HYMN 73.—" Away with our sorrow and fear."—*A Funeral
Hymn.*—TUNE, Sion, 1761.

One of Charles Wesley's " Funeral Hymns," 1744. The imagery used by the poet is taken from that great city, the holy
Jerusalem, and should be read in conjunction with St John's
description in Rev. xxi. It will be seen, on comparison, that
the " divine " apostle and the Methodist poet alike drew their
inspiration from heaven.

Passing through the discipline suitable for a minister's wife,
Martha Smith joined the fellowship of God's people at the age
of thirteen, became a Sunday-school teacher, and laid herself
out for active service in the Lord's vineyard. As the wife of the
Rev. James Smith, and sister of the Rev. Edward Lightwood,
her life seemed to be bound up with the prosperity of the cause
of God. When illness deprived her of the privileges of the sanc-

tuary, she was refreshed by meditations on the Word of God, and especially by repeating the lines—

> " Away with our sorrow and fear,
> We soon shall recover our home ;
> The city of saints shall appear,
> The day of eternity come," &c.

When she came to the verse commencing—

> " By faith we already behold
> That lovely Jerusalem here," &c.,

she dwelt with peculiar emphasis on some of the lines, as realising to her mind the presence of the "city of jasper and gold" already on earth. Her last words were, " He is precious ! "

" A good name is better than great riches." The father of Robert Wood, Wesleyan minister, was James Wood, Wesleyan minister, who, to commemorate his eightieth birthday, had a delightful party at the Conference (1831), consisting, among others, of Messrs Bunting, Newton, Watson, Lessey, James, Hannah, Morley, and Robert Wood. To add to the honour, the venerable man preached before the Conference a sermon on the occasion, full of excellent, affectionate, and faithful counsels. Robert Wood, the estimable son of this venerable sire, was admitted a member of the legal hundred of the Wesleyan Conference at the same time (1831), "being the youngest minister hitherto so honoured." His age was forty-four. Divine Providence, however, cut short his work in righteousness ; he lived but little more than two-thirds the years of his father. During his last illness, which was one of severe suffering and patient endurance, he showed by the tenor of his conversation, the sweetness of his disposition, and his choice of lessons and hymns to be read to him, that he desired to lead the members of his family to concur in the conclusion of the apostle Paul, " To depart and be with Christ is far better." Allusion having been made to the first Great Exhibition in Hyde Park, opened during the previous week, May 1851, in which the sufferer evinced much interest, a hope was expressed that he might so far recover as to be able to visit that "fairy land." He shook his head, and said, " No ; I shall never see the Crystal Palace : but reach the Hymn-book, and read the seventy-third hymn, and you will find that I shall not lose much." The hymn was read to him, and the third verse especially attracted attention :—

E

> " By faith we already behold
>   That lovely Jerusalem here ;
>   Her walls are of jasper and gold,
>   As crystal her buildings are clear," &c.

He survived but a short time, but long enough to testify that his hope for the future was based on the Rock of Ages. Slowly the light of a bright summer's morning in June broke into the chamber of death, and a dawn yet far more glorious burst upon the released spirit.

HYMN 74.—"We know, by faith we know."—*A Funeral Hymn.*
—TUNE, Olney, 1761.

Another of Charles Wesley's " Funeral Hymns," 1744. The second verse of the original is omitted. Dr Watts has a hymn (No. 110, book i.) very similar to this of Mr Wesley's.

Mr John Dyson Fernley was a child of many prayers, and in early life gave his heart to the Lord. After he was-born of God, and had become a new creature, he became eminently a spiritually-minded man. On the Sabbath before he closed his brief earthly career—limited to thirty years—he addressed the children in the Tiviotdale Sunday-school, Stockport, on the subject of sudden death, and the need of constant preparation. Many were much affected, and it is in touching accordance with the whole proceeding that at the close of the service he gave out the seventy-fourth hymn :—

> " We know, by faith we know,
>   If this vile house of clay,
> This tabernacle, sink below
>   In ruinous decay ;
> We have a house above,
>   Not made with mortal hands ;
> And firm, as our Redeemer's love,
>   That heavenly fabric stands."

On the following Sabbath-day apoplexy terminated his useful and happy life.

A godly life is the best test of a real conversion. Thomas Pearson, of Over-Darwen, for a long period efficiently sustained the offices, in Methodism, of leader, local preacher, and steward. His last affliction was painful, but submissively borne. Shortly before his death he asked one of his daughters to pray for the descent of the Holy Ghost upon him. When she ceased, he began to repeat—

> " 'I know, by faith I know,
>   If this vile house of clay,' " &c.,

but before he had finished the verse he had fallen asleep in Jesus.

Robert Chapman retained his fellowship with the Methodists of Wolsingham fifty-six years, and for thirty years was a leader. His religious experience was clear through life, and a day or two before his death, pointing upwards, he said—

> " 'I have a house above, Not made with mortal hands,' " &c.,

with which he closed a life of consistent piety, by a peaceful and happy death.

Medical skill and scientific knowledge of the power of medicine cannot always save their possessor from human suffering. The late James Hunter, Esq. of Islington, was called to endure thirty-eight weeks of weariness and pain, being unable to lie down either by night or day, yet he murmured not for these heavy trials. Within a few days of his death he said, " The Lord is releasing me very gently. I shall soon be free from all suffering. Glory! glory !" The last time he was able to speak, he repeated with emphasis the lines in the seventy-fourth hymn—

> " ' For this in faith we call, For this we weep and pray :
>   O might the tabernacle fall, O might we 'scape away !
>   Full of immortal hope, We urge the restless strife,
>   And hasten to be swallow'd up Of everlasting life.' "

Hymn 75.—"Lift your eyes of faith, and see."—*The Sacrament a Pledge of Heaven.*—Tune, Love-feast, 1761.

This forms No. 105 of Charles Wesley's " Hymns on the Lord's Supper," 1745.

Another instance of early dedication to God we may give from the life of Charlotte Brown, of Bedminster, Bristol, who passed some years in weakness and suffering, during which the consolations of religion were her chief joy. Shortly before her departure, she said to a friend, speaking of Jesus, " I shall see His face—I shall drink from the rivers of His grace ; and these thoughts now create constant joys." Her last words were part of the seventy-fifth hymn—

" ' Palms they carry in their hands,
        Crowns of glory on their heads.'

There is a crown for me, and I shall shortly wear it. I can
sing no more here ; but in heaven, with my palm of victory, I
will sing as loud as any angel there."

HYMN 76.—"What are these array'd in white?"—*The Sacrament
        a Pledge of Heaven.*—TUNE, Arne's, 1761.

The original forms No. 106 of Charles Wesley's "Hymns on
the Lord's Supper," 1745.

Death sometimes makes strange inroads in families. A singular instance occurred in 1824 in Flamborough. The wives of
two brothers died within a few days of each other. Both were
earnest, godly women, and both were connected with Methodism
in that town during the greater part of their lives. Both died
enjoying the clear witness of their acceptance with God, and a
sure hope of heaven. Elizabeth Lamplough, the elder of the
two sisters by two years, when she appeared to be on the extreme verge of mortality, and the realities of the eternal world
were opening to her view, summoned all her remaining strength
and exclaimed—

        " 'What are these array'd in white,
            Brighter than the noon-day sun ?' "

With this inquiry upon her lips, she died.

In peaceful resignation to the divine will, and in sure confidence of her acceptance with God, Sarah Holden, of Brixton,
always delicate of constitution, made preparation for the eternity
which she was awaiting. In calm resignation to the divine will
she committed her family and herself to the disposal of her
heavenly Father. Just before her departure, when failing
strength prevented singing or reading, she opened her Hymn-
book, and pointed to the verse commencing—

        " What are these array'd in white," &c.,

as indicative of her assurance of everlasting happiness, and then
entered into rest.

Sarah, the daughter of the Rev. John Dewhurst, was awakened
to a sense of her sinful state at the age of fourteen, under the
ministry of the Rev. John Bowers. Always delicate in body,
yet she was strong in faith, giving glory to God. The know-

ledge that her life was fast ebbing out, only quickened her desire
to depart and be with Christ.   Some of her last words were part
of the seventy-sixth hymn—

> " These are they that bore the cross,
>   Nobly for their Master stood," &c.

In meek submission to the divine will her released happy spirit
entered paradise.

Methodism at Porte-de-Grave, Newfoundland, was founded
chiefly by the labours of Mr George Ley, a local preacher.
Amongst the early converts there were James and Mary Butler,
whose daughter, Virtue, afterwards became the wife of the son
of George Ley.   She was brought to Christ under the ministry
of the Rev. James Hickson, and during the rest of her life testified to the power of divine grace in renewing her heart.   Shortly
before her death, whilst prostrate by illness, her mind was in
distress through severe temptation.   She was much comforted by a visit from her minister, but the darkness was not
dispelled.   She wrestled with God in her spirit, inwardly, for a
renewal of the divine favour, when she added, " Yes, I will, I
can rejoice in Thee, my Saviour."   The spell was broken, and
with a glowing heart, whilst lying quietly in bed, she began to
sing—

> " ' Out of great distress they came,
>   Wash'd their robes by faith below,
>   In the blood of yonder Lamb,
>   Blood that washes white as snow,' " &c.

In that holy calm she remained to the end, closing her career
with a faint whisper, " Come, Lord Jesus."

HYMN 77.—" The Church in her militant state."—" *The Spirit
    and the bride say, Come,*" &c. (Rev. xxii. 17).—TUNE,
    Funeral, 1761.

The original forms No. 863 of Charles Wesley's " Short Scripture Hymns," 1762, vol. ii.   Two words are altered in the second
verse.

HYMN 78.—" The thirsty are called to their Lord."—" *And let
    him that is athirst come*" (Rev. xxii. 17).—TUNE, Funeral
    1761.

It forms No. 865 of Charles Wesley's " Short Scripture
Hymns," vol. ii., 1762.

HYMN 79.—"A fountain of Life and of Grace."—"*Whosoever will may come,*" &c. (Rev. xxii. 17).—TUNE, Sion, 1761.

Forms No. 866 of Charles Wesley's "Short Scripture Hymns," vol. ii., 1762. James Montgomery has a hymn very similar to these three in language and sentiment.

HYMN 80.—"Terrible thought! shall I alone."—*A thought on hell. For Children.*—TUNE, Wenvo, 1761.

This forms No. 60 of Charles Wesley's "Hymns for Children," 1763, where it has ten verses, four of which are omitted. This commences the sixth section in the Hymn-book, with the title, "Describing Hell." The peculiar idea of this hymn is the utter loneliness of each person when appearing in the presence of God. The same thought is also expressed in these lines by Dr Young—

> " Thy wretched self alone
> Cast on the left of all whom thou hast known,
> How would it wound ! "

Mr Bunting suggests the tune "Bolton" or "St Mary's" for this hymn.

HYMN 81.—"Father of omnipresent grace !"—*For Families.*— TUNE, Welsh, 1761.

In Charles Wesley's "Hymns for Families," No. 13, the original will be found : the last line is changed from "Not a hoof," to "Not a soul," &c.

God has ways of working to human minds unknown. John Langley, of Whitstable, made a rash vow, which he kept till he was forty-five, that he would never enter a Methodist chapel. Convictions for sin set in so strongly at that period of his life, that his friends attributed the disquietude of his mind to insanity. A judicious and pious friend prevailed on him to attend a Methodist service at Canterbury. By this means he found out the evil of his rash vow, began to meet in class, found pardon and peace, and introduced Methodism into Whitstable by opening his own house, forming a society, becoming the leader of the first members there, and afterwards using his talent as an exhorter. The close of his life was sudden. The local preacher appointed for Whitstable had failed to keep his appointment,

and in the afternoon of that Sunday Mr Langley read to the
people Mr Wesley's sermon on Romans v. 15. The intervening
time before the evening service he spent in reading the Scriptures, and Dr Adam Clarke's Commentary thereon. Intending
to read another of Mr Wesley's sermons in the evening, he
took his place, and selected his first hymn, commencing—

> "Father of omnipresent grace," &c.

In the act of rising to open the service, he fell forward, his
friends hastened to his assistance, but his redeemed spirit had
fled !

HYMN 82.—" Shepherd of souls, with pitying eye."—*For the
Outcasts of Israel.*—TUNE, Athlone, 1781.

This forms No. 31 of Charles Wesley's " Redemption Hymns,"
1747. Some of its lines exhibit a dark picture of the heathenism
in Christian England.

HYMN 83.—" Thou Son of God, whose flaming eyes."—*For the
Evening.*—TUNE, Brooks, 1761.

The original forms No. 25 of Charles Wesley's " Hymns for a
Family," 1767, where it is printed as four eight-line stanzas.
The third line in verse four is altered from, "And fill his care-
less heart with grief." In the fifth verse "leper" is changed to
" sleeper."

HYMN 84.—" Come, O thou all-victorious Lord."— *Written
before Preaching at Portland.*—TUNE, Leeds, 1761.

This interesting hymn will be found in Charles Wesley's
" Hymns and Sacred Poems," vol. i., 1749, where it is No. 201.
It was written during the author's visit to Portland in June
1746 ; and some pleasing particulars relating to the circumstances which caused the hymn to be written will be found in
the author's Journal under the date given, as also in the
Wesleyan Magazine for May 1869. The second line of verse
six is altered from—"And make us feel our load," and in the
fourth line, " In Thine" is changed to " In the." The chief
occupation of the residents in the Isle of Portland is that of
quarrymen, and the hymn was written especially to catch their
attention. In the first verse especially this is manifest —

> " Strike with the hammer of Thy word,
> And break these hearts of stone !"

HYMN 85.—" Spirit of Faith, come down."—*For Whitsunday.*—
TUNE, Lampe's, 1746.

The original is No. 27 of Charles Wesley's " Hymns of Petition
and Thanksgiving for the Promise of the Father," 1746, one
verse of which is omitted.   The author's favourite expression in
the third verse, "My dear atoning" is changed to "The all-
atoning."

HYMN 86.—" Sinners, your hearts lift up."—*A Hymn for the
Day of Pentecost.*—TUNE, Irene, 1761.

Was published first by Charles Wesley in "Hymns and Sacred
Poems," 1742.

HYMN 87.—" Come, Holy Ghost, our hearts inspire ; "
   „   88.—" Father of all, in whom alone."
Before Reading the Scriptures.—TUNE, Aldrich, 1761.

These two much admired compositions are found in Charles
Wesley's " Hymns and Sacred Poems," 1740.   Another hymn
designed for the same purpose is No. 746 in the supplement,
written by Miss Steele, commencing, " Father of mercies," &c.

HYMN 89.—" Inspirer of the ancient Seers."—" *All Scripture is
given by inspiration of God,*" &c.—TUNE, Frankfort, 1761.

This forms No. 664 of Charles Wesley's " Short Scripture
Hymns," 1762, vol. ii., and is based on 2 Timothy iii. 16.   The
second verse of the original is omitted.

HYMN 90.*—" Thus saith the Lord of earth and heaven."—*The
forty-fourth chapter of Isaiah.*

This forms No. 3 in Charles Wesley's " Hymns and Sacred
Poems," vol. i., 1749, and is a lengthened paraphrase of Isaiah xliv.
The original has seventeen stanzas of four lines, the first nine of
which are omitted.   This hymn was added to the collection
after Mr Wesley's death, which is indicated by the asterisk.

HYMN 91.—" Long have I seem'd to serve thee, Lord ; "
   „   92.—" Still for Thy loving-kindness, Lord."
The Means of Grace.—TUNE, 91, Fetter Lane ; 92, Wednesbury, 1761.

These two hymns appear as one by Charles Wesley in "Hymns

and Sacred Poems," 1740, where it extends to twenty-three verses. It was written during the prevalence of the disputes between the Wesleys and the Moravians, some of the latter having accepted Antinomian doctrines, whilst some of Mr Wesley's adherents unduly exalted the means of grace. This hymn commences the first section of the second part of the collection, with the title, " Describing Formal Religion."

Few persons connected with Methodism were more faithful in their service than good old Thomas Cordeux, at the book-room store in Paternoster Row. His wife, Hannah Cordeux, feared the Lord from her youth, and in her life testified to the possession of the graces of the Spirit—love, joy, peace, long-suffering, gentleness, goodness, meekness. By these graces she was distinguished. She suffered much from asthma, but she murmured not. Several times during her last days on earth she repeated the eighth verse of hymn 92—

> " I trust in Him, who stands between
> The Father's wrath and me :
> Jesus, Thou great eternal Mean,
> I look for all from thee ! "

In this spirit she closed her earthly career.

HYMN 93.—" My gracious, loving Lord."—*The Backslider.*—
TUNE, Brentford, 1761.

The original is on page 63 of Charles Wesley's " Hymns and Sacred Poems," 1742. It commences thus—"Ah! my dear loving Lord ; " and throughout the hymn the alterations are considerable, and generally improvements. The design of this hymn, and also of No. 94, is to recommend inward and experimental godliness, which was then too generally supplanted by a merely outward and formal observance of religion, a fatal rock on which many have struck and made shipwreck of faith. Mr Bunting suggests that line two of verse 6, should be altered to " I seem'd in human sight."

HYMN 94.—" The men who slight Thy faithful word."—" *The Temple of the Lord are we,*" &c. (Jer. vii. 4).—TUNE, St Paul's, 1761.

Forms No. 1185 of Charles Wesley's "Short Scripture Hymns," 1762, and is founded on Jeremiah vii. 4. It is a strong admonition to formalists. The second verse in the original is omitted. The reason may be obvious when we quote four lines—

> " The church—they from their pale expel
> Whom Thou hast here forgiven ;
> And all the synagogue of hell
> Are the sole heirs of heaven!"

A withering exposure this of the condition of the Church of England one hundred years ago !

HYMN 95.—"Author of faith, eternal Word."—*Faith, the substance of things hoped for.*—TUNE, Anglesea, 1761.

The original of this fine composition, by Charles Wesley, was first printed in " Hymns and Sacred Poems," 1740, where it extends to no less than eighty-eight stanzas, and is entitled, " The Life of Faith Exemplified" (Rom. x.), being a lucid paraphrase and amplification of that chapter.

Every word of this hymn is employed to elicit revealed truth ; it is written in language at once expressive and terse. In the *Wesleyan Magazine* for 1839, page 381, there is a very able critique of this noble composition. The hymn No. 95 is a mere fragment of the whole, and forms here the first of a new section, under the title, " Describing Inward Religion."

Chequered scenes and severe trials have been the portion of many of the Lord's people. John Harper, in early life, entered the king's service on board a transport ship. It soon fell to his lot to suffer many privations, and finally shipwreck and imprisonment. Taken to France as a prisoner of war, he found more than a thousand of his countrymen in the Givet prison, and amongst them some from Shields, his native place, and some who were Methodists. Awakened to a sense of his lost condition as a sinner at the time of his peril in the sea, he gladly accepted the invitation of those few devout men in prison to unite with them in prayer ; and here he saw the greatness of his transgression, and found acceptance with God by faith in Jesus Christ. That blessed sense of the divine favour he then obtained, he retained during the rest of his life. A society was formed in the prison, and all the ordinances of Methodism were observed as far as possible, though with only the same liberty to the person as the captive Jews had in Babylon. Quarterly tickets were regularly issued, neatly written with the pen, and doubtless the Scripture passage which each contained was often a source of comfort to those in bondage. In 1814, when the allied sovereigns entered Paris, the prison doors throughout France were opened, and every man went out free. Mr Harper returned to Shields, became a schoolmaster, joined the Methodists, and continued faithful in the Lord's service. His last illness continued for more than a year, during which time his spirit was ripening for eternity. A little before his death he repeated a verse of the 95th hymn—

> " To him that in Thy name believes
> Eternal-life with Thee is given ;
> Into himself he all receives,
> Pardon, and holiness, and heaven."

This verse correctly described his dying experience. As he neared the port, his testimony became yet more clear, that Christ was all and in all.

The gaieties of youth and the pleasures of the world were cheerfully resigned at the age of twenty by Ann Caudler, of Colchester, when the Spirit of God convinced her of sin. In the fellowship of the Lord's people for two years she found more real delight than she did in the previous twenty years of worldliness. When overtaken by sickness and suffering, her calmness and resignation testified to the preparation of her heart. A few hours before her death her father read some verses of hymns to her, and to those she replied by repeating others. The last she was able to repeat was the closing verse of the 95th hymn—

> " Faith lends its realising light,
> The clouds disperse, the shadows fly ;
> The Invisible appears in sight,
> And God is seen by mortal eye."

To the inquiry, did she feel the truths contained in these words, she said, " Oh yes ; frequently when I cannot speak." Shortly afterwards she entered into rest.

HYMN 96.—" How can a sinner know."—*The Marks of Faith.*
—TUNE, Brentford, 1761.

This forms a combination of a short and common metre hymn by Charles Wesley, in his " Hymns and Sacred Poems," 1749, vol. ii., No. 161, sixteen lines of which are omitted. By the judicious alteration of John Wesley, it is made into a uniform short metre.

The extent of the blessings which flow from early consecration to God we shall know only in eternity. At the early age of twelve years William Barton was under deep religious convictions, and he desired permission of his parents to meet in class. It was a wise decision which consented to the boy's choice. Through the kind instructions of his class-leader, he was soon enabled to realise a sense of pardoned sin. It was on a Sabbath evening, in a prayer-meeting which followed the preaching of the word, that he found peace with God. The minister had given out the first verse of hymn 96—

> "How can a sinner know
>   His sins on earth forgiven?" &c.

The whole of the verse having been sung, the words fixed the attention of the anxious youth, and while singing the second verse—

> " We who in Christ believe
>   That He for us hath died,
>   We all His unknown peace receive,
>   And feel His blood applied," &c.,

he was enabled to commit himself to the Lord Jesus as his Saviour, and felt the peace which passeth understanding. For thirty years he was greatly owned of God as a Wesleyan minister, and died saying, " Happy ! I am resting on Christ."

HYMN 97.*—"Thou great mysterious God unknown."—*Seeking Redemption.*

This forms No. 19 of Charles Wesley's " Redemption Hymns," 1747. Two verses are omitted. It is not found in any edition of the Hymn-book previous to the year 1800.

Mary Wood, of Maltby, near Rotherham, from childhood was under the strivings of the Holy Spirit, but had reached womanhood before she fully gave her heart to the Lord. Nearly forty-five years she was in fellowship with the Methodist society, and was untiring in her efforts to extend the religion which had made her peaceful and happy. She never experienced the rapture of spiritual enjoyment which some professed ; this sometimes discouraged her, but often she found comfort in repeating the first verse of hymn 97, which commences thus :—

"Thou great mysterious God unknown,
Whose love hath gently led me on,
Even from my infant days," &c.

To her to live was Christ, but to die was gain.

HYMN 98.—" Upright, both in heart and will."—" *God hath made man upright*," &c. (Eccles. vii. 29).—TUNE, Kingswood, 1761.

This forms No. 920 of Charles Wesley's "Short Scripture Hymns," 1762, vol. i. There is much force and meaning conveyed in the couplet—

"In ten thousand objects sought
The bliss we lost in one."

HYMN 99.—" Father of lights, from whom proceeds."—*A Prayer under Convictions.*—TUNE, Mourners, 1761.

Written by Charles Wesley, and printed in "Hymns and Sacred Poems," 1739. The last three verses of the original are omitted. It is worthy of note here, that one of the omitted verses is one of three, all by the same author, which are printed in Mr Toplady's works, edition 1837, as though they were written by Toplady. Such an error should not be passed without correction.

HYMN 100.—" Jesus, my Advocate above."—*Try me, O God, and search the ground of my heart.*—TUNE, Smith's, 1781.

This is Charles Wesley's paraphrase of the Prayer-book version of Psalm cxxxix. 23, and is found in "Hymns and Sacred Poems," 1739, page 97. The original has five stanzas ; the fourth is omitted. The first line in the original reads thus :—" Jesus ! my great High Priest above," which John Wesley has altered to "Advocate" above. A change is also made in the last line.

HYMN 101.—" Saviour, Prince of Israel's race."—*A Penitential Hymn.*—TUNE, Dedication, 1781.

This forms No. 33 of Charles Wesley's "Hymns and Sacred Poems," vol. i., 1749. The original has ten verses, only half of which are here given. In the omitted portion reference is made to severe mental suffering and penitence, which lead to the opinion that it was written before the author's conversion in 1738. The hymn is full of fine feeling and power. Mr Bunting suggests that line six, verse 2, should read thus :—" Made Thee shed Thy precious blood."

There are but few remaining links to connect the period of John Wesley's Methodists and those of the present day. Mrs Thomas Gabriel, late of Brixton Hill, was present at the City Road Chapel, London, at the last covenant service conducted there by Mr Wesley, and she was present also at his funeral. In early life she was called to give her heart to the Saviour, and joined the Methodist Society, maintaining her connexion with the body for more than threescore years. In her extreme feebleness the Lord dealt graciously with His aged disciple, whom He called gradually and tenderly from earth to heaven. She was at times buffeted by the adversary, and would always repel his assaults by quoting the last verse of hymn 101 :—

> " O remember me for good,
>   Passing through the mortal vale ;
> Show me the atoning blood,
>   When my strength and spirit fail ;
> Give my gasping soul to see
> Jesus crucified for me.!"

In her ninety-second year she entered into rest, telling her daughters, " I love you all ; but I love Jesus better, and I am going to Him."

In very early life Frances Lewis obtained the pardon of sin, and united herself to the Methodists in 1796, having been converted during a revival in the Spitalfields circuit. She lived a consistent godly life ; and during her last illness, just before her departure to heaven, she repeated, as expressive of her experience, the verse commencing—

> " O remember me for good," &c.

She died resting on the atonement of Christ.

As a little boy, William Lishman wrote a brief prayer to aid his devotions, in which he asked God to give him knowledge, wisdom, and grace. His prayer was answered. Drawn gently by the Spirit's influence, he joined the Methodists in 1816, and was an honoured and attached member to the end of his days. He formed a new society at Coxhoe, and greatly aided the work in the neighbourhood of Gateshead. During a painful illness he found comfort in prayer, and amongst his last utterances he repeated—

> "O remember me for good,
> Passing through the mortal vale."

The earnestness with which he repeated these lines deeply impressed all present. To one who came thirty miles to see him, he said, "Happy! oh yes, happy!" And so passed to his heavenly home.

HYMN 102.—"O that I could repent."—*For one Fallen from Grace.*—TUNE, Olney, 1761.

Forms No. 78 of Charles Wesley's "Hymns and Sacred Poems," vol. i., 1749. The original has four verses, the third and fourth being omitted.

HYMN 103.—"O that I could revere."—*For one Fallen from Grace.*—TUNE, Lampe's, 1746.

This forms No. 82 of Charles Wesley's "Hymns and Sacred Poems," vol. i., 1749. The second verse of the original is left out. "Impendent" in the second verse is changed to "impending."

This striking figure of speech is taken from the story of Damocles, as related by Cicero of Dionysius, king of Italy, and one of his flatterers, B.C. 368. By command of the king, Damocles assumed the sovereignty, and was dazzled by the splendour and luxury of royalty, until he perceived a sword suspended over his head by a single horse-hair. This marred his pleasures, and he relinquished his ambitious assumptions. The Rev. Joseph Stennett employs the same figure thus :—

> "Who laughs at sin, laughs at his Maker's frowns,—
> Laughs at the sword of vengeance o'er his head."

HYMN 104.—"O for that tenderness of heart."—*The Tender Heart*, &c.—TUNE, Mitcham, 1781.

The original forms 609 of Charles Wesley's "Short Scripture Hymns," 1762, founded on 2 Kings xxii. 19–30.

HYMN 105.—"O that I could repent."—*For one Fallen from Grace.*—TUNE, Brentford, 1761.

Forms No. 84 of Charles Wesley's "Hymns and Sacred Poems," vol. i., 1749. The third and fourth verses of the original are omitted.

HYMN 106.—"Jesu, let Thy pitying eye."—*For one Fallen from Grace.*—TUNE, Calvary, 1761.

Forms No. 64 in Charles Wesley's "Hymns and Sacred Poems," vol. i., 1749. The original has twelve verses. The third, fourth, ninth, and tenth are omitted.

The fall, repentance, and recovery of the apostle Peter are related by the poet with much feeling and energy. In the original, the appealing prayer is eleven times offered :—"Turn, and look upon me, Lord, and break my heart of stone." Persevering prayer is rewarded : the last refrain includes in its petition the sufferings, love, and compassion of the Saviour.

> " O my bleeding, loving Lord,
> Thou break'st my heart of stone."

HYMN 107.*—"The Spirit of the Lord our God."—*The Sixty-first Chapter of Isaiah.*

This forms No. 5 of Charles Wesley's "Hymns and Sacred Poems," vol. i., 1749. The original is in two parts, of twenty-two and eighteen verses respectively. Only six verses from the first part are chosen, and several alterations are made in them. It is altered from the first to the third person. The asterisk affixed indicates that this hymn was added to the collection after Mr Wesley's death. Mr Bunting suggests that line four, verse six, should read, "And unto full perfection grow," with the note, " Lame, bad ending of a *very* fine hymn."

HYMN 108.—" Enslaved to sense, to pleasure prone."—*Grace before Meat.*—TUNE, Wednesbury, 1761.

Forms one of Charles Wesley's " Hymns and Sacred Poems," 1739, page 35. This hymn commences a new section, under the title, " For Mourners Convinced of Sin." Mr Bunting changes " actions " to " passions," in verse seven.

HYMN 109.—" Wretched, helpless, and distrest."—*Wretched, and Miserable, and Poor, and Blind, and Naked.*—TUNE, Kingswood, 1761.

This forms one of Charles Wesley's " Hymns and Sacred Poems," 1742, page 43. The second verse of the original is omitted.

Hymn 110.—"Jesus, Friend of sinners, hear."—*A Prayer for Restoring Grace.*—Tune, Kingswood, 1761.

Taken from Charles Wesley's "Hymns and Sacred Poems," 1742, page 67. Mr Bunting suggests changing in verse five, "My struggling spirit" to "My struggling soul set free;" and line two, verse six, to read, "This only I require."

The stupendous magnitude of sin which is indicated in the third verse, is an idea which seems to have been borrowed from Mason's "Songs of Praise," 1682 :—

> "My sins have reach'd up to the skies ;
>   But mercy these exceeds :
>   God's mercy is "above the heavens,—
>   Above my simple deeds."
>   My sins are many, like the stars,
>   Or sand upon the shore ;
>   But yet the mercies of my God
>   Are infinitely more.
>   My sins in bigness do arise
>   Like mountains great and tall ;
>   But mercy is above the skies," &c.

In verse six there is an idea which is very characteristic of Charles Wesley's early poetry, "Take the power of sin away ;" a blessing never more wanted by professing Christians than now.

Hymn 111.*—"Thus saith the Lord ! Who seek the Lamb."— *Fifty-first Chapter of Isaiah.*

This hymn forms No. 4 in Charles Wesley's "Hymns and Sacred Poems," vol. i., 1749. It is a composition in four parts, extending to sixty-two stanzas. The first commences thus :—

> "Hearken to me, who seek the Lamb,
>   Who follow after righteousness," &c.

The hymn as given in the collection consists of the first nine stanzas of the original, omitting the second and seventh. The first line of verse seven reads thus :—"My mercy will I cause to rest," &c. This hymn was added to the collection after Mr Wesley's death, as indicated by the asterisk.

F

HYMN 112.—"Woe is me! what tongue can tell."—*The Good Samaritan.*—TUNE, Kingswood, 1761. .

The original will be found in Charles Wesley's "Hymns and Sacred Poems," 1742, page 101, where it extends to eleven verses, four of which are omitted.

The hymn contains an ingenious and evangelical application of the parable of the Good Samaritan. In the omitted portion the poet seems to imply that the poor sinner was a confessed backslider, in these words :—

> " God was once my glorious dress,
>   And I like Him did shine ;
>   Satan of His righteousness
>   Hath spoil'd this soul of mine."

This poem is considered by the Rev. John Kirk to be " the most chaste, tender, comprehensive, and eloquent poetic exposition of the parable he has met with." The leading features of the parable are very clearly embodied in the poem. The composition is believed to have had its origin in sermons which Charles Wesley was constantly preaching on the Good Samaritan. During a period of nine years there are no less than eighteen records in his Journal, of his showing to sinners the picture of their wretchedness, and the method of their cure, in this parable. He also records not a few instances of good results following these sermons.

HYMN 113.—" O Thou, whom fain my soul would love."—" *My Lord and my God.*"—TUNE, Bradford, 1761.

Taken from Charles Wesley's "Hymns and Sacred Poems," 1742, page 110. It is founded on Genesis xxxii. 24–32. The fourth verse of the original is omitted.

HYMN 114.—" Jesus, in whom the weary find."—*Upon parting with his Friends.*—TUNE, 112th Psalm Tune, 1761.

Written by Charles Wesley in "Hymns and Sacred Poems," 1740, page 49. The original is in four parts, extending to twenty-nine verses. The latter portion is chosen to make this hymn. There is much of genuine poetry in the composition, which is marked with feeling and beauty of thought.

HYMN 115.—" Let the world their virtue boast."—*I am deter-*
    mined to know nothing, save Jesus, and Him crucified.—
    TUNE, Calvary, 1761.

Taken from Charles Wesley's " Hymns and Sacred Poems,"
1742, page 259.   The original has nine stanzas, four of which
are omitted.

The poet takes up the apostle Paul's idea of his own unworthiness, and closes each verse with the expressive declaration, " I the chief of sinners am ;" but adds the comforting
assurance that " Jesus died for me."   This is the language of
unfeigned humility, and of profound self-knowledge.   The allusion in verse three to Gideon is derived from Judges vi. 39, 40.

A venerable old disciple in Methodism was John Tyrer, of
Nineveh, near Birmingham, at the time of his death.   He
founded the first Sunday-school at Handsworth, and by his consistent earnest piety, greatly promoted the cause of God in the
Soho works, where he was long employed.   In death as in
life, the Hymn-book and Bible afforded him constant delight ;
and to a friend who called to see him, when the conflict was
nearly over, he gave, as the only ground of his confidence and
hope—

> " Let the world their virtue boast,
>   Their works of righteousness ;
> I, a wretch undone and lost,
>   Am freely saved by grace."

He passed away in peace to the skies, saying, " All is well ! all
is well ! "

The author of this hymn had but one daughter who arrived
at mature years.   Miss Sarah Wesley was a person of much
mental power, and possessed great general intelligence.   She
was much loved by both her father and the Rev. John Wesley.
Most of her time was spent in literary pursuits.   In her last
illness, which was short, she visited her native city, Bristol,
where she closed her earthly career.   She often said, " I have
peace, but not joy."   When too feeble to converse, she would
repeat the lines—

> " I the chief of sinners am,
>   But Jesus died for me."

These were nearly the last words she uttered.   She died a
member of the Methodist Society.

The chief interest which attaches to this hymn, as a dying testimony, is that afforded from the use by John Wesley himself, and, partly in consequence thereof, the account of his death having been read by so many thousands of persons, it has been so very frequently used by his followers, when under similar circumstances. Of these we have not space for more than a passing allusion. Further instances of the use of this hymn will be found in the index, at the end of the volume.

The only account we have left us of the last days of John Wesley, the founder of the Methodist Societies, was written by Miss Elizabeth Ritchie, one of his most intimate friends, and one of the elect ladies of Methodism. From that account we learn that Mr Wesley preached his last sermon at Leatherhead, in Surrey, February 23, 1791. On the 24th he stopped at Mr Wolff's, at Balham, and on the 25th he returned to his own house at City Road. On the 26th he remained very feeble. On the 27th he seemed to be much exhausted, and said, "Speak to me ; I cannot speak." To the question, "Shall we pray with you, sir ?" he earnestly replied, "Yes." At the end of the prayer, he added a hearty Amen. In the afternoon, as indicating his own consciousness that the end was not far off, he said, "There is no need for more than what I said at Bristol.* My words then were—

> ' I the chief of sinners am,
> But Jesus died for me.' "

Miss Ritchie said, " Is this the present language of your heart ;

* At the Bristol Conference, in 1783, Mr Wesley was taken so ill, neither he nor his friends thought he would recover. Expecting sudden death, and that speedily, he said to Mr Bradford, " I have been reflecting on my past life : I have been wandering up and down between fifty and sixty years, endeavouring in my poor way to do a little good to my fellow-creatures ; and now it is probable there are but a few steps between me and death, and what have I to trust to for salvation ? I can see nothing which I have done or suffered, that will bear looking at ; I have no other plea than this—

> ' I the chief of sinners am,
> But Jesus died for me.' "

This sentiment continued to influence him during the remaining eight years of his earnest active public life and ministry, and was the most prominent feeling of his mind when the fourscore and seven years of his life were ending.

and do you now feel as you then did?" He replied, "Yes."
Soon after, he said to Miss Ritchie, "He is all! He is all!"
To his niece, Miss Wesley, who sat by his bedside, he said,
"Sally, have you zeal for God now?" In the evening, he got
up, and while sitting in his chair, he said, "How necessary is it
for every one to be on the right foundation!—

> "'I the chief of sinners am,
>   But Jesus died for me.'"

We must be justified by faith, and then go on to sanctification."
During the next day, February 28, he slept much. On Tuesday,
March 1, he was restless, but uncomplaining, and tried to
sing part of two hymns. He also tried, but in vain, to write the
memorable words, which he could only speak, "God is with us;"
and afterwards, "The best of all is, God is with us." After
some kindly interchange of affectionate inquiries with Mr
Rogers, Mr Bradford, and his sister-in-law, Mrs Charles Wesley,
he said, "I'll praise! I'll praise!" These were the last words
of the departing saint, excepting that shortly before he drew
his last breath, on Wednesday morning, March 2, a few minutes
before ten o'clock, he said to Mr Bradford, his faithful friend,
who had just then prayed with him, "Farewell!" As his
spirit escaped from its clay tenement, his friends were kneeling
around his bed, commending him to his Father and their
Father in heaven.

HYMN 116.—"*Saviour, cast a pitying eye.*"—*For one Fallen from
Grace.*—TUNE, Foundery, 1761.

Written by Charles Wesley, and forms No. 55 in "Hymns
and Sacred Poems," vol. i., 1749. The second verse is omitted;
and in the third verse, "Thy own sweet mercy," is changed to
"Thy love and mercy."

HYMN 117.—"*God is in this and every place.*"—*For one Convinced of Unbelief.*—TUNE, Fetter Lane, 1761.

Written by Charles Wesley, and forms No. 9 in "Hymns and
Sacred Poems," vol. i., 1749. The original has sixteen stanzas;
the first ten and the fifteenth are omitted. In the last verse the
author shows with what ease he can adopt, even in verse, scriptural ideas and language. There is a singular coincidence

deserving of notice in this, as well as in another of Charles
Wesley's hymns. The first two verses read thus—

> " And have I measured half my days,
>   And half my journey run,
> Nor tasted the Redeemer's grace,
>   Nor yet my work begun ?

> " The morning of my life is past,
>   The noon almost is o'er ;
> The night of death approaches fast,
>   When I can work no more."

When these lines were written, their author was in his fortieth
year ; he died aged eighty. How did he obtain the knowledge
that he had measured half his days ? These facts are indisputable, account for them who may ! There are many statements
in the entire hymn which are certainly not applicable to Charles
Wesley.

HYMN 118.—"Author of faith, to Thee I cry."—"*Ask, and it
shall be given*" (Matt. vii. 7).—TUNE, Snowsfield's, 1761.

The original was written by Charles Wesley, and is the first
of six hymns which are printed at the end of a small tract,
entitled, " A Short View of the Differences between the Moravian Brethren in England, and J. and C. Wesley," 1745. It
is printed also as No. 10 in " Hymns and Sacred Poems," vol.
i., 1749. In the latter portion of the hymn, the poet plainly
states what is the gospel plan of salvation, in contradistinction
to the errors then taught by some of the Moravians.

HYMN 119.*—"Father of Jesus Christ, my Lord."—"*But thou,
when thou prayest, enter into thy closet.*"—TUNE, Aldrich,
1761.

This hymn forms No. 2 in the Moravian tract just named ;
and it is printed also in Charles Wesley's " Redemption
Hymns " in 1747. The title given to it now is, " Before Private
Prayer." In the fourth verse, the poet urges his plea for full
salvation—

> "Blameless before Thy face to live,
>   To live and sin no more."

The seventh verse reads thus in the original—

> " Kindle the flame of love within,
>   That may to heaven ascend ;
> And now in grace the work begin,
>   Which shall in glory end."

This hymn, as well as the next one, was added to the collection after Mr Wesley's death.

HYMN 120.*—"Comfort, ye ministers of grace."—*Groaning for Redemption.*—TUNE, Cary's, 1761.

Charles Wesley's, found in "Hymns and Sacred Poems," 1742, page 109. The original is in four parts, and extends to thirty-seven verses, of which two only are here given.

HYMN 121.—"Expand thy wings, celestial Dove."—*The Creation.* Gen. i. 2, 3, &c.—TUNE, Cary's, 1761.

This is made up by uniting three of Charles Wesley's "Short Scripture Hymns," 1762, Nos. 3, 4, and 635, based on Gen. i. 2, 3, and 2 Chron. vi. 20, 21.

HYMN 122.—"O Thou who hast our sorrows borne."—*For Families.*—TUNE, Travellers, 1761.

This forms No. 19 in Charles Wesley's "Hymns for Families," 1767. One verse is omitted. The poet describes in terse strong language our Lord's sufferings.

HYMN 123.—"Let the redeem'd give thanks and praise."—*For Families.*—TUNE, Aldrich, 1761.

This forms No. 90 of Charles Wesley's "Hymns for Families," 1767. The original is in double verses, and sixteen lines are omitted, whilst others are transposed in their order.

HYMN 124.—"O that I, first of love possess'd."—*On going to a new habitation.*—TUNE, Woods, 1761.

No. 112 of Charles Wesley's "Hymns for Families," 1767. Two verses are left out. It has the appearance of being based on Exodus xxxiii. 20-22. The poet, strangely enough, in the first verse asks to see the Lord, although he knew that such a privilege was denied to mortal eyes—"Ye cannot see my face and live."

HYMN 125.—"O that I could my Lord receive."—*For Love.*—
TUNE, Brockmer, 1761.

This forms No. 159 of Charles Wesley's "Hymns for Families."
Two verses after the second are omitted. -   .

For earnest piety and devoted service, no Methodists can
exceed the Irish. Sarah Jones, of Farnee County, Wicklow,
feared the Lord from a child. At fifteen, during a revival, she
obtained a clear sense of her acceptance with God. As a teacher,
leader, and missionary collector, she laid herself out for daily
service. Her voice, her pen, and her example were all used for
the glory of God, and to help the young on their way towards
heaven. Her last illness was short and severe, but she clung to
the Cross. Her last words were—

> " 'Nothing I ask or want beside,
>   Of all in earth or heaven,
> But let me feel Thy blood applied,
>   And live and die forgiven.' "

HYMN 126.—" Too strong I was to conquer sin."—*Judges* vii. 2,
&c.—TUNE, Welling, 1761.

This is formed by uniting Nos. 400 and 778 of Charles
Wesley's " Short Scripture Hymns," 1762, vol. i., based on
Judges vii. 2 and Job xl. 4.

HYMN 127.—" Wherewith, O God, shall I draw near."—*Micah*
vi. 6, &c.—TUNE, St Luke's, 1761.

Written by Charles Wesley, and found in " Hymns and
Sacred Poems," 1740, page 88. There is a pathos and power in
the pleadings of the poet ; and as the Saviour's intercessions are
represented as accompanying those of the penitent, the blessing
desired is obtained.

Having the advantage in early life of the personal advice of
Mr Wesley, Mrs Fletcher, and Mrs Crosby, Frances Ness
yielded willingly to the strivings of the Holy Spirit, and under
a sermon preached by the Rev. George Story in 1778, she was
brought to God, and during the rest of her days was a faithful and devoted Methodist. She possessed in a remarkable
degree the spirit of the Master, which she tried to diffuse around
her. A little before her death, she said to her minister—

> " 'I nothing have, I nothing am ;'

my trust is alone in Jesus. I am going home, praise the Lord."
She died saying, "Victory!"

At the age of twenty, the Rev. John Fisher was convinced of
sin under a sermon preached by Mr Moon, and soon afterwards
he received the blessing of pardon. From a sense of gratitude
to God, he soon began to exhort, and became a local preacher.
In 1802 he became an itinerant preacher in Methodism, and
laboured with success and acceptance in several circuits. But
his career was brief; illness set in, under which he sunk, but
although tried in affliction, his spirit triumphed over it. Nearly
his last words were—

> "'Jesus, the Lamb of God, hath bled;
> He bore my sins upon the tree;
> Beneath our curse He bow'd His head;
> 'Tis finished! He hath died for me.'"

HYMN 128.—"With glorious clouds encompass'd round."—*For
Families.*—TUNE, St Paul's, 1761.

This forms No. 161 of Charles Wesley's "Hymns for Families,"
1767. In the first line, "encompast" is altered. The sentiment
conveyed in the first verse is also contained in the first verse of
Hymn 130. The line, "Whom angels dimly see," seems to have
been suggested by a similar expression of Milton's :—

> "Who sittest above these heavens,
> To us invisible, or dimly seen."
>   —*Paradise Lost,* v. 157.

Samuel Wesley, jun., in Hymn 561, has the following couplet :—

> "In light unsearchable enthroned,
> Whom angels dimly see."

There is something inexpressibly affecting in the very earnest
appeal in the second verse : —

> "Answer, thou Man of Grief and Love!
> And speak it to my heart!"

Giving her heart to the Lord in early youth, Mrs Marriott, of
Nottingham, became a Sunday-school teacher, missionary collector, and class-leader at Halifax Place Chapel.   Though of
delicate health, she was diligent in all her duties, earnest in her
piety, and generous towards the cause of God and His poor.
When illness laid her low, her faith in God was strong. All
hope of recovery being past, she received the sacrament of the

Lord's Supper. At its close she said, " That offering still continues new ; it is the Lamb newly slain :

> 'I view the Lamb in His own light,
>   Whom angels dimly see ;
>   And gaze, transported at the sight,
>   To all eternity.' "

Her last testimony to the goodness of her heavenly Father was,
" God supports me richly ; He has never left me to feel my weakness. Do not forget the goodness of God."

At the age of eighteen, Thomas Bagshaw, of Rotherham,
joined the Methodist Society, and he continued a steady member to the close of his life, serving with uprightness the offices
of poor, society, and circuit steward. He suffered much for
some months before his death ; but his mind was kept in peace,
and shortly before his spirit escaped to God, he repeated the
verse—

> "I view the Lamb in His own light," &c.,

as the evidence of his acceptance with God.

HYMN 129.—"Adam, descended from above ! "—*Isaiah* xlii. 6, 7.
—TUNE, Guernsey, 1761.

This forms No. 1044 of Charles Wesley's " Short Scripture
Hymns," 1762, vol. i., where it is printed as three eight-line
verses.

Under the heart-searching ministry of the Rev. William
Bramwell, George Sargent, of Huddersfield, the son of a Wesleyan minister, was awakened to a sense of his sinful condition,
at the early age of six years. Those convictions ripened into
penitence and pardon, and were followed by a life of earnest,
sincere godliness. At Kingswood School, as an apprentice, and
as a medical student, he feared the Lord, and walked in His ways,
always delighting in the means of grace and in the company of
the Lord's people. On February 7, 1840, he was apparently in
his usual health, and Mrs Sargent commenced the family devotions. When she had read the 129th hymn, after this verse—

> " Open mine eyes the Lamb to know,
>   Who bears the general sin away ;
>   And to my ransom'd spirit show
>   The glories of eternal day,"

Mr Sargent's mind seemed carried above all earthly things, and absorbed in contemplating the truths contained in the hymn ; forgetting himself, he knelt down to prayer without the customary lesson from the Word of God. Observing the omission, he rose and read Psalms cxxi., cxxii., and after prayer retired to rest. Shortly afterwards, he complained of pain in his head. Assistance was at once procured ; but the last messenger had arrived : he became insensible, and within an hour he quietly passed to his rest with God.

HYMN 130.—" Thou God unsearchable, unknown."—*Isaiah*
xlv. 15.—TUNE, Mourners, 1761.

This is made up of Nos. 1055 and 1056 of Charles Wesley's " Short Scripture Hymns," vol. i., 1762. Two of the lines are altered.

HYMN 131.—" Lord, I despair myself to heal."—*" Looking unto Jesus,"* &c.—TUNE, Evesham, 1761.

Charles Wesley's, from " Hymns and Sacred Poems," 1739, page 91. It is based on Hebrews xii. 2. The first and second verses of the original are left out ; the hymn commences thus—

> " Weary of struggling with my pain ;
> Hopeless to burst my nature's chain ;
> Hardly I give the contest o'er,
> I seek to free myself no more."

HYMN 132.—" Jesus, the Sinner's Friend, to Thee."—*Galatians*
iii. 22.—TUNE, Complaint, 1761.

Charles Wesley's, in "Hymns and Sacred Poems," 1739, page 92. The original has thirteen stanzas. This hymn consists of the 1st, 2d, 5th, 6th, 10th, and 12th verses.

The strong language used in the third verse—

> " Tread down Thy foes, with power control
> The beast and devil in my soul,"

the Wesleys and Whitefield learned from Bishop Hall and William Law. Southey, in his " Life of Wesley," relates the story of a merry-andrew who, attending the preaching of Whitefield, finding no common acts of buffoonery of any avail, to divert the attention of the audience, climbed into a tree and exposed himself in so disgraceful a manner as to make the brutal mob shout ; but the more decent people were abashed.

Whitefield himself was for a moment confounded with such a spectacle, but recovering himself, he appealed to his audience, whether he had wronged human nature in saying with Bishop Hall, that " man, when left to himself, is half a fiend and half a brute ; " or in calling him, with William Law, " a motley mixture of the beast and the devil ? "—*Southey's "Life of Wesley,"* vol. ii. page 192.

HYMN 133.—"Jesu, whose glory's streaming rays."—*The Change.*
—TUNE, Islington, 1761.

The original is a German hymn, written by Wolfgang Christian Deszler in 1692 ; the translation was made by John Wesley, and is found in " Hymns and Sacred Poems," 1739, page 99, where it is in six double verses, the first three only of which are here given, and divided into single verses. The remaining verses form hymn No. 196. The German author was the son of a pious author of Nuremberg ; he was born in 1660, and died in 1722. He published several devotional books, containing fifty-six hymns of his own, many of which are very beautiful.

HYMN 134.—"Jesus, if still the same Thou art."—*Matthew* v. 3-6.—TUNE, Frankfort, 1761.

Charles Wesley's, from " Hymns and Sacred Poems," 1740, page 66.

HYMN 135.—" Jesu, if still Thou art to-day."
       „   136.—" While dead in trespasses I lie."
" *These things were written for our instruction.*"—TUNE, Mitcham, 1761.

Charles Wesley's, from " Hymns and Sacred Poems," 1740, page 71. The two hymns form one in the original, extending to twenty-one verses, the thirteenth only being omitted, which reads thus—

> " While torn by hellish pride I cry,
>   By legion lust possest,
>   Son of the living God, draw nigh
>   And speak me unto rest."

The tenth verse is altered from " Long have I waited in the way."

Janeway's " Token for Children " was a book which afforded great delight to Fanny Wrightson, when only a child, and its teachings induced in her a love of piety and prayer which ripened into a sincere godly life.   During an illness, at the age of fifteen, she obtained remission of sin, and after her recovery, she began to meet in class, became a Sunday-school teacher, and ultimately was married to the Rev. Henry Ranson, Wesleyan minister.   During life she remained a thorough and consistent Methodist, and in her last illness, even in extreme suffering, she displayed perfect submission to the will of God, and strong confidence in His power to deliver, often repeating—

> " If Thou impart Thyself to me,
>   No other good I need :
>   If Thou, the Son, shalt make me free,
>   I shall be free indeed."

In her last utterance she tried to say, " Thanks be to God, who giveth us the victory; " but faintly saying " thanks ! " she sweetly entered into rest.

HYMN 137.—" When shall Thy love constrain ? "—*The Resignation.*—TUNE, Lampe's, 1746.

Charles Wesley's, found in " Hymns and Sacred Poems," 1740.   The original has twenty-two verses, the first eight and the last two being omitted.   The first line reads thus, " And wilt thou yet be found ? "   This is a great favourite with the people, probably arising from the simplicity of the language. Like many of the poet's hymns, the rhyme of this is occasionally imperfect.

HYMN 138.—" O that thou wouldst the heavens rent."
  „   139.—" Jesu ! Redeemer, Saviour, Lord."
A Prayer against the Power of Sin.—TUNE, Brockmer, 1761.

Charles Wesley's, in " Hymns and Sacred Poems," 1740, page 79.   The original has seventeen verses.   The hymn presents a grand and sustaining view of the omnipotence of the Deity, arguing from His power over the physical to that over the moral and spiritual.   It is a sublime and characteristic composition.

Hymn 140.—" Come, O thou Traveller unknown."

     „   141.—" Yield to me now, for I am weak."

Wrestling Jacob.—Tune, Travellers, 1761.

Charles Wesley's, found in "Hymns and Sacred Poems," 1742. The original consists of fourteen verses. In the earlier editions of the collection it was printed as one hymn; the editors of the edition in 1797 were the first to mar its uniformity by dividing it. The hymn is founded on the events recorded in Genesis xxxii. 26-29.

Of this noble composition, so many have written in praise, it is difficult to select from the high testimonies. John Wesley, in his brief notice of his brother's death, observes: "His least praise was his talent for poetry, although Dr Watts did not scruple to say that that single poem, 'Wrestling Jacob,' was worth all the verses he himself had written." James Montgomery, the Sheffield lyric poet, in his "*Christian Psalmist*," records that "among Charles Wesley's highest achievements may be recorded, 'Come, O thou Traveller unknown,' in which with consummate art he carries on the action of a lyrical drama; every turn in the conflict with the Mysterious Being against whom he wrestles all night being marked with precision by the varying language of the speaker, accompanied by intense increasing interest, till the rapturous moment of the discovery, when he prevails and exclaims, 'I know Thee, Saviour, who Thou art,' &c." This lyric was also an intense favourite with John Wesley, who frequently selected it to be sung in the public services. After his noble brother had in peaceful triumph passed away to his rest, John was always moved with intense emotion, visible to all who heard him, when he read that intensely touching couplet—

> " My company before is gone,
> And I am left alone with Thee."

The Rev. John Kirk writes of "its wonderful conciseness, yet perfect and finished picturing of the scene on the Transjordanic hills, beyond the deep defile where the Jabbok, as its name implies, wrestles with the mountains through which it descends to the Jordan. The dramatic form, so singular in hymnic composition, shadowing forth the action of the conversation; the great force of its thoroughly English expression; the complete finish and rhythm of its verse; its straightforward ease, without any mere straining at elegance; and the minuteness and general beauty of its application of the narrative, have won the commendation of all competent critics." Wrestling Jacob was the theme of Charles Wesley's preaching as well as of his poetry. Before the hymn was published in 1742, he records having preached on Jacob wrestling for the blessing, on two occasions, on May 24, and July 16, 1741. On six occasions after the hymn appeared, he mentions in his Journal having discoursed on the deeply interesting theme : at the Foundery, in London, October 6, 1743, and again in London, June 12, 1744, " when many wept with the angel and made supplication, and were encouraged to wait upon the Lord ;" at Bristol, January 29, 1749, when the power of the Highest overshadowed the audience ; in Dublin, February 7, and also on March 7, 1748, when hearers went to their houses justified ; and finally, in Bristol, May 20, 1748, when many were stirred up to lay hold on the Lord, like Jacob. The Rev. Thomas Jackson, in his " Life of Charles Wesley," vol. i., page 306, remarking on this poem, says, " It applies with admirable ingenuity and tact the patriarch's mysterious conflict, and the happy result to which it led, in the process of an awakened sinner's salvation." To have heard the poet's sermon on this mighty wrestling, with all the play of a fine fancy arranging the eminently evangelical topics in glowing colours before a crowded assembly, and then to have closed that discourse with the singing of part of that grand hymn, must have been a privilege of surpassing interest and delight.[*]

That theme which had been made a blessing to many through the author's preaching, has been also blest to others through the poet's verse. Solomon Burrall, of Tuckingmill, Cornwall, was in

---

[*] Mr George Macdonald has recently (1869) published in the Sunday Library, a volume entitled "England's Antiphon," in which he professes to give a review, with examples of the religious poetry of England. In this somewhat large collection of religious verse, Charles Wesley is represented by only one piece—"Wrestling Jacob ;" and to this the critic volunteers his opinion, that the hymns of this author "do not possess much literary merit." Is literary merit the only quality of a hymn worth noticing? Will Mr Macdonald furnish evidence of the practical use of the hymns he has chosen, as those which do contain merit of other kinds, and which have been useful in leading sinners to Christ and to heaven? If he cannot furnish such evidence, his depreciatory remarks on Charles Wesley's hymns will have but little weight with competent judges.

early life restrained from sin by the Spirit of God, and at the age of twenty, yielded his heart to the service of God. During forty-five years he was a member of the Methodist Society, and a useful worker in the Lord's vineyard, living in the uninterrupted enjoyment of the perfect love of God. The evening before his death, he put forth all his strength in singing the verse—

> " ' Come, O thou Traveller unknown,
>   Whom still I hold, but cannot see !
> My company before is gone,
>   And I am left alone with Thee :
> With Thee all night I mean to stay,
>   And wrestle till the break of day.' "

After this he spoke but little, and only to express his strong confidence in God.

HYMN 142.—" Drooping soul, shake off thy fears."—*Waiting for the Promise.*—TUNE, Foundery, 1761.

Charles Wesley's, found in " Hymns and Sacred Poems," 1742, page 237. The original is in six verses, the fifth and sixth being omitted.

HYMN 143.*—"Jesu, Lover of my soul."—*In Temptation.*—TUNE, Hotham, 1761.

Charles Wesley's, found in " Hymns and Sacred Poems," 1742, page 67. This hymn was not added to the collection till the year 1797. The original has five verses, the third being omitted. It delineates so correctly the views, feelings, and desires of all true Christians, that it has become a favourite among the pious of all denominations.

"A fine, intelligent young Virginian, while residing in the Western States of America, became an infidel and a blasphemer of the name of God. From this state he was delivered by reading a work by Soame Jenyns, but whilst he became convinced of the truth of revelation, he did not feel its power. A lingering illness and fatal disease led him to reflection and prayer. Three Christian friends sometimes visited him to spend the tedious hours in singing hymns. They one day entered his room and began to sing, 'There is a fountain fill'd with blood,' followed by 'The voice of free grace,' &c. He then said to them, 'There is nothing I so much like to hear as the first

hymn you ever sung to me, 'Jesu, Lover of my soul.' We sung
it again to the tune Martyn, and found the solemnity which had
reigned in the room while singing the former hymn was changed
to weeping. We struck the very touching strain of the second
stanza, 'Other refuge have I none.' The weeping became
loud. The heart of him who had reviled Christ was broken ; we
feared to sing the remaining stanzas owing to the prostration of
the sufferer. A few days afterwards he said, 'I don't think I
shall ever hear,' 'Jesu, Lover of my soul,' sung again, it so excites
me that my poor body cannot bear it."—*Belcher's Historical
Sketches of Hymns.*

Mrs Harriet Beecher Stowe, describing the last hours of her
distinguished father, Dr Lyman Beecher, says : "The last indication of life, on the day of his death, was a mute response to
his wife, repeating—

> ' Jesu, Lover of my soul,
>   Let me to Thy bosom fly.' "

The Rev. H. W. Beecher of New York has written : " I would
rather have written that hymn of Wesley's—

> ' Jesu, Lover of my soul,
>   Let me to Thy bosom fly,'

than to have the fame of all the kings that ever sat on the earth.
It is more glorious. It has more power in it. I would rather
be the author of that hymn than to hold the wealth of the richest
man in New York. He will die. He *is* dead, and does not
know it. He will pass, after a little while, out of men's thoughts.
What will there be to speak of him ? What will he have done
that will stop trouble, or encourage hope ? His money will go
to his heirs, and they will divide it. It is like a stream divided
and growing narrower by division. And they will die, and it
will go to their heirs. In three or four generations everything
comes to the ground again for redistribution. But that hymn
will go on singing until the last trump brings forth the angel
band ; and then, I think, it will mount up on some lip to the
very presence of God. I would rather have written such a
hymn than to have heaped up all the treasures of the richest
man on the globe. A man may be very useful and influential,
and not be rich."

" Righteousness to children's children," was a rich heritage,
enjoyed by Julia E. Jordan. Her grandfather, the Rev. George

M'Elwaine, spent fifty-six years in the Methodist ministry; whilst she herself commenced her Christian career in childhood, in answer to prayers offered by her parents. Symptoms of consumption having set in, she was taken from Nova Scotia to Bermuda, but no advantage being manifest, she returned home to die. Her life had been one of brightness and purity, and her last days testified to the holiness of her heart. In her last hours she saw Jesus in His power to save to the uttermost, and sang—

> " Jesu, Lover of my soul,
>   Let me to Thy bosom fly.'

She called all her friends around her that she might encourage them to trust in the Lord ; and with grace triumphing over nature, she entered into rest.

The consolation afforded to the young disciple by Mr Wesley's touching lines, was quite as acceptable by, and accessible to, the aged divine. Thomas Hartwell Horne, the painstaking theologian and learned author, was convinced of sin under a sermon by the Rev. Joseph Benson, and at once united himself to the Methodists. As a clerk to Mr Butterworth, and under the religious instruction of the Rev. Dr Adam Clarke, he served Methodism faithfully for some years, and ultimately got ordination in the Church of England. His great work, " The Introduction to the Critical Study of the Holy Scriptures," originated in Methodism. He was faithful in the discharge of his duties as one of the metropolitan clergy, and died in honoured age, often repeating during his sickness—

> " Other refuge have I none,
>   Hangs my helpless soul on Thee," &c.

In this calm and resigned frame of mind, he exchanged mortality for life, aged 82.

Perhaps there does not exist a hymn which has been more extensively quoted on death-beds. A volume, of considerable dimensions, might be made up of such examples, from Methodist sources alone. Some of these have a record at the end of this volume, in the index.

HYMN 144.—" Thee, Jesu, Thee, the Sinner's Friend."—*Desiring to Love.*—TUNE, Musician's, 1781.

Charles Wesley's, found in " Hymns and Sacred Poems,"

1742, page 242. The original has eleven verses, the second and third being omitted. "Dear Lord" is altered to "O Lord" and "My Lord" in two places. This hymn has much of the sentiment and imagery of Wrestling Jacob. The sixth verse refers to the passing by of the Almighty before Moses, and the concluding verses glance at the parable of the Lost Sheep and the death of Moses, thus showing how thoroughly scriptural is Charles Wesley's poetry.

HYMN 145.—"O Jesus, let me bless Thy Name!"—*Desiring to Love.*—TUNE, Chapel, 1761.

Charles Wesley's, found in "Hymns and Sacred Poems," 1749, vol. i. The sixth and seventh verses of the original are left out. In the first line "kiss" is changed to "bless." Mr Bunting suggests that line four, verse 5, should read thus: "The surety who my debt has paid."

HYMN 146.—"Still, Lord, I languish for Thy grace."—*Desiring to Love.*—TUNE, Snowsfield's, 1761.

Charles Wesley's, from "Hymns and Sacred Poems," 1749, vol. i., the second and fourth verses of the original being left out.

HYMN 147.—"O Love Divine, how sweet thou art!"—*Desiring to Love.*—TUNE, Chapel, 1761.

Charles Wesley's, from "Hymns and Sacred Poems," 1749, vol. i., three verses of the original being omitted.

This hymn contains an extraordinary depth of feeling and desire, eager, impatient, resolute, combined with an extended view of the love of God, such as only a poet of much heart experience like Charles Wesley could write. This fine, bold, poetical language may help private devotion, but is scarcely proper for general use in the sanctuary. Interruptions in the regular order of divine service are seldom to be commended, but we have an instance before us in which the monotony was broken with good effect. William Dawson, of Barnbow, Leeds, had once preached a very impressive sermon, and at its close gave out this hymn. When the choir were singing the third verse, "God only knows the love of God," he stopped them, and said, "Stop, friends! If angels, the first-born sons of light, cannot understand the height, the breadth, the depth, the length of the love of God, how can we expect to fathom it while here below?"

He then repeated, with deepest feeling, thrilling his large auditory—

"'God only knows the love of God.'

Let us sing it again, friends, for we shall all have to sing it in heaven—

'God only knows the love of God.'"

It need hardly be said that a profound feeling of majestic awe pervaded the vast assembly.

Pardon to a sinner who has felt the agonies of deep repentance is often followed by an ecstasy of joy. Thomas Carter, of Catterick, after entering into the society of the children of God, and feeling the witness within him of his acceptance with God, one Sabbath morning, in the parish church, after the absolution had been pronounced, modestly stood up in the gallery, and asked permission to tell the people what God had done for his soul, as he could confirm the truth just read, for God had pardoned him, being penitent. Such testimony is of rare occurrence ; the world would be the better, and the Church too, for the frequent repetition of such assurance. The good man lived according to that beginning, serving the office of prayer-leader on Sunday morning at seven o'clock, class-leader, steward, and trustee, with uprightness and fidelity. Only a few hours before his death he sang his favourite hymn, commencing—

"O Love Divine, how sweet thou art."

But voice and speech had well-nigh gone ; he seemed to pray to the last, and to "enter heaven by prayer."

The labours of the late Mr Crabbe, of Southampton, were instrumental in bringing John Bailey, of Crowdhill, to the Saviour. He soon afterwards became useful in the Methodist Society as a class-leader and local preacher, and spent a long life, like Enoch, walking with God. The testimony of his friends was, "that he was a faithful man, and feared God above many." For three years he was afflicted with paralysis, but without complaint he endured all his privations. On the Sabbath before he died, he awoke with the words on his mind—

"O Love Divine, how sweet thou art," &c.

When unable to speak, he made signs that he was happy.

HYMN 148.—" Father of Jesus Christ, the Just."—*Seeking Redemption.*—TUNE, Mourners, 1761.

Is No. 14 in Charles Wesley's " Redemption Hymns," 1747. The original has five verses, two of which are omitted.

HYMN 149.*—" Thus saith the Lord,—'tis God commands."— *Isaiah* lxii.

Charles Wesley's, from " Hymns and Sacred Poems," 1749, vol. i., where it forms the sixth, and extends to thirty verses. This hymn commences with the twenty-first of the original, but the first line of that verse is altered from " Go through the gates, 'tis God's command." Twenty-four of the verses are omitted.

HYMN 150.—" Thou hidden God, for whom I groan."—*Seeking Redemption.*—TUNE, Wednesbury, 1761.

Forms No. 27 of Charles Wesley's " Redemption Hymns."

HYMN 151.—" Out of the deep I cry."—*Seeking Redemption.*— TUNE, West Street, 1761.

Is No. 20 of Charles Wesley's " Redemption Hymns."

HYMN 152.—" Ah! whither should I go?"
    „   153.—" Lo! in Thy hand I lay."
God will have all Men to be Saved.—TUNE, Lampes, 1746.

No. 14 in Charles Wesley's " Hymns on God's Everlasting Love," 1741. The two form one in the original, and it is based on 1 Timothy ii. 4. Nine verses are omitted, and several lines are altered.

HYMN 154.—" Fain would I leave the world below."—*A Hymn for Midnight.*—TUNE, Mourners, 1761.

Charles Wesley's, from " Hymns and Sacred Poems," 1739, pp. 55, 56, where the first verse commences thus : " While midnight shades the earth o'erspread." The original has six verses, the first and second being left out. This hymn commences with the third verse ; the last line of verse 3 is altered from " And look my *midnight* into day," to "*darkness* into day ;" and the first line of verse 4, "*error*" is changed to "*sorrow ;*" and line 6, verse 1, "since *death*" is changed to "since *faith.*"

This hymn was written by Charles Wesley about the year 1737, before his conversion, and he gave it then the title, "A Midnight Hymn, for one under the Law." It describes, in melancholy, plaintive language the distressing state of spiritual gloom of the author himself. John Wesley, in selecting this hymn for his collection in 1779, aptly placed it in the section "For Mourners convinced of Sin," and altered it in several places. "In its altered state," observes the Rev. Thomas Jackson, "it no longer appears as the desponding language of a real Christian, expecting to be made free from sin and misery by the body's dissolution, but as the prayer of a weeping penitent convinced of his guilt, and looking for present deliverance through faith in the blood of Atonement."

HYMN 155.—"God of my life, what just return."—*After Recovery from Sickness.*—TUNE, Athlone, 1761.

Charles Wesley's, from "Hymns and Sacred Poems," 1739, page 82.

"This hymn," says Mr Jackson, "is a fine specimen of Charles Wesley's poetic genius, unimpaired by disease." Mr Bunting suggests that a better title would be, "For Evening Worship." For that purpose he used it. The original has seventeen verses, the first seven, and two others, being left out. The first line commences thus—"And live I yet by power divine?" Whilst at Oxford, during the year of his conversion (1738), the poet was so dangerously ill, he did not expect to recover. Feeling the same sense of gratitude to God for his restoration to health as did King Hezekiah under similar circumstances, the poet bases his thoughts on the account of the king's recovery (2 Kings xx. 1–11), and from thence he has produced a truly sublime hymn. These stanzas, in sublimity of thought and strength of expression, surpass Addison's fine hymn, written under similar circumstances, which commences, "When rising from the bed of death," &c.

HYMN 156.—"O disclose Thy lovely face."—*My soul gaspeth for Thee as the thirsty land,*" &c.—TUNE, Dedication, 1781.

Charles Wesley's, from "Hymns and Sacred Poems," 1740, page 60. This hymn is a composite, made up in this way: the first verse forms in the original the second of five, the remaining four of that hymn being left out. The first line of the hymn commences, "Lord, how long," &c. To that one verse is added two others from another hymn on the next page, entitled, "A Morning Hymn," which commences, "Christ, whose glory fills the skies."

In Toplady's works, part of this hymn is inserted as belonging to that author, which is a misappropriation. Similar sentiments are found in a hymn by Sir Robert Grant, and quoted by Mr Punshon in his sermon on the "Christian Inheritance."

At Oxhill, Kineton, preaching by the Methodists was held for a long period only fortnightly, on a week evening ; and this was about to be given up, when Mrs Gardner and three other persons formed a society, began to meet in class, and then there followed a gracious revival. For forty-eight years she continued in fellowship with the Methodists, manifesting her love to God by her care for the preachers, her diligent attention on the ordinances of religion, and her liberal support of church funds. During her last illness she was severely tried by the enemy ; but prayer was made for her, and she obtained the victory, saying, "Precious Jesus ! His blood cleanseth from all sin." She often repeated, and tried to sing verses of hymns, especially the lines—

> "Haste, my Lord, no more delay,
> Come, my Saviour, come away."

Thus calmly did she wait till the heavenly convoy escorted her home.

HYMN 157.—"My sufferings all to Thee are known."—*Written in stress of Temptation.*—TUNE, Dresden, 1761.

Charles Wesley's, from "Hymns and Sacred Poems," 1740, page 84. The original has twenty verses, twelve of which are omitted, and two are transposed.

Mrs Bennett, of Tempsford, from her youth, had been subject to a painful contraction of the throat. The aperture for food was so narrow as to threaten death by starvation. Medical skill was tried in vain. Thirty years she had lived happily with her husband and family, but taking a cold whilst visiting two of her sons in Norfolk, the malady was increased, her sufferings were very severe, and she wasted away to a mere shadow of her former self. In this extreme trial, she found support from her confidence in God, and her reliance on His promises. Charles Wesley's beautiful and pathetic hymn was never more appropriately used than by this sorely-tried Christian. Often did she repeat—

" My sufferings all to Thee are known,
   Tempted in every point like me ;
   Regard my grief, regard Thy own ;
   Jesus, remember Calvary !

" Art Thou not touch'd with human woe ?
   Hath pity left the Son of man ?
   Dost Thou not all my sorrows know,
   And claim a share in all my pain ?"

She had to struggle for life ; the claims of her family seemed
to produce a wish to be spared ; the world itself had no charms
for her. She at length gave up all to the care of her heavenly
Father, and patiently waited the release of her happy spirit from
her suffering body.

It is only as "last-words" that we value some things which
would otherwise pass without notice. John Clarkson Sutcliffe,
of Barnsley, was for many years an earnest Christian, giving to
God a portion of every day's time, his journals being headed
on alternate pages "eternity" and "time ;" and under each,
daily, was usually made some entry, indicating his methodical
way of living, and his spiritual-mindedness. Here is one entry
worth writing in letters of gold, "I have not had a barren class-
meeting for several years." When smitten with paralysis, he
suffered much ; but on the Sabbath before his death, his speech
was partly restored to him, and he read with delight the hymn
commencing—

   " My sufferings all to Thee are known."

He was then engaged in closet prayer, about four hours before
the final stroke ; thus he consecrated his latest consciousness
to his loved employ, and retiring to rest, he slept in Jesus.

HYMN 158.—"O my God, what must I do ?"—"*The heart is
   deceitful,*" &c. (Jer. xvii. 9).—TUNE, Brays, 1761.

Charles Wesley's, from "Hymns and Sacred Poems," 1742,
page 41. The original has twelve verses. The first commences
thus : "O my false deceitful heart." The first eight verses are
omitted.

Some of the expressions in this hymn are so strong as scarcely
to be reconcilable with man's free agency. For example, in the
second verse—

   " Force me, Lord, with all to part ;
   Tear these idols from my heart."

Mr Bunting suggests an improvement in three lines : line five, verse one, to read thus : " Over all, if God Thou art ; " and the last line of the second and third verses to read as follows: "Make me a new creature now."

HYMN 159.—" Lay to Thy hand, O God of Grace !"—*Groaning for Redemption.*—TUNE, Whitsunday, 1791.

Charles Wesley's, from " Hymns and Sacred Poems," 1742, page 79. The original is in four parts, extending to thirty-six verses. This hymn consists of the last three verses of part iii. The tune is not in any of Mr Wesley's music books.

HYMN 160.—" O Jesus, my hope, For me offer'd up."—*A Penitential Hymn.*—TUNE, Passion, 1761.

Charles Wesley's, from " Hymns and Sacred Poems," 1749, vol. i., No. 38, where it is printed in six-line stanzas, like the New-Year's Hymn. The second verse is left out. The doctrine of Christian perfection is strongly expressed in some parts of this hymn.

HYMN 161.—" Stay, thou insulted Spirit, stay."—*A Penitential Hymn.*—TUNE, Welling, 1761.

Charles Wesley's, from " Hymns and Sacred Poems," 1749, vol. i., No. 41. The sixth verse is left out.

In this, as in a former hymn, the poet refers to his own age, the original having been written just in the middle of his early life ; and it indicates deep feelings of penitential sorrow in his own heart.

> " Though I have steel'd my stubborn heart,
>   And still shook off my guilty fears ;
> And vex'd and urged Thee to depart
>   For forty long rebellious years."

The word "forty" John Wesley changed into "many," and some other judicious alterations were made by him in other parts of it.

HYMN 162.*—" O my offended God."—*God's Everlasting Love.*

Forms No. 5 of Charles Wesley's " Hymns on God's Everlasting Love," 1741. The original has seventeen stanzas, twelve of which are omitted. This was added after Mr Wesley's death.

HYMN 163.—" When, gracious Lord, when shall it be."—*Come, Lord Jesus.*—TUNE, Complaint, 1761.

Charles Wesley's, from " Hymns and Sacred Poems," 1742, page 201. The original has thirteen stanzas, the fourth to the ninth being left out. The first line in the original commences, " When, 'dearest' Lord," which is altered to " gracious." The idea contained in the second verse, " O dark! dark! dark! I still must say," is similar to a line in Milton's " Samson Agonistes," line 80, as follows: "O dark! dark! dark! amid the blaze of noon." The last verse of the hymn commencing, " Lord, I am blind," may have been suggested to Milton's fertile mind by the fact of Samson's blindness, or by his own blindness, or both.

Never was the " beauty of holiness " more marked in a Christian's life, than in that of Mary Isaac, wife of the Rev. Daniel Isaac, who was born in York, and died there at the patriarchal age of ninety-seven years. How early in life she began to serve the Lord is not now known ; she was a matured Christian when married in 1808, and for twenty-five years was a help-meet indeed to her husband. During many years of widowhood, her cry was, " Not my will, but Thine be done." Her piety was deep ; her love of the Bible, of the means of grace, and of the Lord's people, was intense. Though long past fourscore years, scarcely a wrinkle marked her beautiful countenance ; her complexion was fair and clear as that of a child, and that of her face serenity itself. Although a martyr to pain, no complaint escaped her lips, but rather, " Thy will be done, O Lord, not mine." During the watches of her last night on earth, she repeated—

" When, gracious Lord, when shall it be,
   That I shall find my HOME in Thee?"

She breakfasted in the morning at eight, after which her niece assisted her out of bed, when she said, " I believe I am dying," and in a few moments, in great peace, she departed to be with Christ.

HYMN 164.—" Lord, regard my earnest cry."—" *The Woman of Canaan* " (Matt. xxv. 22-28).—TUNE, Calvary, 1761.

Charles Wesley's, from " Hymns and Sacred Poems," 1742, page 96, where there are nine verses, three of which are left out.

HYMN 165.—"Come, holy, celestial Dove."—*For Whitsunday.*
—TUNE, Thou Shepherd of Israel, 1761.

Charles Wesley's, from "Hymns of Petition and Thanksgiving for the Promise of the Father," page 29.

HYMN 166.—"Jesus, take my sins away."—" *The Pool of Bethesda* " (John v. 2, 9).—TUNE, Kingswood, 1761.

Charles Wesley's, from "Hymns and Sacred Poems," 1742, page 98. The original has eleven verses, five of which are left out, and the sixth verse is made up of parts of two other verses.

HYMN 167.—"Lamb of God, for sinners slain."—*Looking to Jesus.*—TUNE, Kingswood, 1761.

Charles Wesley's, from "Hymns and Sacred Poems," 1742, page 49. Two of the six verses in the original are left out.

HYMN 168.—"Depth of mercy, can there be."—*After a Relapse into Sin.*—TUNE, Savannah, 1761.

Charles Wesley's, from "Hymns and Sacred Poems," 1740, page 82. The original is in thirteen stanzas of four lines each, one of which is omitted, and the eighth is transposed. This hymn commences the third section of the collection, with the title, "For Persons Convinced of Backsliding."

An actress in one of the provincial towns, whilst passing along the street, had her attention arrested by singing in a cottage. Curiosity prompted her to look in at the open door, when she saw a few poor people sitting together, one of whom was giving out hymn 168—

> " Depth of mercy, can there be
> Mercy still reserved for me ? "

which they all joined in singing. The tune was sweet and simple, but she heeded it not ; the words had riveted her attention, and she stood motionless, until she was invited to enter. She remained during a prayer which was offered up by one of the little company, and which, though uncouth in language, carried with it the conviction of sincerity. She quitted the cottage, but the words of the hymn followed her, and she resolved to procure a copy of the book containing it. The hymn-book secured, she read and re-read this hymn. Her convictions deepened, she attended the ministry of the gospel, and sought and found that pardon which alone could give her peace. Having given her heart to God, she resolved henceforth to give her life to Him also; and, for a time, excused herself from attending on the stage. The manager of the theatre called upon her one morning and urged her to sustain the principal character in a new play. This character she had sustained in other towns with admiration, but now she gave her reasons for refusing to comply with the request. At first the manager ridiculed her scruples, but this was unavailing; he then represented the loss which her refusal would be to him, and promised, if she would act on this occasion, it would be the last request of the kind he would make. Unable to resist his solicitations, she promised to appear at the theatre. The character which she assumed required her, on her entrance, to sing a song, and as the curtain rose the orchestra began the accompaniment. She stood like one lost in thought; the music ceased, but she did not sing; and, supposing she was embarrassed, the band again commenced, and they paused again for her to begin, but she opened not her lips. A third time the air was played, and then, with clasped hands and eyes suffused with tears, she sang—not the song of the play, but

> " Depth of mercy, can there be
> Mercy still reserved for me?
> Can my God His wrath forbear?
> Me, the chief of sinners, spare?"

The performance suddenly ended; many ridiculed, though some were induced from that memorable night to "consider their ways,"—to reflect on the power of that religion which could influence the heart and change the life of one hitherto so vain. The change in the life of the actress was as permanent as it was singular; and after some years of a consistent walk, she at length became the wife of a minister of the gospel of Christ.

At an early period of life, Ralph Ravenscroft, of Runcorn, was converted to God. He retained an unbroken sense of his acceptance with God to the end of life. His last visit to his class was a season of special blessing. His ambition was to have the faith which endured as did that of Abraham. Shortly before his death he was heard pleading for immediate and full salvation, exclaiming, "Why not now?" Then breaking out in singing—

> "Depth of mercy! can there be," &c.

God graciously prepared him for the final hour, which found him waiting to enter into the "mansions" of the redeemed.

Forty years was the limit of time allotted to Mrs Glass, of Chichester, for twenty of which she was a consistent member of the Methodist Society. Her piety was deep, and her conduct exemplary. She was able to testify that the blood of Jesus Christ cleansed from all sin. Not long before she died, she said, with emphasis—

> "God is love! I know, I feel ;
> Jesus weeps, and loves me still ! "

Her last words were, "I am going to glory," and breathed out her spirit to God.

Amongst the first members of the Methodist Society in London were the parents of Elizabeth Dowsett ; her father was one of the local-preachers at the old Foundry, where she herself worshipped, being a regular attendant at the five o'clock morning preaching by Mr Wesley for many years, and she was honoured with the personal friendship of that great and good man. Her conversion was thorough, and her religion that of love. For nearly eighty years she was a member of the Methodist Society. Her life was one of holy service, and her experience was that of quietness and assurance. As she drew near her end, her peace seemed to flow as a river. Some of her last words were—

> "God is love ! I know, I feel ;
> Jesus weeps, and loves me still ! "

and in peaceful triumph she went to heaven.

HYMN 169.*—"Jesus, the all-restoring Word."—*A Morning Hymn.*

Charles Wesley's, from "Hymns and Sacred Poems," 1740, page 25. This was first added to the collection in 1797, and included all the six verses, the sixth having been omitted since the year 1830.

HYMN 170.—"O 'tis enough, my God, my God !"
     ,,   171.—"O God, if Thou art love indeed."
God's Everlasting Love.—TUNE, 22d and 112th Psalm Tune, 1761.

These form together No. 9 in Charles Wesley's "Hymns on

God's Everlasting Love," 1741, page 16. It has eleven verses, four of which are omitted. The first nine verses will be found in the first number of the *Arminian Magazine*, 1778, with the title, " Salvation depends not on Absolute Decrees."

HYMN 172.—" O unexhausted Grace !"—*After a Recovery.*— TUNE, Olney, 1761.

Charles Wesley's, forming No. 93 in " Hymns and Sacred Poems," 1749, vol. i. The original has seven verses, the first three of which are omitted.

HYMN 173.—" Jesus, I believe Thee near."—*For one Fallen from Grace.*—TUNE, Dedication, 1781.

Charles Wesley's, forming No. 79 in " Hymns and Sacred Poems," 1749, vol. i. The third verse of the original is omitted.

HYMN 174.—" How shall a lost sinner in pain."—*For one Fallen from Grace.*—TUNE, Funeral, 1761.

Charles Wesley's, forming No. 71 in " Hymns and Sacred Poems," 1749, vol. i.

HYMN 175.—" God of my salvation, hear."—*After a Relapse into Sin.*—TUNE, Kingswood, 1761.

Charles Wesley's, from " Hymns and Sacred Poems," 1742, page 139.

The Rev. William Barton, of whom previous mention has been made, after thirty years of service in the Methodist ministry, became an invalid from heart disease, but was able to realise peace through the atonement of Christ. His favourite hymn was the 175th, and he delighted to repeat

" Friend of sinners, spotless Lamb,
Thy blood was shed for me."

These lines he repeated the night before his death; and the last word he was heard to utter was " Happy ! "

HYMN 176.—" O God, Thy righteousness we own."—*For one Fallen from Grace.*—TUNE, Mourners, 1761.

Charles Wesley's ; forming No. 74 in " Hymns and Sacred Poems," 1749, vol. i.

HYMN 177.—" Jesus, Thou know'st my sinfulness."—*Groaning for Redemption.*—TUNE, Bradford, 1761.

Charles Wesley's, from " Hymns and Sacred Poems," 1742, page 76. The original is in four parts, and extends to thirty-six verses. This hymn is selected from the second part, but seven verses out of twelve are omitted. In the first line " simpleness " is changed to " sinfulness."

HYMN 178.—" Yes, from this instant now, I will " (Jer. iii. 4, 5). —TUNE, Cary's, 1761.

Forms No. 1168 of Charles Wesley's "Short Scripture Hymns," 1762, vol. ii.

HYMN 179.—"Father, if Thou must reprove" (Jer. x., &c.)— TUNE, Kingswood, 1761.

Forms Nos. 1191 and 1211 of Charles Wesley's "Short Scripture Hymns," 1762, vol. ii., based on Jer. x. 24, and Jer. xxiv. 7.

HYMN 180.—" Saviour, I now with shame confess."—*For the iniquity,*" &c. (Isa. lvii. 17-19).—TUNE, Pudsey, 1761.

Forms No. 1113 of Charles Wesley's "Short Scripture Hymns," 1762, vol. i.

HYMN 181.—" Thou Man of griefs, remember me."—" *Who in the days of his flesh,*" &c. (Heb. v. 7, 8).—TUNE, Palmi, 1761.

Forms No. 686 in vol. ii. of Charles Wesley's " Short Scripture Hymns."

HYMN 182.—" I will hearken what the Lord."—*Waiting for Christ the Prophet.*—TUNE, Amsterdam, 1761.

Charles Wesley's, from " Hymns and Sacred Poems," 1742, page 210. This hymn is the first in the fourth section of the collection, with the title, " For Backsliders Recovered."

HYMN 183.—" Jesu, Shepherd of the sheep,"—*After a Recovery.* —TUNE, Foundry, 1761.

Charles Wesley's, No. 94 in " Hymns and Sacred Poems," 1749, vol. i. Two verses of the original are left out. In line two of verse 3, Mr Bunting suggests this reading : "All my carnal mind control."

HYMN 184.—"My God, my God, to Thee I cry."—*After a Relapse into Sin.*—TUNE, Wenvo, 1761.

Charles Wesley's, from "Hymns and Sacred Poems," 1740, page 154.

Attending a love-feast at Weeton, near Knaresborough, where several young men, recent converts, related their experience, John Atkinson was convinced of sin, and at a prayer-meeting held in his father's barn at five o'clock in the morning, where those young men assembled often for prayer, he received a sense of pardon and adoption into the family of God. During forty years' membership with the Methodists, he never dishonoured his profession. Just before the end of his pilgrimage, when contending with his last enemy, he began to sing—

> "My God, my God, to Thee I cry ;
> Thee only would I know."

And after prayer he said, "My God is reconciled, His pardoning voice I hear." Then praying for his family, on pronouncing the benediction, immediately his happy spirit joined the company of the redeemed in heaven.

HYMN 185.—"After all that I have done."—*After a Recovery.*—TUNE, Magdalen, 1761.

Forms No. 91 in Charles Wesley's "Hymns and Sacred Poems," 1749, vol. i. The original has seven verses, the fifth and sixth being selected for this hymn. In the last verse, so intense is the poet's grief for having sinned, that rather than fall again into sin, he twice asks that he may die before such an act of wickedness should overtake him !

HYMN 186.—"Weary of wandering from my God."—*After a Recovery.*—TUNE, 113th Psalm, 1761.

Charles Wesley's, being No. 89 in "Hymns and Sacred Poems," 1749, vol. i.

HYMN 187.—"Son of God, if Thy free grace."—*After a Recovery.*—TUNE, Kingswood, 1761.

Charles Wesley's, from "Hymns and Sacred Poems," 1742. The original has six verses, two of which are omitted.

HYMN 188.—"Lord, and is Thine anger gone?"—*After a Recovery.*—TUNE, Kingswood, 1761.

Charles Wesley's, from "Hymns and Sacred Poems," 1742. The original has eight verses, the two last being omitted.

HYMN 189.—"Now I have found the ground wherein."— *Redemption Found.*—TUNE, Norwich, 1761.

Written in German by John Andrew Rothe, who was born in 1688, many years a friend of Count Zinzendorf, was pastor of the Moravian church at Hernhutt, and died in 1758. He wrote forty-five hymns, many of which are very beautiful. This one has in the original ten verses. John Wesley's translation is faithful and free ; it has made the hymn a great favourite with many Christians, and is much sung by his people. From its first publication in "Hymns and Sacred Poems," 1740, page 91, it has found multitudes of admirers. Perhaps there is not in the whole collection a hymn which is so full of Scripture truth in Scripture phraseology. One lover of this hymn has been led to compare it with the Word of God, and he has found no less than thirty-six separate passages of Scripture which, in language or spirit, correspond with the several lines of this hymn. When the translation of this hymn was finished, John Wesley sent a copy of it to P. H. Molther, one of the German Moravians in London, and under date of January 25, 1740, M. Molther returns the translation with his approval of all but one verse, which Mr Wesley altered as suggested. We learn from M. Molther's letter, first, that Mr Wesley willingly asked advice of others whose knowledge was reliable ; and secondly, that he readily adopted such advice when given. This hymn has won the admiration of thousands, and it will be admired to the end of time. The third stanza was translated by Molther, whose rendering Mr Wesley adopted.

The last two lines—

> "While Jesu's blood, through earth and skies,
> Mercy, free, boundless mercy cries ! "

were almost the last words spoken by the saintly John Fletcher, of Madeley, whose faith in the truths they contain was so strong that his feeble voice re-echoed with surprising energy the words, "boundless—boundless mercy!"

H

In the *Wesleyan Magazine* for April 1861, we read of the
Rev. John Haigh, that on one occasion, at the end of a
long life, while repeating the 189th hymn, on coming to the
fourth verse, "With faith I plunge me in this sea," &c., he
appeared completely absorbed, and with his eyes upraised, and
his hands clasped, he at length broke silence with "Glory be to
God! Glory be to God!" continuing to repeat, whisperingly,
the verses following, and then sank into sleep with the last lines
trembling on his lips—

> "Mercy's full power I then shall prove,
> Loved with an everlasting love."

Mr Wesley visited Thorne in April 1766, when he was welcomed to the hospitable home of Mr Meggitt; eleven such visits
did the good man pay to that home, and from that date till 1855
the messengers of salvation were hospitably entertained by
father and son. Samuel Meggitt succeeded to the house, and
had the piety of his father, and his love of good men. From
infancy he was under godly influences. In 1793, the Rev.
Alexander Mather preached at Thorne, and under that sermon,
young Meggitt, then only thirteen, was convinced of sin, and
two years later he found pardon during a visit of George and
William Masby, the praying colliers. For seventy-five years he
greatly aided the cause of God at Thorne, then removed to
Hull, where the influence of his family in promoting Methodism
has been considerable. When paralysis laid the strong man
low, he patiently endured his sufferings. Often in the night
season he would awake with a verse of Scripture or of a hymn
upon his lips. His rich and matured Christian experience
delighted and instructed his visitors. Often did he request them
to join him in singing to the tune of Euphony—

> "Now I have found the ground wherein
> Sure my soul's anchor may remain," &c.

Seldom was it sung without his face becoming illumined with a
heavenly halo, and tears of joy told of his happy heart. He
passed away in peace to the haven of rest.

Testimonies to the usefulness of this hymn are so numerous,
the reader will find a summary of them in the index at the end
of the volume. This hymn forms the first of the fourth part,
with the title, "For Believers Rejoicing."

HYMN 190.—"Jesus, Thy Blood and Righteousness."—*The Believer's Triumph.*—TUNE, Cannon, 1761.

Translated from the German of Count Zinzendorf, by John Wesley, and published in "Hymns and Sacred Poems," 1740, page 177.

Nicholas Lewis, Count and Lord of Zinzendorf and Pottendorf, was born at Dresden, May 26, 1700. His pious father was the prime-minister of Saxony. He became one of the most useful men in promoting religion, both in Germany and in England, though sometimes there was with it an admixture of dangerous error. He was for many years a most attached and endeared friend of the Wesleys, and his life by Spangenberg is one of the most interesting books of religious biography in the English language. He wrote many hymns, to which his noble wife and son added others also original, and he printed at his own private press at Chelsea two volumes of hymns, dated 1754, which there had then been nothing to compare with in England for variety and deep spiritual experience. These two volumes are the basis of nearly all subsequent collections of hymns made in England. From a copy before us, with authors' names affixed, we find most of the translations made by the Wesleys. The count died very happy in May 1760. The original of this hymn has twenty-four stanzas; and John Wesley made, in 1739, a free and faithful, though abridged, translation of this truly beautiful composition. A more complete translation will be found in "The United Brethren's Hymn-Book," No. 326, extending to twelve verses.

The interest which attaches to this hymn will be unceasing. It has been used by hundreds of Christians on their death-beds; allusion to some of these will be found in the index.

When divine things are seen in their true light, worldly things get into their right place. The father of the Rev. James Smetham was brought to a knowledge of the truth as it is in Jesus, through the prayers of his son. When father and mother were converted, the eldest son began to pray for his brothers, and James followed the happy example. After many years of useful labour in the Wesleyan ministry, he was laid aside by illness. Addressing his son one day, he said, " I have had such a sight of my own defects and unfaithfulness, and such a view of the purity and holiness of God, as almost made me despair of

finding mercy at the last. I remembered that when your brother
John was dying, he was delivered from his last fear by remembering and repeating the verse—

> Jesus, Thy blood and righteousness
> My beauty are, my glorious dress :
> 'Midst flaming worlds, with these array'd,
> With joy shall I lift up my head.'

I asked that the hymn-book might be given me,—I opened it,
and the first lines on which my eye rested were those commencing—

> 'Jesus, Thy blood and righteousness.'

All my fear, doubt, and distress vanished, when, at the reading
of that verse, I cast my soul on the Atonement ; and since that
time I have enjoyed perfect peace." In his last hours he seemed
to have sweet and mysterious manifestations of the heavenly
world. His pleasant smiles, rapt looks, and upward pointing
of the finger, indicated glorious visions to his own eyes, and he
said, " I am coming !"

Sunday-schools were till quite recently unknown on the Continent. In a letter from a German missionary, dated Carlsruhe,
October 1865, we read some particulars of the death in that
place of the first German Sunday-school superintendent. At
his funeral the missionary read the first four lines of this hymn,
as containing the creed of the departed man of God. Those
simple and powerful words made a deep impression on all.

An interesting story is told of Queen Christiana of Prussia,
who, having seen a beautiful child, the little daughter of one
of the palace gardeners, playing amongst the flowers, had
the child brought to her in the palace the next day, and placed
on a chair near her at dinner-time. The queen, by anticipation,
enjoyed the delight and surprise she thought the child would
express. But, to the astonishment of the queen, the little girl,
looking quietly down at the table, repeated the following prayer
for a blessing—

> "Christ's dear blood and righteousness
> Be to me as jewels given,
> Crowning me when I shall press
> Onward through the gates of heaven."

No one spoke for a time ; but it seemed as though the innocent
child, seeing the dinner provided, was asked to sing her blessing
before meals, and she said it accordingly.

HYMN 191.—" Thee, O my God and King."—*Hymn of Thanksgiving to the Father.*—TUNE, Irene, 1761.

Charles Wesley's, from " Hymns and Sacred Poems," 1739, page 107.   The fifth verse of the original is omitted.

HYMN 192.—" Oft I in my heart have said."—*Romans* x. 6.—TUNE, Amsterdam, 1761.

Charles Wesley's, from " Hymns and Sacred Poems," 1742, page 179.   The original has six verses, the last three of which are omitted.

HYMN 193.—" O Filial Deity."—*Hymn to the Son.*—TUNE, West Street, 1761.

Charles Wesley's, from " Hymns and Sacred Poems," 1739, page 73.   It contains an admirable poetical exemplification of the titles and offices of Christ ; the metre is of an unusual kind—a feature in which the author excelled.

> HYMN 194.—" Arise, my soul, arise."
> „   195.—" High above every name."
> *On the Titles of Christ.*—TUNE, West Street, 1761.

Charles Wesley's, from " Hymns and Sacred Poems," 1739, page 165.   The original has fifteen verses, six of which are omitted.   This hymn is very similar in sentiment and line of thought to the preceding.   Dr Watts has a hymn also similar, which commences—

> " Join all the names of love and power."

These two were printed as one hymn by Mr Wesley ; it was divided in 1830.

HYMN 196.—" Into Thy gracious hands I fall."—*The Change.*—TUNE, St Luke's, 1761.

From " Hymns and Sacred Poems," 1739, page 99.   Translated by John Wesley from the German of Wolfgang C. Deszler. The original has six verses ; the other three form hymn 133, which see, for notice of author.

HYMN 197.—" Happy soul, who sees the day."—*The Twelfth Chapter of Isaiah.*—TUNE, Love-feast, 1761.

Charles Wesley's, from " Hymns and Sacred Poems," 1742, page 189.   The original is in four-line stanzas.

HYMN 198.—"O what shall I do My Saviour to praise."—*A Thanksgiving.*—TUNE, Walsal, 1761.

Charles Wesley's, from "Hymns and Sacred Poems," 1742, page 118. In Mr Wesley's "Sacred Melody," this hymn is printed to the tune of Tallis.

When Methodism was a new thing in the land, and was everywhere spoken against, Elizabeth Toase, mother of the Rev. William Toase, at the age of fourteen, was converted to God, became a member of Society, and for seventy-three years remained faithful to her trust. She knew many of the first race of Methodist preachers. She was very happy in her last illness; and when she was dying, she sang with a clear voice the verse commencing—

"O what shall I do my Saviour to praise," &c.

Ann Roberts, of Polruan, Liskeard, was converted to God, and joined the Methodist Society at the age of twenty-one, and for more than half a century maintained a consistent connexion with the people of her choice. She delighted in the ordinances of religion, and was never willingly absent from the much-loved class-meeting. In her last illness she delighted in repeating texts of Scripture and hymns, especially the one commencing—

"O what shall I do my Saviour to praise," &c.

When drawing her last breath, she said, "Glory shall end," and as her daughter added, "what grace has begun," she entered into glory.

Having been favoured by hearing Mr Wesley preach at York, Margaret Dickenson never forgot the privilege she then enjoyed. She had for a long time a lingering attachment to the Methodists, and through the instrumentality of Messrs Spence and Burdsall, she was led to seek the Saviour. At a meeting, at which the verse was given out for singing—

"O what shall I do my Saviour to praise," &c.,

the truth conveyed by the words of the hymn were so powerfully applied to her mind, that she was enabled to believe for herself, to enter into liberty, and to rejoice with joy unspeakable and full of glory. After a life of usefulness in the Church, in honoured age, she entered into rest.

HYMN 199.—" O Heavenly King, Look down from above."—*A Thanksgiving.*—TUNE, Triumph, 1761.

Charles Wesley's, from " Hymns and Sacred Poems," 1742, page 119.

Early training in a Methodist Sabbath-school resulted in Elizabeth Nocke, of Newtown, becoming a teacher therein, then, after her conversion, a useful member of society. Whilst still young in years, an illness set in, which soon ended her earthly career, and, fixing her affections entirely on God, she realised as much of heaven upon earth as was possible for humanity to enjoy. She once said, " I heard music and singing ! Oh, the innumerable company that have washed their robes, and made them white in the blood of the Lamb ! " Shortly before the mortal strife was over she said, " Thy rod and staff they comfort me." When passing away to her inheritance she was heard to say—

> "O heavenly King, Look down from above ;
> Assist me to sing Thy mercy and love :
> So sweetly o'erflowing, So plenteous the store,
> Thou still art bestowing, And giving us more."

Her spirit escaped whilst she was saying, " Come, Lord Jesus."

HYMN 200.—" My Father, my God, I long for Thy love."—*A Thanksgiving.*—TUNE, Tallis, 1761.

Charles Wesley's, from " Hymns and Sacred Poems," 1742, page 119.

The three hymns, of which this is the third, appear to have been written about the same time, and each has been made a blessing. Stephen Watson, of Sunderland, was under the happy influence of religious parents ; and when his elder brother joined the Society his worldly companions tried to induce him to give up his opinions. In reply, he entreated several of them to accompany him to the sick-bed of a young Christian, whose admonitory counsels produced conviction in their minds that they were in error. They began to seek the Lord ; their example influenced many others, and a blessed revival followed: amongst those with whom the Holy Spirit strove was Samuel Watson. For a fortnight his convictions were severe, and his anguish of spirit deep. Accustomed frequently to repeat verses of hymns, one day, whilst meditating on this verse—

" My Father, my God, I long for Thy love ;
  O shed it abroad ; send Christ from above !
  My heart, ever fainting, He only can cheer ;
  And all things are wanting, till Jesus is here,"

his soul was filled with joy unspeakable, and all things around
him wore a new aspect. Love to all men, especially the people
of God, was immediately made manifest in his life and conduct,
and he lived a consistent Christian course for more than fifty
years.

HYMN 201.—"And can it be that I should gain."—*Free Grace.*—
TUNE, Birmingham, 1761.

Charles Wesley's, from " Hymns and Sacred Poems," 1739,
page 117. The original has one verse more than is here printed.
   It was written in 1738, immediately after the poet's conversion,
and was printed in the scarce volume of " Psalms and Hymns "
which appeared in that year. Read in the light of this fact, it
is remarkable how minutely the poet describes his own personal
experience, gratitude, and joy. When, at ten o'clock of the
evening on which John Wesley entered into liberty, he, with
several friends, went to Charles's room, in Little Britain, he
informs us, "We sung the hymn with great joy, and parted
with prayer." It is now difficult to determine which of two
hymns, written on this occasion, was then sung, but it was either
this or hymn 30. The fourth verse contains an expressive
allusion to the deliverance of Peter from prison by an angel.
   That a hymn written under such circumstances should be
made a blessing to thousands is not surprising. Every verse,
and nearly every line of it, has been made useful in comforting
some Christian. To notice all these is not possible : but it may
be profitable to give an example of the use of each verse.
   In early life, Mrs Joseph Stocks, of Cudworth, Barnsley,
became savingly acquainted with God, and testified to the
genuineness of the change, by a long life of uniform devotedness to Christ and the interests of His Church and people. For
fifty years she was made a blessing to many as a class-leader.
Amongst the poor she was as an angel from heaven. In her
last illness her countenance indicated the growing meekness of
her spirit, and the faithfulness of God in assuring her of acceptance with Him. She exulted in the prospect of reunion with
sainted relations, but added, " It will be the Father's glory

shining in the face of Jesus, that will be the crowning joy."
She often repeated her favourite hymn, commencing—

> "And can it be that I should gain," &c.

Dwelling with admiration and emphasis on the closing lines of
that verse—

> "Amazing love! how can it be,
> That Thou, my God, should'st die for me!"

In holy triumph she passed away to her rest, her last words
being a request that her class should be attended to with care
and diligence.

Favoured with the drawings of the Holy Spirit even in childhood, Mrs Christopher Dove, of Darlington, gave her heart to
God in her nineteenth year, and joined the Methodist Society.
Her life was brief, but one of continued joy and peace, and in
her last illness she enjoyed a clear and strong evidence of her
interest in Christ. Shortly before she died, she called the nurse
to her bedside, and broke out with these lines—

> "And can it be that I should gain
> An interest in the Saviour's blood?"

On the nurse observing, "I trust you *have* gained," she sweetly
smiled, and pressed her hand in token of assurance. When she
came to the closing lines of the third verse—

> "'Tis mercy all, immense and free,
> For, O my God, it found out ME,"

her soul seemed to be filled with adoring gratitude and love;
and she again repeated, with stronger emphasis—

> "For, O my God, it found out ME."

In the swellings of Jordan she had peace, and her soul cast its
anchor within the vail.

"To a mother's prayers, and a father's counsel and example,
their children are indebted under God for their religious convictions, and their status in the Church of God." Such is the record
made by a son of George Hobill, who, at the age of twenty-four,
joined the Methodist Society at Daventry, and for more than
fifty years maintained an unblemished reputation for integrity
and consistency, and for more than forty-five years was a useful
and laborious local-preacher. Though his career in life was
a chequered one, he had confidence in God's promises; and

though in his affliction he was sorely tried, he found rock for his feet whilst passing over Jordan. Some of his last words were—

> "'Tis mystery all!   The Immortal dies !
> Who can explore His strange design !"

During an illness of some duration, Mrs Arnett, the wife of the Rev. Thomas Arnett, was sustained by the grace she had sought and enjoyed in health. As the end of her life drew near, she greatly exalted the mercy of Christ ; and shortly before her departure, while her husband was engaged in prayer, she joyfully exclaimed—

> "'Tis mercy all, immense and free,
> For, O my God, it found out me !"

Living for more than half a century in a spirit of cheerfulness and worldly gaiety, esteemed by her neighbours for her integrity and kindness, Mrs Sarah Obee, of Cawood, Selby, was awakened, during a revival, to a sense of her lost condition as a sinner. For two days and nights her anguish was so deep, she could neither take food nor rest. One of her friends, on hearing of her troubled mind, and being unacquainted with spiritual religion, said, " The Lord have mercy on us ! If Sally Obee needs to be converted, what is to become of us ? " In the depth of her contrition she exclaimed, " A wounded spirit, who can bear ? " During the second night of her sorrow, after pleading earnestly for mercy, whilst walking in her bedroom, she repeated the hymn commencing—

> " And can it be that I should gain," &c. ;

and when she came to the fourth verse—

> " Long my imprison'd Spirit lay
> Fast bound in sin and nature's night
> Thine eye diffused a quick'ning ray ;
> I woke ; the dungeon flamed with light ;
> My chains fell off, my heart was free,
> I rose, went forth, and follow'd Thee,"

she was enabled to believe in Christ ; she received the witness of the Spirit to her adoption ; was filled with joy and peace through believing ; joined the Methodists ; and for thirty years, witnessed a good confession for Christ. Soon a class was commenced in her house, and ultimately her husband also was brought to know the Saviour.

Amongst the first-fruits of the labours of the Methodist missionaries in Jamaica, was the first wife of Mr Charles Davis. Her godly example lived after her ; and although her husband had persecuted her for her religion, yet about the time of her decease he became terribly alarmed by the untimely death of one of his ungodly associates. He began to attend the Methodist ministry, sought and found mercy in Parade Chapel, Kingston, and never lost the evidence of his acceptance with God to the day of his death. During the illness which closed his life, his soul was happy in God. On the day of his departure, when he supposed himself to be alone, he exclaimed, with much feeling, "Glory be to God !

> ' No condemnation now I dread ;
> Jesus, and all in Him, is mine !' &c.

' Thy sins, which are many, are all forgiven ; glory be to God !' " On his daughter approaching him, and asking, "Is Christ with you in the valley?" he tried to reply ; and in the act of saying "Jesus Christ," the weary wheels of life stood still, and in peaceful triumph he entered into the joy of his Lord.

In an account of the death of Mr Richard Murlin, brother of the Rev. John Murlin, the "weeping prophet," in the *Methodist Magazine*, under date of St Austell, May 27, 1804, we read, that a week after his last illness commenced, the Rev. J. Anderson visited him, and he gave his religious experience in part of this hymn—

> " No condemnation now I dread ;
> Jesus, and all in Him, is mine."

He added, " I feel the Spirit of God within me, and He will bring me triumphantly through." He suffered much, but passed quietly away at last, saying, "Jesus hath died ; and God is love."

A revival of religion in her native village was the means of bringing Mary Lewis, of Berriew, to a knowledge of sins forgiven. Soon afterwards she was married to a godly husband, and they devoted their lives to the interests of religion. At the age of sixty-three she was left a widow, and from that time she sought richer manifestations of the Divine presence, especially in the class-meetings, to which she was often carried, rather than be

absent. On the Sabbath before her death, she realised entire
sanctification, and exclaimed—

> " 'No condemnation now I dread ;
> Jesus, and all in Him, is mine.'

Glory to God ! Jesus is all in all ;" and quietly fell asleep with
the name of Jesus on her lips.

At the early age of thirteen, Mary Ann Gardner, of Shore-
ditch, London, joined the Methodist Society, and soon afterwards
was appointed the leader of a class of young females, over whom
she watched with fidelity and affection. She was long a visitor
of the Strangers' Friend Society, and engaged in other useful
labours to promote the glory of God, until by illness she was
laid aside. The last words she uttered, just as she was expiring, were—

> " Bold I approach the eternal throne,
> And claim the crown, through Christ my own."

This hymn being associated with the conversion of the
founders of Methodism, we give the omitted verse—

> " Still the small inward voice I hear,
> That whispers all my sins forgiven :
> Still the atoning blood is near,
> That quench'd the wrath of hostile heaven.
> I feel the life His wounds impart ;
> I feel my Saviour in my heart."

HYMN 202.—*"Arise, my soul, arise."*—*Behold the Man !*—
TUNE, Fonmow, 1761.

Charles Wesley's, from " Hymns and Sacred Poems," 1742,
page 264. It is utterly impossible to conceive how many tried
believers have had their faith strengthened and their hope of
heaven brightened by this inestimable hymn. It is full of that
self-appropriation of the work of the Redeemer which is a
marked feature in Charles Wesley's poetry. This feature is
noticed by John Wesley himself in his " Journal."

This hymn, like the one preceding it, has been made a blessing to multitudes of Christians, and almost every line of it has
been used by persons in dying circumstances. Nor has it been
less useful in bringing sinners to realise a sense of sins forgiven,
of which many instances are on record.

The necessity of constant preparation for heaven was never

made more manifest than in the case of the sudden death of
Mr James Collinson, of Liverpool, who, from being in a state of
robust health, was, in thirty hours, numbered with "the dead
who die in the Lord." At the age of twenty he gave his heart
to the Lord, and served Methodism faithfully for nearly twenty
years more. Though his last illness was short and severe, yet
he gave clear evidence of his reliance alone on the atonement
of Jesus. Raising himself up, with a strong effort, just before
he died, he exclaimed, with marked feeling—

> " Arise, my soul arise, Shake off thy guilty fears ;
> The bleeding Sacrifice On my behalf appears ;
> Before the throne my Surety stands ;
> My name is written on His hands."

Shortly afterwards he fell asleep in Jesus.

In another, and somewhat similar instance of sudden death,
the second verse of this hymn was used as a dying testimony.
The Rev. John Strawe had arrived at his new home in the
Sheffield East Circuit only a few days, when he became indis-
posed. Typhus fever set in, and recovery at once became
hopeless. His trust in Christ for salvation was unshaken, and
among his last words were these, " Christ is my Saviour :

> ' He ever lives above, For me to intercede.'

Glory be to God ! all is bright, bright above."

Amongst those honoured men who took part, in 1813, in
forming the Wesleyan Missionary Society, the name of the Rev.
James Buckley has a deservedly foremost place, he having
preached one of the official sermons at Leeds on that interesting occasion. A somewhat lengthy and laborious service in
the ministry of Methodism was followed by a short illness, in
which he enjoyed much of the Divine presence ; and during his
last night on earth he repeated, with much feeling, the second
and third verses of the 202d hymn ; after which he spoke but
little : his last words were, " For me the Saviour died."

In early life, Mary H. Thorneloe, wife of the Rev. W. B.
Thorneloe, gave her heart to the Lord, and became a useful
member of the Methodist Society. She was convinced of her
sinful condition under a sermon preached by the Rev. John
Moulton. Her after-life was spent in doing good ; and when
prostrate by illness, her mind was kept in peace. After she had
taken leave of those she loved on earth, she repeated the verse—

> " Five bleeding wounds He bears, Received on Calvary;
>   They pour effectual prayers, They strongly speak for me ;
>   ' Forgive him, O forgive ! ' they cry,
>   ' Nor let the ransom'd sinner die.' "

After this, she spoke only to say, " Come, Lord Jesus," and then peacefully escaped with a convoy of angels to heaven.

The privileges of Christian fellowship are too lightly appreciated by many Christian professors. William Hiskins, of Fexham, Wilts, in conveying a ticket of membership to a Methodist living at a distance, remarked, " I value my ticket more than a pound-note, for it is the token of my connexion with a praying people : and they pray for me. I feel I need their prayers." A class-leader of such a spirit could not fail of being useful, and by doing good to others, being much loved in return. He was for seventy-four years in fellowship with the people of God. At the age of ninety, his love for the services of the sanctuary was unabated ; and on the day of his death, speaking of the evening service, he said, " I believe we shall have a good time this evening." The sermon that night was on the intercession of Christ. To a verse in the Hymn-book relating to this subject he was very partial, wishing to have it in recollection both in life and death. It was given out at that service ; and when his favourite verse was lined out for singing—

> " Five bleeding wounds he bears, Received on Calvary," &c.,

he sang them with considerable energy. He asked the preacher to pray for his son-in-law, then near death, and to every petition he subjoined a hearty " Amen." After the service, he hastened to visit his afflicted son-in-law. His road lay by the side of the canal. He took his lantern and departed. Half an hour afterwards inquiry was made for him, but he could not be heard of, until his body was found in the canal. In trying to avoid a heap of stones, he had passed too near the water and fell in.

In the year 1824, probably the oldest member of the Methodist Society in Ireland was Theophilus White, of Emo, Queen's County. He became a member of Society at the age of nineteen, and for seventy-four years sustained the Christian character with unblemished reputation. He maintained a clear sense of his acceptance with God, and only half an hour before his death he said, " Happy, happy ! sing, sing—

> " ' My God is reconciled,
>   His pardoning voice I hear ;
>   He owns me for His child.' "

Here his voice failed, and in a few minutes his spirit took its flight to the house of his Father and God.

For thirty-one years the Rev. William Nother laboured as a useful minister of Jesus Christ in the Wesleyan itinerancy. When health failed, and protracted heavy affliction overtook him, he lost not his confidence in God. As the end drew near, on being asked the state of his mind, he said his prospect heavenwards was bright, and added—

> "My God is reconciled,
>   His pardoning voice I hear."

But his breath failed, he was unable to finish the verse, and shortly afterwards fell asleep in Jesus.

When feeble flesh is failing, and the consciousness of the nearness of eternity is experienced, to be able to say of Christ that He is felt to be " a rock," " a refuge in a weary land," is a source of comfort both to the dying and to those who receive the testimony. Such was the dying utterance, faintly breathed by George Dracott, of Wootton-under-Wood, who was for thirty years an attached Methodist. Almost the last words he was heard to speak were—

> " With confidence I now draw nigh,
>   And boldly, Abba, Father, cry."

While reading the second of the Ten Commandments, Ann Barnsley, of Oldbury, was deeply convinced of sin, and soon afterwards, in company with some friends who were pleading for her, she realised the blessing of pardon. Ten years subsequently she was " made perfect in love ; " and from that time she maintained a life of perfect consistency. Shortly before she died, she spoke reverently of God the Father, the Son, and the Holy Ghost as ONE God, adding, " I shall soon see Him. I have no fear, no pain.

> ' With confidence I now draw nigh,
>   And boldly, Abba, Father, cry.'

The blood of Jesus Christ cleanseth from all sin." Thus triumphantly she entered upon her eternal rest in heaven.

Probably the most remarkable, not to say astonishing, result

from the use of a hymn is the following record, which has come
to hand from the Rev. Matthew Cranswick, who laboured in the
West Indies, and who has since his communication personally
certified to the writer the truth of the statement hereafter made.
Mr Cranswick observes : "I feel it due to the honour and glory
of God, to inform you of the utility of one hymn in particular, No.
202, commencing, 'Arise, my soul, arise,' &c. I have a record of
upwards of two hundred persons, young and old, who received
the most direct evidence of the forgiveness of their sins while
singing that hymn [at different services and at various periods].
The conversion of the greatest number of these persons took
place whilst I was a missionary abroad. My plan [of using the
hymn] was the following :—After ascertaining as far as possible
that the professed sorrow of the penitent was godly sorrow, we
then commenced singing that hymn, requesting the penitent to
join. Some of them would hesitate to sing the last verse ; in
that case, I would begin to sing the whole or part of the hymn
again, until the penitent had obtained courage to sing every
part. I have never known one instance of a sincere penitent
failing to receive a joyous sense of pardon while singing that
hymn.

"I could give interesting circumstances of the use of this
hymn both to the living and dying. Upon one occasion,
seven young persons, under concern for their salvation, visited
me ; after about two hours' engagement, praying, &c., while
singing that hymn six of them obtained a clear sense of pardon.
A lady, about eighty years old, on being seized with paralysis,
became much concerned about her soul. I was requested to
visit her. After explaining the plan of salvation to her (though
belonging to the Church of England, she had a Methodist hymn-
book in the house), I repeated this hymn to her, and requested
her to let the servant read it to her. She got several of the
verses off by heart, and died most happy. On another occasion,
I was called to visit a man dying of cancer in the throat ; the
same plan as already mentioned was adopted. I requested his
wife to read that hymn to him ; he found peace while it was
being read, and died happy."

The missionary goes on to remark : "I do not think it possible for any sincere person to read or sing that hymn without
profit. There is in it direct reference to the Trinity, and the
apparent office of each—the intercession of Christ, the atoning

blood; the assistance of the Holy Spirit; the love of the Father; and in the last verse, the necessary effort of faith made by the penitent." May multitudes more realise a sense of pardon in the same way!

The Rev. T. O. Keysell, when at Bury, in Lancashire, was visited by a woman in deep distress of mind. Awakened, and terrified by her lost condition as a sinner, thinking herself to be mad, she related to the preacher the story of her past life. After directing her mind to many very encouraging promises in the Word of God, he urged her to fix her mind's eye on the Crucified One, and to look especially to the blood of atonement. To assist her faith he quoted the verse of this hymn—

> " Five bleeding wounds He bears,
>   Received on Calvary ;
> They pour effectual prayers,
>   They strongly speak for me," &c.

Instead of following the preacher in the recitation, she hurried on before him, she knowing the lines. When she said, " They strongly speak for me," " Stop ! stop !" said Mr Keysell ; "they strongly speak for whom ?" " For *me*," replied the seeking soul. Divine light burst in upon her mind ; she saw her interest in the atonement, and she found redemption in His blood, even the forgiveness of her sins. She exclaimed, " Bless the Lord ! my load is gone, and I am free ! Oh, what a mercy that I did not drown myself ! Thank God !"

HYMN 203.—" Glory to God, whose sovereign grace."—*For the Kingswood Colliers.*—TUNE, Islington, 1761.

Charles Wesley's, from " Hymns and Sacred Poems," 1740, page 104. It also forms hymn 80 in the " Select Hymns and Tunes," the tune chosen for it being Zoar, in Wesley's " Sacred Harmony," 1761, in which place the hymn closes with Bishop Ken's doxology, " Praise God, from whom all blessings flow."

The Kingswood colliers had for many years been a horde of lawless foresters, ignorant, depraved, brutal. When Whitefield last visited Bristol, before his embarkation for America, he spoke of converting the savages in that great western continent ; his friends said to him, "What need of going abroad for this? Have we not Indians enough at home ? If you want to convert Indians, there are colliers enough at Kingswood !" The preaching of the Wesleys and Whitefield did result in their conversion, and in the entire renovation of the whole neighbourhood. This hymn is Charles Wesley's triumphant song of thanksgiving that the sovereign grace of God had "animated senseless stones!"

The original has eleven stanzas, the two last and the doxology being omitted. The hymn contains such terms as "senseless stones," "reprobates," and "outcasts," as indicating the character of the people of whom he wrote.

HYMN 204.—"Jesus, Thou soul of all our joys."—*The true use of Music.*—TUNE, Musician's, 1761.

It has also the additional title of "I will sing with the Spirit, and I will sing with the understanding also." 1 Cor. xiv. 15. Charles Wesley's, No. 90 in "Hymns and Sacred Poems," 1749, vol. ii. The best title for this composition would be, the Christian Musician's Hymn. It was probably written in connexion with an incident in the life of Mr Lampe, a musician of note, who first composed tunes to the hymns written by the Wesleys.

HYMN 205.—"My God, I am Thine, What a comfort divine."— *For Believers.*—TUNE, Old German, 1761.

Charles Wesley's, from "Hymns and Sacred Poems," 1749, vol. i. The original is printed in three-line stanzas, so that each verse includes two of the original ones. The sentiment and metre of the hymn are in happy accordance.

Portions of this hymn have been used by many of the Lord's people when dying or in trying circumstances.

Richard Walker, of Colne, was upwards of thirty years a useful member of the Methodist Society. His last illness was protracted over more than two years, but he had a glorious hope of immortality amidst his sufferings. His last words were—

> " 'My God, I am Thine, What a comfort divine,
> What a blessing to know that my Jesus is mine!' "

Mrs Kezia Shepherd, of whom a memoir appears in the *Methodist Magazine* for March 1800, was early brought under religious influence. Visiting some friends at Oxford, she was introduced to the Methodists. Feeling deep penitence on account of her sins, she wept one day as she walked along the streets, telling her companion that she mourned for the Friend of sinners. They called at a house where several pious persons were present, when the state of her mind was readily perceived. One

of them gave out a hymn ; and whilst they were singing the first
part of hymn 205—

> " My God, I am Thine, What a comfort divine,
> What a blessing to know that my Jesus is mine ! "

the Lord spoke peace to her soul. The assurance of her
acceptance through Jesus was so strong, that she could hardly
help crying out aloud, " He is mine ! He is mine ? " She held
fast her confidence through life ; and in death she dedicated
her soul to God, by singing entirely through Dr Watts' hymn,
commencing, " I 'll praise my Maker while I 've breath."

Faithful in the service of God and Methodism, Mr J. P.
Hawkesworth, of Wetherby, Tadcaster, for more than half-a-
century filled the offices of class-leader, local preacher, steward,
and trustee. In his last illness he found rest in the atonement
of Christ, while it yielded peace and comfort to his mind. Shortly
before he died, with victory in his countenance, he said, " I am
going home ; in my Father's house are many mansions :

> ' My God, I am Thine, What a comfort divine,
> What a blessing to know that my Jesus is mine.' "

The religious character of Mrs Agnes Douglas, Sutherland,
was felt in its happy influences in both the United States of
America, and in Scotland, her native country. She built,
almost entirely at her own cost, a Methodist chapel in Stirling,
and a good minister's house, both of which, free of debt, were
secured to the connexion. She built another good chapel at
Doune, where, for several years, she supported a minister also.
She bequeathed £200 towards building a third chapel for the
benefit of the colliers at Wallacestone. Her last affliction was
short, but severe, and she was unable to converse much ; but
on one occasion, in the midst of extreme suffering, she
exclaimed—

> " ' My God, I am Thine, What a comfort divine. ' "

In reply to the last question put to her, she said to her friend,
" Jesus died for me."

Early in life Henry Budgett, of Kingswood, was converted
to God, and united himself to the Methodists. About the year
1800, he removed to Kingswood, near Bristol, which was then
infested by a lawless gang of banditti, whose depredations
extended far beyond that locality. Mr Budgett undertook the

task of putting down these savage hordes, and aided by two of his neighbours and the kind providence of God, he secured to the village rest and quietness. His next benevolent work was to establish a Sunday-school, which was done on the spot where the robbers had their colony; one of whom became converted, and was very zealous in the cause of the Redeemer. Receiving evidence from on high that his providential lot had been cast in that village, his diligence in business and fervency of spirit were rewarded by both temporal and spiritual prosperity. He liberally distributed his substance to support the cause of God, and served Methodism faithfully as steward, class-leader, local preacher, and Sunday-school superintendent. When, through illness, he was unable to attend the house of God, he was more diligent in his private devotions, and enjoyed greatly the class-meeting held in his own house weekly. A short time before he died, he sent a message to the members of his class, charging them "not to rest with Christ *about* them, but to have Christ IN them, the hope of glory," and repeated, with intense feeling—

> " 'My Jesus to know, And feel His blood flow,
> 'Tis life everlasting, 'tis heaven below."

His last request was, to have Psalm xxiii. read to him, after which he calmly fell asleep in Jesus.

A scene of violence committed on a poor but pious local preacher, about the year 1754, was the cause of Bryan Proctor's thorough awakening to a sense of his danger as a sinner before God. The good man had preached near Harewood, and at the close of the sermon, which was from "Ye must be born again," the rabble Yorkshiremen dragged their religious adviser several times through a pond, till he was all but drowned. That which was nearly the physical death of one, proved to be the spiritual life of another. Young Proctor took his tale of sorrow home to his widowed mother at Pannel, near Harrowgate, who, from that time, opened her house to receive the preachers, and for preaching. Here, soon afterwards, came Christopher Hopper, who, after preaching, formed a class of those seriously disposed. Those who first joined that class were John Pawson, Richard Burdsall, Bryan Proctor, and fourteen others, who formed the first Methodist Society in that neighbourhood. From that time, and for about seventy years, Mr Proctor never omitted to receive from the preacher himself his quarterly society ticket. For many years, Mr Proctor accompanied Richard Burdsall on his Sabbath-day preaching excursions. He often said, that the business of his life was "to live a godly quiet life." At the end of his pilgrimage, he said, "I disputed in my younger days whether God did indeed dwell with men on the earth ; but now, in my old age (ninety-two), the Lord dwelleth in my heart, and I do assuredly enjoy a heaven upon earth." Shortly before he died, he said, " The blood of Jesus cleanseth us from all sin :

> ' My Jesus to know, And feel His blood flow,
> 'Tis life everlasting, 'tis heaven below.' "

He expired, faintly whispering, " My Jesus, my Jesus, glory, glory ! "

A period of bodily suffering in early life became to William Robinson, of Cleathorpe, a season of salvation. Recovering from a second severe attack of illness, he resolved to seek the salvation of his soul, and through the preaching of Mr Thomas Edman, about 1750, he found the Lord. His eagerness to see the conversion of his father and other relatives induced him to give up more lucrative employment, where there were no Methodists, that he might remain under the influences of religion. He read the Bible and Wesley's Hymns daily in his family before prayer, established and himself conducted a public prayer-meeting, and had Methodist preaching in his house for more than fifty years. He rejoiced in seeing his father happy in the pardoning love of God. His conversion was remarkable. In youth the father had a scythe-wound in his knee, which healed, leaving him with a stiff knee which had prevented his running for forty years. When under conviction of sin, his distress was painful, arising from a conviction that he had sinned beyond the reach of mercy, and he thought nothing less than a miracle could convince him that his sins were pardoned. The Lord gave him a double blessing. During his convictions, the knee-joint became pliant without any human means being used, and on the following Sabbath father and son met after the service at Grimsby, and whilst crossing the common, with joyful tears he told his son that the Lord had worked a double miracle, by speaking peace to his soul and healing his body, and to convince his son of its reality, he ran some yards on the common to demonstrate the completeness of the cure. They rejoiced together at the mercy and goodness of God. William, in his last

illness, exhorted all around him to turn to the Lord. While
unable to rest, he lay in bed repeating—

> " 'My Jesus to know, And feel His blood flow,
> 'Tis life everlasting, 'tis heaven below.
> Yet onward we haste To the heavenly feast :
> That, that is the fulness ; this is *but the taste.*' "

Shortly afterwards his spirit entered the port in full sail.

At the early age of twenty-four, William Gibson, of Braith-
waite Green, Kendal, gave his heart to the Lord, and became a
zealous and successful class-leader and local preacher to the
end of his life. In his last illness his experience was clear and
deep, resting alone on the merits of the Redeemer. To the
vicar and curate of the village, who took pleasure in visiting
him, he often said, "I am on the Rock of ages." His last words
were—

> " 'My Jesus to know, And feel His blood flow,
> 'Tis life everlasting, 'tis heaven below.' "

Whilst engaged in his work at the mill, Christopher Chapman, of Knaresborough, sought and found the Lord. His religious life was greatly aided by reading the " Spiritual Letters
and Christian Experience " of Hester Ann Rogers. His last
illness was long and painful. His last night on earth was spent
entirely in prayer, in praise, in reading the Word of God, and
verses of hymns. Just before he died, he whispered—

> " 'My Jesus to know, And feel His blood flow,
> 'Tis life everlasting, 'tis heaven below ;' "

and while praying, " Lord, save me to the end," he fell asleep
in Jesus.

HYMN 206.—"What am I, O Thou glorious God !"—*For Believers.*—TUNE, Sheffield, 1761.

Charles Wesley's, forming No. 114 in " Hymns and Sacred
Poems," 1749, vol. i. The poet seems to base part of this hymn
on 2 Sam. vii. 18, and Ezek. xvi. 6.

In early life, the mind of the Rev. Joseph Agar, of York, was
wrought upon by divine influences ; but at the age of twenty-
one, he gave his heart fully to the Lord, became an exhorter,
and shortly afterwards was admitted into the full ministry of
Methodism. He was a man of much usefulness, of overflowing
kindness of heart, great simplicity and integrity of purpose, and

of unquenchable ardour for the promotion of the glory of God and the salvation of souls. He lived a life of faith on the Son of God, and in his last illness delighted to dwell on the goodness of God in early life, especially in giving him parents who brought him up in the fear of the Lord. He often expressed his grateful feelings in the verse—

> " What am I, O Thou glorious God !
>   And what my father's house to Thee,
> That Thou such mercies hast bestow'd
> On me, the vilest reptile, me ?
> I take the blessing from above,
> And wonder at Thy boundless love."

Thus serenely he waited the closing scene, saying, just before his departure to heaven, " Pray for me, praise for me ; Jesus comforts me. Sing, sing aloud, I cannot."

HYMN 207.—" Jesus is our common Lord."—*Receiving a Christian Friend.*—TUNE, Hotham, 1761.

Charles Wesley's, from " Hymns and Sacred Poems," 1742, page 157. The original has four verses, the first and second being left out. The first line is as follows :—" Welcome, friend, in that great name."

HYMN 208.—" Come, let us, who in Christ believe."—*On God's Everlasting Love.*—TUNE, Cornish, 1761.

Forms No. 8 in Charles Wesley's " Hymns on God's Everlasting Love," 1741. The original has fourteen verses, of which ten are omitted.

HYMN 209.—"Thou hidden Source of calm repose."—*For Believers.*—TUNE, Birmingham, 1761.

Charles Wesley's, forming No. 143 of " Hymns and Sacred Poems," 1749, vol. i. The poet's idea in this hymn is to exalt Christ, and he selects various circumstances in life, which he gives in striking antitheses, to set this forth. Christ is the Christian's rest in toil, his ease in pain, his peace in war, his gain in loss, his liberty in bondage, and, last of all, comes this marvellous climax—his heaven in hell ! This cannot be taken as it is literally expressed ; it is a poet's license with language, which requires to be received in a careful and modified sense.

The Rev. Samuel Coley has related, that a gentleman of large business transactions was known for his great spirituality of mind, and was once asked by a friend how he was enabled to preserve such a frame. He replied, " By making Christ all in all." After a time, he sustained heavy losses in a commercial crisis, when his friend again asked him how he still maintained his cheerfulness and buoyancy. He replied, " By finding my all in Christ."

During a revival in the Pateley-Bridge circuit, Sarah Harkness, at the age of fifteen, was enabled to believe in Christ for salvation. From that time her love to Christ was manifest throughout life. In her last illness she was dead indeed to the world ; but even in pain she rejoiced in God. When her end was near, her husband repeated the second verse of Hymn 209, " Thy mighty Name salvation is," &c. She cried out, " Salvation ! glory ! praise Him ! bless Him ! " She continued in this happy strain of exultation till she entered on the beatific vision.

Gentle, kind, generous, sincere, faithful, and intelligent, Elizabeth Mary Ash, eldest daughter of the Rev. William Ash, in very early life gave her heart to the Lord, and devotedly promoted the interests of Methodism. When unable to teach by her voice, she wrote her counsels to the young in Wesleyan periodicals, under the signature of H. Y. H. In her last illness she rested entirely on the atonement made by Christ ; and almost the last words she spoke were part of a favourite hymn—

> " Jesus, my all in all Thou art,
> My rest in toil, my ease in pain," &c.

Awakened to a sense of sin at the age of twenty, Mary Reynolds attended a watch-night service held in 1801, and, about the midnight hour, it pleased the Lord to reveal His Son in her heart, and fill her with joy and peace in believing. From that time, and through a long life as the wife of the Rev. John Reynolds, she "walked with God." She was much devoted to works of piety and benevolence, and as a class-leader was faithful and affectionate. Her last illness was short, but she patiently waited the coming of her Lord ; and the last words she was heard to speak were those by Charles Wesley—

> " Jesus, my all in all Thou art,
> My rest in toil, my ease in pain," &c.

HYMN 210.—" Thee will I love, my strength, my tower."—
Gratitude for our Conversion.—TUNE, Frankfort, 1761.

Translated from the German of John Angelus, 1657, by John
Wesley, and found in " Hymns and Sacred Poems," 1739, page
198.   The poet's theme seems that of David in Psalm xviii. 1, 2.
As early as the age of ten years, Mary Joyce, of Tonge,
Ashby-de-la-Zouch, joined the Methodist Society, having been
taught the way of truth by the preachers who visited her father's
house.   A long life of unassuming usefulness was crowned by
a peaceful end.   On the day before her death, she dwelt much
on this verse—

> " I thank Thee, uncreated Sun,
>   That Thy bright beams on me have shined ;
> I thank Thee, who hast overthrown
>   My foes, and heal'd my wounded mind ;
> I thank Thee, whose enlivening voice,
> Bids my freed heart in Thee rejoice."

HYMN 211.—" Let all men rejoice, By Jesus restored."—*For
the Kingswood Colliers.*—TUNE, Newcastle, 1761.

Charles Wesley's, from " Hymns and Sacred Poems," 1749,
vol. ii., No. 184.

HYMN 212.—" My brethren beloved, Your calling ye see."—*For
the Kingswood Colliers.*—TUNE, Triumph, 1761.

Charles Wesley's, No. 185, in " Hymns and Sacred Poems,"
1749, vol. ii.   The second verse of the original is omitted.

HYMN 213.*—" My God, the spring of all my joys."—*God's Presence is Light in Darkness.*—TUNE, Leeds, 1761.

Dr Watts', from Book ii., Hymn 54, date 1707.   Several improvements have been made in it, and it has been added to the
collection during the present century.   In the 18th edition, 1805,
it formed Hymn 87, with an asterisk.

"This hymn," says Milner, in his "Life of Watts," "is almost
without spot or blemish," if we except the last line of verse 4,
which was amended by John Wesley.   " T' embrace my dearest
Lord," wrote Watts.   Wesley made other improvements in the
hymn, which are generally adopted.   An able critic in the

"Wesleyan Methodist Magazine" says of this hymn, that "it is the very best Watts wrote, and breathes the intense earnestness, and passionate, kindling fervour of Wesley himself. It is an effusion of irrepressible joy and triumphant faith."

Every verse of this hymn, and almost every line, has been a source of comfort and joy to some suffering Christian. Sarah Bickerton was made a partaker of saving grace at the age of twenty, and during a long and terribly severe illness, whilst residing at Compstall Bridge, New Mills, she bowed in humility to the Divine will—saying of her Heavenly Father, "For all, I bless Thee, most for the severe." Her end was triumphant. She requested those around her bed to sing the hymn beginning—

> "My God, the spring of all my joys," &c.

in which she joined with all her might, often repeating—

> "The wings of love, and arms of faith,
> Will bear me conqu'ror through."

From a child, John Dewhurst, of Mytholmroyd, Todmorden, was under the influence of the drawings of the Holy Spirit, and at the age of seventeen he received a clear sense of pardon, and joined the Methodist Society. The confidence in God he now realised he never lost to the day of his death. To his class he was much attached; as a prayer-leader and Sunday-school teacher he was diligent. At an early period of life he was called away to heaven; but in his sufferings his face beamed with joy, and his heart was joyful and happy. In the last hour of life he began to sing—

> "My God, the spring of all my joys,
> The life of my delights,
> The glory of my brightest days,
> And comfort of my nights!"

He then added, "Glory be to God: come Lord Jesus!" and peacefully entered into rest.

The erection of the first Methodist Chapel at Farnley, near Leeds, was mainly due to the efforts put forth by Mr Thomas Pawson, a churchman, who, seeing the prosperity of the cause under his fostering care, was induced to join the Society, and ultimately became a useful class-leader, serving the Lord and Methodism with fidelity for more than thirty years. On the day before his death he said, "I bless God I am happy and comfortable ; " and added—

> " 'In darkest shades, if Thou appear,
>   My dawning is begun :
>   Thou art my soul's bright morning star,
>   And Thou my rising sun.' "

He afterwards said, " I have strong confidence ; worthy is the Lamb ! " and then entered into rest.

During a period of nearly forty years, Mrs Batho, of Whitchurch, Salop, welcomed the visits of the Methodist preachers, till one was located in the place. She lived to see a prosperous Society rise from small beginnings. She suffered much in her last illness, but she was enabled to " Shout victory through the blood of the Lamb." Nearly her last words were—

> " The opening heavens around me shine,
>   With beams of sacred bliss,
>   If Jesus shows His mercy mine,
>   And whispers, I am His."

" Them that honour me I will honour," was never more remarkably manifested than in the case of Mr John Lofthouse, of Sheffield. Beginning to meet in class as a youth, he resolved to find out what were the joys of the people of God ; and he soon realised his determination. On removing to London, his first concern was to secure the privilege of class-meeting, and this he did by meeting with Mr Butterworth, M.P., as leader in a Sunday-morning class, at seven o'clock. His earnest, consistent piety, at Rotherham and Sheffield, for some years endeared him to the people of God. In his last illness, he was exceedingly happy. During the night before his death, remembering that an American physician had expressed an opinion that singing may greatly soothe the dying, the third and fourth verses of Hymn 213 were sung, and verses 38, 39, of Romans viii. were read, which roused the dying energy of the man of God, who cried out, " My soul takes hold of these truths, and triumphs through them. Glory be to God ! " He spoke no more, but, just as the Rev. George Mather was offering a brief prayer, he breathed out his spirit to God.

Sarah Vasey received a conscious sense of sins forgiven in her twentieth year, and diligently attended the means of grace, till a long affliction overtook her, during which she was very severely

tried. The reading of the Beatitudes in St Matthew's Gospel
broke the power of the tempter, and she exclaimed, in a transport of holy joy, " Call the children up, let us join together to
praise the Lord "—

> " Fearless of hell and ghastly death,
>   I 'd break through every foe ;
> The wings of love, and arms of-faith,
>   Would bear me conqu'ror through.' "

HYMN 214.—" Talk with us, Lord, Thyself reveal."—*On a
Journey.*—TUNE, Liverpool, 1761.

Charles Wesley's, from " Hymns and Sacred Poems," 1740,
page 127. The first verse is left out ; it commences, " Saviour,
who ready art to hear." The original is written in the first person, thus—" Talk with me, Lord," &c. ; which John Wesley
has altered to the plural—" Talk with us, Lord," &c.

The idea and sentiment conveyed in the second verse are
borrowed from Milton, who represents Eve as saying, in one of
her addresses to Adam—

> " With thee conversing, I forget all time,
>   All seasons and their change ; all please alike."

But how is the sentiment elevated and dignified when Christian
believers are taught, in approaching their Heavenly Father, to
say—

> " With Thee conversing, we forget
>   All time, and toil, and care ;
> Labour is rest, and pain is sweet,
>   If Thou, my God, art here."

In the " Life of Dr Payson," we read that when the last sands
were running out of the glass of Time, he said, " I have been
ready to doubt whether pain be really an evil ; for though more
pain was crowded into last week than any other week of my life,
yet it was one of the happiest weeks I ever spent. And now I
am ready to say, Come sickness, pain, agony, poverty, loss of
friends; only let God come with them, and they shall be
welcome."—(*Life*, p. 344.)

In very early life, Ann Pool, of Wakefield, was under the
influence of the Divine Spirit, and whilst yet young she began
to meet in her mother's class. Having given her heart to the
Lord, she never regretted the choice she had made. She was

much tried during her last illness, but she had enduring peace and joy ; and only an hour before her death she said, " Jesus is precious ; He loves me." After that, when labouring under severe pain, she exclaimed—

> " ' Labour is rest, and pain is sweet,
>   If Thou, my God, art here.' "

Several hymns having been read to her relating to the merits of the Saviour and the happiness of heaven, she then began to pray, and in that happy frame she fell asleep in Jesus.

One of the native Wesleyan ministers of Sierra Leone, Rev. George Harding Decker, was first brought to a knowledge of sins forgiven through the preaching of the Methodists in Freetown in 1836. His intelligence and piety soon recommended him for service in the Church, and he was appointed an assistant missionary. In this capacity he was untiring in his efforts to do good, and unsparing in his labours, which brought on cold and illness, and these soon terminated in death. To an inquiry as to his having a clear manifestation of Divine love, he replied he had that assurance. " I could not have preached the gospel so long and not be assured of this. Yes, I feel—

> ' Labour is rest, and pain is sweet,
>   If Thou, my God, art here.'

I feel that God is love, and that He has loved me, and that if I die at this moment, I shall die in the Lord. He is my rock and shield." A few hours afterwards his spirit went to God.

HYMN 215.—" Glorious Saviour of my soul."—*On God's Everlasting Love.*—TUNE, Amsterdam, 1761.

Charles Wesley's, forming No. 6 of his " Hymns on God's Everlasting Love," 1741. The original has seven verses, three of which are omitted. It was inserted by Mr Wesley in the *Arminian Magazine.* Mr Bunting suggests the changing of the first word in verse 4 from " yet " to " now."

HYMN 216.—" Infinite, unexhausted Love."—*After a Recovery.* —TUNE, Liverpool, 1761.

Charles Wesley's, forming No. 92 in " Hymns and Sacred Poems," 1749, vol. i., where it extends to eighteen verses, the first eight and the tenth being left out. The first line of the original is, " O what an evil heart have I ! "

HYMN 217.—"Jesus, to Thee I now can fly."—*After a Relapse into Sin.*—TUNE, Morning Song, 1761.

Charles Wesley's, from "Hymns and Sacred Poems," 1742, page 141. The original has ten verses, the first five and the seventh being omitted.

The Rev. F. W. Briggs, in a brief biography of Mrs Maria Fernly, of Manchester, who died at Stockport, says that, though her sufferings were extremely severe, yet she retained clearness and collectedness of mind, and found much comfort in repeating portions of Scripture and verses of hymns. Those plaintive lines of Charles Wesley's, " In age and feebleness extreme," &c., were in her constant recollection, and also the last verse of Hymn 217—

> "Jesus, my Strength, my Life, my Rest,
> On Thee will I depend,
> Till summon'd to the marriage-feast,
> When faith in sight shall end."

HYMN 218.—" See how great a flame aspires."—*After Preaching to the Newcastle Colliers.*—TUNE, Magdalen, 1761.

Charles Wesley's, and forms No. 199 in " Hymns and Sacred Poems," 1749, vol. i. There are in the volume four hymns under this title, this being the fourth. It was written as an evidence of thanksgiving to God for the success of the gospel amongst the colliers of the North. The imagery of the first verse was suggested by the furnace-blasts and burning pit-heaps which even now are scattered thickly over the district for some miles around Newcastle-on-Tyne, and which illuminate the whole neighbourhood. In the last verse allusion is made to the prophet Elijah and the coming rain (1 Kings xviii. 44, 45).

The imagery of the poet in this hymn is so exceedingly characteristic of the spread of vital religion, that it has become a favourite at missionary services in other Churches besides Methodist ones.

HYMN 219.—"All thanks be to God."—*Thanksgiving for the Success of the Gospel.*—TUNE, Derby, 1781.

Charles Wesley's, forming No. 3 in " Redemption Hymns." The original has eight verses, the fourth being left out.

Gwennap, in Cornwall, is a place made famous by the successful preaching of the Wesleys in the famous amphitheatre—

a circular green hollow, covering a surface of fourscore square
yards, gently sloping down about fifty feet deep, and known as
the Gwennap Pit. Here the two founders of Methodism
preached often to immense multitudes, once to twenty-five
thousand persons. On one occasion, after Charles Wesley had
preached at Gwennap, in July 1744, such blessed results followed that he commemorated the incident by a dialogue hymn,
entitled "Naomi and Ruth ; adapted to the Minister and the
People." In August 1746, Charles Wesley paid his last visit to
that memorable locality, where he "found at least five thousand
miners waiting for the glad tidings of salvation." "On Sunday,
August 10," writes Charles Wesley, in his journal, "for nearly
two hours nine or ten thousand, by computation, listened with
all eagerness," while he commended them to God and to the
word of His grace. "Never," he continues, "had we so
large an infusion of the Holy Spirit as in the Society. I
could not doubt at that time either their perseverance or my
own." The next day, August 11, 1746, he joyfully surveyed the
glorious progress of his labours in that deeply interesting
locality, and expressed his gratitude of heart in the hymn of
thanksgiving commencing—

> "All thanks be to God,
> Who scatters abroad," &c.

HYMN 220.—"All glory to God in the sky."—*The Nativity.*—
TUNE, Thou Shepherd of Israel, 1761.

Charles Wesley's, forming No. 18 in "Hymns for the Nativity of our Lord." This hymn is a fine poetical picture of the
results of Christianity as foretold in Isaiah xxxii. 17—the effects
of righteousness being quietness and assurance for ever. John
Wesley said this was the best of his brother's Nativity hymns.
The metre is appropriate, and the diction of the hymn is smooth
and harmonious.

For thirty years George Fowler, farmer, Gunhouse, near
Epworth, lived according to the fashion of this world. In 1800
he was prevailed upon to attend a Methodist service, held in a
cottage, on Christmas-day, at Scotton. On hearing the hymn
given out—

> "All glory to God in the sky," &c.,

his attention was arrested, his convictions for sin deepened to
sincere repentance ; he saw the way of salvation, believed,

obtained pardon, and was made happy in God. The change
was entire and abiding, and for more than thirty years he
maintained his confidence in God, and died happy.

HYMN 221.—" Meet and right it is to sing."—*For the Watch-
night.*—TUNE, Amsterdam, 1761.

Charles Wesley's, forming No. 97 in " Hymns and Sacred
Poems," 1749, vol. ii. The second verse of Hymn 221 is similar
in idea to the second verse of Hymn 316, by Dr Watts, memorable as the last words of the late Rev. Dr Joseph Beaumont.

HYMN 222.—" How happy, gracious Lord! are we."—*For the
Watch-night.*—TUNE, Snowsfields, 1761.

Charles Wesley's, forming No. 96 in " Hymns and Sacred
Poems," 1749, vol. ii. The language used by the poet in this
and the preceding hymn is peculiarly appropriate to the occasion for which they were written.

HYMN 223.—" When Israel out of Egypt came."—*Psalm* cxiv.
—TUNE, Sheffield, 1761.

This is Charles Wesley's version of Psalm cxiv., found in a
" Collection of Psalms and Hymns," published by John and
Charles Wesley, second edition, page 109, date 1743; and also in
Charles Wesley's version of the Psalms by H. Fish. Mr Bunting
suggests the changing of the word " rod " to " nod," at the end of
line five, verse four. It has been wrongly attributed to Addison
and to Andrew Marvell. Dr Watts commences his version of
this psalm in similar language :—

> " When Israel, freed from Pharaoh's hand,
> Left the proud tyrant and his land."

When these notes first appeared in the " Methodist Recorder,"
Mr Stelfox, of Belfast, supplied to that paper the following
additional information. In a collection of hymns prepared for
the use of the United Methodist Free Churches, edited by the
Rev. James Everett, this psalm is assigned to Addison, though
it is undoubtedly Charles Wesley's. Mr Stelfox thus proceeds :—" In No. 461 of the ' Spectator ' there is given one of
several versions of this psalm, and this, probably, was the occasion of Mr Everett's mistake ; especially as the two first words,
' When Israel,' are in *both* versions. But even the hymn in the
' Spectator ' is not Addison's, but Dr Watts'. It is somewhat

remarkable that Milton has given two renderings of the same psalm, one English, one Greek. I will just set down the English version (made when the author was fifteen), and that of Dr Watts :—

"MILTON.

" ' When the blest seed of Terah's faithful son,
    After long toil their liberty had won,
    And past from Pharian fields to Canaan land,
    Led by the strength of the Almighty's hand ;
    Jehovah's wonders were in Israel shown,
    His praise and glory was in Israel known.
    That saw the troubled sea, and shivering fled,
    And sought to hide his froth-becurled head
    Low in the earth ; Jordan's clear streams recoil,
    As a faint host that hath received the foil.
    The high huge-bellied mountains skip, like rams
    Amongst their ewes ; the little hills, like lambs.
    Why fled the ocean ? And why skipt the mountains ?
    Why turned Jordan toward his crystal fountains ?
    Shake earth ; and at the presence be aghast
    Of Him that ever was, and aye shall last ;
    That glassy floods from rugged rocks can crush,
    And make soft rills from fiery flint-stones gush.'

"DR WATTS.

" ' When Israel, freed from Pharaoh's hand,
    Left the proud tyrant and his land ;
    Their tribes with cheerful homage own
    Their king, and Judah was His throne.

    Across the deep their journey lay ;
    The deep divides to make them way;
    Jordan beheld their march, and fled
    With backward current to his head.

    The mountains shook like frighted sheep,
    Like Lambs the little hillocks leap ;
    Not Sinai on her base could stand,
    Conscious of sovereign power at hand.

    What power could make the deep divide ?
    Make Jordan backward roll his tide?
    Why did ye leap, ye little hills ?
    And whence the fright that Sinai feels ?

K

Let every mountain, every flood
Retire, and know the approaching God,
The king of Israel : see Him here !
Tremble, thou earth, adore and fear.

He thunders, and all nature mourns,
The rock to standing pools He turns;
Flints spring with fountains at His word,
And fires and seas confess the Lord.'"

HYMN 224.—"I 'll praise my Maker while I've breath."—*Praise to God for His Goodness.*—TUNE, 113th Psalm, 1761.

This memorable composition forms Dr Watts' version of Psalm cxlvi., published 1719. The original has six verses, the second and third being omitted. The first line John Wesley has altered from " I 'll praise my Maker *with my* breath ;" and verse three in the original reads thus :—

"The Lord hath eyes to give the blind,
The Lord supports the sinking mind."

These and other judicious alterations made by John Wesley add much to the value of the hymn. The thought of the poet in the third verse seems to be borrowed from Pope's " Messiah "—

"All ye blind, behold !
He from thick films shall purge the visual ray,
And on the sightless eyeballs pour the day."

The venerable founder of Methodism died in great peace. On Monday, February 28, 1791, he was exceedingly weak, slept much, and spoke but little. On Tuesday morning, he sang two verses of a hymn, then, lying still, as if to recover strength, he called for pen and ink, but could not write. Miss Ritchie proposed to write for him, and asked what to say. He replied, " Nothing, but that God is with us." In the forenoon he said, " I will get up." While they were preparing his clothes, he broke out in a manner that astonished all who were about him in singing—

"I 'll praise my Maker while I've breath ;
And when my voice is lost in death,
Praise shall employ my nobler powers ;
My days of praise shall ne'er be past,
While life, and thought, and being last,
Or immortality endures."

Having finished the verse, and got him into his chair, they observed him change for death. But he, regardless of his dying body, said with a weak voice, "Lord, Thou givest strength ; speak to all our hearts, and let them know that Thou loosest tongues." He then sung one of his brother's doxologies :—

> " To Father, Son, and Holy Ghost,
> Who sweetly all agree."

Here his voice failed. After gasping for breath he said, " Now, we have done all." He was then laid on the bed, from which he rose no more. Later in the day he tried again to speak, and with all his remaining strength said, " The best of all is, God is with us." During the night following, and early on Wednesday morning, March 2, he often attempted to repeat Dr Watts' Psalm cxlvi., but could only get out—

> " I 'll praise ; I 'll praise."

His end drew near. His old and faithful friend, Joseph Bradford, now prayed with him ; and the last word he was heard to articulate was " Farewell." A few minutes before ten o'clock on Wednesday morning, March 2, 1791, while a number of friends were kneeling round his bed, died John Wesley, without a groan, in his eighty-eighth year.

The interest which attaches to this composition, from the circumstances just related, has caused its use by many saints departing hence, allusions to some of whom will be found in the Index.

HYMN 225.—" Praise ye the Lord ! 'tis good to raise."—*The Divine Nature, Providence, and Grace.*—TUNE, Kettlesby's, 1761.

Dr Watts' version of Psalm cxlvii., from Wesley's "Collection of Psalms and Hymns," third edition, 1743. The original has eight verses, the second and fourth being omitted.

HYMN 226.—" Eternal Wisdom ! Thee we praise."—*Song to Creating Wisdom.*—TUNE, Hallelujah, 1761.

Dr Watts', from "Horæ Lyricæ," 1705. It is found in Wesley's "Collection of Psalms and Hymns," third edition, 1743, where it appears with some of John Wesley's judicious alterations. Four verses of the original are omitted.

HYMN 227.—"How do Thy mercies close me round!"—*At lying down.*—TUNE, Evesham, 1761.

Charles Wesley's, from "Hymns and Sacred Poems," 1740, page 129. The original has ten verses, the three last being omitted. The language of this hymn adapts it especially for singing at the close of the day.

Converted to God at the age of twenty, Mrs Hunter, of Barton-on-Humber, zealously sought to bring others to a knowledge of Christ. She was meek, consistent, and earnest; given to hospitality, a lover of the sanctuary and of the Lord's people. In her last illness, and when recovery was hopeless, she spoke much of her mercies, often repeating—

> "How do Thy mercies close me round!
> For ever be Thy name adored;
> I blush in all things to abound;
> The servant is above his Lord!"

She died very happy, a "mother in Israel."

As early as the age of sixteen, Mrs Bush, of Bath, joined the Methodist Society, and remained an exemplary member for fifty-nine years. Gratitude, humility, and anxiety for the welfare of others characterised her long Christian course. In her last illness she was subject to much suffering, weakness, and conflict, but she enjoyed much of the Saviour's love; and in the face of her spiritual foes, when her lips were trembling, her friends were rejoiced to hear her exclaim—

> "Jesus protects; my fears, begone!
> What can the Rock of Ages move?
> Safe in Thy arms I lay me down,
> Thy everlasting arms of love."

Her faith was vigorous, and her prospect clear as she entered the Canaan of rest.

The conversion of Samuel Scholes, of Higher-Moor, near Oldham, occurred in this wise. In the year 1777, being in his garden on a Sunday viewing his flowers, an earthquake occurred. This convulsion so alarmed his fears that he ran into the house for his Prayer-Book, and read from the Litany, "From lightning and tempest; from plague, pestilence, and famine; from battle and murder, and from sudden death—Good Lord, deliver us." Through the same occurrence his wife also became convinced

of sin. Both joined the Methodist Society, and soon afterwards
they found peace with God. Samuel was made a class-leader,
and during fifty-three years all the members of his class who
departed this life died happy. During a severe illness he maintained his peace with God, and when recovering from a sharp
paroxysm, addressing himself to his Heavenly Father, he said—

> " Me for Thine own thou lov'st to take,
>   In time and in eternity :
> Thou never, never wilt forsake
>   A helpless worm that trusts in Thee."

On the day following he departed in great peace.

The influence of early parental instruction, example, and
prayer, under the Divine blessing, was evinced by the conversion
to God of Hannah Kitson, at the age of eighteen, and she
joined the class of her father, Mr Kitson of Wakefield. From
that period till the time of her death her piety was manifest in
all the duties of life. She was afterwards married to the Rev.
William Vevers. Owing to the excitement attending the Leeds
Conference of 1837, her residence being at the Conference Chapel
House, an attack of paralysis seized her, which was followed
by others, but during her sufferings her mind was unclouded,
and her spirit was at peace. Her father, at the age of eighty-
four, took to his bed on the same day as Mrs Vevers, and survived her only a few days. On hearing of his illness, she said,
"Tell my father and sister I die happy." A few hours before
her death, after a night of restlessness, she sweetly said, " He
will lay no more upon me than he will enable me to bear.

> ' He never, never will forsake
>   A helpless soul that trusts in Him.' "

Shortly afterwards she breathed her spirit in great tranquillity into the hands of her Saviour.

HYMN 228.*—" Thou Shepherd of Israel, and mine."—" *Tell me,
O Thou, whom my soul loveth.*"—TUNE, Thou Shepherd
of Israel, 1761.

Forms No. 931 of Charles Wesley's " Short Scripture
Hymns," vol. i. It is a rich evangelical exposition and application of Solomon's Song i. 7. This was added in the year 1797.

Mrs Wilson, of Waterford, received the evidence of her
adoption into the family of God whilst reading Isaiah vi. in her

closet at the age of eighteen. While reading "Thy iniquity is taken away, and thy sin is purged," she was "filled with joy and peace in believing." She became a useful Christian ; and, as the mother of a large family, saw her eldest son engaged as a local preacher at the age of nineteen, and five of her daughters in early life converted to God, who met with her in the same class. She lived to enjoy that "perfect love" which casteth out fear. The day before her death she prayed with each of her children, and to the physician and parish clergyman who visited her she spoke with earnestness on the preciousness of Christ, and frequently repeated the hymn commencing—

> " Thou Shepherd of Israel, and mine,
>   The joy and desire of my heart ;
> For closer communion I pine,
>   I long to reside where Thou art."

On one occasion, after repeating this hymn, Mr Doolittle engaged in prayer, after which she said, " The enemy is kept far from me ; thanks be to God, who giveth me the victory." Whilst repeating "Victory through the blood of the Lamb," she entered into rest.

HYMN 229.—"God of my life, to Thee."—*On his Birthday.*—
TUNE, Miss Edwins, 1761.

Charles Wesley's, forming No. 123 in "Hymns and Sacred Poems," 1749, vol. i. The fifth verse of the original is left out.

The singular idea in the last two lines is founded on a tradition amongst the Jews, that the Almighty drew the soul or spirit of Moses out of his body by a kiss. Dr Watts, in his lyric poem on the death of Moses, gives the same idea thus—

> " Softly his fainting head he lay
>   Upon his Maker's breast ;
> His Maker kissed his soul away
>   And laid his flesh to rest."

The opinion thus conveyed is Jewish rather than Christian in its character, and is delicate, touching, and sublime in its phraseology.

As early as her thirteenth year, Mary Hardy, of Duffield, Derby, afterwards of Falcon Street, London, was convinced of sin under a sermon preached by the Rev. Mr Gill, of Matlock, and soon afterwards she entered into full liberty from sin. Her love of the world was now changed for love to the Scriptures, the services of the Sanctuary, and the people of God ; and she became a zealous Sunday-school teacher and collector for the cause of God. Happy in her marriage, she adorned her godly profession by a useful Christian life, and lived to realise the blessing of entire sanctification. During a brief illness she found Christ to be precious, and delighted in repeating some favourite hymns, especially the lines—

> " Then when the work is done,
> The work of faith with power ;
> Like Moses, to Thyself convey,
> And kiss my raptured soul away."

Her last words were—"Angels wait to convey me to glory. Very happy !" and thus she peacefully entered into rest.

HYMN 230.—"Fountain of life and all my joy."—*On his Birthday.*—TUNE, Whitsunday, 1761.

Charles Wesley's, from "Hymns and Sacred Poems," 1742, page 122. The original has ten verses, the first three and three others being left out. It was written December 18, 1741, and in the omitted verses the poet alludes to that singular desire for death which has found its way into many of his early effusions.

HYMN 231.—"Away with our fears! The glad morning appears." —*On his Birthday.*—TUNE, Builth, 1761.

Forms No. 191 in Charles Wesley's "Hymns and Sacred Poems," 1749, vol. ii. The original is in fourteen six-line stanzas. In the first line, " my fears " is altered to " our fears." Two verses are left out. Some of the lines are strikingly appropriate to the founder of Methodism. Few persons besides the brothers Wesley could say of friends what Charles Wesley says in one of the omitted verses :—

> " How rich in the friends Thy providence sends
> To help my infirmity on !
> What a number I see Who could suffer for me,
> And ransom my life with their own !"

Forty-two years after this hymn was written, and after the poet had entered the realms of the blessed, John Wesley made this affecting reference to this hymn : "I this day (June 17, 1788)

enter on my eighty-fifth year ; and what cause have I to praise
God, as for a thousand spiritual blessings, so for bodily blessings
also ! How little have I suffered yet by the rush of numerous
years ! . . . Even now, though I find daily pain in my eye, or
temple, or arm, yet it is never violent, and seldom lasts many
minutes at a time. Whether or not this is sent to give me
warning that I am shortly to quit this tabernacle, I do not
know ; but, be it one way or the other, I have only to say—

> ' My remnant of days I spend in His praise,
> Who died the whole world to redeem :
> My days are His due, Be they many or few,
> And they all are devoted to Him.' "

Fifty years' labour as a Methodist preacher during the last
century, and five of them passed in travelling the almost un-
trodden wilds of America, as a pioneer missionary and superintendent, prior to 1780, represents an amount of toil and service
of which few in these days can have any knowledge. Such a
career was that of the Rev. Thomas Rankin. The whip which
accompanied the good man during his five years' journeyings in
America on horseback, has long been a treasured relic belonging to the author of these notes. His zeal for the glory of God,
and his love to souls, suffered no abatement during a long life :
he continued to preach with much acceptance and profit to
the close of his days. During his last illness he said to a friend,
" I did not immediately join the Methodists when awakened and
converted ; I hesitated for some time ; but glory be to God that
He inclined me to cast in my lot among them !" Then referring
to one of his favourite hymns, he quoted part of it as expressing
his feelings and experience at the end of his pilgrimage :—

> " From Jehovah I came, For His glory I am,
> And to Him I with singing return ;
>   *   *   *   *   *
> What a mercy is this ! What a heaven of bliss !
> How unspeakably happy am I !
> Gathered into the fold, With Thy people enrolled,
> With Thy people to live and to die."

He lived a long life of honourable usefulness, and died rejoicing
in God his Saviour, and was buried in City Road Chapel ground ;
his character being sketched at the time of his funeral by three
Presidents of the Conference, his friends in the ministry, the Rev.
Walter Griffith, the Rev. Henry Moore, and the Rev. Joseph

Benson. Great crowds of people attended at his funeral, and to hear the funeral sermon which was preached afterwards.

HYMN 232.—" Young men and maidens raise."—*For Children.*
—TUNE, Trumpet, 1761.

This forms No. 65 of Charles Wesley's " Hymns for Children," and is a spirited paraphrase of Psalm cxlviii. 12, 13.

HYMN 233.—"Happy man whom God doth aid!"—*For Children,*
—TUNE, Hotham, 1761.

Forms No. 18 of Charles Wesley's " Hymns for Children."

HYMN 234.—" Let all that breathe Jehovah praise."—*For*
Children.—TUNE, Fulham, 1761.

Forms No. 90 of Charles Wesley's " Hymns for Children."

HYMN 235.—" Father of all, whose powerful voice."
  „   236.—" Son of Thy Sire's eternal love."
  „   237.—" Eternal, spotless Lamb of God."
The Lord's Prayer.—TUNE, London and Palmis, 1761.

John Wesley's " Paraphrase of the Lord's Prayer," found in " Hymns and Sacred Poems," 1742, page 275. It possesses all the characteristics of the poet's classical pen. It is probably the finest paraphrase of that inimitable prayer to be found in the English language.

HYMN 238.—" Meet and right it is to praise."—*For a Family.*
—TUNE, Ascension, 1761.

Forms No. 11 in Charles Wesley's " Hymns for a Family." The original has five verses, the last one being omitted.

HYMN 239.—" Hail! Father, Son, and Holy Ghost!"—*Of God.*
—TUNE, Cornish, 1761.

Forms the first of Charles Wesley's " Hymns for Children."

HYMN 240.—" O God, Thou bottomless abyss !"
  „   241.—" Thou, true and only God, lead'st forth.'
  God's Greatness.—TUNE, Italian, 1761.

John Wesley's translation from the German of Ernest Lange, found in " Hymns and Sacred Poems," 1739, page 161. Two lines in the second verse of Part II. are borrowed from Tate and Brady's version of Psalm ciii. The lines commence "Thy wakened wrath," &c. The latter part of the first verse of this grand hymn is manifestly not suited for use in public worship. This is "an awe-inspiring hymn ; serious without being heavy ; bold without being extravagant." Mr Wesley has placed this hymn under the sub-title "On the Attributes of God."

Ernest Lange, the author of this much-admired hymn, was born at Danzic, in 1650, where he became magistrate and burgomaster. In February 1711, when sixty-one years old, he published sixty-one hymns, "to praise the mercy of God," who had delivered him from the pestilence which prevailed in 1710. He died at Danzic in 1727. Another translation of the same hymn forms No. 183 in the "United Brethren's Hymn-Book." Only three of this author's hymns have been put into English.

HYMN 242.—"Glorious God, accept a heart."—*For Children.*—
TUNE, Hambleton's, 1761.

This hymn forms No. 11 of Charles Wesley's "Hymns for Children." The expressive importunity of the pleadings in the last verse, where the personal pronoun ME is five times repeated, demonstrates how natural earnestness becomes true eloquence.

HYMN 243.—"Thou, my God, art good and wise."—*For Children.*—TUNE, Amsterdam, 1761.

Forms No. 22 of Charles Wesley's "Hymns for Children."

HYMN 244.—"Thou, the great, eternal God."
„   245.—"Good Thou art, and good Thou dost."
For Children.—TUNE, Kingswood, 1761.

Forms No. 94 of Charles Wesley's "Hymns for Children." The fourth verse of the original is left out, and the fifth verse is made the commencement of Hymn 245, which latter has been made extensively useful.

Religious impressions received in the Wesleyan Sunday-school, St Nicholas, Margate, led Ann Young to seek the Lord, and at the age of fourteen, she became converted, and joined the Methodist Society. As a domestic in the family of Captain Wood, of Birkenhead, she adorned her profession by an humble walk with God. When her end was approaching, she expressed her confidence in God, and with all her strength she repeated the hymn—

> " Good Thou art, and good Thou dost,
>   Thy mercies reach to all," &c.

laying particular emphasis on the line, " Watches every numbered hair." In this calm and resigned state of mind she fell
asleep in Jesus.

Mrs Broad, of Sewdley, in the Newent circuit, received her
first ticket of membership from the Rev. Jonathan Crowther,
when she was at school. Her joy was unbounded when she
received the blessing of pardon. When laid aside by illness,
her last hours were solemnly delightful. She said, " I cannot
sink, I hang on my Saviour's merits." Bidding her husband
farewell, she said, "Give your heart to God." She then repeated the verse—

> " Good Thou art, and good Thou dost,
>   Thy mercies reach to all," &c.

" He is mine, and I am His." Her last words were, " Washed
all my sins away."

HYMN 246.—" My soul, through my Redeemer's care."—" *Thou
hast delivered my soul from death,*" &c.—TUNE, Stanton,
1761.

Charles Wesley's, forming No. 858 of " Short Scripture
Hymns," vol. i., based on Psalm cxvi. 8.

The mother of the Rev. Oliver Henwood was brought up in
the Church of England. During the last fifteen years of her
life she was united to the Methodists, and her solicitude was
afterwards increased for the salvation of her children, especially
her son, who became a Wesleyan minister. She passed away
from earth to heaven, repeating, with difficulty, yet word for
word—

> " My soul, through my Redeemer's care,
>   Saved from the second death, I feel,
>   My eyes from tears of dark despair
>   My feet from falling into hell."

It was the privilege of Mrs Barrett, of Hull, mother of the
Rev. Alfred Barrett, to attend a love-feast held in Norfolk
Street Chapel, Sheffield, conducted by the late William Bramwell. The meeting was conducted in the usual manner for
some time. "As the meeting was drawing to a close there was
a pause ; none seemed willing to rise ; and there fell upon the

assembly a stillness and an awe as deep as that of the grave.
Every soul seemed to be absorbed and overwhelmed by the
influence from above. None desired or dared to break the
hallowed and awful silence of that hour, but all sat communing
with heavenly and eternal things, until the preacher arose, and
said, 'Now who can say that God is not here?' which appeal,
made with much force and feeling, enabled the assembly to
relieve themselves by subdued ejaculations and tears." The
powerful impression produced on the mind of Mrs Barrett never
wore off; and, supported as it was by the drawings of the Holy
Spirit, in early life she was led to join the Methodist Society, when
she removed to Hull, and there found peace through believing.
In 1832, she gave up her son to the ministry, to whom she wrote
frequently letters which indicated a growing in grace, and a
lively interest in promoting religion.   Her last illness was brief.
Though the valley of suffering was dark, she said, "All is light
beyond." Her husband said it was a happy circumstance to be
able to appropriate the words of the hymn commencing—

> " My soul, through my Redeemer's care,
>   Saved from the second death, I feel," &c.

" Indeed it is," she replied, " and, through the mercy of the
Redeemer, I have no fear of death." Her faith was triumphant ;
and shortly afterwards her redeemed spirit fled to paradise.

The Rev. William Bird, in describing the last hours of Mrs
Bird on earth (" Methodist Magazine," 1817) remarks :—"When I
inquired into her spiritual state, she replied, ' I hope you will
strive to make yourself easy concerning me ; because all *is* and
will be well with me for ever. Jesus is my all. The Lord liveth,
and blessed be my Rock ! He is a sure foundation." Observing
me weep on account of her approaching dissolution, she requested
me not to grieve, " Because (said she) I shall be happy for ever ;
and I *now* feel perfectly resigned to the Divine will. Towards
the end of her last day her speech began to falter. A few
minutes before her departure, she, pressing my hand, said, ' I *do*
love you, but I love God Almighty *better :* my obligations to
Him are infinitely greater.   Yes—

> " My soul, through my Redeemer's care,
>   Saved from the second death I feel ;
> My eyes from tears of dark despair,
>   My feet from falling into hell."

And then immediately added, 'My sight is going, and *I* am going !' and in a moment fell asleep in Jesus."

HYMN 247.—" Holy as thou, O Lord, is none !"—" *There is none holy as the Lord,*" &c.—TUNE, Palini, 1761.

Forms No. 448 of Charles Wesley's " Short Scripture Hymns," vol. i., based on 1 Sam. ii. 2.

HYMN 248.—" Blest be our everlasting Lord."—" *Blessed be the Lord,*" &c.—TUNE, Brooks, 1761.

Made up of three of Charles Wesley's " Short Scripture Hymns," vol. i. Nos. 623–625, based on 1 Chron. xxix. 10–13.

HYMN 249.—" Great God ! to me the sight afford."—" *The Lord descended in the cloud,*" &c.—TUNE, Trinity, 1761.

This forms three of Charles Wesley's " Short Scripture Hymns," vol. i., Nos. 166-168, founded on Exod. xxxiv. 5, 6.

HYMN 250.—" Thy ceaseless, unexhausted love."—" *The Lord God, merciful and gracious,*" &c.—TUNE, Trinity, 1761.

This is also composed of three of Charles Wesley's " Short Scripture Hymns," vol. i. Nos. 169–171, founded on Exod. xxxiv. 6.

Matthew Henry has, in his Commentary on this passage, very similar thoughts to those expressed by the poet. It is known that Mr Wesley made free use of Henry's Notes in ascertaining the interpretation of many portions of Holy Scripture.

For fifty years Thomas Thompson, of Brompton, Kent, was a useful member of the Methodist Society, a Sunday-school teacher, and leader. He was truly a pattern to believers in his integrity, simplicity, and devotedness to the cause of God. On the Sabbath before his death he addressed the school with his usual earnestness, but during the week he met with an accident, by which he sustained severe internal injuries. He became at once resigned to the certainty of speedy dissolution, saying, " My Saviour is about to take me home ; I have left all the future to Him." Among his last words, he repeated the verse —

> " Faithful, O Lord, Thy mercies are !
> A Rock that cannot move
> A thousand promises declare
> Thy constancy of love."

His end was peace, and his home heaven.

HYMN 251.—" Father of me, and all mankind."—" *Our Father which art in heaven,*" *&c.*—TUNE, Spitalfields, 1761.

This forms part of two of Charles Wesley's "Scripture Hymns," vol. ii., No. 342 and No. 343, founded on Luke xi. 2, being a paraphrase of the first three clauses of the Lord's Prayer. Three verses of the original are left out.

HYMN 252.—" Come, Father, Son, and Holy Ghost."—" *The Lord bless thee, and keep thee,*" &c.—TUNE, Hallelujah, 1761.

Formed of Nos. 200-202 of Charles Wesley's "Scripture Hymns," vol. i., founded on Numb. vi. 24-26.

HYMN 253.*—" Father, in whom we live."—*To the Trinity.*

Charles Wesley's, forming No. 34 in "Redemption Hymns." This was added to the collection in 1797.

HYMN 254.—" The day of Christ, the day of God."—*The Divinity of Christ.*—TUNE, Smith's, 1761.

Charles Wesley's, from "Hymns on the Trinity," founded on 2 Peter iii. 12.

HYMN 255.—" Spirit of Truth, essential God."—" *All Scripture is given by inspiration of God,*" &c.—TUNE, Norwich, 1761.

Charles Wesley's, from "Hymns on the Trinity," founded on 2 Tim. xvi., and 2 Peter i. 21.

HYMN 256.—" Hail! Father, Son, and Spirit great."—*The Plurality and Trinity of Persons.*—TUNE, Trinity, 1761.

Charles Wesley's, from page 58 of "Hymns on the Trinity." Its tendency is to show the connexion between the creation and redemption of man.

HYMN 257.*—" Glory be to'God on high."—*Gloria in Excelsis.*— TUNE, Salisbury, 1761.

Charles Wesley's paraphrase of the *Gloria in Excelsis*, in the Sacramental Service, found in "Hymns and Sacred Poems," 1739, page 128. It is printed in John Wesley's "Select Hymns, with Tunes annext," and was added to the collection after Mr Wesley's death.

HYMN 258.—" Jehovah, God the Father, bless."—" *The Lord bless thee, and keep thee,*" &c.—TUNE, Brooks, 1761.

Charles Wesley's, from " Hymns on the Trinity," founded on Numb. vi. 24. The last verse of the original is left out, in which occurs the line, " The incommunicable name."

HYMN 259.—" Hail! holy, holy, holy Lord."—" *Holy, holy, is the Lord of Hosts,*" &c.—TUNE, Trinity, 1761.

Charles Wesley's, from " Hymns on the Trinity, page 69, founded on Isaiah vi. 3, and Rev. iv. 8.

HYMN 260.—" Holy, holy, holy Lord."—*To the Trinity.*—TUNE, Salisbury, 1761.

Charles Wesley's, from page 96 of " Hymns on the Trinity." It is a hymn full of noble thoughts, conveyed in fine and appropriate language. Dr Watts, in one of his lyrics, has the same idea which Charles Wesley has conveyed in the second stanza—

> " Thy dazzling beauties while he sings,
> He hides his face behind his wings,
> And ranks of shining thrones around
> Fall worshipping, and spread the ground."

Dr Young, in his " Complaint," Night Second, has this line—

> " Time, in advance, behind him hides his wings."

HYMN 261.—" Come, Father, Son, and Holy Ghost."—*To the Trinity.*—TUNE, Sheffield, 1761.

Charles Wesley's, from page 98 of " Hymns on the Trinity."

HYMN 262.—" A thousand oracles divine."—*To the Trinity.*—TUNE, Hallelujah, 1761.

Charles Wesley's, from " Hymns on the Trinity," page 100. The original is printed in eight-line stanzas. Dr Edward Young, in his " Night Thoughts," Night Four, line 440, has the following, which exactly corresponds with the seventh verse of this fine hymn—

> " They see on earth a bounty not indulged on high,
> And downward look for heaven's superior praise."

HYMN 263.* —" Father, how wide Thy glory shines !"—*God glorious, and Sinners saved.*

Dr Watts', from " Horæ Lyricæ," 1705. The original has nine verses, the fifth and seventh being omitted. This hymn was added to the collection many years after Mr Wesley's death, and does not appear in the edition of 1805.

Through the instrumentality of an awakening dream, George Rolstone was brought to God at the age of eighteen. He joined the Methodist Society, and during fifty years maintained a consistent godly profession. For forty years he was a useful classleader. During his last illness, whilst he suffered much, he had a glorious assurance of his acceptance with God. He looked forward with joyous anticipation to the employment of glorified saints, and sometimes said—

> " 'O may I bear some humble part,
> In that immortal song.' "

In this patient and happy frame of mind, he departed from the militant to join the triumphant church.

HYMN 264.—" O All-creating God."—*Of the Creation and Fall of Man.*—TUNE, Brentford, 1761.

Charles Wesley's, forming the second of his " Hymns for Children." The third verse is omitted.

HYMN 265.—" O may Thy powerful word."—" *The kingdom of heaven suffereth violence,*" &c.—TUNE, Lampe's, 1746.

Charles Wesley's, forming No. 137 of "Short Scripture Hymns," vol. ii., founded on Matt. xi. 12. This hymn commences another section of the book with the title of "Believers Fighting."

> HYMN 266.—" Soldiers of Christ arise."
> „   267.—" But, above all, lay hold."
> „   268.—" In fellowship, alone."

The whole armour of God.—TUNE, Handel's March, 1761.

Charles Wesley's, forming together No. 140 in "Hymns and Sacred Poems," 1749, vol. i. ; founded on Eph. vi., and extending to sixteen verses, four of which are omitted. It is inserted in "Select Hymns with Tunes annext."

HYMN 269.—"Surrounded by a host of foes."—*This is the
Victory!*—TUNE, Norwich, 1761.

Charles Wesley's, from "Hymns and Sacred Poems," 1749,
vol. ii., No. 113.

A fierce epidemical fever in July 1826, entered the dwelling
of William Treffry, of Cuby, Cornwall. Its first victim was
Ann Treffry, a venerable widow, a godly woman, who had for
fifty years maintained a consistent membership in the Methodist
Society; she died ascribing "Glory to God!" Immediately
afterwards, Charles Treffry, a youth of eighteen, enjoying unutterable peace of mind, yielded to the same disease. Then
followed the head of the household himself. He had been
afflicted for some years, and hence he fell a more ready victim;
but his loins were girded, and his light was burning. Shortly
before his departure, he delighted all about him by declaring
his unshaken confidence in God in these lines—

> "What though a thousand hosts engage,
>   A thousand worlds, my soul to shake?
> I have a shield shall quell their rage,
>   And drive the alien armies back:
> Portray'd it bears a bleeding Lamb;
> I dare believe in Jesu's name."

HYMN 270.—"Equip me for the war."—*On God's Everlasting
Love.*—TUNE, Olney, 1761.

Charles Wesley's, forming No. 12 of "Hymns on God's Everlasting Love." The first and eighth verses of the original are
left out. The first commences—

> "O all-atoning Lamb."

This long poem was written at a time when the Antinomian
and high Calvinistic doctrines were boldly enforced; and in
the omitted portions will be found some very strong thoughts
against "the five points."

HYMN 271.—"O Almighty God of Love."—*On going into a
Place of Danger.*—TUNE, Amsterdam, 1761.

Charles Wesley's, from "Hymns and Sacred Poems," 1742.
The first and second verses of the original are left out.

L

HYMN 272.—"Peace! doubting heart; my God's I am!"—*Isaiah*
xliii. 2, 3.—TUNE, 23d Psalm, 1761.

Charles Wesley's, from "Hymns and Sacred Poems, 1739,
page 153. This hymn is one of rare excellence, abounding in
scriptural images and metaphors, and is full of instruction and
encouragement.

The early life of James Hoby, of London, was a testimony to
the truth of the scriptural record that "The thoughts of the heart
are evil, and that continually." A more giddy round of gaiety,
worldliness, and sin never attended a young man than was the
lot of Mr Hoby when young. His mind next became entangled
with almost every variety of religious opinion—Jewish, Popish,
Mohammedan, and infidel. During all this time he thought
himself to be a good churchman. Having been led to the
Methodist Chapel at Greenwich, he heard a sermon by the
Rev. Richard Watson on holiness, from which he learned that in
his heart there was none of it. The next Methodist sermon he
heard was by the Rev. Jabez Bunting, from which he saw, to
his sorrow, that for thirty years he had been deceiving his own
heart. Another sermon, by the Rev. Charles Atmore, led him
to begin family prayer. On Christmas day, 1825, he began to
meet in Mr Butterworth's class, and received his first ticket
from the Rev. John Stephens. From that time to the end of
his life, so deeply conscious was he of the greatness of God's
mercy to him in rescuing him from so low a degradation, that
his utmost energies were employed in furthering the kingdom
of Christ in the world, and in making known his salvation.
When informed that the disease of the heart from which he was
suffering would terminate suddenly, and obliged to keep his
room he requested that, when he was dying, his friends would
join in singing the hymn beginning—

> "Peace! doubting heart; my God's I am!
> Who form'd me man, forbids my fear."

On the first Sunday of 1863, he had hoped to have again joined
in the Annual Service at Great Queen Street, but the call of the
Divine Master on that day was, "Come up higher;" and just
after saying "He will give the Holy Spirit to them that ask
Him," his soul entered the rest above.

No tale of sorrow and distress could exceed in intensity of

interest that of the loss of the *Maria* mail-boat, in the West Indies, in 1826. The account of the shipwreck of the Apostle Paul near Malta is the nearest approach to the one just named for variety of incident, and for the unbounded faith which was exercised on the occasion. Five missionaries, three wives of missionaries, with several children and nurses, were returning to Antigua. In sight of land, a storm arose, and before its fury the mail-boat was wrecked, the five missionaries were drowned, and in fact the only one of the large party who escaped with life was Mrs Jones, the wife of one of the missionaries, who endured many deaths in saving her own life; but through mercy she was saved, and some years afterwards was married to Mr Hincksman, and died in great peace at Lytham, in April 1859. When the storm arose, one of the missionaries' sons, a little boy, gave out the verse beginning—

"Though waves and storms go o'er my head," &c.

After this had been sung, a holy inspiration came over the child, and he astonished the party in the boat by the address he gave on the shipwreck of Jonah. A strange feeling came over those who heard the child. Mrs Jones (Hincksman) tried to pray, but could not. At length, she cried, "Lord! Lord! help me." Scarcely had she uttered the words when she became composed, and repeated the verse—

"Jesus protects; my fears, begone!"

In that time of trouble and sorrow she gladdened her own heart and those of her companions by singing, for the last hymn most of them heard on earth—

"When passing through the watery deep,
  I ask in faith His promised aid,
The waves an awful distance keep,
  And shrink from my devoted head;
Fearless their violence I dare;
They cannot harm, for God is there!"

She was the only one who could sing in that distressing hour, and the only one saved in that redeemed company!—*Vide Methodist Magazine*, 1826, page 486, and 1861, page 195.

Another incident of like character, the peril and preservation of a missionary, and the use of this hymn on the occasion, will be found in a letter from Mr Wallace, in the *Methodist Magazine*, May 1846, page 977.

When Methodism was little more than a by-word and reproach, Mrs Gaulter chose for her companion in life one of John Wesley's preachers. When about fourteen years old she joined the Methodist Society, and for more than sixty years she maintained a truly consistent godly profession, and in all things lived and acted under the influence of the fear and love of God. She suffered much during life, and in her last illness she had but little strength for resistance ; but the enemy of souls tried to distress her mind even at the end of a very long pilgrimage. Shortly before her death, after one of these spiritual conflicts, she repeated with much energy—

> "Still nigh me, O my Saviour, stand !
>   And guard in fierce temptation's hour :
> Hide in the hollow of Thy hand ;
>   Show forth in me Thy saving power ;
> Still be Thy arm my sure defence :
> Nor earth nor hell shall pluck me thence."

Her last words were but faint breathings—"A world of light and glory "—and that world she then entered.

HYMN 273.—"Omnipotent Lord, My Saviour and King."— *The Good Fight.*—TUNE, Triumph, 1761.

Charles Wesley's, from "Hymns and Sacred Poems," 1742, page 137.

Elizabeth Deane, of Ightham, Sevenoaks, was a zealous and liberal member of the Methodist Society during thirty years, and greatly aided the erection of a chapel on her property. She was a timid follower of the Lord Jesus, but in death she was enabled to triumph. Fearing a sudden death, in answer to prayer she was saved from her apprehensions, and gave the most satisfactory evidence of being ready for her change. The last words she was heard to say were—

> "Omnipotent Lord, my Saviour and King
> Thy succour afford, Thy righteousness bring ;
> Thy promises bind Thee Compassion to have,
> Now, now let me find Thee Almighty to save."

HYMN 274.—"O my old, my bosom foe."—*After a Recovery.*— TUNE, Amsterdam, 1761.

Charles Wesley's, from "Hymns and Sacred Poems," 1749, vol. i., No. 95.

HYMN 275.—" The Lord unto my Lord hath said."—"*Lord, Thou hast been our dwelling-place*," &c.—TUNE, Liverpool, 1761.

Charles Wesley's, from " Hymns and Sacred Poems," 1742, page 89, being a paraphrase of the Ninetieth Psalm, first verse. The original has fifteen verses, six of which are left out.

HYMN 276.*—" Worship, and thanks, and blessing."—*Written after a Deliverance in a Tumult.*—TUNE, Dying Stephen, 1761.

Charles Wesley's, forming No. 20 of his " Redemption Hymns."

At this distance of time, it is difficult to decide which of several tumultuous riots, from which the poet of Methodism so narrowly escaped with his life, gave rise to this elegant and spirited hymn of gratitude and praise. The Rev. John Kirk, in a very discriminating article on this subject, traces the origin of this hymn to what are known as the Wednesbury riots of 1743, in which " Honest Munchin" was the captain of the mob, till divine grace reached even him, and after enduring from him, his followers, and maddened bull-dogs, what might be termed "deaths often," Charles Wesley himself received the broken-spirited Munchin on trial as a Methodist. If the Wednesbury riots gave birth to this hymn, it was composed on October 26, 1743 ; and was afterwards used on other occasions rivalling in violence and ferocity the scenes which it commemorates. Another tumult is thus referred to by Mr Charles Wesley, as part of a long and exciting narrative of the doings of an infuriated wicked mob at Devizes : " In 1747, after riding two or three hundred yards, I looked back and saw Mr Merton on the ground in the midst of the mob, and two bull-dogs upon him. One was first let loose, and leaped at the horse's nose ; but the horse, with his foot, beat him down. The other fastened on his nose and held there till Mr Merton, with the butt-end of his whip, felled him to the ground. Then the first dog fastened on the horse's breast ; the beast reared, and Mr Merton slid gently off. The dog held on till the flesh tore off. Then some of the men took off the dogs, others cried, " Let them alone." But neither beast nor man had any commission to hurt. I stopped the horse and delivered him to my friend ; he remounted with great composure, and we rode on leisurely till out of sight ; then we mended our pace, and in an hour came to Sçen, having rode three miles about, and by seven to Wrexall. The news of the danger was got thither before us, but we brought the welcome tidings of our deliverance. We joined in hearty praises to our Deliverer, singing the hymn—

"Worship, and thanks, and blessing," &c.

Men who could thus suffer and thus sing were as ready for the "lions' den" or the "fiery furnace" as for such infuriated madness of men and beasts. The hymn was inserted in the collection after Mr Wesley's death.

HYMN 277.—"Jesus, the Conqueror, reigns."—*Thanksgiving.*— TUNE, Handel's March, 1761.

Charles Wesley's, forming No. 139 in "Hymns and Sacred Poems," 1749, vol. i.

The original is in sixteen stanzas, the first six only being used. These when first added to the collection formed three hymns of two verses each. They were united in 1797.

HYMN 278.—"Who is this gigantic foe?"—*David and Goliath*, I *Samuel* xvii.—TUNE, Amsterdam, 1761.

Charles Wesley's, from "Hymns and Sacred Poems," 1742, page 176.

In its construction the history of the triumph of David over the Philistine is applied most effectively to the triumph of believers over inbred and besetting sin.

HYMN 279.—"Shall I, for fear of feeble man."—*Boldness in the Gospel.*—TUNE, Canon, 1761.

From the German of John Joseph Winkler, published in 1703, and translated by John Wesley during his residence in Georgia as a missionary. It appeared first in "Psalms and Hymns," issued by the Wesleys in 1738, and is also added to their "Hymns and Sacred Poems," 1739.

"This," says Miss Winkworth, "is one of the standard hymns of Germany." John Wesley endured severe persecution whilst in America for his stern fidelity in reproving sin, and in the language of this hymn he found comfort and encouragement.

John Joseph Winkler was born at Luckau, in Saxony, December 23, 1670. He was first pastor in Magdeburg, afterwards chaplain in the army, and accompanied the troops to Holland and Italy. Subsequently he returned to Magdeburg, where he became chief minister at the Cathedral, and member of the Consistory. He died there, August 11, 1722. He was an excellent man, of a highly-cultivated mind, and wrote ten very good hymns.

HYMN 280.—"The Lord is King, and earth submits."—"*He that believeth shall not make haste.*"—TUNE, Zoar, 1761.

Charles Wesley's, from "Hymns and Sacred Poems," 1742, page 274.

HYMN 281.—"Are there not in the labourer's day."—*The Way of Duty the Way of Safety.*—TUNE, Snowsfields, 1761.

Charles Wesley's, from "Hymns and Sacred Poems," 1749, vol. i., No. 124.

HYMN 282.—"But can it be, that I should prove."—*In Temptation.*—TUNE, Chapel, 1761.

Charles Wesley's, from "Hymns and Sacred Poems," 1749, vol. i., No. 113.
The original has six verses, the third being left out. This has the words "second part" at the head of the hymn, probably through an oversight ; it is a separate hymn in the original, and under a different head to the previous one.

HYMN 283.—"O God, my hope, my heavenly rest."—*For a Preacher of the Gospel.*—TUNE, Marienburn, 1761.

Charles Wesley's, from "Hymns and Sacred Poems," 1749, vol. i., No. 178, with a separate title, "Moses' Wish."

HYMN 284.—"To Thee, great God of Love! I bow."—*For a Preacher of the Gospel.*—TUNE, Cary's, 1761.

Charles Wesley's, forming No. 180, in "Hymns and Sacred Poems," 1749, vol. i. The second verse of the original is left out.

HYMN 285.—"Come, Saviour, Jesus, from above."—*Renouncing all for Christ.*—TUNE, Angel's Song, 1761.

The original of this hymn was written in French about the

year 1640, by Madame Antoinette Bourignon, whilst she was
suffering from her father's anger on account of the mercenary
suitors who solicited her hand. It expresses her resolution to
devote herself entirely to the service of God. The French is in
five eight-line verses. Madame Bourignon was born in 1616,
and died in 1680. Her life was one of extraordinary suffering,
privation, and endurance. Her self-denying industry and devotion were the marvel of many, and her writings fill twenty
volumes. John Wesley made the translation in 1736, when he
was suffering from reproach and calumny in America. It first
appeared in "Hymns and Sacred Poems," 1739, page 123.
It is also found in Dr John Byrom's "Miscellaneous Poems,"
2 vols., Manchester, 1773, vol. ii., page 211, with the title, "A
Hymn to Jesus." This publication has led some to suppose,
erroneously, that it was written by Byrom.

A reminiscence of sadness is associated with this hymn in
connexion with the last service conducted by the Rev. George
Manwaring. That service was the administration of the Lord's
Supper in Carver Street Chapel, Sheffield, August 14, 1825.
Little more than fourteen days sufficed for a violent fever to end
the mortal strife. During the wanderings of the mind, the man
of God was occupied with divine things, and the evening before
his death it was affecting to his attendants to hear him give out
the hymn—

> "Come, Saviour Jesus, from above !
> Assist me with Thy heavenly grace ;
> Empty my heart of earthly love,
> And for Thyself prepare the place."

This he did with a distinct and audible voice, as he lay insensible in bed, proceeding through the whole of the Communion
Service and the form of administering the elements, just as he
had done during his last earthly service. In imagination he
was commemorating the Lord's death with His saints on the
earth, and almost immediately afterwards his released spirit
joined the marriage-supper of the Lamb in the courts above.
Mrs Manwaring was just recovering from an illness when her
husband was smitten down, and her watchful care of him she
loved induced the same malady in herself. The children were
removed to the care of friends. She was taken to the dwelling of the Rev. Daniel Isaac, to whose care her ultimate recovery was mainly attributable ; nor was it deemed prudent or

safe to tell her of her widowed condition till her husband had been buried two days.

HYMN 286.—" Abraham, when severely tried."—" *The life of faith exemplified,*" &c.—TUNE, Complaint, 1761.

Charles Wesley's, from " Hymns and Sacred Poems," 1740, page 12. This is a portion of one of the longest of this poet's compositions ; it extends to more than eighty verses, and is a paraphrase of Heb. xi. 17-19.

HYMN 287.—" Omnipresent God ! whose aid."—*At lying down.*—TUNE, Magdalen, 1761.

Charles Wesley's, No. 119 of " Hymns and Sacred Poems," 1749, vol. i. The original has eight verses, four of which are omitted.

Under the ministry of the Rev. William Henshaw, Mrs Wilson, wife of the Rev. Joseph Wilson, was convinced of sin, and shortly afterwards, during a revival amongst young people in the Rye circuit, she obtained the blessing of pardon. In a humble and consistent walk before God, she manifested the power of divine grace in her heart. During her last illness, the Bible, Wesley's Hymns, and the " Pilgrim's Progress," afforded her much encouragement. It was her practice every night to repeat upon her knees the whole of the hymn commencing—

" Omnipresent God ! whose aid
No one ever ask'd in vain," &c.

A more suitable evening prayer was scarcely ever done in verse. It is matter of surprise if thousands of the Lord's people have not made a similar and daily use of this admirable summary of devotion and self-dedication.

HYMN 288.—" O God, Thy faithfulness I plead ! "—*In Temptation.*—TUNE, Wood's, 1761.

Charles Wesley's, forming No. 106 of " Hymns and Sacred Poems," 1749, vol. i. The original has eight verses, three of which are omitted.

It is a delightful record which a daughter has written of her mother, " That the light of purity and holiness which made the character of Mrs Mary Miller so lovely in the eyes of others was invisible to herself." What is recorded of this holy " mother

in Israel" may be with equal truth affirmed of her excellent
husband, the pure, transparent, and holy William Edward
Miller, Wesleyan minister.   The writer of these lines has a delightful recollection of hearing the living testimony of the good
man, delivered at a love-feast in Carver Street Chapel, Sheffield,
in 1840, that for years sin had had no place in his thoughts or
heart.   The thirty-eight years passed by Mrs Miller in the
Methodist Society were marked by inward and abiding peace,
irreproachable uprightness, and a holy life.   She walked in
light.   She frequently repeated the three last verses of Hymn
288, more especially the closing lines—

> " Thy love shall burst the shades of death,
>   And bear me from the gulf beneath,
>   To everlasting day."

What was said of the holy patriarch was equally appropriate to
her, " She was not, for God took her."

HYMN 289.— " God of my life, whose gracious power."—*At the
Approach of Temptation.*—TUNE, Invitation, 1761.

Charles Wesley's, from " Hymns and Sacred Poems," 1740,
page 149.   The original has fifteen verses, seven of which are
omitted.

Shortly before the close of the last century, the first Methodist services were held in the village of Walton, near Brampton,
Cumberland.   One of the first-fruits of that preaching was the
conversion of a youth of sixteen, named Joseph Taylor.   From
that time his whole life and energies were devoted to the service
of God, and abundantly was he owned and blessed in his work.
He accompanied a young friend of his to Liverpool to see him
sail as a Wesleyan missionary to the West Indies : but when the
seraphic Dr Coke saw the two young men together, he was so
impressed with the superior fitness of Mr Taylor for the work,
that he was appointed and sent in the place of his friend.
Reaching Barbadoes on a Sunday morning, accompanied by
another missionary, they hasted, on landing, to the Methodist
chapel.   The missionary in charge was so overjoyed that, at the
conclusion of the reading of the lesson, he left the pulpit and
hasted to welcome the two brethren before the whole congregation.   They fell on each other's necks, and wept tears of joy and
gratitude.   Mr Taylor's labours were abundantly owned of God

in that mission, scarcely a service being held without souls being saved ; and, as he once observed when stationed in London, he saw more souls saved in the West Indies on one Sabbath than he saw saved in the metropolis in three months. At one mission-station he had to sleep in a room near the chapel with no human being near. A good black woman prepared him his supper, and then left him alone with God. But he found these sweet and happy seasons of communion with heaven. After some years' earnest labours, he was brought to the margin of the grave by fever and ague, as well as by the perils of the sea. When, in subsequent life, he referred to these times of affliction and jeopardy, he would devoutly lift his eyes and hands heavenward, and with strong feeling repeat the stanza—

> " Oft hath the sea confess'd Thy power,
>   And given me back at Thy command ;
> It could not, Lord, my life devour,
>   Safe in the hollow of Thine hand.
>
> " Oft from the margin of the grave
>   Thou, Lord, hast lifted up my head ;
> Sudden, I found Thee near to save ;
>   The fever own'd Thy touch, and fled."

Then he would add, " I will sing of mercy and judgment : unto Thee, O Lord, will I sing." Few men have done more real service in promoting the kingdom of Christ, not only in the West Indies, but in various important circuits at home, and especially as one of the general missionary secretaries, and as president of the Conference in 1834. He was a devout and earnest Christian. He died in peace at Bass Lane House, Bury, Lancashire, the residence of J. R. Kay; Esq., and had his last resting-place in the burial-ground of Cheetham-hill Wesleyan Chapel, Manchester, honoured in death as he had deservedly been in life.

HYMN 290.—" My God, if I may call Thee mine."—*Justified, but not Sanctified.*—TUNE, Pudsey, 1761.

Charles Wesley's, from " Hymns and Sacred Poems," 1739, page 150. The original is in nine double verses, five of which are omitted.

HYMN 291.—" Fondly my foolish heart essays."—*In Desertion or Temptation.*—TUNE, Athlone, 1761.

Charles Wesley's, from " Hymns and Sacred Poems," 1739.

page 149. The original has fourteen verses, the first ten of which are left out.

HYMN 292.—"To the haven of Thy breast."—*Isaiah* xxxii. 2.
TUNE, Kingswood, 1761.

Charles Wesley's, from "Hymns and Sacred Poems," 1742, page 145. The latter half of the fourth, and the first half of the fifth verses in the original are left out.

HYMN 293.—"Jesus, my King, to Thee I bow."—*Fight the Good Fight of Faith.*—TUNE, Italian, 1761.

Charles Wesley's, from "Hymns and Sacred Poems," 1742, page 251. The original has nineteen verses, the fourth, and all after the tenth, being omitted.

HYMN 294.—"Jesus, Thou sovereign Lord of all."—*Desiring to Pray.*—TUNE, Mourners, 1761.

Charles Wesley's, forming No. 26 in "Hymns and Sacred Poems," 1749, vol. ii. One-half of the original is left out. The necessity and efficacy of prayer is strongly set forth in this hymn. "The God-commanding plea" of the fourth verse is founded on Isa. xlv. 11, where the Almighty says, "Command ye me." This commences the third section of the book, with the title, "For Believers Praying."

HYMN 295.—"Come, ye followers of the Lord."—"*Men ought always to pray, and not to faint,*" (Luke xviii. 1).—TUNE, Kingswood, 1761.

Charles Wesley's, first printed at the end of a tract, entitled, "A Short View of the Differences between the Moravian Brethren lately in England, and the Rev. Mr John and Charles Wesley, 1741." It is also printed in "Hymns and Sacred Poems," 1749, vol. ii., No. 28. One verse is omitted.
Under the preaching of the first missionaries at English Harbour, Trinity Bay, Newfoundland, the heart of George Ivamy was graciously opened to receive the gospel; after he received the evidence of pardon and assurance he was abundantly happy, and during the rest of his short life he enjoyed uninterrupted peace with God. Fever and consumption followed

each other in quick succession, and in the midst of his sufferings, after a violent paroxysm, he broke forth into singing—

> "Be it weariness or pain
> To slothful flesh and blood ;
> Yet we will the cross sustain,
> And bless the welcome load."

He died, saying to his mother, "Death is gain ; I am going to Jesus."

HYMN 296.—"The praying Spirit breathe."—*In a Hurry of Business.*—TUNE, Olney, 1761.

Charles Wesley's, No. 145, from "Hymns and Sacred Poems," 1749, vol. i. The original commences "Help, Lord! the busy foe," &c., but the first verse is left out. In the fourth line the original reads, "Call off my anxious heart ; " and by changing the word "anxious" to "peaceful," the intention of the poet is quite diverted.

HYMN 297.—"Shepherd Divine, our wants relieve."—*Desiring to Love.*—TUNE, Aldrich, 1761.

Charles Wesley's, No. 27 in "Hymns and Sacred Poems," 1749, vol. ii.

HYMN 298.—"Oh, wondrous power of faithful prayer."—*For those that seek Redemption.*—TUNE, Canterbury, 1761.

Charles Wesley's, from "Redemption Hymns," page 49. There is great fervency of manner and strength of language in this hymn. The all-powerful intercession of the Redeemer is set forth in the line, "Jesus forces me to spare."

HYMN 299.—"Jesus, Thou hast bid us pray."—*Avenge me of mine Adversary.*—TUNE, Kingswood, 1761.

Charles Wesley's, from "Hymns and Sacred Poems," 1742, page 199, founded on Luke xviii. The original has ten verses, two of which are left out.

HYMN 300.—"Jesus, I fain would find."—*Revelation* iii. 19.—TUNE, Lampe's, 1746.

It forms No. 846 of Charles Wesley's "Short Scripture Hymns," vol. ii.

HYMN 301.—" Jesus, my strength, my hope."—*A Poor Sinner.*
—TUNE, Lampe's, 1746.

Charles Wesley's, from "Hymns and Sacred Poems," 1742, page 146. The fourth verse of the original is left out, and the second is placed at the end and forms the sixth.

Brought to a knowledge of the truth under the ministry of the Rev. William Jenkins in 1791, Ann Austen, of Kimbolton, joined the Methodist Society in early life. For many years she was a diligent tract-distributor, sick-visitor, and class-leader. For five years she was confined to the house by severe suffering, but no complaint escaped her lips. In a paroxysm of pain she would sometimes say—

" I want a heart to pray, To pray and never cease,
    Never to murmur at Thy stay, Nor wish my sufferings less."

Her last words were expressive of her confidence in God, and sure hope of heaven.

HYMN 302.—" Lord, that I may learn of Thee."—*Isaiah* xxviii. 9.
—TUNE, Minories, 1761.

Forms No. 1005 of Charles Wesley's "Short Scripture Hymns," vol. i.

HYMN 303.—" Ah, when shall I awake ?"—*God's Everlasting Love.*—TUNE, Lampe's, 1746.

Forms No. 7 in Part II. of Charles Wesley's " Hymns on God's Love." The original has eleven verses, five of which are omitted.

HYMN 304.—" Saviour, on me the want bestow."—*The Beatitudes.*—TUNE, Travellers, 1761.

This is made up of Nos. 19, 21, 22, 23, 24, 26, and 27 of Charles Wesley's " Hymns on the Beatitudes," found in the "Short Scripture Hymns," vol. ii.

HYMN 305.—"Gracious Redeemer, shake."—*For the Watchnight.*
—TUNE, Olney, 1761.

Charles Wesley's, being No. 85 in "Hymns and Sacred Poems," 1749, vol. ii. The original has ten verses, the first four of which are omitted. This hymn commences the fourth section of the collection, with the title, " For Believers Watching."

HYMN 306.—" Father, to Thee I lift mine eyes."—*For the Morning.*—TUNE, 112th Psalm, 1761.

Charles Wesley's, from " Hymns and Sacred Poems," 1749, vol. i., No. 142.

HYMN 307.—" God of all grace and majesty."—*For the fear of God.*—TUNE, Wenvo, 1761.

Charles Wesley's, from "Hymns and Sacred Poems," 1749, vol. ii., No. 166. In line six, verse four, Mr Bunting suggests changing the first word "And" for "Oh !"

HYMN 308.—" I want a principle within."—*For a Tender Conscience.*—TUNE, Wenvo, 1761.

Charles Wesley's, forming No. 167 of " Hymns and Sacred Poems," 1749, vol. ii. The first verse, and the halves of verses four and five of the original, are omitted.

HYMN 309.—" Help, Lord, to whom for help I fly."—*In Temptation.*—TUNE, Musicians, 1761.

Charles Wesley's, forming No. 110 of " Hymns and Sacred Poems," 1749, vol. i.

HYMN 310.—" Into a world of ruffians sent."—*For the Watchnight.*—TUNE, St Paul's, 1761.

Forms No. 89 of Charles Wesley's " Hymns and Sacred Poems," 1749, vol. ii., the first verse of the original being left out. Mr Bunting has suggested an entirely new and much improved reading of the first verse :—

> " Into a world of tempters sent,
>   I walk on hostile ground ;
>   Where fools, on self-destruction bent,
>   And bent on mine, surround."

HYMN 311.—"Bid me of men beware."—*For the Watchnight.*—TUNE, Olney, 1761.

Forms No. 90 of Charles Wesley's " Hymns and Sacred Poems," 1749, vol. ii., the first verse of the original being left out, and the next slightly altered.

HYMN 312.—"Jesu, my Saviour, Brother, Friend;"
    „   313.—"Pierce, fill me with an humble fear."
Watch in all things.—TUNE, Purcells, 1761.

Charles Wesley's, from "Hymns and Sacred Poems," 1742, page 214. The original of these two forms one hymn, extending to fifteen stanzas, the last four being left out.

John Wesley and Methodism had no truer friends than were Ann and Sarah Loxdale, two of the daughters of Thomas Loxdale, Esq., of Shrewsbury. Ann was the intimate personal friend of the Rev. John Wesley and the Rev. John Fletcher, and afterwards became the second wife of the Rev. Dr Coke. Sarah, the younger sister, was converted to God in early life, and was afterwards married to Mr Hill, of Shrewsbury, son of the estimable Mrs Hill, who was her first class-leader. Her life was one uninterrupted round of goodness and mercy, and cannot be better described than in the words of the Rev. P. M'Owan :—" Her Christian experience was deep; her discourse was spiritual, edifying, and intelligent; and her entire deportment and conduct evinced the closeness of her walk with God. Her attachment to Methodism was ardent; and her liberality in supporting its institutions exemplary. Her understanding was strong and well cultivated; her judgment was sound and discriminating; and her disposition was generous and tenderly affectionate. Her piety was cheerful, evangelical, and catholic. She was a faithful friend, a condescending teacher of youth, a wise counsellor, and an efficient class-leader." To this justly-deserved eulogium may be added, that she was, from the commencement of her religious course, accustomed to early rising and habitual industry. In later years, when unable to rise early, she generally had her Bible, hymn-book,* and writing desk in requisition about six in the morning. This custom she observed till she was half way between eighty and ninety years of age. Only five days' illness preceded her death, but her mind was unclouded, and she enjoyed perfect peace. The thought of joining the glorious

* A copy of Charles Wesley's "Hymns and Sacred Poems," 1749, two volumes, with Mrs Sarah Hill's name written across both title-pages, and formerly used by that lady, has been used by the writer of these notes to compare with the originals all the hymns selected from that work, and it is prized by him for that pleasant association.

company before the throne, made her joyful. Naming several, her departed friends, she added—" They are waiting for me; it is enrapturing to think of joining them." The day but one before her death, she appeared to be favoured with some peculiar manifestation of the Divine presence, and said—

"And, hovering, hides me in His wings."

In serene tranquillity, her happy spirit entered paradise.

HYMN 314.—" Hark, how the watchmen cry."
  „   315.—" Angels your march oppose."
For the Watchnight.—TUNE, Handel's March, 1761.

From No. 91 in Charles Wesley's "Hymns and Sacred Poems," 1749, vol. ii. The original forms one hymn of twelve verses, five of which are omitted.

HYMN 316.—" Eternal Power, whose high abode."—*God exalted above all praise.*—TUNE, Palmis, 1761.

Dr Watts', from Horæ Lyricæ, 1705. The original has six verses, the second being left out. It is as follows :--

" The lowest step above Thy seat,
  Rises too high for Gabriel's feet.
  In vain the tall archangel tries,
  To reach thine height with wondering eyes."

The third verse commences thus :—

" Thy dazzling beauties whilst he sings,"

which Mr Wesley has greatly improved by altering to—

" Thee, while the first archangel sings."

There is an interest attaching to this hymn for all Methodists which cannot be left unnoticed. On Sunday morning, Jan. 23, 1855, the Rev. Dr Beaumont prepared to preach, in Waltham Street Chapel, Hull, the anniversary sermons for the Sunday school. He had been suffering much from acute rheumatism, and had declined taking any medicine for relief that morning, lest it should distress him in his work. The morning was cold, and the street slippery with the frozen snow, yet, with the aid of one of his daughters, he reached the chapel safely, making but few observations by the way. On entering the vestry, he made inquiries about the condition of the schools, for whose aid he was about to preach. He ascended the pulpit-stairs with elasticity, in order as much as possible to conceal the lameness

M

from which he was suffering.   He opened the service with much solemnity, giving out Hymn 316, commencing—

> " Eternal Power, whose high abode."

Without reading the first verse, he gave out the first two lines of the second—

> " Thee, while the first archangel sings,
> He hides his face behind his wings."

These lines he delivered with an awful pathos, his lips quivering as he uttered the solemn words. His emotion was doubtless increased by the loosening of the silver cord of life at that moment. Whilst the congregation were singing the second of those lines, the preacher looked partially round (as if in search of something), sank down on the spot where he stood, and his beautiful spirit was at once admitted to chant the praises of God before His throne in heaven, and to witness that beatific vision which leads even the " first archangel " in heaven to " hide his face behind his wings."   Without a sound, or sigh, or motion, or without even a single instant's premonition, did that eminent servant of God pass away to the skies, with a mind full of sweet peace and steadfast trust, overflowing with sacred joy in the full performance of his holy duties.

HYMN 317.—"*Ah, Lord, with trembling I confess.*"—*Matthew v.* 13.—TUNE, Welling, 1761.

Forms No. 30 of Charles Wesley's " Short Scripture Hymns," vol. ii.   This hymn has long been " a stone of stumbling and a rock of offence " to many Calvinists.

Forty years of the active life of John Early were devoted to God ; during the whole of which, he was the chief support of the cause of Methodism in Witney.   For several of his latter years, he was deprived of his sight, and was otherwise infirm, but in all these sufferings he complained not, for God was the strength of his heart and his portion.   In his last illness he was very happy ; praising God, speaking of the precious blood of Jesus, and quoting the promises of God, and a couplet of a favourite hymn—

> " And lead me to the mount above,
> Through the low vale of humble love."

His last words were—" I feel that heaven is my home."

HYMN 318.—"A charge to keep I have."—*Leviticus* viii. 35.—
TUNE, Olney, 1761.

This is No. 188 of Charles Wesley's "Short Scripture Hymns," vol. i. ; a hymn full of weighty and impressive thought, and often sung ; a great favourite, as it will ever remain, owing to its special adaptation to the experience of life.

HYMN 319.—"Watch'd by the world's malignant eye."—
Nehemiah v. 9.—TUNE, Welsh, 1761.

Charles Wesley's, forming No. 685 of "Short Scripture Hymns," vol. i. It shows the poet's great power of embodying Gospel duty and principle upon Old Testament history.

HYMN 320.—"Be it my only wisdom here."—"*Behold the fear of the Lord, that is wisdom,*" &c.—TUNE, Chapel, 1761.

Charles Wesley's, forming No. 757 of "Short Scripture Hymns," vol. i., founded on Job xxviii. 28.

HYMN 321.—"Summon'd my labour to renew."—*To be sung at work.*—TUNE, Mitcham, 1761.

Charles Wesley's, from "Hymns and Sacred Poems," 1739, page 194. This hymn commences the Fifth Section, with the title—"For Believers Working."

HYMN 322.—"Servant of all, to toil for man."—*To be sung at work.*—TUNE, Bexley, 1761.

Charles Wesley's, from "Hymns and Sacred Poems," 1739, page 193. The first verse of the original, omitted, reads as follows :—

> "Son of the carpenter, receive
> This humble work of mine ;
> Worth to my meanest labour give
> By joining it to Thine."

HYMN 323.—"God of almighty love."—*An Hourly Act of Oblation.*—TUNE, Lampes, 1746.

Charles Wesley's, forming No. 149 in "Hymns and Sacred Poems," 1749, vol. i.

In the third verse of the original the first line is, "Spirit of grace inspire," and the last line is, "A worm into a god." The alterations are to be preferred; but the idea conveyed in the last line exactly corresponds with a passage in the first book of Young's "Night Thoughts"—

> " How poor, how rich, how abject, how august,
> How complicate, how wonderful, is man !
>
> Midway from nothing to the Deity !
> A beam ethereal, sullied, and absorpt !
> Though sullied and dishonour'd, still divine !
> Dim miniature of greatness absolute !
> An heir of glory, a frail heir of dust !
> Helpless immortal, insect infinite !
> A worm ! a god !"

Young, as a poet, was a favourite with the Wesleys, but probably both Young and the Wesleys had in their minds the recollection of the words of the Saviour, " Is it not written in your law, I said, Ye are gods ?" John x. 34; see also Gen. i. 26.

HYMN 324.—" Forth in Thy name, O Lord, I go."—*Before Work.*
—TUNE, Angels' Song, 1761.

Charles Wesley's, forming No. 144 in "Hymns and Sacred Poems," 1749, vol. i.

HYMN 325.—" Lo! I come with joy to do."—*For a Believer in Worldly Business.*—TUNE, Kingswood, 1761.

One of Charles Wesley's " Redemption Hymns."

HYMN 326.—" Captain of Israel's host, and Guide."—*Exodus* xii. 21.—TUNE, Norwich, 1761.

Forms No. 133 of Charles Wesley's " Short Scripture Hymns," vol. i.

HYMN 327.—" O Thou who camest from above."—*Leviticus* vi. 13.—TUNE, Palmis, 1761.

Forms No. 183 of Charles Wesley's " Short Scripture Hymns," vol. i.

The words here versified are, " The fire shall ever be burning upon the altar ; it shall never go out." Samuel Bradburn, in his sketch of the character of the founder of Methodism, says, " The Rev. John Wesley told me, when with him in Yorkshire,

in the year 1781, that his experience might always be found in
the following lines :—

> " 'O Thou who camest from above,
>   The pure celestial fire to impart,
> Kindle a flame of sacred love
>   On the mean altar of my heart.
>
> " ' There let it for Thy glory burn
>   With inextinguishable blaze ;
> And trembling to its source return,
>   In humble prayer and fervent praise.'

That flame of sacred love was always kept burning in Mr
Wesley's heart, and it always kept him in the path of duty,
which was the path of safety.   Hence, when, on another occasion, he was asked how he would act if he knew that in two days
he must die, he simply repeated the programme of the duties he
had marked out in his diary for those days."

In early childhood, Eliza Hill, of York, grand-daughter of
Richard Burdsall, gave her heart to the Lord, and His service
ever after became her chief joy.   Her reliance on the merit and
death of Christ was habitual ; her sense of acceptance with God
was generally clear, and her peace and joy unbroken.   Knowing
the shortness of life and certainty of death, she crowded her
life's short day with works of faith and labours of love.   The
night before she died, she sang the hymn through, commencing—

> " O Thou who camest from above,"

and ending with—

> " Ready for all Thy perfect will,
>   My acts of faith and love repeat,
> Till death Thy endless mercies seal,
>   And make the sacrifice complete."

On the last day of her earthly pilgrimage, she was sending out
garments to the poor.   She lived only a few hours after a seizure
of paralysis.

HYMN 328.—" When quiet in my house I sit."—*Leviticus* vi. 7.
                    TUNE, Canterbury, 1761.

Formed of four of Charles Wesley's " Short Scripture
Hymns," vol. i., Nos. 289–292, based on these words, " Thou
shalt talk of them when thou sittest in thy house ; when thou
walkest by the way ; when thou liest down ; and when thou

risest up." This, like many other hymns in the collection, has, in every verse and line, been made a blessing to some of the Lord's people.

Previous to the introduction of Methodism into Fakenham and Walsingham, in Norfolk, in 1781, by Mr Wesley, there were none but female preachers in that locality ; but twelve of these eminently holy gifted women were the means of kindling the fire of the Lord, till the work spread, and many villages and towns were blessed by the revival which followed their labours. Amongst the converts resulting from these labours were many of the relatives and friends of Ann Hill Taylor, who afterwards became the wife of the Rev. George Taylor. One of these converts was her mother's brother, Josiah Hill, who became an eminent Methodist preacher ; another was his brother, James Hill, a third was also named James Hill, all three of whom adorned the Christian profession during long lives. A fourth, Mr Harrison, became a useful local preacher : then followed a sister, who became the wife of Richard Fisher, a Methodist preacher, and mother of Thomas R. Fisher, also a Methodist preacher. The parents of Ann Hill Taylor also shared in the rich outpouring of the Spirit of God ; and she herself partook of the heavenly fire, which consumed the sin from the soul, and produced a life devoted to God and to His service. When scarcely twenty years of age, she was made the leader of a class, and wisely used the office for many years. Her love to the Word of God was great : she studied its truth, lived in obedience to its precepts, partook largely of its blessings, and drank in its hallowed inspirations, diffusing as a consequence light and joy on every hand. From youth she almost daily sang—

> " When quiet in my house I sit,
>   Thy book be my companion still ;
> My joy Thy sayings to repeat,
>   Talk o'er the records of Thy will,
> And search the oracles divine,
> Till every heart-felt word be mine.'

She delighted in the services of the sanctuary, and especially in prayer meetings, and for many years attended one held at an early hour on the Sabbath morning. Her life was one of sincerity, integrity, usefulness, and prayer.

In very early life, Ann, the wife of the Rev. William Naylor, devoted herself to the Lord, and through many years maintained a close and uniform walk with God. In the church she was ready for every good work, and her labours of love were blessed to many. As a class-leader she was diligent, faithful, and successful. The Word of God was her daily companion ; and she was accustomed to sing—

> " O may the gracious words divine
> Subject of all my converse be :
> So will the Lord his follower join,
> And walk and talk Himself with me."

By her life, she taught her family how to live, and in her death, which took place at' Hammersmith, showed how peacefully the Christian can die. Her last words were, speaking of heaven, " My treasure and my heart is there."

Music, which has been the charm of so many, has been the snare of many more. Samuel Potter, of Culmstock, Devon, was for some years a member of the choir in the parish church, and often during that period resisted the strivings of the Spirit of God, by his love of the frivolity of his companions. A letter containing earnest godly advice, from a relative of his, the venerable John Moon, one of the early Methodist preachers, was to his guilty conscience like the message of Nathan to David ; he left his ungodly companions, joined the Methodists, found peace in believing, opened his house for preaching, and ever afterwards devoted his best efforts to the extension of the work of God. On the last Sabbath he spent on earth, he called his family together for evening prayer, and they sang at his request the whole of Cowper's hymn which begins—

> " God moves in a mysterious way."

Having closed the devotions of the day, he sang for himself, as he had done on many previous occasions, the verse—

> " Oft as I lay me down to rest,
> O may the reconciling word
> Sweetly compose my weary breast !
> While, on the bosom of my Lord,
> I sink in blissful dreams away,
> And visions of eternal day."

He was very fervent in prayer the evening before he died, and rested peacefully during the night. Rising in the morning refreshed, he cheerfully said, "Well, I think my work is almost done," and before he left his bed-side, the messenger of mercy arrived, he quietly sank down on the bed, and fell asleep in the Lord. Crowds from the surrounding villages attended his funeral to do honour to the memory of a useful godly man.

Methodism was introduced into Beeston, chiefly through the residence there of Mr and Mrs Kirkland. When residing in Nottingham, Mrs Kirkland was brought to Christ by means of a sermon preached in Halifax Place Chapel, by the Rev. Edward Hare. In 1819, on removing to Beeston, Mr Kirkland opened a room on his ground for preaching. The cause grew and prospered, until a large chapel was erected, in which twelve classes of members were gathered, and a large Sunday-school established. Two of these classes were met by Mrs Kirkland, whose life was marked by so many of the fruits of the Spirit, that one of her neighbours said of her, "she had for many years lived next door to heaven, and had only to step over the threshhold." During many of her later years, she every evening repeated the verse—

> " Rising to sing my Saviour's praise,
>   Thee may I publish all day long ;
>   And let Thy precious word of grace
>   Flow from my heart, and fill my tongue ;
>   Fill all my life with purest love,
>   And join me to the Church above."

That prayer was fulfilled in her life : and after a short illness, she departed to be " for ever with the Lord."

HYMN 329 —" Thee, Jesus, full of truth and grace."—*The Trial of Faith.*—TUNE, Wednesbury, 1761.

Charles Wesley's, from " Hymns and Sacred Poems," 1749, vol. ii., No. 18. The original is in two double verses, and is evidently founded on the fiery trial of the three Hebrew children in Babylon and their astonishing deliverance.

"The doctrine of a particular providence," observes Mr D. Creamer, " which breathes throughout Charles Wesley's poetry, is very forcibly expressed in the second stanza of this hymn—

> ' We now Thy guardian presence own,
>   And walk unburn'd in fire.' "

This hymn commences the sixth section of the book, with the title, " For Believers Suffering."

At the early age of twelve, John Elam, of Fartown, Huddersfield, gave himself to the Lord, and ever afterwards, his unceasing efforts to do good gave abundant evidence of a renewed heart. He became a useful Sunday-school teacher, a successful local preacher, and for a few years was an earnest preacher in the itinerant ministry. When seized by illness, he continued to preach till within fourteen days of his death. His sufferings were severe, but borne with Christian fortitude. Shortly before he died, he lifted his eyes toward heaven, and began to repeat the hymn—

> " Thee, Jesus, full of truth and grace," &c.

On coming to the third verse, he changed the pronoun, and continued the hymn with emphasis thus—

> " Thee, Son of Man, by faith I see,
> And glory in my guide,
> Surrounded and upheld by Thee,
> The fiery test abide," &c.

In this spirit of resignation, he waited but a few hours longer, and the spirit returned to God who gave it.

When about sixteen years of age, Miss Barritt, wife of the Rev. J. W. Barritt, was enabled to give her heart to the Lord, and her life to His service. Cheerfully relinquishing the pleasures of the gay, in which she had found delight, she left all that was merely worldly to follow the Lord. When she became a pastor's wife, she found many ways of usefulness in the Church; and she was especially helpful in forming new classes, and many members whom she gathered into the fold will, in the last day, be the crown of her rejoicing. She patiently endured illness for three months; and when conscious that her end was near, she summoned her family for a farewell act of worship. Hymn 329 she selected to be sung, and on coming to the last verse, her voice was heard clearly and distinctly singing forth—

> " The fire our graces shall refine,
> Till, moulded from above,
> We bear the character divine,
> The stamp of perfect love."

This was her last song upon earth; shortly after, her speech failed, and she quietly passed into the heaven of rest.

HYMN 330.—" Saviour of all, what hast Thou done !"—*The Trial of Faith.*—TUNE, 23d Psalm, 1761.

Charles Wesley's, forming No. 6 of " Hymns and Sacred Poems," 1749, vol. ii. There is a mighty power of poetic imagination in this fine hymn, particularly in the closing lines—

> " I take my last triumphant flight
> From Calvary's to Sion's height."

An " old disciple," of a cheerful disposition, was John Webster, of Leeds. Having good health, an active mind, an intense love to Christ, and an anxious desire to bring sinners to Christ, he devoted himself, and much of his income, to promoting the cause of God. He joined the Methodist Society in 1780, and was a class-leader for forty years. On one Sunday afternoon, he met his class with more than his usual fervour and affection. In the evening he attended the service at Brunswick Chapel, in good health, and joined heartily in singing the concluding verse of Hymn 330—

> " This is the strait and royal way
> That leads us to the courts above," &c.

He knelt down with the congregation to pray, and whilst so engaged he was heard to groan, and, without speaking a word he ceased to breathe.

HYMN 331.—" Thou, Lord, hast blest my going out."—*After a Journey.*—TUNE, Leeds, 1761.

Charles Wesley's, from " Hymns and Sacred Poems," 1740, page 128. In the original, three hymns follow each other—" On a Journey," hymn 214 ; " After a Journey," hymn 331 ; " At Lying Down," hymn 227.

HYMN 332.—" Master, I own Thy lawful claim."—*If any man will come after me.*—TUNE, Marienbourn, 1761.

Charles Wesley's, from " Hymns and Sacred Poems," 1749, vol. ii., No. 13. The original has eleven verses, six of which are omitted, and in some of them the more glaring sins of that age as well as of this, are fearlessly exposed.

HYMN 333.—"Come on, my partners in distress."—*For the Brotherhood.*—TUNE, Snowsfields, 1761.

Charles Wesley's, forming No. 22 in "Hymns and Sacred Poems," 1749, vol. ii. The third verse of the original is left out. This hymn is distinguished for its special adaptation to the circumstances of the tried and suffering people of God. Montgomery says of the hymn that it anticipates the strains of the redeemed, "and is written almost in the spirit of the Church triumphant." Two or three only out of many examples, illustrative of the value of this hymn, can be here given; others will be found referred to in the Biographical Index.

Under date of "Coleraine, June 7, 1778," Mr Wesley writes particulars of "a pleasing sight." A young gentlewoman entered into the Methodist Society there, as the result of Mr Wesley's first preaching in that town in the open air. Unexpectedly meeting her sister in the preaching-room, she fell upon her neck, wept over her, and could only say, "O sister, sister!" and sank down on her knees to praise God. Both sisters were in tears, so were many others in the room; Mr Wesley himself was so affected that he hastened into another apartment to conceal his emotion and to praise God. These two sisters were Ann Young and Isabella Young. Ann became the beloved wife of the estimable and venerable Henry Moore, one of Mr Wesley's executors; and Isabella became the wife of another excellent Methodist preacher, Thomas Rutherford. There did not live a person who stood higher in Mr Wesley's estimation, for every grace and virtue which can adorn humanity, than Ann Moore; nor was she less beloved by Mrs Charles Wesley, Dr Adam Clarke, and by other distinguished Methodists who knew her. In her last illness she had no desire but "to depart and be with Christ;" and when, on one occasion, reference was made to some dear departed relatives, she said she should soon see them all in heaven; and, addressing Mrs Rutherford, said, "Sing,

> 'Come on, my partners in distress,
> My comrades through the wilderness,
> Who still your bodies feel,'" &c.

Nearly her last words to her husband were, "God is good; God is love; glory be to the Father, and to the Son, and to the

Holy Ghost." She peacefully entered into rest, with a heavenly smile resting on her countenance ; and her remains were deposited with those of her honoured husband, close to the east wall of City Road grave-yard, behind the chapel.

Amongst the "noble army of martyrs," few will occupy a more prominent position than the missionary of the cross ; and amongst that self-denying band, few will take higher rank than those of ·Sierra-Leone. Three successive terms of service in Western Africa were undertaken and completed by Thomas Dove. Up to that period, 1846, no missionary had rendered so much service in that terrible climate, and escaped with his life. He was converted in early life, received his first ticket from the Rev. John Gaulter, when president of the Conference, became a useful local preacher, and was encouraged by the Rev. Dr Adam Clarke to offer himself for the mission work. The record of his labours, as furnished by his brethren, is an ample testimony that he loved the "happy toil," and was abundantly owned and blessed. Through the mercy of God, he was permitted to return to England, after seeing so many colleagues fall in the foreign field around him, and occupied several home circuits with acceptance ; but the toil of that service induced a somewhat premature termination of his useful labours. He bowed in submission to the Divine will ; and in his severest pain and weakness, only a short time before his death, he said—

> " Who suffer with our Master here,
> We shall before His face appear,
> And by His side sit down."

On the day of his death he said, " I have not a cloud on my mind ; I die at peace with God and all mankind." Afterwards he said, " I shall soon be landed," and in twenty minutes he expired without a sigh.

Amongst the connecting links uniting the Methodism of Mr Wesley with that of his immediate successors, none held a more useful position than Thomas Cordeux, the official printer to the connexion. Mrs Cordeux was a most excellent, useful, and exemplary Christian, in early life seeking the kingdom of heaven and its righteousness, and finding all other blessings attendant thereupon. Their journal is a most interesting record of Christian experience. When illness had prostrated her strength, and death was near, she said, " Lord, I am Thine, and Thou art mine." Her husband, seeing that life was ebbing fast, said—

> "Your conflicts here will soon be past!"

To which she most distinctly rejoined—

> " And you and I ascend at last,
> Triumphant with our Head."

With these words she closed her earthly career. The venerable man, her husband, lived many years afterwards, and died triumphing through Christ.

In the *Wesleyan Magazine* is an account of Miss Barbara Jewitt, of whom we read as follows : " On the day of her death she was sitting in the chair, in which she had sat for three weeks, and broke out into singing in a loud tone the delightful hymn—

> " 'On Jordan's stormy banks I stand,
> And cast a wishful eye
> To Canaan's fair and happy land,
> Where my possessions lie.'

Her relatives were alarmed, for she had only been able to speak in a whisper for some weeks. After singing half-an-hour, she requested Hymn 383 to be given out—

> " 'Come on, my partners in distress,' &c.,

in the singing of which she joined at intervals with earnestness. 'Sing on, sing on,' she frequently said to her friends. Then, as if talking to angelic spirits, she said, 'Stay, stay, I am not ready yet.' She requested the hymn to be sung—

> " 'O glorious hope of perfect love,' &c.

Her sight now failed her, and she asked her friends to come nearer and sing on. Whilst they were thus engaged she waved her hand round in triumph, and with much emphasis sang—

> " 'And makes me for some moments feast
> With Jesu's priests and kings.'

She then fell back in her chair, and in a moment her spirit fled to the skies."

HYMN 334.—"Lord, I adore Thy gracious will."—"*The Lord hath said unto him, Curse David.*"—TUNE, Snowsfields, 1761.

Forms No. 519 of Charles Wesley's "Short Scripture Hymns," vol. i., founded on 2 Sam. xvi. 10.

Dr Adam Clarke gives frequent commendation of the poetry

of Charles Wesley in his "Notes on the Bible;" and on this short hymn the discriminating biblical critic makes these observations in his notes on this passage of Holy Writ : "No soul of man can suppose that ever God bade one man to curse another, much less that he commanded such a wretch as Shimei to curse such a man as David ; but this is a peculiarity of the Hebrew language, which does not always distinguish between, permission and commandment. Often the Scripture attributes to God what He only permits to be done, or what in the course of His providence He does not hinder. David, however, considers all this as being permitted of God for his chastisement and humiliation." The doctor then quotes this hymn with these words : "I cannot withhold from my readers a very elegant poetic paraphrase of this passage, from the pen of the Rev. Charles Wesley, one of the first of Christian poets."

HYMN 335.—"Cast on the fidelity."—*For a woman near the time of her travail.*—TUNE, Kingswood, 1761.

Forms one of Charles Wesley's "Hymns for a Family," page 54. In the second verse there is a spirited personification of mercy, death, pain, and sorrow.

Many who visited Margate a few years ago were struck, on entering the Wesleyan chapel, with the appearance of two brothers, both in the evening of life, one of whom read the liturgy with deep and reverent feeling, while the other led the responses of the congregation. One of these was George Rowe, who early gave his heart to the Lord, and became a useful member of the Methodist Society, conducting a class for nearly forty years, and serving the offices of Society and Circuit Steward with efficiency. When laid aside by illness, he retained his confidence in God, and when near his end, his brother visited and prayed with him, and at the close of the prayer he uttered the beautiful lines—

" Cast on the fidelity Of my redeeming Lord,
    I shall His salvation see, According to His word :
    Credence to His word I give ; My Saviour in distresses past
    Will not now His servant leave, But bring me through at last."

His faith was nourished by devout meditation and prayer, and in peace he entered heaven.

One of the worthies of Methodism in Nottingham was Mr Sampson Biddulph, M.R.C.P. At the early age of eighteen, he was brought to a knowledge of the truth in the Methodist chapel at Hockley, was admitted on trial by the Rev. J. S. Pipe, and received his first member's ticket from the holy William Bramwell, who ever afterwards was his friend. He took an active part in the first missionary meeting held at Nottingham, and in whatever tended to spread the knowledge of divine truth, and promote personal holiness. The parties held in Methodism in his days were really means of grace ; the time was spent in Christian communion and in prayer ; this was their delight, and the secret of their power, and one result was, that often in those days from fifteen to twenty thousand members, and even more, were annually added to the Church. In his last illness, and on the last Sabbath he spent on earth, he said, " I now feel the power of grace to sustain me ; " and afterwards, whilst being supported in bed, he tried to repeat—

> " Cast on the fidelity Of my redeeming Lord,
> I shall His salvation see," &c.

Here his voice failed ; but a friend read the hymn through, which eminently expressed the feelings of his heart, and in this spirit he departed, to be " for ever with the Lord."

The parents of Mrs D. Bealey were both intimate personal friends of Mr Wesley in London. In early life she resided on the Continent, enduring many trials. Returning to England in 1800, Miss Marsden became the wife of Mr Richard Bealey, of Radcliffe, near Manchester. During sixty years, this family has rendered most important and substantial help to Methodism in Bury, and around that locality. Mrs Bealey was called to suffer the separation from several members of her family, and ultimately her own health gave way, and this confined her much at home. Through these trials she found great consolation in reading the Scriptures and Wesley's Hymns. Every night she used to have two or three hymns read to her, until she could repeat them from memory. A few days before her death, whilst her sufferings were most acute, she was relieved by verses of Scripture or hymns. She frequently repeated two lines from her favourite hymn, the 335th—

> " To Thy bless'd will resign'd,
> And stay'd on that alone."

And when memory failed, every few minutes she would say,

"Repeat *my* lines." In perfect calm, without a struggle, her redeemed spirit returned in triumph to God.

HYMN 336.—" Father, in The name I pray."—*For a Woman near the time of her travail.*—TUNE, Kingswood, 1761.

Charles Wesley's, from "Hymns for a Family," page 54. The first and second verses of the original are left out. Objection has often been taken to the last line of the first verse, "And agony is heaven." The severity of the contrast implied in the language used we may become more reconciled to, when the design for which the hymn was written is known. This is expressed in the title. Under any circumstances, can it be shown that "agony is heaven"?

The influence of Methodism, in promoting the salvation of the members of its homes, compares favourably with that of other sections of the Christian Church. One example of the truth of this opinion may be found in the blessed effect following the home training in the domestic circle of Mr George Osborn, of Rochester. At the age of eighteen he gave his heart to the Lord, and during the rest of his life he became the most active and influential member of the Methodist society in his native city. On several occasions he had the privilege of meeting Mr Wesley, and on one of the visits of that excellent man to the locality, he walked with a few friends to one of the hills behind the town of Chatham, from which a delightful prospect of the surrounding country is obtained. All were pleased, and when they had freely expressed their admiration, Mr Wesley took off his hat and began to sing—

" ' Praise ye the Lord, 'tis good to praise,' " &c.

When they had sung the hymn, they returned home ; but the lesson learned by Mr Osborn was, whenever he saw fine scenery, to praise, not the landscape only, but the Author of it also. When he was married, he had wished that the Rev. John Newton should perform the ceremony ; but the time not being favourable, the venerable city rector invited his two Chatham friends to tea with him, when a religious service was held, the happy effects of which were never forgotten. Two of the sons of Mr Osborn—the Rev. George Osborn, D.D., and the Rev. James Osborn—have occupied no mean place in the Methodist ministry now for many years, and some grandsons also are taking positions in the same sphere of labour.   For thirty years Mr Osborn, sen., led the service of song in the Methodist chapel, Rochester, with propriety, and some-times with delightful effect.   His love of psalmody was great and enduring ; and daily family worship was never considered complete without a hymn.   He held with acceptance and effici-ency in turn every office of influence and trust in the Rochester Society.   In his last illness, his preparation for the great change had not to be made ; he was ready to depart and to be with Christ.   During the last few days of his life, he asked often for three favourite hymns to be read to him, the 336th, 616th, and 624th.   Nearly the last hymn which occupied his attention begins—

> " Father, in the name I pray
>   Of Thy incarnate Love," &c. ;

and nearly the last words he spoke were, " I will trust and not be afraid."

From childhood, Mary Bailey, daughter of the Rev. John Nelson, was taught to walk in wisdom's ways ; and, when quite young, under a sermon preached by the Rev. Robert Newton, she was enabled to believe to the salvation of her soul.   She was educated for the pursuit of school duties, but her health gave way ; yet she was very useful in helping to spread the knowledge of salvation where her lot was cast.   Consumption cut short her earthly course ; but though her sufferings were severe, her prayer in the language of her favourite hymn was answered—

> " Father, Son, and Holy Ghost,
>   For good remember me !
> Me, whom Thou hast caused to trust
>   For more than life on Thee :
> With me in the fire remain,   ⋅
>   Till like burnish'd gold I shine ;
> Meet, through consecrated pain,
>   To see the face divine."

She died in so much peace, that they who stood watching scarcely perceived when her happy spirit fled.

HYMN 337.—" Eternal Beam of Light Divine."—*In Affliction.*
—TUNE, Welling, 1761.

Charles Wesley's, from " Hymns and Sacred Poems," 1739,

N

page 144. The power of the presence of Christ to comfort and heal is strongly set forth in the fourth verse.

Whilst attending a social prayer-meeting at a friend's house, Elizabeth Calvert, afterwards wife of the Rev. Richard Johns, was made happy in the pardoning love of God when little more than eighteen years of age. Shortly after becoming the wife of a Methodist preacher, she had to take charge of a class, but illness prevented her using so much active energy in the cause of religion as she desired. She was a source of much help and comfort to the Rev. Philip Garrett during the sickness which ended his days on earth. As the leader of a class at Walworth she was made a blessing to many. When illness set in, she sought recovery in change, but she soon found that her earthly labours were drawing to a close. When life appeared to ebb away, and her friends in tears surrounded her, she would suddenly break out in singing the verse of her favourite hymn—

> " Thankful I take the cup from Thee,
> Prepared and mingled by Thy skill ;
> Though bitter to the taste it be,
> Powerful the wounded soul to heal."

Amongst her last words were these—"The Lord does sustain me," and " Mine eyes shall behold the Lamb."

HYMN 338.—" Thou Lamb of God, Thou Prince of Peace."— *In Affliction or Pain.*—TUNE, Purcells, 1761.

John Wesley's translation, from the German of Christian Frederic Richter, and appears in " Hymns and Sacred Poems," 1739, page 145. The original has been attributed, in error, to both Tersteegen and Gerhardt.

Dr Richter was born in 1676. He studied medicine, and afterwards divinity, at Halle, and in 1699 became medical adviser at Franke's Orphan-house in that town. Here he discovered a remarkable medicine which yielded him large profits, all which he gave to orphan-houses. He was a remarkably plain, simple man, bent only on doing good. He began to compose hymns at the age of twenty. He died at the early age of thirty-five, and left twenty-three hymns full of spiritual thoughts, and showing a deeply-contemplative Christian mind.

For many years, John Bramwell, of Colne, lived a rigid Pharisee ; but under a Methodist sermon he was convinced of his sinful condition, and, after severe mental anguish, found pardon. He used to say that the 93d Hymn described his character and his conversion. He ever afterwards spent his time in advancing the cause of God. In his last illness he had settled peace of mind, and generally replied to inquiries in a verse of Scripture or of a hymn, some of which he much loved. To a friend who asked how he was, he replied—

> " When pain o'er my weak flesh prevails,
>   With lamb-like patience arm my breast ;
> When grief my wounded soul assails,
>   In lowly meekness may I rest."

A few hours later, he whispered, " Well, well," and died in the Lord.

After many years' laborious toil in the ministry of Methodism, the Rev. Daniel Jackson retired from the full work, after which he was severely afflicted, first by losing his sight, then his hearing, and lastly, by a painful spasmodic asthma. In the midst of these complicated sufferings he manifested Christian submission, finding relief often by quoting the verse—

> "Thou, Lord, the dreadful fight hast won;
>   Alone Thou hast the wine-press trod ;
> In me Thy strengthening grace be shown,
>   O may I conquer through Thy blood!"

He afterwards added, " I have sweet peace, sweet confidence in God ;" and with his last breath he calmly uttered, " Jesus, in death remember me."

HYMN 339.—"O Thou, to whose all-searching sight."—*The Believer's Support.*—TUNE, Pudsey, 1761.

John Wesley's translation from the German of Count Zinzendorf, which was published first in his " Collection of Psalms and Hymns," 1738, and afterwards in the edition, enlarged, in 1739, page 154.

HYMN 340.—"The thing my God doth hate."—*Jeremiah* xxxi. 33 and xliv. 4.—TUNE, Lampes, 1746.

This hymn is made up of two of Charles Wesley's " Scripture Hymns " (1762), vol ii., Nos. 1240 and 1232.

There is a remarkable thought in the third verse, " Soul of my soul." " Christ and the true believer become, as it were, identified ; for he that is joined to the Lord, is one spirit." Sir

Richard Blackmore has the same thought in his "Ode to the Divine Being"—

> "Blest object of my love intense,
> I Thee my joy, my treasure call,
> My portion, my reward immense,
> Soul of my soul, my life, my all!"

This hymn commences the seventh section, with the title of "Seeking for Full Redemption."

The death of the father of Robert Spanton, of Malton, was the cause of the son's conversion at about the age of eighteen, and for nearly fifty years he was a consistent member of the Methodist society, faithfully and lovingly filling the duties of class-leader, local preacher, and circuit steward during a great portion of that period. He never lost an opportunity to recommend religion to all he came in contact with ; declaring to a young gentleman on one occasion, that it afforded "pleasure in possession, pleasure in the retrospect, and pleasure in the prospect." He seemed to live in the spirit enjoyment of the text, "Rejoice evermore ;" and when, just before his pilgrimage was ended, he was unable to sing himself, he desired this verse to be sung to him—

> "Thy nature be my law, Thy spotless sanctity,
> And sweetly every moment draw My happy soul to Thee.
> Soul of my soul remain ! Who didst for all fulfil,
> In me, O Lord, fulfil again Thy heavenly Father's will."

"Yes," he said, "there is more divinity in that one verse than some persons write in their life-time." Nearly his last whisper was, "My heavenly Father calls me. Glory, glory !"

HYMN 341.—"O Jesus, let Thy dying cry."—*Matt.* xxvii. 46, and *Ezek.* xxxvi. 26.—TUNE, Palmis, 1761.

This is formed of two of Charles Wesley's "Scripture Hymns" (1762), Nos. 269 and 1269, based on Matt. xxvii. 46, and Ezek. xxxvi. 26.

HYMN 342.—"God of eternal truth and grace."—*Perfect Love.*
—TUNE, Mitcham, 1781.

This hymn is formed by joining three of Charles Wesley's "Scripture Hymns" (1762), Nos. 1376, Micah vii. 20 ; 174, Matt. xv. 28 ; 297, Mark ix. 23.

HYMN 343.—"O for a heart to praise my God!"—"*Make me a Clean Heart,*" &c.—TUNE, St Paul's, 1761.

Charles Wesley's, from "Hymns and Sacred Poems" 1742, page 80, founded on Psalm li. 10.

The holy John Fletcher, of Madeley, says of this hymn, "Here is undoubtedly an evangelical prayer for the love which restores the soul to a state of sinless rest and scriptural perfection."

Faint not, Christian, though the way be dreary, and though clouds and gloom be spread around—there is light above and beyond. Just one hundred years ago, when John Hampson and Robert Pillmore were itinerating in and around Nottingham, and Messrs Warwick, Willis, Kerring, and Jeffries, as local preachers, were carrying the word of life with them to the outlying villages, the prospect of success was so cheerless that one day, after preaching, one of the above-named local brethren said, as they had visited the place Calverton so long, and no apparent good had been done, they purposed to discontinue the preaching at that place. The word had taken hold of some hearts, and amongst the persons thus blest was Mrs Morley, who, fearing to be deprived of the privileges of the gospel altogether, told the preacher that he had been mistaken, that good had been done, that she, with others, desired their visits; and thereupon these few sisters in the Lord were formed into a society, which has continued in that place ever since. By the preaching of the word, Mrs Morley had been convinced of her sinful state; by the other means of grace which were set up, the class and prayer meeting, she found peace through believing in Jesus, and lived through fourscore years and five to testify to the power of Christ to forgive sin, and to keep the believer from falling. When, shortly before her death, she was asked if Christ was precious to her, she promptly replied, "O yes, precious indeed;" and then, with uncommon energy in her manner, she said—

> "O for a heart to praise my God,
>   A heart from sin set free!
> A heart that always feels Thy blood
>   So freely spilt for me!"

And delighted to dwell on the last appropriating word, "For me, for me!" With this assurance, her happy spirit went to keep an eternal Sabbath before the throne of God.

Religion does not exempt a man from trials, but it does supply him with needful grace to help him to endure and overcome them. Ball-Green, Sowerby, was known during the greater part of a century as the home for the Methodist preachers on their visits to that place ; and in the dwelling of John Haigh (whose wife was sister to the Rev. Matthew Lumb, and mother-in-law to the Rev. John Aslin), not a few of the early presidents of the Conference found a hearty welcome. This good man was often in the furnace of trial, yet, though he lived through ninety winters save one, he lost not his confidence in God ; and in all his trials he delighted in the ordinances of religion, and in the spiritual conversation of the Lord's people. In his last affliction he had settled peace, and shortly before his speech failed him, he repeated very earnestly the verses—

"O for a heart to praise my God!" &c.

And also—

> "A heart in every thought renew d,
> And full of love divine ;
> Perfect, and right, and pure, and good ;
> A copy, Lord, of thine !"

He added, "This will do, and nothing else ;" and in that spirit he entered into rest.

Clustering round this hymn are other memories sacred and precious, which it is difficult to pass by. One of Mr Wesley's chosen class and band leaders in London was Mrs Langford, whose husband was a local preacher in the last century, and of whose trial sermon, Mr Bradburn reported to the founder of Methodism, "he preached like a prince." The Sunday morning prayer meeting now held in Lambeth Chapel vestry was commenced by Mrs Langford in her kitchen ; and the first female class formed in Lambeth owes its origin to this godly woman. Her daughter Mary began to meet in class when about twelve years old, and for more than sixty successive years she remained in fellowship with the same people, and maintained an unblemished reputation. When very young she became one of the collectors for the building of City Road Chapel, and continued the good work till local claims diverted the flow of her generous sympathy. In 1791 Mary Langford became the wife of Mr Corderoy, and afterwards the mother of Messrs John, Edward, George and William Corderoy. all of whom were

or are honoured and useful members and officers of the Methodist
Societies in London.   Her husband was placed in a position of
trust and responsibility under the Government, but it involved
the employment of many workmen on the Sabbath-day.   To
this Mr Corderoy not only demurred, but positively declined to
work himself, choosing rather the fear and love of God than the
fear of any man, even the sovereign himself ; it involved the
breaking of the Divine law.   His integrity as a man was as
great as his resolution to keep the Sabbath was firm ; and his
firmness of character was rewarded by his being exempted from
work on the Lord's Day, and by his having still greater confidence and responsibility reposed in him.   In these things he was
supported and encouraged by his excellent wife, who, after she
became a widow, continued to maintain an unwavering confidence
in God.   " The Lord sustains you, dear mother," said one of her
children on the morning of her death.   Her lips moved in prayer,
" The Lord support me."   Shortly afterwards she added with
emphasis, "The Lord Jehovah is my strength."   One of her last
acts was to take her purse, and with her own hand pay for a
Bible to be used in the pulpit of a Primitive Methodist Chapel
in a village where she had lately visited.   Immediately afterwards, at her request, Psalm ciii. was read to her.   On coming
to the 17th verse the reader said, " You see, dear mother, the
promises are to your children and grandchildren."   Her reply
was, " They must seek the Lord."   She then began—

<blockquote>" O for a heart to praise my God ! "</blockquote>

but could not get through even the first line.   Her child caught
up the strain and finished the verse ; a smile was the only
reward the sufferer could bestow, as the departing spirit entered
paradise.

HYMN 344.—"Thou hidden love of God, whose height."—
  Divine Love.—TUNE, Careys, 1761.

  John Wesley's translation of a German hymn, written by
Gerard and Tersteegen.   It first appeared in the collection of
" Psalms and Hymns," 1738, also in " Hymns and Sacred
Poems," 1739.   Tersteegen wrote the fourth and eighth verses.

  John Wesley, in his " Plain Account of Christian Perfection,"
records that he wrote (translated) this hymn while at Savannah,
Georgia, in the year 1736, and he quotes the line in verse four,

commencing—"Is there a thing beneath the sun," to show his religious sentiments at that period. Dr Southey, confusing dates, gives the affection for Grace Murray as the origin of this hymn. Mr B. Love, in his "Records of Wesleyan Life," describes this hymn as the pious contemplation of a soul seeking for full redemption. In a translated "Life of Tersteegen," by the Rev. Samuel Jackson, a version of this hymn is given with two verses, the fourth and fifth, more than John Wesley had translated.

Gerard Tersteegen was born November 25, 1697, in the town of Mors, in Westphalia, and was the son of a godly tradesman, who died soon after his birth. He early showed great talents, and made progress at school; but his mother's circumstances compelled him to go to business instead of the University at the age of fifteen. At sixteen the grace of God reached his heart, and soon afterwards, in a remarkable manner, he surrendered himself to God, and became unspeakably happy. Though poor himself he gave much to the poor, so that he was often in want. At the age of thirty he began to exhort in private meetings, and soon became widely known from the simplicity, power, and excellence of his addresses. He began to travel and to address large audiences, chiefly on the love of God, till his health failed. He belonged to no sect, though the Moravians tried to secure him. He gradually became so weak as to look like a corpse, but he continued his labours till he was seventy-three, when dropsy set in, and he died April 3, 1769. He left 111 hymns, chiefly on three subjects—namely, "Lo, God is here," "God in us," and "Communion with God and Christ." This hymn, No. 344, was written by Tersteegen in 1731, and was originally in eight verses, of which John Wesley translated six. This is a decided favourite, and is printed in all the Wesleyan collections—in Mercer's "Church Psalter," in Roundell Palmer's "Book of Praise," and also in the Moravian collection, No. 669, where it will be found in another rendering, and in the original metre.

HYMN 345.—"Ye ransom'd sinners, hear."—*Rejoicing in Hope.*— TUNE, Resurrection, 1761.

Charles Wesley's, from "Hymns and Sacred Poems," 1742, page 180. The second verse of the original is left out, and the first line of the original is altered from "Ye happy sinners, hear," but the alteration was made after John Wesley's death.

HYMN 346.—"For ever here my rest shall be."—*Christ our Righteousness.*—TUNE, Wednesbury, 1761.

Charles Wesley's, from "Hymns and Sacred Poems," 1740, page 96. The original has seven verses, the first, commencing, "Jesus, Thou art my righteousness," and the second, are left out. It is also inserted in John Wesley's "Select Hymns with Tunes" in the "Sacred Melody," 1761, with the tune "Spitalfields."

That excellent, godly woman, Martha Lessey, wife of the Rev. Theophilus Lessey, and mother of the President of the Conference of that name, walked closely with her God by a life of true piety, evincing the genuineness of her religion by fruits of righteousness which are by Christ Jesus. In her last illness, and shortly before her death, when assailed by her spiritual enemy, she often cried out—

> " For ever here my rest shall be,
>   Close to Thy bleeding side,
>   This all my hope, and all my plea,
>   For me the Saviour died."

Her end of life was a triumph of joy.

One of the many losses of those self-denying men, the missionaries to Shetland, was the death of Mrs Allen, wife of the Rev. Richard Allen, at North Mavin. She gave her heart to God in early youth, and served him faithfully to the end of her days. When conscious of her end, she wished once more to see and bless her children ; but as seas rolled and mountains rose between her and the desire of her heart, she bowed in submission to the will of God. Amongst her last words she said—"My anchor is cast within the veil"—

> " For ever here my rest shall be,
>   Close to Thy bleeding side," &c.

and when articulation was failing she whispered, "O the mercies of God," and entered paradise.

A veteran of fourscore years, and of fifty-five years' service in the Methodist ministry, was John Reynolds of Penzance, Cornwall. He began to travel in 1799 with Dr Bunting and Dr Newton, and laboured with zeal and acceptance whilst

health was continued to him. He died just before the Conference, to which body he sent this message two days before
he died—"Tell the Conference I die in peace, in love to the
preachers and the connexion. I am going into eternity glorying
in the cross of Christ !

> ' This all my hope, and all my plea,
>   For me the Saviour died.' "

He left most of his property to the funds of Methodism, and
died in much peace.

Miss Frances Dalby, of Newark, was converted to God in
early life under a sermon preached by Squire Brooke. She had
a fine talent for music, but for some years she had been nearly
blind. On the last Sunday she spent on earth she requested her
sister to play her a tune once more, and to sing the hymn commencing,

> "For ever here my rest shall be,"

adding, " I shall sing it too." Her sister having re-entered the
room where she lay, she said, " You managed your part better
than I did mine. I could only sing,

> 'For ever here my rest shall be ; ' "

but she added with emphasis, " I shall remain close to the bleeding side of my Saviour." And so she passed away in peace.
But just before her departure, she had glorious manifestations of
the Divine presence to cheer her in the dark valley.

A poor but industrious man named Martin, who lived near
Leeds, had been valiant for Satan, but after his conversion was
as earnest for his Saviour. It was his custom, on returning
home from his work in the evening, to have a thorough washing,
and whilst doing so he continued to sing the third verse of
Hymn 346:—

> "Wash me, and make me thus Thine own,
>   Wash me, and mine Thou art ;
>   Wash me, but not my feet alone,
>   My hands, my head, my heart."

Several other examples of the use of this hymn will be found
named in the index.

HYMN 347.—"Jesus, my life ! Thyself apply."—*Christ our
      Sanctification.*—TUNE, Aldrich, 1761.

Charles Wesley's, from " Hymns and Sacred Poems," 1740,

page 97. The last verse of the original is left out. It is also printed in John Wesley's "Select Hymns with Tunes annext," 1761, in the "Sacred Melody," with the tune "Spitalfields."

HYMN 348.—"Heavenly Father, sovereign Lord."

„ 349.—"Where the ancient Dragon lay."

Isaiah xxxv.—TUNE, Hotham, 1761.

Charles Wesley's, from "Hymns and Sacred Poems," 1740, page 107. The original is in twenty four-line stanzas, and was divided after Mr Wesley's death.

HYMN 350.—"Holy Lamb, who Thee receive."—*Redemption Found.*—TUNE, Savannah, 1761.

John Wesley's translation, made in 1740, from the German of Anna Dober, originally written in 1735. It was published in "Hymns and Sacred Poems," 1740, page 93. The German was written for a children's school-feast. The eighth and ninth verses are not translated. It is a fine embodiment of sound scriptural doctrine.

When Oldham was part of the Manchester circuit in Methodism, and Thomas Tennant the stationed preacher in 1790, Hannah Mills received her first ticket of membership; and for half a century her walk was such as became the gospel of Christ. In her last illness her mind was kept in perfect peace, and she often called on her friends to help her to praise the Lord. The day before she died, she was favoured with a special sight of the heavenly world; whereupon she said, "If the Lord will but allow me to spend my next Sabbath in heaven, I will praise Him louder than any that are there. Oh that I could sing! I would sing my favourite verse,—

> "Dust and ashes though I be
> Full of sin and misery.'"

Then, after a pause, she repeated the third and fourth lines with great emphasis,—

> "Thine I am, Thou Son of God,
> Take the purchase of Thy blood."

Shortly afterwards, robed in righteousness divine, she entered the New Jerusalem above.

HYMN 351.—"Come, Holy Ghost, all-quickening fire !"—*Hymn to God the Sanctifier.*—TUNE, York, 1761.

Charles Wesley's, from "Hymns and Sacred Poems," 1740, page 45.

HYMN 352.—"Jesus, Thou art our King !"—*Hymn to Christ the King.*—TUNE, Irene, 1761.

Charles Wesley's, from "Hymns and Sacred Poems," 1739, page 174.

HYMN 353.—"O Jesu, source of calm repose !"—*Christ Protecting and Sanctifying.*—TUNE, 113th Psalm, 1761.

From "Hymns and Sacred Poems," 1739, page 181, translated by John Wesley from the German of John Anastasius Freylinghausen. This hymn throws much light on the doctrine of Christian perfection ; but the petition in verse five,

"No anger may'st Thou ever find,"

must be understood as referring only to sinful anger, and not as condemning all anger whatever ; for it is a precept, Be ye angry, and sin not.

John Anastasius Freylinghausen was born December 2, 1670, at Gundersheim, in the small principality of Wolfenbüttel, where his father was a tradesman and the burgomaster. His pious mother early taught him the truths of Christianity. In 1689 he entered the University of Jena, but in 1692 he removed to Halle under A. H. Francke, and became his assistant-minister at Glancha, near Halle. In 1715 he was raised to the assistant charge of St Ulric's Church, Halle, and married his god-child, Francke's only daughter, with whom he lived in great peace and blessedness. On the death of Francke in 1723, Freylinghausen was appointed chief minister of St Ulric's, and director of the Orphan Houses. He suffered much from most violent toothache, during which, however, he composed some of his best hymns. In 1737 his tongue became paralysed, and he had to give up preaching. He died February 12, 1739. He left the Church a legacy of forty-four hymns which are full of sound piety and tender godliness, combined with great beauty and warmth of expression. Freylinghausen was the chief hymn-writer of the pietist school in Germany, and collected the best hymns of all the poets belonging to that class of writers, together with their tunes, in a large book of two volumes, the first edition dated 1704, the second 1714 : it was designed chiefly for the use of the Orphan Houses at Halle.

HYMN 354.—" Ever fainting with desire."—*A Prayer for Holiness.*—TUNE, Kingswood, 1761.

Charles Wesley's, from " Hymns and Sacred Poems," 1742, page 219. The original has ten verses, four of which are left out.

HYMN 355.—" Jesu, shall I never be."—" *Let this mind be in you which was also in Christ Jesus.*"—TUNE, Plymouth, 1761.

Charles Wesley's, from " Hymns and Sacred Poems," 1742, page 221, based on Phil. ii. 5. The original has twenty verses, seven of which are omitted. The line in verse nine,

" I shall have no power to sin,"

has been supposed to inculcate the doctrine of final perseverance of the saints, but really it seems to be no more than a little extra fervour in the poet's feelings.

HYMN 356.—" Lord, I believe Thy every word."—" *They that wait upon the Lord shall renew their strength.*"—TUNE, Wenvo, 1761.

Charles Wesley's, from " Hymns and Sacred Poems," 1742, page 225, founded on Isaiah xl. 31. The original has fourteen stanzas, four of which are omitted.

HYMN 357.—" Jesus, the Life, the Truth, the Way."—"*Thy will be done on earth,*" &c.—TUNE, Brooks, 1761.

Charles Wesley's, from " Hymns and Sacred Poems," 1742, page 230. The original has twelve verses, four of which are omitted. It is founded on part of the Lord's Prayer, Matt. xi. 10.

HYMN 358.—" Open, Lord, my inward ear."—*Waiting for Christ the Prophet.*—TUNE, Amsterdam, 1761.

Charles Wesley's, from " Hymns and Sacred Poems," 1742, page 206, with the first verse omitted.

HYMN 359—."God of Israel's faithful three."—*The Three Children in the fiery furnace.*—TUNE, Amsterdam, 1761.

Charles Wesley's, from " Hymns and Sacred Poems," 1742, page 210, founded on Daniel iii. The second verse of the original is left out.

HYMN 360.—" Father of Jesus Christ, my Lord."—" *Therefore it is of faith, that it might be by grace.*—TUNE, Bexley, 1761.

Charles Wesley's, from " Hymns and Sacred Poems," 1742, page 248, founded on Romans iv. 13, &c. The original has twenty verses, nine of which are left out. The poet seeks with much care to guard this hymn against the faith of the Antinomian ; hence the faith of which he writes is obedient faith ; it waits on God in a diligent use of the means of grace.

In early life, Fanny Wedgwood, of Wybunbury, Nantwich, was converted to God ; she joined the Methodist Society, and walked circumspectly. A rapid consumption cut short her earthly career. Her sleepless nights were occupied in holy meditation, prayer, and praise. A little before her death she exclaimed—

> "Faith, mighty faith, the promise sees,
>   And looks to that alone ;
> Laughs at impossibilities,
>   And cries, It shall be done !"

" I shall go to heaven ; the promise cannot fail :" so she slept in Jesus.

Mrs Riles, wife of the Rev. John Riles, suffered a painful affliction with exemplary patience. Her husband praying by her bedside, she joined heartily, and at the close exclaimed, with great emotion—

> "Faith, mighty faith, the promise sees,
>   And looks to that alone ;
> Laughs at impossibilities,
>   And cries, It shall be done !"

Adding, " I long to be gone," and her wish was very soon afterwards granted.

HYMN 361.—" My God ! I know, I feel Thee mine.' —*Against
    hope, believing in hope.*—TUNE, Mitcham, 1761.

Charles Wesley's, from " Hymns and Sacred Poems," 1740,
page 156.   The eleventh verse of the original is left out.

HYMN 362.—" Be it according to Thy word."—" *He that loseth
    his life for My sake shall find it.*"—TUNE, St Paul's, 1761.

Charles Wesley's, from " Hymns and Sacred Poems," 1742,
page 212.   The original has twelve verses, three of which are
omitted.

HYMN 363.—" What ! never speak one evil word."—*James*
    iii. 2 ; *and Psalm* ciii. 3.—TUNE, Evesham, 1761.

Charles Wesley's, from " Scripture Hymns," 1762.   The first
and second verses form No. 753 (James iii. 2) ; the third and
fourth verses form No. 854 (Psalm ciii. 3).

HYMN 364.—" Jesus, the gift divine I know."—*John* iv. 10, 14 ;
    and James i. 27.—TUNE, 123d Psalm, 1761.

Charles Wesley's, from " Scripture Hymns," 1762.   Verses
1 and 2 form No. 413 (John iv. 10, 14) ; verses 3, 4, and 5 form
No. 738 (James i. 27).   " A fine hymn," writes Mr Bunting ;
" but patched up and disjointed, and requires emendation."

> HYMN 365.—" O God of my salvation, hear."
> "   366.—" I soon shall hear thy quick'ning voice."
> *A Thanksgiving.*—TUNE, York, 1761.

Charles Wesley's, from " Hymns and Sacred Poems," 1742,
page 167.   The original forms but one hymn of eighteen stanzas,
four of which are left out ; it was not divided till after Mr
Wesley's death.   " Several lines in this hymn," writes Mr
Bunting, " lame and bad."

HYMN 367.—" O come, and dwell in me."—" *Seeking for full
    Redemption.*—TUNE, Olney, 1761.

The original forms three of Charles Wesley's " Scripture
Hymns, 1762, vol. ii.   Verse 1 forms No. 619 (2 Cor. iii. 17) ;
verse 2 forms No. 578 (2 Cor. v. 17) ; verse 3 forms No. 713
(Hebrews xi. 5).

The mother of Mr James Musgrave, of Leeds, was a Methodist

for sixty years, and her father was one of the first members of
Society in that town. James Musgrave was brought to God
during a revival in 1797, when he was twenty years of age.
His convictions of sin were so deep, he retired into a field to
plead with God for pardon, and there he found it. Forty-six
years afterwards, at a band meeting, he testified to the reality
of the change of heart he then underwent. Several hundred
young persons were brought to God in that revival, and amongst
them was the Rev. James Blackett, and the father of the Rev.
Robert Spence Hardy. A class formed of these young men
was taken in charge by the Rev. William Inglis, whose judicious
counsels greatly contributed to their establishment in the faith.
One of his valued admonitions was, "When the world assaults
you, watch and pray; when the flesh, flee and pray; when the
devil, fight and pray." He was successively appointed a local
preacher, class-leader, and trustee of several chapels, in which
duties he acted with fidelity and judgment. Oxford Place Chapel
owes much to his activity, diligence, and benevolence; and a
tablet to honour his memory is erected within that edifice. He
was present at the great Centenary Meeting held in Manchester
in 1839, and his portrait is engraved in the great picture commemorating that event. On Sunday, May 6, 1844, he attended
the seven o'clock morning prayer meeting at the Oxford Place
Chapel, and shared in conducting the service. He selected and
gave out hymn 367—

> "O come, and dwell in me, Spirit of power within!"

With impressive earnestness he gave out the last verse—

> "I want the witness, Lord, That all I do is right,
> According to Thy will and word, Well-pleasing in Thy sight.
> I ask no higher state: Indulge me but in this;
> And sooner or later then translate To my eternal bliss."

With the giving out of that hymn, and its accompanying prayer,
his public work for God on earth may be said to have closed.
He attended the forenoon service at the chapel, and in the
evening was proceeding to the same place, when he was seen
by a person in the street to stagger, and fall. Medical assistance was obtained in a few minutes, but life was extinct; disease
of the heart had translated the Lord's servant, "to sing the
Lamb in hymns above."

The pioneer mother of Methodism in South Africa was Ann

Shaw, the excellent wife of the Rev. William Shaw. Early in
life she sought and found the Lord. The Rev. J. Wilcox, curate
of Long Sutton, was the immediate cause of her conversion, but
it was at a Methodist prayer-meeting that she found peace
through believing. In South Africa there are multitudes to
witness how holily, and justly, and unblamably, she lived during
a long life afterwards. In 1854 she was seized with paralysis.
The last entries she was able to make in her journal were the
following :—

> "O come and dwell in me!
>
> .   .   .   .
>
> And make my heart Thy loved abode,
> The temple of indwelling God."

These indicate the devout and heavenly state of her mind. She
breathed her spirit quietly into the hands of God.

  The brother of Ann Pennington was for a time a servant in
the family of R. C. Brackenbury, Esq., of Raithby Hall, where
he learned the way of God perfectly, and returned to his native
village full of love to perishing sinners, and several members of
his family became converted. Ann, soon after her conversion,
was married to a local preacher, Samuel Pennington, who was
for many years at the head of the Lincoln plan. They licensed
their house for preaching, and in every way sought to promote
the glory of God. During her last affliction she often quoted—

> "'I want the witness, Lord, That all I do is right,
> According to Thy will and word, Well-pleasing in Thy sight.'"

Her last words to her daughter were, " Happy, happy !"

HYMN 368.—" Father, see this living clod."—*Seeking for full
Redemption.*—TUNE, Kingswood, 1761.

  This is formed out of several of Charles Wesley's " Scripture
Hymns," 1762 ; verse 1 forms No. 8 (Gen. ii. 7) ; verse 2 forms
No. 197 (Lev. xxvi. 13); verse 3 forms No. 55 (Gen. xvii. 1);
and verse 4 forms No. 5 (Gen. i. 26).

HYMN 369.—"O God, most merciful and true !"—*Ezekiel* xvi.
62, 63.—TUNE, Athlone, 1761.

  This forms No. 1258 of Charles Wesley's " Scripture Hymns,"
1762, vol. ii., where it is printed in three double stanzas.

  An appreciative writer in the *Wesleyan Magazine*, 1839, page
382, refers this hymn " to one of a class including everything

O

that is contained in communion with God, whether of prayer or praise. It is free from figurative language : but how shall we express otherwise than in the language of the hymn itself the seraphic solemnity, the spirit of prayer, which are evinced in this composition—that prostration of soul before the Infinite Three-in-One, which none but the saved sinner can feel, and which seems to imitate that of the angels in heaven? It is only the Spirit in the first, and those consecrated by Him in the second place, which can search into the deep things of God."

HYMN 370.—"Deepen the wound Thy hands have made."— *Seeking for full Redemption.*—TUNE, Brockmer, 1761.

This is made up of two of Charles Wesley's "Scripture Hymns," 1762, vol. i. Verses 1 and 2 form No. 342 (Deut. xxxii. 39), and verses 3 and 4 form No. 869 (Psalm cxix. 96).

HYMN 371.—"What now is my object and aim?"—*Seeking for full Redemption.*—TUNE, The Shepherd of Israel, 1761.

This is made up of Nos. 805 and 810 of Charles Wesley's "Scripture Hymns," 1762, based on Psalm xxxix. 8, and xlii. 2, of the Prayer-book version.

Mrs Agar, of York, mother of the Rev. Joseph Agar, was privileged with the special personal friendship of the founder of Methodism, who sojourned under her roof during his last visit to York. She had then two young children, on whose heads that venerable man of God laid his hands, and blessed them. Previous to her marriage, she had been privileged to attend the Conference at Leeds in 1784, when she was edified with the conversations of Mr Wesley, Mr and Mrs Fletcher, Miss Ritchie, and others of Mr Wesley's special friends. She gave her heart to God in early life ; but after that Conference, religion was with her more than ever a reality. In her last illness her mind was kept with perfect peace. When a hope of her recovery was expressed by her friends, she answered, "For me to live is Christ, and to die is gain." And again,—" I am in great peace ; all is Rock !

> 'I thirst for a life-giving God,
>   A God that on Calvary died !
> I gasp for the stream of Thy love,
>   The Spirit of rapture unknown :
> And then to re-drink it above,
>   Eternally fresh from the throne.'"

Her last words were, " Jesus is precious ; He is with me in the valley." Thus her spirit peacefully entered into rest.

HYMN 372.—" Give me the enlarged desire."—*Seeking for full Redemption.*—TUNE, Amsterdam, 1761.

This is No. 841 (Psalm lxxxi. 10) of Charles Wesley's " Scripture Hymns," 1762. It was a favourite hymn of the Rev. John Fletcher's, when president of Lady Huntingdon's College at Trevecca. At that time Mr Benson was the head-master of that college.

HYMN 373.—" Jesu, Thy boundless love to me."—*Living by Christ.*—TUNE, Cary's, 1761.

John Wesley's translation of Paul Gerhardt's German hymn. It appears in " Hymns and Sacred Poems," 1739, and also in the United Brethren's Collection. The original has nineteen verses, seven of which are left out. For a notice of the author see under Hymn 23. Several verses of this hymn, and especially the last one, have been used as dying testimonies.

The first Methodist who visited Prince Edward's Island is believed to have been Benjamin Chappel, whom Mr Wesley mentions in his " Journal," vol. iii., page 369 :—" Benjamin and William Chappel, who had been here (at Inverness) three months, were waiting for a vessel to return to London. They had met a few people every night to sing and pray together, and their behaviour, suited to their profession, had removed much prejudice." Benjamin was a wheelwright, and, going out to Prince Edward's Island, began to call upon the islanders to turn to God. He died as he had lived, rejoicing in his Saviour, and faintly singing with his expiring breath—

> " O Love, how cheering is thy ray !
> All pain before thy presence flies."

Before he died, he saw the cause of God established and prospering on the island.

At the age of fourteen, Eleanor Dickinson received confirmation in the Church of England, and learned, by heart, prayers adapted to every circumstance of life. Wrapt in a cloak of self-righteousness, she continued till more than twenty, when she was induced to hear a sermon by the Rev. Thomas Hanby amongst the Methodists, under which she was convinced of her sinful state by nature. She began to pray, and earnestly sought the Lord, and entirely lost all recollection of the forms she had learned by heart. She was invited to a class meeting, feeling, at the same time, that her heart was "as hard as the nether mill-stone." As she entered the room, the leader was giving out the verse, in Hymn 373—

> "More hard than marble is my heart,
>   And foul with sins of deepest stain ;
> But Thou the mighty Saviour art,
>   Nor flow'd Thy cleansing blood in vain ;
> Ah ! soften, melt this rock, and may
> Thy blood wash all these stains away !"

These lines so exactly described her case, that she was greatly affected ; her mind was earnestly engaged in prayer, and before the meeting closed she was enabled to believe on the Lord Jesus Christ for pardon, and went home happy in God. After her marriage, she was providentially visited by Mrs Fletcher, who became an intimate friend, and they lived on terms of happy fellowship to the end of their lives, dying within a few days of each other. Mrs Dickinson was an example of all godliness, and the last words she was able to utter were in answer to the observation of her friend the Rev. Walter Griffith, "It is easy to die when the sting of death, which is sin, is drawn." She faintly whispered, "Yes, yes." Soon after, her redeemed spirit entered the mansions of the blessed.

It is worthy of remark, that the same hymn was dwelt upon with evident delight by the same Walter Griffith when on the verge of eternity, just ten years afterwards. Being somewhat disappointed in the plans he had himself formed in youth, he sought revenge by a determined purpose to enter the army, but Divine Providence frustrated his plans ; and when his disappointment was deepest, he was led to hear a sermon by the Rev. Joseph Pilmoor, in Whitefriars' Street Chapel, Dublin, which resulted in his being received a member of the Methodist Society by that excellent minister. He was admitted on trial as a travelling preacher by the Irish Conference in 1784 ; and the account of the labours of this truly devoted servant of God in early life is a most interesting record, as found in the *Methodist Magazine* for 1827. In 1813 he was elected President of the Conference, and continued to labour with great acceptance and usefulness till within a few months of his death. During his last illness he said to Dr Adam Clarke, "You know, Doctor, Mr

Pawson was disturbed by fears that when he and some others of the old preachers were removed, Methodism would come to nothing. I once told Mr Pawson that Methodism did not depend upon his life, or on that of any of the preachers ; that if it were a work of God, He would raise up men to carry it on. You see, Doctor," said Mr Griffith, with animation, " I spoke the truth : and never fear but that it will spread." Shortly before he died, St John xiv. and Hymn 373 were read to him, after which he said, " What a sweet chapter and hymn are these which you have read !" and with particular delight he repeated the last verse of the hymn—

> " In suffering be Thy love my peace ;
>> In weakness be Thy love my power ;
>> And when the storms of life shall cease,
>> Jesus, in that important hour,
>> In death as life be Thou my guide,
>> And save me, who for me hast died."

His weakness became extreme ; but ere his spirit departed he raised his voice in holy triumph, and cried aloud, " Glory ! glory ! glory ! The blood of Jesus Christ cleanseth from all sin. I have gained the victory through the blood of the Lamb ! " With this testimony he peacefully closed his earthly career, and entered the rest of heaven. He was interred in Mr Wesley's grave at the City Road Chapel.

HYMN 374.—" Come, Holy Ghost, all-quick'ning fire."—*Hymn to the Holy Ghost.*—TUNE, Mourners, 1761.

Charles Wesley's, from " Hymns and Sacred Poems," 1739, page 184. The first verse is repeated, in the original, as the last.

HYMN 375.—Saviour from sin, I wait to prove."—" *Groaning for Redemption.*"—TUNE, Psalm 112, 1761.

Charles Wesley's, from " Hymns and Sacred Poems," 1742, page 80. The original forms one long hymn, in four parts, of which this forms the fourth, with the third verse omitted.

HYMN 376.—" I want the Spirit of power within."—" *Groaning for the Spirit of Adoption.*"—TUNE, Bradford, 1761.

Charles Wesley's, from " Hymns and Sacred Poems," 1740, page 131. The first verse of the original, which commences, " Father. if Thou my Father art," is omitted.

HYMN 377.—"Father of everlasting grace."—*For Whit-Sunday.*
—TUNE, Psalm 113, 1761.

Charles Wesley's, from "Hymns of Petition and Thanksgiving for the Promise of the Father," 1746, page 3.

HYMN 378.—"What shall I do my God to love?"—*Desiring to Love.*—TUNE, Canterbury, 1761.

Charles Wesley's, from "Hymns and Sacred Poems," 1742, page 24. The third verse of the original is left out.

HYMN 379.—"O love, I languish at thy stay!"—*Desiring to Love.*—TUNE, Psalm 112, 1761.

Charles Wesley's, from "Hymns and Sacred Poems," 1742, page 25.

HYMN 380.—"Prisoners of hope, lift up your heads."—"*The Word of our God shall stand for ever.*"—TUNE, Frankfort, 1761.

Charles Wesley's, from "Hymns and Sacred Poems," 1742, page 232. Four verses are omitted.

HYMN 381.—"When, my Saviour, shall I be."—*Submission.*—
TUNE, Paris, 1781.

Charles Wesley's, from "Hymns and Sacred Poems," 1742, page 152. The original is in five double verses, of which three are omitted.

HYMN 382.—"O great Mountain, who art thou?"
„ 383.—"Who hath slighted or contemn'd?"
Zechariah iv. 7, &c.—TUNE, Amsterdam, 1761.

Charles Wesley's, from "Hymns and Sacred Poems," 1742, page 234. The second part, like the first, consists of five verses, of which two are omitted.

HYMN 384.—"I know that my Redeemer lives."—"*Rejoicing in Hope.*"—TUNE, Liverpool, 1761.

Charles Wesley's, from "Hymns and Sacred Poems," 1742, page 180. The original has twenty-three verses, of which fourteen are omitted.

A plain simple-hearted, unlettered, but godly man, was John

Warters, of Norton, near Malton, where he became a useful
local preacher, and lived to be at the head of the plan in the
Malton circuit. The poor uneducated people heard him gladly,
from his plainness of speech. He long prayed for the conversion
of his family, and lived to see his prayers answered. He suffered
much and severely in his last illness, but comforted himself by
quoting verses of hymns. One of his last efforts at quotation
gave evidence of his assured faith in Christ. He repeated the
first verse of Hymn 384—

> "I know that my Redeemer lives,
> And ever prays for me ;
> A token of His love He gives,
> A pledge of liberty."

On coming to the second verse, he dwelt with pleasure on the
line—

> "He brings salvation near."

Amongst his last utterances were the words, "Christ is precious
—precious Christ—precious blood—precious promises." After
a connexion of more than sixty years with the church militant,
he joined the triumphant host in the city of God.

Isaac Pape was brought to know God, in the city of York, and
made a prayer-leader and exhorter. In 1822 he removed to
Ripon, where he became a local preacher, and, aided by his
brother, commenced a Sunday-school at Borough-Bridge. He
was long a most faithful and earnest class-leader. When illness
set in, he saw no hope of recovery, and was fully resigned to the
will of God. To a friend who visited him the day before his
death he said, "Whatever you do, give your heart to God ;
and do it without delay." To another friend he said, " I have
built on a Rock, and that Rock is Christ." And to Mr Stevenson, one of the preachers, who asked if he found Jesus near, he
replied—

> " I find Him lifting up my head,
> He brings salvation near :
> His presence makes me free indeed,
> And He will soon appear."

After partaking of the sacrament of the Lord's Supper, he seemed
lost to all earthly things, and talked of nothing but chariots and
angels, shining garments, crowns, and music, shouting hallelujah,
until his exulting spirit entered the paradise above.

Hymn 385.—"Love Divine, all loves excelling."—*For those that seek Redemption.*—Tune, Westminster, 1761.

Charles Wesley's, from "Hymns for those that seek and those that have Redemption in the Blood of Jesus Christ," 1747.

The second verse of the original is left out, arising probably from two lines which are thought to be defective in doctrinal accuracy. The omitted verse is as follows—

> " Breathe, O breathe Thy loving spirit
>   Into every troubled breast ;
> Let us all in Thee inherit,
>   Let us find that second rest :
> Take away the power of sinning,
>   Alpha and Omega be,
> End of faith, as its beginning,
>   Set our hearts at liberty."

Upon the two doubtful lines in the centre of this stanza, that refined critic, Mr Fletcher of Madeley, has remarked :— " Mr Wesley says *second rest*, because an imperfect believer enjoys a first, inferior rest ; if he did not, he would be no believer." And of the line, " Take away the power of sinning," he asks, " Is not this expression too strong ? Would it not be better to soften it by saying, ' Take away the love of sinning ' ? [or the bent of the mind towards sin]. Can God take away from us our *power of sinning*, without taking away our power of free obedience ? "

As early as the age of ten years, Elizabeth, the first wife of the Rev. Francis Athow West, began to meet in class, and to none of the many means of grace offered by Methodism was she more attached than to the class-meeting. Instructed and delighted by the preaching of the Rev. Robert Newton, her joy was greatly increased when she became an inmate of his house to take charge of his children. In 1826, she was married ; and in 1829, she had some strong presentiments of changes in the family by death. The death of two of her sisters, and of Mr West's mother, confirmed these impressions, and shortly afterwards she had further indications of a similar character, which really preceded her own early death. She suffered much and severely, and was very prostrate. To her husband's inquiry, " Is Jesus precious ? " she made no reply for some time. After she had gathered a little strength, she began singing—

> " Jesus, Thou art all compassion ;
>   Pure, unbounded love Thou art ;
>   Visit us with Thy salvation ;
>   Enter every trembling heart," &c.

On the day before her death she had a fierce conflict with the tempter, but overcame by earnest and importunate prayer. She then exclaimed, " I do love thee, O God ; for I feel thy love ! " She continued spending all her time and strength in praising God and singing, till her released spirit fled from its clay tenement to the land of rest.

The desolation of widowhood was the awakening cause which led Mrs Rowbotham to seek the Lord. From a desire " to flee from the wrath to come," she joined the class led by Mrs Morley, wife of the Rev. George Morley, at Macclesfield, and found pardon whilst praying in private. Soon afterwards she became the affectionate, faithful, and successful leader of the same class. The whole tenor of her life was changed after her conversion, and her delight was in the ordinances of religion, and in fellowship with the people of God. On the day of her death this promise was constantly in her mind, " Fear not, worm Jacob ; I will help thee, saith the Lord." A few hours before she exchanged mortality for life, she expressed herself as especially sensible of the Divine presence, saying—

> "Angels are hovering round us ; "

then adding—

> " Finish, then, Thy new creation,
>   Pure and spotless let us be ;
>   Let us see Thy great salvation,
>   Perfectly restored in Thee :
>   Changed from glory into glory,
>   Till in heaven we take our place,
>   Till we cast our crowns before Thee,
>   Lost in wonder, love, and praise."

HYMN 386.—"Arm of the Lord, awake, awake ! "—*Isaiah* li. 9.
—TUNE, St Luke's, 1761.

Charles Wesley's, from " Hymns and Sacred Poems," 1739, page 222. This forms the last hymn in the work which is known as the 1739 book. It is printed also in " Hymns and Sacred Poems," 1749, vol. i., where it is in four parts, this hymn forming a portion only of the second part. This appeared at the end of the first, second, and third editions only of this work, but was withdrawn from the fourth and fifth editions, and inserted as a complete paraphrase of the chapter in the 1749 book, as stated above.

One of "God's worthies" was Mrs Sarah Benson, wife of the Rev. Joseph Benson. Very early in life she felt the strivings of the Spirit of God. When she was sixteen, she attended the Methodist chapel in Leeds, where she was convinced of sin, and was enabled to believe for pardon. From the time of her acceptance with God, to the end of her earthly pilgrimage, her uprightness and conscientiousness of conduct were manifest to all who knew her, and she was spoken of as "an Israelite indeed, in whom there was no guile." She was much and heavily afflicted in body through weakness, but her faith and patience enabled her to bear all submissively. Her last confinement was a time of peculiar and protracted trial, and occurring at the time of the Conference in 1799, her husband was unable to leave her to attend the first session, and a time of special prayer was observed by the whole Conference for the deliverance of His servant. In answer to these fervent, heartfelt, believing prayers, the goodness of God was manifested, the youngest son in the family was born, and Mr Benson was enabled to go to Conference before it was half over. That child was called Samuel, "heard of God," and was known for years as "Mr Benson's Conference Child." Dedicated from before his birth to the Lord, and by the earnest prayers of the whole Methodist Conference, he grew up a God-fearing, God-loving, and God-serving man, and has been for forty-five years one of the clergymen of St Saviour's Church, at the foot of London Bridge. In her last illness, Mrs Benson suffered much and long, but her joy and peace with God were unbroken. When she had taken to bed for the last time, she asked her daughter Ann to read three verses to her—

> "By death and hell pursued in vain,
>   To Thee the ransom'd seed shall come ;
> Shouting, their heavenly Sion gain,
>   And pass through death triumphant home.

> "The pain of life shall there be o'er,
>   The anguish and distracting care ;
> There sighing grief shall weep no more,
>   And sin shall never enter there.

> " Where pure essential joy is found,
>   The Lord's redeem'd their heads shall raise,
>   With everlasting gladness crown'd,
>   And fill'd with love, and lost in praise."

Upon this she said, " Oh, what a blessed hymn ! Let me hear it again." She then gave instructions to be buried behind City Road Chapel, and soon afterwards entered on her eternal rest.

It is worthy of remark, that the last time the Rev. Joseph Benson was out to tea, the Rev. Jabez Bunting was present, who records how Mr Benson delighted all present by the solemn manner in which he recited the same three verses, and gave a heavenly tone to the whole conversation of the evening.

A woman at Alnwick had a dream that she saw a young man sitting under the gallery of the Methodist chapel there, in a pensive mood. On the next evening, being at the chapel, and seeing a young man in the place she had seen in her dream, she sent her brother to ask him to accompany him to a class-meeting. He had previously been convinced of sin under a sermon by Mr R. C. Brackenbury in 1780, and soon afterwards he obtained pardon, and ultimately entered the Methodist ministry. Such was the commencement of the religious life of the Rev. Robert Johnson. When prostrated by illness, and expecting his death, he rejoiced in the fact that he had preached a full gospel, and especially the doctrine of Christian perfection. Then, calling for the Hymn-book, he repeated the hymn—

> " Arm of the Lord, awake, awake !
>   Thine own immortal strength put on ! " &c. ;

adding emphasis to the third verse—

> "Thy arm, Lord, is not shorten'd now ;
>   It wants not, Lord, the power to save," &c.

A perpetual smile beamed from his countenance, and in tranquillity he entered heaven.

During half his life-time, James Scott, father of the Rev. William Scott, missionary, was a useful class-leader at Lincoln. A little before he died, he said, " All is bright ; all is clear," and then repeated the verse—

> " By death and hell pursued in vain,
>   To Thee the ransom'd seed shall come," &c. ;

and after quoting the next verse, he peacefully fell asleep in Jesus.

HYMN 387.—"Prisoners of hope, arise."—*For those that wait for full Redemption.*—TUNE, Olney, 1761.

Charles Wesley's, forming No. 133 in "Hymns and Sacred Poems," 1749, vol. ii. The fourth verse of the original is left out.

HYMN 388.—"O that my load of sin were gone!"—"*Come unto ME,*" &c. (Matt. xi. 28).—TUNE, Purcell's, 1761.

Charles Wesley's, from "Hymns and Sacred Poems," 1742, page 91. It is also in John Wesley's "Select Hymns with Tunes Annext," bound with the Sacred Melody, 1761, the tune there given being "Evesham."

Having been brought to God in early life during a revival in 1837, the sympathies of Catherine Workman were naturally entwined round the young; and both in the Sabbath-school, and in her own family, her love and regard for young people was manifested in an earnest desire for their salvation. As the wife of the Rev. J. S. Workman, her zeal for the glory of God, her piety and consistent example, her love of God's Word, of prayer, and of the means of grace, won for her a circle of attached friends. Nine days of intense suffering, whilst residing at Patricroft, Manchester, terminated her earthly course. On the night before her death, Mr Workman asked if she felt Christ precious, to which she replied, "*Very,* very; full of Christ!" She then repeated, with surprising animation—

> " Come, Lord, the drooping sinner cheer,
> Nor let Thy chariot-wheels delay ;
> Appear, in my poor heart appear!
> My God, my Saviour, come away !"

She suffered much in her last hours, but rejoiced in a present Saviour ; and waving her feeble hand in triumph, with a smile on her lips, her released spirit entered the realms of the blest.

HYMN 389.—"O Jesus, at Thy feet we wait."—*For those that wait for full Redemption.*—TUNE, Trinity, 1761.

Charles Wesley's, from "Hymns and Sacred Poems," 1749, vol. ii., No. 134. Three verses of the original are left out.

It is an honourable record to the memory of James Bond, of Warminster, that from 1780, for fifty years, he acted as an earnest, faithful local preacher ; and during that time he preached four thousand sermons, and to do so had to walk twenty thousand miles. He was a man of sincere piety, and the utmost simplicity in conversation, habits, and preaching. The opinion of all his neighbours, after he had lived fourscore and seven years amongst them, was, that "he was a good man." He was able to praise and rejoice in God through a long affliction ; and just before closing his earthly pilgrimage, he raised himself up in bed, and said, " Sing my favourite hymn—

> 'O Jesus, at Thy feet we wait,
> Till Thou shalt bid us rise,
> Restored to our unsinning state,
> To love's sweet paradise.' "

His last words were, " A full reward ; but all through grace."

HYMN 390.—" Since the Son hath made me free."—" *Ask, and ye shall receive.*"—TUNE, Dedication, 1781.

Charles Wesley's, from " Hymns and Sacred Poems," 1739, pages 219, 220 ; founded on John xvi. 24.

HYMN 391.—" God of all power, and truth, and grace."
    „   392.—" Father, supply my every need."
    „   393.—" Holy, and true, and righteous Lord."
Pleading for the Promise of Sanctification.—TUNE, Zoar, 1761.

From Charles Wesley's " Hymns and Sacred Poems," 1742, page 261 ; founded on Ezek. xxxvi. 23, &c.

The whole of this fine hymn may be found at the end of Mr Wesley's fortieth sermon, the subject of which is Christian Perfection.   It was a great favourite with both John Wesley and John Fletcher, who made good use of it in their controversies with the opponents of the doctrine of sanctification. Mr Fletcher, in his " Last Check to Antinomianism," says of his opponents' antagonism to the doctrine, " it doubtless chiefly springs from his inattention to our definition of it, which I once more sum up in those comprehensive lines of Mr Wesley." Then follow the lines of this hymn.

No Christian poets but the Wesleys have so clearly stated and so fearlessly enforced the doctrine of spiritual perfection. Many have taken exception thereto. Mr Fletcher gives a reason for this, which it may be desirable to record here.   In a letter which the Vicar of Madeley had then lately received from the Rev. C. Wesley, the latter observes :—" I was once on the brink of Antinomianism, by unwarily reading Crisp and Salt-marsh. Just then, warm in my first love, I was in the utmost danger, when Providence threw in my way Baxter's treatise en-titled 'A Hundred Errors of Dr Crisp Demonstrated.' My brother was sooner apprehensive of the dangerous abuse which would be made of our unguarded (Calvinistic) hymns and ex-pressions than I was." From that time and circumstance the clearness, purity, and demonstrative power of scriptural holiness was frequently manifested in Charles Wesley's compositions.

HYMN 394.—"O God of our forefathers, hear."—*The Holy Eu-charist as it implies a Sacrifice.*—TUNE, Marienbourn, 1761.

Charles Wesley's, and appears in "Hymns on the Lord's Supper," 1745, page 106.

HYMN 395.—"O God, to whom, in flesh reveal'd."—*Jesus Christ, the same yesterday, to-day, and for ever.*"—TUNE, Invitation, 1761.

Charles Wesley's, forming No. 43 in "Hymns and Sacred Poems," 1749, vol. i. ; founded on Hebrews xiii. 8.

Of this hymn Mr Bunting observes, that it is "quite as appro-priate, and indeed more so, to a penitent sinner on his first coming to Christ for pardon and purity."

HYMN 396.—"O Thou, whom once they flocked to hear."— "*Jesus Christ, the same yesterday, to-day, and for ever.*"— TUNE, Evesham, 1761.

Charles Wesley's, being No. 46 in "Hymns and Sacred Poems," 1749, vol. i. Four verses of the original are left out.

HYMN 397.—"Jesu, Thy far-extended fame."—"*Jesus Christ, the same yesterday, to-day, and for ever.*"—TUNE, Dresden, 1761.

Charles Wesley's, being No. 44 in "Hymns and Sacred Poems," 1749, vol. i. The original has twelve verses, four of which are omitted.

HYMN 398.—"Saviour of the sin-sick soul."—*For those that wait for full Redemption.*—TUNE, Brays, 1761.

Charles Wesley's, forming the latter half of No. 116 in "Hymns and Sacred Poems," 1749, vol. ii. The original is in four eight-line stanzas, commencing "Jesus cast a pitying eye." The first and second verses are omitted. The second line of verse 2 in the hymn reads in the original, "Take away my power to sin,' which is the same as in Hymn 393.

For more than sixty years John James, of Sancreed, St Just, was a consistent Methodist, and sustained the offices of class-leader and local preacher for more than fifty years, with acceptance and faithfulness. His assurance of the Divine favour was clear, his attachment to the ministry strong, and his regular early attendance at the means of grace a consistent and worthy example to many. In his eighty-ninth year he died a tranquil and happy death. Some of his last words were, " I am on the Rock."

> " None but Christ to me be given !
> None but Christ in earth or heaven."

" Christ is my all in all." Thus peacefully he entered into rest.

The repetitions used in verse 3, just quoted, and also in the fourth verse, are no less a beauty than a peculiarity in Charles Wesley's poetry ; and the antithesis in the first two lines of verse 3, and in the last two of verse 4, taken in connexion with the reiteration of words, renders these two stanzas among the most remarkable of any in the volume, both for singularity of expression and sublimity of sentiment.

HYMN 399.—" Light of life, seraphic fire."—*For those that wait for full Redemption.*—TUNE, Westminster, 1761.

Charles Wesley's, being No. 120 in " Hymns and Sacred Poems," 1749, vol. ii. The third verse of the original is omitted.

HYMN 400.—" Jesus comes with all His grace."—*For those that wait for full Redemption.*—TUNE, Cookham, 1761.

Charles Wesley's, from "Hymns and Sacred Poems," 1749, vol. ii., No. 135. Three verses of the original are omitted.

HYMN 401.—" All things are possible to him."—"*All things are possible to him that believeth.*"—TUNE, Norwich, 1761.

Charles Wesley's, being No. 112 in " Hymns and Sacred Poems," 1749, vol. ii., founded on Mark ix. 23. Two verses are omitted. The hymn contains a clear statement of the doctrine of Christian perfection, a feature which John Wesley specially commends in this edition of his brother's works.

HYMN 402.—" O might I this moment cease."—*Waiting for the Promise.*—TUNE, Amsterdam, 1761.

Charles Wesley's, from " Hymns and Sacred Poems," 1742, page 240. Three verses are left out. The first commences—

" O the cruel power of sin."

HYMN 403.—" Lord, I believe a rest remains."—" *There remaineth therefore a rest for the people of God.*"—TUNE, Wednesbury, 1761.

Charles Wesley's, from " Hymns and Sacred Poems," 1740, p. 204, founded on Heb. iv. 9. The original has twenty-seven stanzas, and forms the last in the book. In some of the omitted stanzas there are a few rather extravagant thoughts.

Multitudes of Methodists have experienced delight in committing to memory Wesley's hymns ; but few, probably, in a higher degree than Emma Ann, the wife of the Rev. John B. Charles. At the early age of twelve she joined the Methodist Society, and when only twenty-two, she was called to exchange mortality for life. Her chief delight was to speak of Jesus ; and she would often, during her last illness, ask her friends to sing to her of Him. On one occasion, when those near were looking on her in silence, she tried to sing—

" Lord, I believe a rest remains, To all Thy people known,
A rest where pure enjoyment reigns, And Thou art loved alone."

Her last advice was, " Live to purpose," and " Meet me in heaven."

HYMN 404.—" O glorious hope of perfect love ! "—*Desiring to Love.*—TUNE, Musicians, 1761.

Charles Wesley's, from " Hymns and Sacred Poems," 1742, page 245. The original has eight stanzas, the first three of which are left out. The first commences—

" Come, Lord, and help me to rejoice."

It contains an admirable contrast between the earthly and the heavenly Canaan.

During a revival of religion at Runcorn, Sarah Rhodes, of Rotherham, was convinced of sin, whilst a girl at school. She joined the Methodists, and some time afterwards was appointed

to the charge of a class of young persons, by the Rev. Jabez
Bunting. She had been but a short time married when con-
sumption set in, and carried her to an early grave. She left
behind her a glorious testimony of her acceptance with God.
Having partaken of the Lord's Supper, given by the Rev. R.
Heyes, she was perfectly resigned and happy. She asked Mrs
Law to read her some hymns. When she had finished one, she
said, " Now then another, and let it be—

> ' O glorious hope of perfect love !
>   It lifts me up to things above,' " &c.

After hearing this, she repeated the last verse with deep emotion—

> " Now, O my Joshua, bring me in !
>   Cast out Thy foes ; the inbred sin,
>   The carnal mind, remove ;
>   The purchase of Thy death divide !
>   And O ! with all the sanctified
>   Give me a lot of love ! "

Her prayer was soon answered ; for she died exclaiming, " Victory in death : the love of God in the heart."

Methodism was early planted in Cornwall, and has been the
greatest blessing God ever sent there. When Dr Adam Clarke
was a stripling, he was stationed in that county in 1785. The
pulpit Bible and Hymn-book in the chapel at Launceston were
so torn and worn, that Robert Pearse, a Presbyterian, who heard
the young preacher, sent to him next morning a handsome Bible
and Hymn-book for the use of the congregation. William
Pearse, the second son of this good man, became a Methodist,
and contributed greatly to the establishment of Methodism in
the town, and to its extension all around. He also contributed
time, influence, and substance to the cause of foreign missions,
as carried on by Dr Coke. Going together one day to call on
a reverend doctor in divinity, a man of wealth, and a magistrate,
to plead for the cause of missions, they were coldly refused any
help or countenance by the so-called divine : and, on leaving the
room, the gown of Dr Coke was caught in the door. When
liberated, the warm-hearted little doctor said, " Brother Pearse,
I would not have that man's soul in my body for all the world."
After a consistent, upright, useful, godly life of seventy-five
years, a short illness closed his earthly career. But as he had
been accustomed throughout life to express his sorrows and

P

joys in the language of Wesley's hymns; so just before his sufferings on earth were closed, he said, in reply to the inquiry of
one of his family—

> " Rejoicing now in earnest hope,
> I stand, and from the mountain top
> See all the land below :
>
> .   .   .   .   .   .
>
> There dwells the Lord our Righteousness,
> And keeps His own in perfect peace,
> And everlasting rest."

After this he gradually sank, until his happy spirit fled to God.

HYMN 405.—" O joyful sound of gospel grace! "—" *The Spirit
and the Bride say come.*"—TUNE, Bexley, 1761.

Charles Wesley's, forming the last piece in " Hymns and
Sacred Poems," 1742.   The original has twenty-two stanzas, the
first nine and four others being omitted.   This is one of the
few hymns to which the poet has added, in the omitted portion,
a note of explanation of the terms he has made use of in one
verse.

Few can boast the privilege which was well earned by Mrs
Hay, of Louth, of having entertained the travelling and local
preachers at her house for more than half a century.   For
seventy-two years she adorned her religious profession as a member of the Methodist Society, and for ninety-two years the providence of God prolonged her life.   When prostrated by illness
she rejoiced in Christ as her Saviour, and had pleasure in quoting the verse commencing—

> " The glorious crown of righteousness
> To me reach'd out I view."

To which she added, " Yes ; I shall wear it as my own through
Jesus."   Just before her departure, she added, "Angels are come;
surely they are come to fetch me home ; " and so she entered into
rest.

Martha Meek, the mother of Mr Alderman Meek, of York,
was brought to know God when very young, and through a long
life she was a sincere follower of the Lord Jesus Christ.   When
old age and infirmities set in, she was still able to rejoice in God,
and frequently before her departure she delighted to repeat the
verse—

> "The promised land, from Pisgah's top,
>   I now exult to see ;
> My hope is full (O glorious hope !)
>   Of immortality."

She left behind her a clear and pleasing testimony that she was going to be for ever with the Lord.

HYMN 406.—"What is our calling's glorious hope."—"*Who gave Himself for us,*" &c.—TUNE, Aldrich, 1761.

Charles Wesley's, from "Hymns and Sacred Poems," 1742, page 246, founded on Titus ii. 14. The original commences, "Jesus, Redeemer of mankind," and has fourteen stanzas, the first nine being omitted.

HYMN 407.—"None is like Jeshurun's God."—*Deuteronomy* xxxiii. 26–29.—TUNE, Amsterdam, 1761.

Charles Wesley's, from "Hymns and Sacred Poems," 1742, page 248. The original has nine stanzas, the two last being omitted. It is remarkable for its admirable adaptation of Scripture history, combined with evangelical sentiment.

It was the privilege of Mrs Witty to hear Mr Wesley preach in George Yard Chapel, Hull, and also to hear Mr Benson preach the opening sermon of that renowned house of prayer. There she received her first ticket from the Rev. Thomas Taylor, in 1791, and during a long life spared no pains or cost in extending the kingdom of Christ in the world. During a protracted affliction her mind was kept in peace, and a few minutes before she expired she faintly uttered—

> "Round me and beneath are spread
>   The everlasting arms ;"

and directly afterwards entered into her heavenly rest.

HYMN 408.—"He wills that I should holy be."—"*Holiness to the Lord.*"—TUNE, Athlone, 1781.

Charles Wesley's, being made up of four of his "Short Scripture Hymns." Verses 1 and 2 form No. 631, vol. ii. ; verses 3 and 4 No. 325, vol. i. ; verses 5 and 6 No. 838, vol. i. ; and verses 7 and 8 No. 171, vol. ii.

From having been a gay, thoughtless, impetuous, worldly young man, John Anderson, through the grace of God, became one of the most honoured and successful preachers of right-

eousness which Methodism has known. Born in the garrison of
Gibraltar, where his father was a soldier, he grew up with a proud
and unyielding spirit, till the death of his mother awakened him
to a state of conscious sinfulness, and at a love-feast held in
London when he was seventeen, his convictions were deepened,
and at another love-feast, held on Whit-Tuesday 1808, at Poplar,
he entered into the liberty of the children of God. One day,
whilst reading the experience of one of the early Methodist
preachers, he became convinced of a call to enter the ministry;
and, advised to that effect by the Rev. Richard Reece, he soon
entered upon that course of useful and efficient service with which
his name is blessedly associated even to this day. In 1820, a
remarkable visitation from heaven resulted in his entire consecration of all his powers of mind and body to the service of
God, and in the entire sanctification of his nature, and this personal holiness stood alternately in the relation of cause and
effect to fidelity in the duties of his calling. Ever afterwards his
soul was full of glory. The struggle by which he entered on
this blessed experience is so full of instruction, that it may be
briefly stated here. The reading of "Rutherford's Letters" had
created a panting in his soul after God, and in that spirit he had
prepared two sermons and preached them. "On Monday," observes Mr Anderson, "I was musing on the past day's labours,
and praying for a blessing. The subject of Christ's manifestation occurred to me. I fostered the delightful topic. I longed
for Jesus to come and dwell in me. My heart was soft and tender; my soul clear and peaceful. I broke out in praise of God.
In this frame I took up our Hymn-book, and read and sang
the hymn beginning—

> "He wills that I should holy be;
>   That holiness I long to feel," &c.

Proceeding to examine other hymns in the same strain, I then
fell upon my knees, and prayed for the free gift of God in Jesus
Christ. I soon found the powerful visitation of the Spirit. I saw
the glorious fulness of Jesus Christ. I felt it was only by faith.
Satan tempted, when I was on the eve of believing, that I should
not confess the blessing. I saw the impious design, and in that
moment my whole soul opened by faith, and the plenitude of God
entered in and took possession of my heart. My full soul uttered,
'I can, I will, I do believe!' and it immediately sank into a
calm and heavenly state." Oh! for such a baptism on all the

ministers of the Church of Christ !   The glorious manifestations
of Divine power to save sinners which attended his ministry ever
afterwards should induce others of the Lord's servants to seek
the same blessed experience.

HYMN 409.—"Jesus, my Lord, I cry to Thee."—*Seeking for
full Redemption.*—TUNE, Leeds, 1761.

Charles Wesley's, formed of Nos. 299, 341, and 1004 of "Short
Scripture Hymns."

HYMN 410.—"Father, I dare believe."—*Seeking for full Redemption.*—TUNE, Brentford, 1761.

Charles Wesley's, formed of Nos. 881, 1178, and 1179.   In
the second verse Mr Bunting proposed to alter "Take, empty
it," to "Empty my heart ;" and in the next line read "My soul,
with purity."   Hymns 395, 396, and 397 treat on the same subject

HYMN 411.—"Why not now, my God, my God?"—*Seeking for
full Redemption.*—TUNE, Dedication, 1781.

Charles Wesley's, forming No. 850 of "Short Scripture Hymns,"
based on Psalm ci. 2.   The second verse is altered from "At the
close of life's short day."

HYMN 412.—"Thou God that answerest by fire."—*Seeking for
full Redemption.*—TUNE, Smith's, 1781.

Charles Wesley's, formed from Nos. 845 and 846 of "Scripture Hymns," vol. i., founded on 1 Kings xviii. 38, 39.   The first
eight lines of the original are left out, which refer to the unavailing character of the prayers of the priests of Baal.

HYMN 413.—"Once thou didst on earth appear."—*Seeking for
full Redemption.*—TUNE, Kingswood, 1761.

Charles Wesley's, made up of No. 790, and part of No. 649,
of "Short Scripture Hymns," vol. i., the fourth verse being the
first of Hymn 28 in the "Family Hymns."

HYMN 414.—"Now, even now, I yield, I yield."—*Seeking for
full Redemption.*—TUNE, Hamilton's, 1781.

Charles Wesley's, formed of No. 1197, Jer. xiii. 27, and No.
1209, Jer. xxiii. 29, of "Short Scripture Hymns," vol. ii.   The
second verse in the original reads thus :—

> "Jesus, Lord, our hearts inspire
> With that true word of Thine."

HYMN 415.—" Jesus hath died that I might ive."—" *Believe in the Lord Jesus Christ and thou shalt be saved.*"—TUNE, Liverpool, 1761.

Charles Wesley's, from " Hymns and Sacred Poems," 1742, page 95, commencing with the ninth stanza of the original, eight being omitted ; and founded on Acts xvi. 31. There are no two lines more widely known amongst Methodists than the closing lines of this hymn, which are :—

> " Thy presence makes my paradise,
> And where Thou art is heaven."

The poet Cowper has written a stanza which contains a somewhat similar sentiment :—

> " But O, Thou bounteous Giver of all good !
> Thou art of all Thy gifts Thyself the crown ;
> Give what Thou canst—without Thee we are poor,
> And with Thee, rich—take what Thou wilt away."

The truth of the declaration of the Psalmist, " When thy father and mother forsake thee, the Lord taketh thee up," was verified in the experience of Sarah Pearson, who, losing both her parents before she was sixteen, found a pious home in a Methodist family, was early married " in the Lord," and early called to her reward. After she had taken the final leave of her relatives, she said, " Oh how happy I am !

> " ' My soul breaks out in strong desire
> The perfect bliss to prove ;
> My longing heart is all on fire
> To be dissolv'd in love.' "

Whilst breathing out " faith and patience," she escaped to the mansions of light.

HYMN 416.—" I ask the gift of righteousness."—" *Whatsoever things ye desire, when ye pray, believe,*" &c.—TUNE, Brockmer, 1761.

Charles Wesley's, forming No. 313 in " Short Scripture Hymns," vol. ii., founded on St Mark xi. 24, with the first eight lines of the original left out. Mr Bunting says, that " This, with some other hymns and verses in this section, belongs properly to ' Mourners Convinced of Sin.' " The line in verse 3, " Thy fulness I require," Mr Bunting alters to " Thy whole salvation I require ;" and the last line he alters to " Shall ne'er commit it more."

HYMN 417.—" Come, O my God, the promise seal."—" *What things ye desire, when ye pray, believe,*" &c.—TUNE, Chimes, 1761.

Charles Wesley's, forming No. 314 of " Scripture Hymns," vol. ii., founded on St Mark xi. 24 ; with two verses considerably altered. Mr Bunting observes, " This hymn might be taken as an expression of the first triumph of a new-born believer."

HYMN 418.—" God ! who didst so dearly buy."—*For Believers Saved.*—TUNE, Kingswood, 1761.

Charles Wesley's, formed by uniting three of the "Short Scripture Hymns," numbered 554, 823, and 822 ; founded on 1 Cor. vi. 20 ; Rev. i. 5 ; Rev. i. 4, 5,—the transposed order being frequently resorted to by Mr John Wesley in arranging his brother's verses. This commences the eighth section of the collection, with the title " For Believers Saved."

HYMN 419.—" Quicken'd with our immortal Head."—" *God hath not given us the spirit of fear,*" &c.—TUNE, Palmis, 1761.

Charles Wesley's, being No. 655 of " Short Scripture Hymns," vol. ii., founded on the words, " God hath not given us the spirit of fear, but of power, and of love, and of a sound mind " [Gr. sobriety] 2 Tim. i. 7.

HYMN 420.—" Ye faithful souls, who Jesus know."—*Resurrection.* —TUNE, Palmis, 1761.

Charles Wesley's, formed of Nos. 625 and 626 of " Short Scripture Hymns," vol. ii., founded on Col. iii. 1–4.

HYMN 421.—" I the good fight have fought."—" *Fight the good fight of faith.*"—TUNE, Brentford, 1761.

Charles Wesley's, formed of Nos. 665 and 667 of " Short Scripture Hymns," founded on 2 Tim. iv. 7.

At the age of fifteen, Mrs Joseph Smith, of Market-Weighton, found peace in God through faith in Jesus Christ. For many years she retired several times daily to hold communion with God by prayer. She suffered from six attacks of paralysis.

After the last seizure she was very happy, and just before she expired, she repeated and sung—

> "I the good fight have fought,
> O when shall I declare?
> The victory by my Saviour got,
> I long with Paul to share," &c.

The enthusiasm which was shown in worldly pursuits by Margaret Vasey, of Whitby, was turned in its full tide into the cause of God and religion when she became converted; and as the affectionate faithful leader of a class for many years, she was made a blessing to many. When told that recovery, in her last illness, was hopeless, in calm resignation she accepted the position, and continued some time in prayer, afterwards adding, " May I bring glory to God in my last hour.

> "' O may I triumph so,
> When all my warfare's past;
> And, dying, find my latest foe
> Under my feet at last!'"

Her dying breath was a prayer for her youngest son, "Lord, save him! Lord, save him!"

In her seventeenth year, Agnes Hall, wife of the Rev. Thomas Hall, was brought to a saving knowledge of the truth through the instrumentality of Methodism, and from that time her resolution was taken: "This people shall be my people, and their God my God." As the wife of a minister, she sought in every way to extend the Redeemer's kingdom. After a brief illness, in calm resignation she lay waiting for her change, and repeated the lines—

> "O may I triumph so,
> When all my warfare's past;
> And, dying, find my latest foe
> Under my feet at last!"

Her children rise up and call her blessed.

HYMN 422.—" Let not the wise his wisdom boast."—" *Let not the wise man glory in his wisdom*," &c.—TUNE, Angels' Song, 1761.

Charles Wesley's, being No. 1090 of "Short Scripture Hymns," vol. ii., founded on Jer. ix. 23.

Hymn 423.—"Who can worthily commend?"—"*Unto Him that loved us,*" &c.—Tune, Kingswood, 1761.

Charles Wesley's, forming No. 824 of "Short Scripture Hymns," vol. ii., founded on Rev. i. 5, 6. There is a noble boldness in the opening verses which is continued throughout. The poet vividly and sweetly points out what the love of Christ has done for man.

Hymn 424.—"Us, who climb Thy holy hill."—"*Showers of blessing,*" &c.—Tune, Kingswood, 1761.

Charles Wesley's, forming No. 1263 and part of No. 1264 of "Short Scripture Hymns," vol. ii., founded on Ezek. xxxiv. 26, 27.

Hymn 425.—"The voice that speaks Jehovah near."—"*What doest thou here, Elijah?*" &c.—Tune, Palmis, 1761.

Charles Wesley's, forming No. 550 of "Short Scripture Hymns," vol. i., founded on 1 Kings xix. 13.

Hymn 426.—"Lord, in the strength of grace."—*Self-Consecration.*
—Tune, Lampe's, 1746.

Charles Wesley's, being No. 621 of "Short Scripture Hymns," vol. i., founded on 1 Chron. xxix. 5.

From childhood Charles Hulme was an indefatigable reader. At the age of twelve years his father died, and the family was brought under the influence of Methodism, by which means he became seriously impressed. When eighteen years old, by prayer and faith he was enabled to believe on Christ for pardon, and from that time used his utmost efforts to bring others to a knowledge of the truth. After passing the offices of prayer-leader, exhorter, and local preacher, he was proposed by the Rev. Joseph Entwisle for the Wesleyan ministry, and accepted, and for twelve years laboured with very gratifying success in several circuits. He had a third year's appointment at Dudley in 1823, where a violent inflammation of the liver prostrated his strength and closed his life and ministry. In his last hours he exalted Christ, and urged his friends to rely on the Saviour. He also sang with energy—

> "Lord, in the strength of grace,
> With a glad heart and free."

Here his strength for singing failed, and he repeated—

> "Myself, my residue of days,
> I consecrate to Thee."

With his last breath he was extolling the merits of the atonement made by Christ.

HYMN 427.—"God of all-redeeming grace."—*Concerning the Sacrifice of our Persons.*"—TUNE, Foundery, 1761.

Charles Wesley's, from "Hymns on the Lord's Supper," 1745, No. 139. The second verse in the original reads thus :—

> "Just it is, and good, and right."

HYMN 428.—"Let Him to whom we now belong."—*Concerning the Sacrifice of our Persons.*—TUNE, Spitalfields, 1761.

This forms No. 157 of Charles Wesley's "Hymns for the Lord's Supper," 1745.

The self-consecration expressed in this and the previous hymn is, as Dr Brevint remarks, inclusive of all which we are, and which we can give to God, even to the least vessel in our houses ; all are made holy in this one consecration, according to the words of Zech. xiv. 20, 21. The poet sums up the whole in the couplet—

> "The Christian lives to Christ alone,
> To Christ alone he dies !"

In early life Sally Thomas, of Haworth, Keighley, was converted to God, and continued to witness a good confession till called home. She delighted much in the means of grace. To the Methodist ministers, who were for many years entertained in her family, she evinced the most sincere attachment. In her last affliction her mind was kept in peace ; death had lost its sting, and she often exclaimed—

> " The Christian lives to Christ alone,
> To Christ alone he dies !"

In this spirit of happy resignation she entered into rest.

HYMN 429.—"Behold the servant of the Lord."—*An Act of Devotion.*—TUNE, Whit Sunday, 1781.

Taken from Charles Wesley's " Hymns and Sacred Poems," 1749, vol. i., No. 120.

This hymn was first published by John Wesley at the end of the first part of his "Further Appeal to Men of Reason and

Religion," which is dated December 22, 1744. That the hymn was written by Charles Wesley is certified by the fact that it is printed in the first volume of hymns published by him in 1749, with which work John Wesley's name is not associated.

The thoroughly scriptural character of Wesley's hymns has been so often demonstrated, that the Bible may be said to be embodied in the Hymn-book. Some of the more careful students of both those books have given proofs of the hymns abounding in scriptural language; indeed, during the preceding century, in which the hymns were written, some of them had scriptural proofs published with them. To show only one example of this interesting fact, this hymn was lately given by a Wesleyan minister to the young ladies of a Bible-class, to trace out the scriptural allusions therein, line by line. The result was as follows :—

Lines.	Scrip. passages.	Lines.	Scrip. passages.
1.	Luke i. 38.	13.	2 Chronicles vi. 7–9.
2.	Psalm xxii. 8.	14.	Proverbs xvi. 9.
3.	Luke xii. 28.	15.	1 Corinthians xvi. 10.
4.	Romans xii. 2.	16.	John xvii. 4.
5.	Hebrews iv. 10.	17.	John viii. 29.
6.	Matthew iii. 15.	18.	Mark vii. 37.
7.	Ephesians iii. 7.	19.	1 Cor. vi. 19, 20.
8.	1 Corinthians xv. 9.	20.	Isaiah lxiv. 8.
9.	Isaiah vi. 8.	21.	Psalm xvii. 15.
10.	Hosea xiv. 8.	22.	Psalm cxix. 6.
11.	John iii. 21.	23.	Matthew vi. 22.
12.	Hebrews xiii. 20, 21.	24.	Philippians i. 21.

HYMN 430.—Father, Son, and Holy Ghost."—*Concerning the Sacrifice of our Persons.*—TUNE, Dedication, 1781.

Forms No. 155 of Charles Wesley's " Hymns on the Lord's Supper," 1745.

" Directed by his own choice to the medical profession, Daniel M'Allum was subsequently called by the great Head of the Church to minister in holy things. In obedience to this call, he exercised his ministry among the Wesleyans until (by a mysterious dispensation of Providence) he was removed, in the midst of his years and of his usefulness, from his labours on earth to his reward in heaven." When, in 1819, he asked the consent of the Conference to be relieved from the law which prohibits the marriage of probationers, he was successful, and

he makes the following entry in his journal on the occasion :—
" As it respects temporal things, my desire is to live honestly in
the sight of all men ; and my prayer is that which Agur offered
up. As it regards heavenly things, my wish is expressed in the
following lines :—

> " ' If so poor a worm as I
> May to Thy great glory live,
> All my actions sanctify,
> All my words and thoughts receive.' "

His last testimony was, " My labours are done, but I build only
on the merits of my Saviour. I feel that Jesus died for me."

HYMN 431.—" O God, what offering shall I give ?"—*A Morning Dedication of ourselves to Christ.*—TUNE, Bradford, 1761.

John Wesley's translation of a German hymn, written by
Ernst Lange, 1650–1727, and appears in "Hymns and Sacred
Poems," 1739, page 179. The first verse commences thus in
the original—"Jesu, Thy light again I view," but it is omitted.
It forms a very earnest and plain poetical condemnation of
" the putting on of gold and costly apparel," which is prohibited
also by the original rules of the " United Societies."

HYMN 432.—" Father, into Thy hands alone."—*Concerning the
Sacrifice of our Persons.*—TUNE, Liverpool, 1761.

Forms No. 145 of Charles Wesley's " Hymns on the Lord's
Supper," 1745. The substance of this hymn is embodied in
some remarks by Dr Brevint, which generally precede Charles
Wesley's " Sacramental Hymns."

HYMN 433.—" Give me the faith which can remove."—*For a
Lay Preacher.*—TUNE, Welsh, 1761.

Charles Wesley's, being No. 188 in " Hymns and Sacred
Poems," 1749, vol. i., the first, second, and eighth verses being
omitted. The individuality of this hymn, as expressed in the
title, is confined chiefly to the three omitted verses. In the
second verse the poet breathes a " strong desire" for " a calmly-
fervent zeal"—

> " To save poor souls out of the fire,
> To snatch them from the verge of hell,
> And turn them to a pardoning God,
> And quench the brands in Jesu's blood."

Pollok, in his "Course of Time," has a passage which has a strong resemblance to these lines (Book II., line 157) :—

> "The Holy One for sinners dies,
> The Lord of Life for guilty rebels bleeds,
> Quenches eternal fire with blood divine.

HYMN 434.—"Jesus, all-atoning Lamb."—*For Believers.*—
TUNE, Savannah, 1761.

Forms No. 126 of Charles Wesley's "Hymns and Sacred Poems," 1749, vol. i. The first line of the original is as follows —"Gentle Jesus, lovely Lamb." This hymn is an extension of the sentiment of the apostle, "He that dwelleth in love dwelleth in God, and God in him."

At the early age of eleven years Georgiana Gladwin was awakened to a sense of her sinful condition whilst attending the Wesleyan Chapel, Romney Terrace, Westminster, and was, two years afterwards, converted to God, and became a useful member and class-leader, and an infant-school teacher, years before a Normal school was thought of for Methodism. She was seized with illness in the house of God, and in a few weeks finished her earthly career. Shortly before she died, she laid her hand on her bosom and said, "The Prince of Peace is here. Oh, yes, I feel Him here!" Afterwards, lifting her hands towards heaven, she exclaimed—

> "Jesus, all-atoning Lamb,
> Thine, and only Thine, I am ;
> Take my body, spirit, soul ;
> Only Thou possess the whole."

Then adding, "Yes, I am thine. Oh, what peace I feel! Well may it be called the peace of God, for it passes understanding."

The sudden death of an uncle was the cause of the conversion of John Horrill, of Higham Ferrars. From the time of his joining the Methodist Society he delighted in the means of grace, and for several years was a respected and useful class-leader and local preacher. In his last affliction the enemy was never suffered to interrupt his peace : he was always happy, and resigned to the will of God. The day on which he died he seemed to be unusually happy, and repeated—

> "Jesus, all-atoning Lamb,
> Thine, and only Thine, I am ;
> Take my body, spirit, soul ;
> Only Thou possess the whole."

He added, " He has been with me for twenty-two years, and oh! what pleasure I have had in meeting my class ! But now I am more happy than ever," and so he entered into rest.

The labours of Mr Wedlock, as a missionary in Jamaica, were made a blessing to many, and amongst them to Rebecca Ballah, of Montego Bay. She became an earnest and sincere Christian. In early life she was called to heaven, but before she departed she left a blessed testimony of her acceptance with God. To her leader who visited her she said, " Sing me my favourite hymn—

> " ' Jesus, all-atoning Lamb,
> Thine, and only Thine, I am ;
> Take my body, spirit, soul ;
> Only Thou possess the whole.' "

She sat up and sung the whole with those present, dwelling with great emphasis on the line—

> " Thine, and only Thine, I am."

" Thank God," she said, " I fear no evil days."

HYMN 435.—" Father, to Thee my soul I lift."—"*It is God that worketh in you to will and to do,*" &c.—TUNE, Mitcham, 1761.

Charles Wesley's, forming No. 168 of " Hymns and Sacred Poems," 1749, vol. ii. Note one very characteristic line of the poet's, " His blood *demands* the purchased grace !"

HYMN 436.—" Jesu, my Truth, my Way."—*For Believers.*— TUNE, Olney, 1761.

Charles Wesley's, being No. 127 in " Hymns and Sacred Poems," 1749, vol. i. The original is in seven double stanzas, the third and fourth being left out.

The affluent circumstances of the parents of John Ripley, of Leeds, did not prevent them placing their son in a position to earn his own living by his own industry. When he grew to approaching manhood, he hesitated for some time to join the Lord's people in fellowship ; but under a sermon preached by the Rev. A. E. Farrar, he saw that religion was necessary to qualify a man for business in the world, for worshipping in the Church, and for walking before God with a perfect heart. He at once joined his father's class. A short time afterwards, after

a sermon preached by the Rev. George Marsden, he was given
to realise a sense of pardon and adoption into the family of
God.   He was an instructive Sunday-school teacher, and a
useful and acceptable local preacher.   He was not strong,
physically, and one Sunday in 1828, when returning from one of
his preaching appointments, he was drenched through with rain,
and incautiously went into a chapel and sat to hear one of his
brethren preach.   He returned home ill, and from that night
did not recover his health.   During his illness he spoke as one
on the confines of heaven.   He earnestly sought till he found
the blessing of perfect love, and then, with peculiar emphasis
he gave out the hymn, which had long been a favourite with
him—

> " Let me Thy witness live,
>   When sin is all destroyed :
> And then my spotless soul receive,
>   And take me home to God "

When he had realised the full blessing of sanctification, the
weakness of the man was swallowed up in the strength of the
Christian : and he reproached himself that he had so long remained without the blessing.   He died in great peace, whispering " Glory ! glory !"

HYMN 437.—" O God, my God, my All Thou art !"—*Psalm*
lxiii.—TUNE, Italian, 1761.

This hymn is from the Spanish, translated by John Wesley
when he was in America in 1735, and first published in his
"Collection of Psalms and Hymns," 1738 ; it is also in "Hymns
and Sacred Poems," 1739, page 196.   The fourth verse of the
original is left out.

A writer in the *Christian Miscellany* for 1846 observes, respecting this hymn, "This is one which stands pre-eminent, and
which is almost unrivalled for its elevated devotional feeling, its
rich evangelical sentiment, its simple elegance of language, and
the accurate and beautiful manner in which, without any
apparent effort, the poet has interwoven the thoughts and expressions of the Psalmist in his own sacred ode."   It is a version
of Psalm lxiii.   The author has not yet been ascertained, and it
is the only one of John Wesley's translations which has not been
traced to its source.

The mind of Elizabeth Stockdale was disposed towards religion from early life. In reading religious books, and especially Christian biography, she took delight. She did not receive the blessing of acceptance with God until a short time before her death. She was alone with her husband, and they were speaking of the beauties of the hymn beginning, "Thou great mysterious God unknown," &c., when she was much affected. She asked to have the Hymn-book, that she might find her favourite hymn. With much feeling, she read the first verse—

> " O God, my God, my All Thou art !
> Ere shines the dawn of rising day,
> Thy sovereign light within my heart,
> Thy all-enlivening power, display."

She continued to read till she came to the sixth verse, when she increased the emphasis—

> " Abundant sweetness, while I sing
> Thy love, my ravished heart o'erflows ;
> Secure in Thee, my God and King,
> Of glory that no period knows."

And then, with no ordinary feeling, she repeated—

> "O God, my God, my All Thou art."

She was enabled to exercise faith in the promises of God, and to believe on Him for her acceptance through Christ. Strangely mysterious are the ways of God sometimes to the eyes of human observers. A few hours after this blessed change was realised, it was evident that death was at hand, and just before the change came, her only child was suddenly seized with croup, and was suffocated before relief could be applied, and a youthful mother and her only infant entered heaven together !

HYMN 438.—" O God of peace and pardoning love."—"*Now the God of peace*," &c.—TUNE, York, 1761.

Charles Wesley's, being No. 734 of "Short Scripture Hymns," vol. ii., founded on Heb. xiii. 20, 21. This hymn and the two following ones are of a measure so peculiar that they are very seldom used in the service of song.

HYMN 439.—"Thy power and saving truth to show."
,,   440.—"Thou, Jesu, Thou my breast inspire."
For a Person called forth to bear his Testimony.—TUNE, York, 1761.

From Charles Wesley's "Hymns and Sacred Poems," 1749,

vol. i., No. 209. The original has nine verses of twelve lines each, four of which are left out. The first line of the fifth verse reads thus :—" Thy power and saving grace to show." " Grace" is altered to "truth" by John Wesley. Mr Jackson, in his Life of the poet, and speaking of the noble and energetic lines which form these two hymns, says :—" Mr Charles Wesley has strikingly depicted the mighty faith, the burning love to Christ, the yearning pity for the souls of men, the heavenly-mindedness, the animating hope of future glory, which characterised his public ministry, and which not only enabled him to deliver his Lord's message before scoffing multitudes, but also carried him through his wasting labours, and the riots of Bristol, Cornwall, Staffordshire, Devizes, and of Ireland, without a murmur."

HYMN 441.—" Let God, who comforts the distrest."—" *For all Mankind.*"—TUNE, Canterbury, 1761.

Charles Wesley's, forming the first of " Hymns of Intercession for all Mankind," 1758. This is the first hymn in Section IX., with the title, " For Believers Interceding."

HYMN 442.—" Our earth we now lament to see."—*For Peace.*— TUNE, Canterbury, 1761.

The second of Charles Wesley's " Hymns of Intercession."

HYMN 443.—" Sun of unclouded Righteousness."—*For the Turks—Mohammedans.*—TUNE, Marienburn, 1761.

Charles Wesley's, being No. 33 of his "Hymns of Intercession."

HYMN 444.—" Lord over all, if Thou hast made."—*For the Heathen.*—TUNE, Welsh, 1761.

Appears as No. 34 of Charles Wesley's " Hymns of Intercession."

The third stanza is quoted by John Wesley at the end of his " Thoughts upon Slavery." The Unitarian and Mohammedan both denying the divinity of our Lord Jesus Christ, are classed together in this hymn ; and though the language of the poet is particularly strong against Unitarianism, yet it is not more so than the dangerous character of that heresy deserves.

HYNN 445.—"O come, Thou radiant Morning-Star."—*Balaam's Prophecy.*—TUNE, Bradford, 1761.

Charles Wesley's, made up of portions of Nos. 257, 258, and 259 of "Short Scripture Hymns," vol. i., founded on Num. xxiv., 17, 18, with two verses omitted.

HYMN 446.—"Jesu, the word of mercy give."—"*Let thy priests be clothed with salvation,*" &c.—TUNE, Cornish, 1761.

Charles Wesley's, made up of portions of two "Short Scripture Hymns," Nos. 638 and 397, founded on 2 Chron. vi. 41, and Judges v. 31.

HYMN 447.—"Messiah, Prince of Peace!"—"*Neither shall they learn war any more,*" &c.—TUNE, Olney, 1761.

Forms No. 960 of Charles Wesley's "Scripture Hymns," vol. i., based on the words, "Neither shall they learn war any more" (Isa. ii. 4).

HYMN 448.—"Prince of universal peace."—"*The wolf shall dwell with the lamb,*" &c.—TUNE, Kingswood, 1761.

Forms No. 989 of Charles Wesley's "Scripture Hymns," vol. i., based on Isa. xi. 6, 7.

HYMN 449.—"Happy day of union sweet!"—"*Ephraim shall not envy Judah,*" &c.—TUNE, Kingswood, 1761.

Forms No. 995 of Charles Wesley's "Scripture Hymns," vol. i., based on Isa. xi. 13.

HYMN 450.—"Messiah, full of grace."—"*The Israelites as dried bones.*"—TUNE, Brentford, 1761.

Forms No. 1277 of Charles Wesley's "Scripture Hymns," vol. ii., based on Ezek. xxxvii. 11, 12.

HYMN 451.—"Father of faithful Abraham, hear."—*For the Jews.*—TUNE, Mourners, 1761.

This is No. 32 of Charles Wesley's "Hymns of Intercession," 1758, a rare tract, and seldom reprinted.

HYMN 452.—"Almighty God of Love."—*A Sign and an Offer-ing.*—TUNE, Olney, 1761.

This is made up of Nos. 1157, 1158, and 1159 of Charles Wesley's "Scripture Hymns," based on Isa. lxvi. 19, 20.

HYMN 453.—"Sinners, the call obey."—*For England.*—TUNE, Lampe's, 1746.

Forms the fifth of Charles Wesley's "Hymns for Times of Trouble and Persecution," 1744; the third, fourth, and fifth verses of the original omitted.

HYMN 454.—"God of unspotted purity."
    „   455.—"O let us our own works forsake."
Unto the Angel of the Church of the Laodiceans.—TUNE, Athlone, 1781.

Charles Wesley's, forming part of a long hymn of thirty-six stanzas, in "Hymns and Sacred Poems," 1742, p. 296, founded on Rev. iii. 14–19. There are twenty-four verses of the original left out. Hymn 454 commences with verse 3 of the first part.

HYMN 456.—"Father, if justly still we claim."
    „   457.—"On all the earth Thy Spirit shower."
On the Descent of the Holy Ghost at Pentecost.—TUNE, Fulham, 1761.

These form part of a hymn written by Dr H. More (1614–1637), and altered by John Wesley. The first five verses of the original are left out; the first line reads thus :—

" When Christ had left His flesh below."

This fine Pentecostal hymn has formed the theme of a most interesting paper, in a recent issue of the *Wesleyan Magazine*, from the pen of the Rev. G. Osborn, D.D., in which the reader is presented with parts of the original by Dr More, and the altered version by John Wesley; exhibiting the masterly hand of Wesley, and how "the fulness of the gospel salvation shines out in Wesley's rendering even more brightly than the genius of the poet."

Henry More, D.D., was an able divine, born in 1614, at Grantham, and educated at Eton and Christ College, Cambridge. In 1675 he was made a prebend of Gloucester, but as

he renounced the Calvinistic principles in which he had been
rigidly brought up, he resigned his position in the church, and
retired on a small competency, refusing high preferment, which
was offered him. He died in 1687. Besides the two hymns
which Mr Wesley used in an altered form, he was the author of
"Song of the Soul," a Platonic poem, which was reprinted in
1647 with additions.

HYMN 458.—"Author of faith, we seek Thy face."—*Of Intercession.*—TUNE, Smith's, 1781.

Charles Wesley's, from No. 64 of "Hymns and Sacred
Poems," 1749, vol. ii. Three verses of the original are left out.

HYMN 459.—"Shepherd of Israel, hear."
    „ 460.—"God of all power and grace."
For the Fallen.—TUNE, Brentford, 1761.

These form together No. 65 in Charles Wesley's "Hymns
and Sacred Poems," 1749, vol. ii. The fourth and fifth verses
of the original are left out. The last line of verse 4 is
changed from "In perfect charity" to "harmony."

HYMN 461.—"Saviour, to Thee we humbly cry!"—*For the
Fallen.*—TUNE, Mourners, 1761.

Charles Wesley's, from "Hymns and Sacred Poems," 1749,
vol. ii., No. 72. This hymn appeared first at the end of a tract
on the "Differences between the Moravians and the Wesleys,"
1745. The Moravians had taught that if a person professed
faith in Christ, there was no necessity that he should manifest
any sorrow on account of sins, past or present; but that he
should acknowledge himself to be a *happy* sinner, and rest satis-
fied in that state. The term *happy* sinner being thus prostituted
to unholy purposes, was reprobated in this hymn by the poet.
Another of their errors was that of recommending an unscrip-
tural *stillness*—teaching people to refrain from the use of religious means and ordinances. This error is condemned by Mr
Wesley in Hymn 295, verse 2, in the line—

"While Satan cries—Be still."

HYMN 462.—"O let the prisoners' mournful cries."—*Hymn of
Intercession.*—TUNE, Evesham, 1761.

Charles Wesley's, from "Hymns and Sacred Poems," 1749,

vol. ii., No. 63. The original has eighteen stanzas. This hymn
commences with the sixth verse, and includes all to the fourteenth ; the first five and the last four being omitted.

HYMN 463.—" Lamb of God, who bear'st away."—*For Times
    of Trouble and Persecution.*—TUNE, Dedication, 1781.

Charles Wesley's, from "Hymns for Times of Trouble and
Persecution," for the year 1745. The original has eight stanzas ;
the first four only are given ; and the fifth and sixth lines of verse
3 are transposed with the same lines of verse 4.

HYMN 464.—"Jesus, from Thy heavenly place."—*Intercession.*—
        TUNE, Kingswood, 1761.

Charles Wesley's, being No. 1025 of "Short Scripture Hymns,"
vol. i., founded on Isa. xxxiii. 5, 6. In the first line "holy" is
changed for "heavenly," and in line 5 "salvation" is changed
for "protection."

HYMN 465.—" Sovereign of all ! whose Will ordains."—*A Prayer
    for his Majesty King George [II.].*—TUNE, Brockmer's,
    1761.

Charles Wesley's, forming the tenth of " Hymns for the Times
of Trouble and Persecution," 1744. The divine right of kings
is strongly asserted in the first verse. At the time the hymn
was written that dogma was in high dispute throughout the
nation. The opinion of the Wesleys is clearly enough stated in
the hymn.

HYMN 466.—" A nation God delights to bless."—*Intercession.*—
        TUNE, Snowsfield's, 1761.

Charles Wesley's, being No. 771 of " Short Scripture Hymns,"
vol. i., founded on Job xxxiv. 29. The first and second verses
of the original are left out.

HYMN 467.—" Father of all, by whom we are."—*For Parents.*—
        TUNE, Islington, 1761.

Charles Wesley's, being No. 63 of " Hymns for a Family."
The original is in eight-line stanzas. The dangers to which
many children are exposed by the neglect of parents are lucidly
stated in the hymn. The need for divine wisdom in the train-

ing of a family is impressively taught in the history of many households known as religious ones.

HYMN 468.—" God only wise, almighty, good."—*For a Family.*
—TUNE, Mitcham, 1781.

Charles Wesley's, from " Hymns for Families," No. 65.   This fine and practical hymn inculcates some really invaluable lessons for the proper government of a family.   The " sacred clew " of the fourth verse, which guides persons in a labyrinth, and keeps them in the right way, is especially striking and suggestive.

HYMN 469.—" Father of Lights !   Thy needful aid."—*For a Family.*—TUNE, St Paul's, 1761.

Charles Wesley's, from " Hymns for Families."   The fourth verse is omitted.

HYMN 470.—" Master supreme, I look to Thee."—*The Master's Hymn.*—TUNE, Angels' Song, 1761.

Charles Wesley's, being No. 135 of " Hymns for Families." It is written in eight-line stanzas, and is well worthy of daily perusal.

HYMN 471.—" How shall I walk my God to please."—*The Master's Hymn.*—TUNE, Snowsfield's, 1761.

Charles Wesley's, forming No. 136 in " Hymns for Families." Two verses are left out.

HYMN 472.—" I and my house will serve the Lord."—*The Master's Hymn.*—TUNE, Travellers, 1761.

Charles Wesley's, being No. 137 of " Family Hymns."

HYMN 473.—" Come, Father, Son, and Holy Ghost."—*At the Opening of a School in Kingswood.*—TUNE, Marienburn, 1761.

Charles Wesley's, being No. 40 of his " Hymns for Children," 1763.   It exhibits in a few words the true basis of education— "knowledge and piety ;" " learning and holiness."

HYMN 474.—" Captain of our salvation, take."
    „   475.—" But who sufficient is to lead."
    For Children.—TUNE, Frankfort, 1761.

Charles Wesley's, forming Nos. 41 and 42 of " Hymns for

Children," the original title being " At the Opening of a School in Kingswood."

HYMN 476.—" Come, Father, Son, and Holy Ghost."—*At the Baptism of Adults.*—TUNE, Palmis, 1761.

. Charles Wesley's, from No. 182, in " Hymns and Sacred Poems," 1749, vol. ii.

HYMN 477.—" Father, Son, and Holy Ghost."—*At the Baptism of Adults.*—TUNE, Hamilton's, 1781.

Charles Wesley's, being No. 183 in " Hymns and Sacred Poems," 1749, vol. ii. The original was written for a female, as the seventh line reads—

"Bless for her the laving flood ;"

and the feminine pronoun is used throughout.

HYMN 478.—" And are we yet alive."—*At the Meeting of Friends.*—TUNE, Lampe's, 1746.

This hymn forms No. 236 of Charles Wesley's " Hymns and Sacred Poems," 1749, vol. ii., page 321.

The fourth verse of the original is omitted ; but it is given here because of its connexion historically with Methodism, this being the hymn which has been sung, more or less, at the opening of the Conference, for probably more than a century. It is also used at the opening of the conferences of other sections of the Methodist family. The last verse is as follows :—

"Jesus, to Thee we bow, ·
And for Thy coming wait ;
Give us for good some token now,
In our imperfect state ;
Apply the hallowing word ;
Tell each who looks for Thee,
Thou shalt be perfect as thy Lord,
Thou shalt be all like me."

There seems to be something of discord between the sentiments conveyed in the third and fourth verses : in the former we read of the power of redeeming grace, which saves " Till we can sin no more ;" whilst in the latter verse, as given above, we read of our present being " our imperfect state." Taken together, it is evident that the poet means the sinless state of the third verse to refer to the state of the glorified saints. This seems the more evident from the two lines following:—

> "Let us take up the cross,
> Till we the crown obtain."

The singing of this hymn at the opening of Conference seems now to be an essential part of the graver duties of that venerable and deliberative assembly. This is the first hymn in the fifth part of the collection, the first section, with the title, "For the Society on Meeting."

HYMN 479.—"Peace be on this house bestow'd."—*The Salutation.*—TUNE, Foundery, 1761.

Charles Wesley's, from "Hymns and Sacred Poems," 1742, page 157. In the fourth line of the third verse, "pardoned" is substituted for "washed."

HYMN 480.—"Glory be to God above."—*At the Meeting of Christian Friends.*—TUNE, Foundery, 1761.

Charles Wesley's, from "Hymns and Sacred Poems," 1742, page 158. The original has six stanzas, the last three being left out. The seventh and eighth lines of the original read thus:—

> "Lasting comfort, steadfast hope;
> Solid joy, and settled peace."

HYMN 481.—"All thanks to the Lamb, Who gives us to meet."— *At Meeting of Friends.*—TUNE, Newcastle, 1761.

Charles Wesley's, from "Hymns and Sacred Poems," 1749, vol. ii., No. 238.

HYMN 482.—"Saviour of sinful men."—*At the Meeting of Friends.*—TUNE, Lampe's, 1746.

Charles Wesley's, forming No. 232 in "Hymns and Sacred Poems," 1749, vol. ii. The fourth verse of this hymn has been often used by the Lord's people in their extremities of life and suffering.

When only seventeen years old, Jane, the wife of the Rev. Matthew Day, was convinced of sin; and at the Watch-night service following, she was enabled to believe in Christ to the saving of her soul. Her friends not being Methodists, her path became one of trial; but she remained firm in her religious course, and the Lord opened her way into a pleasant path, in which she walked with unfaltering fidelity during the rest of her pilgrimage. Her last illness was long and painful, but she manifested great patience, and her mind was stayed on God. When eternity was at hand, her joy absorbed every other feeling. Her last words to her husband were, "I hardly know anything but Jesus; but very soon all will be new." After pausing a few moments, with unusual vigour she said—

> "O! what a mighty change
> Shall Jesu's sufferers know,
> While o'er the happy plains they range,
> Incapable of woe! ˉ
> No ill-requited love
> Shall there our spirits wound."

She could say no more; but after remaining a short time speechless, without a struggle, she ceased to breathe.

For fifty-seven years, Richard Wade, of Sturton-Grange, Leeds, maintained a consistent Christian character. For many years he was a trustee, circuit and society steward, and the leader of a class. When laid aside by paralysis, he found comfort in repeating Wesley's hymns; and shortly before he died, he said to his son—

> "O! what a mighty change
> Shall Jesu's sufferers know,
> While o'er the happy plains they range,
> Incapable of woe!"

Thus peacefully he fell asleep in Jesus.

Methodism was introduced into Marston, in the Isle of Wight, nearly a century ago. Under a sermon preached by Mr J. Moon, Mrs Caws was convinced of sin, and soon found peace by believing on Christ. Her parents opposed her union with the Methodists, but she held fast her profession, and the trial gave firmness to her character. She cherished a very high sense of the value of class-meetings, and never wilfully absented herself from them. While housekeeper to the Rev. Legh Richmond, author of the "Dairyman's Daughter," she maintained her membership with the Methodists; and her Christian deportment was so exemplary that for some years after her marriage, and removal to Portsmouth, she was favoured with the cordial friendship of that eminent clergyman. During many years she sustained the office of class-leader with marked fidelity. Her last illness was short, but her joy at the prospect of heaven was unbounded.

She said, " I am going home ; going to my Saviour ; going to glory !" The last night of her pilgrimage of eighty-six years was one of suffering ; but instead of murmuring, she said, " Oh that the cord were broken ; then would I fly away, and be at rest ;" adding—

> "O ! what a mighty change
> Shall Jesu's sufferers know,
> While o'er the happy plains they range,
> Incapable of woe ! "

The dying saint then said, with an ecstasy of joy, "My Sabbath will be in heaven ;" and at midnight of Saturday her released spirit fled to the mansions of light.

We read in the *Wesleyan Magazine* of the last hours of Mrs Jane Keys, of Lurgan, in Ireland, who at intervals so delightfully realised the glories of heaven, that she appeared in a state of rapture. With her hands clasped, and her eyes lifted up, she sweetly sang—

> "O ! what a mighty change
> Shall Jesu's sufferers know,
> While o'er the happy plains they range,
> Incapable of woe !"

In her last hour she said, "All is sunshine before me." How many thousands have thus been helped to realise heaven upon earth by the sweet hymns of Charles Wesley ?

HYMN 483.—" Jesu, to Thee our hearts we lift."—*At Meeting of Friends.*—TUNE, Norwich, 1761.

Charles Wesley's, from " Hymns and Sacred Poems," 1749, vol. ii., No. 235. The fifth verse of the original is omitted, and alterations are made in three others.

HYMN 484.—" Appointed by Thee, We meet in Thy name."— *For Christian Friends.*—TUNE, Tallis, 1761.

Charles Wesley's, from " Hymns and Sacred Poems," 1749, vol. ii. The original is in six eight-line stanzas, single measure, the first being omitted.

The hymn, as first written, commences thus :—

> " How happy the pair
> Whom Jesus unites," &c.

These lines suggest thoughts which are not fully conveyed by the hymn in its abridged form as it appears in the Hymn-book. Its author, Charles Wesley, had spent nearly forty years in single blessedness that he might give himself up entirely to the work of preaching the gospel. In the very prime of life the thought crossed the poet's mind, "How know I whether it is best to marry or no?" This thought soon attained maturity ; and having met with a fair young lady during his evangelistic labours in Wales, he consulted his brother John, who "neither opposed nor much encouraged" the interesting intercourse. Taking the still further advice of his estimable friend, good Vincent Perronet, vicar of Shoreham, that man of God encouraged him "to pray, and wait for a providential opening." He thought, and waited ; and "expressed the various searchings of his heart in many hymns on the important occasion." Charles Wesley was married by his brother John to Miss Sarah Gwynne, in a Welsh village church, at Garth, on Saturday, April 8, 1749, a day so fine that "not a cloud was to be seen from morning till night." Praise, prayer, and thanksgiving was the sole occupation of that day. John Wesley says of that occasion, "It was a solemn day, such as became the dignity of a Christian marriage." The opening verses of this marriage hymn are as follows :—

> "How happy the pair Whom Jesus unites
> In friendship to share Angelic delights,
> Whose chaste conversation Is coupled with fear,
> Whose sure expectation Is *holiness here !*

> "My Jesus, my Lord, Thy grace I commend,
> So kind to afford My weakness a friend,
> Thy only good pleasure On me hath bestowed
> A heavenly treasure, A servant of God."

There were other hymns written on this occasion, amongst which portions will be found in the Hymn-book as Hymns 499, 510, 512, 513, 514, and 524.

At the age of forty, Watkin Lewis, of Berriew, Montgomery, was convinced of sin owing to a bereavement, and found peace whilst wrestling with God alone. After a few years' membership, he was made a Methodist class-leader, which office he held nearly forty years. He was tried in his last illness, and asked for Isaiah xlix. to be read to him. He then said, "The promises there have often been my support," and added :—

"O Jesus, appear ! No longer delay
To sanctify here, And bear us away :
The end of our meeting On earth let us see,
Triumphantly sitting In glory with Thee !"

He died saying, " Praise the Lord ! Though He slay me, yet
will I trust in Him !"

HYMN 485.—" Jesu, we look to Thee."— *At Meeting of Friends.*
—TUNE, Brentford, 1761.

Charles Wesley's, from " Hymns and Sacred Poems," 1749,
vol. ii., No. 237, the last verse being omitted.

HYMN 486.—" See, Jesus, Thy disciples see."—*At Meeting of
Friends.*—TUNE, Swanling-Bar, 1791.

Charles Wesley's, from " Hymns and Sacred Poems," 1749,
vol. ii., No. 239, with two verses omitted.

HYMN 487.—" Two are better far than one."—*For Christian
Friends.*—TUNE, Amsterdam, 1761.

Charles Wesley's, from " Hymns and Sacred Poems," 1749,
vol. ii., No. 227, with one verse of the original omitted.

HYMN 488.—" How happy are we, Who in Jesus agree."—*To be
Sung at the Tea-table.*—TUNE, Builth, 1761.

Charles Wesley's, being No. 146 of " Hymns for Families."
This commences the second section of the fifth part, with the
title, " For the Society giving Thanks." There is a quickening
and edifying spirit pervading this admirable hymn.

HYMN 489.—" How good and pleasant 'tis to see."—*For a
Family.*—TUNE, York, 1761.

Charles Wesley's, being No. 12 of " Hymns for Families."

HYMN 490.—" Behold, how good a thing."—*Psalm* cxxxiii.—
TUNE, Trumpet, 1761.

Charles Wesley's version of Psalm cxxxiii., from "Hymns and
Sacred Poems," 1742, page 174. This was added after Mr
Wesley's death.

HYMN 491. —" Come away to the skies, My beloved, arise."—
On the Birth-day of a Friend.—TUNE, Smith, 1761.

Forms No. 165 of Charles Wesley's " Hymns for Families." It was composed for the anniversary of the birth of his wife, Oct. 12, 1755.

HYMN 492.—"What shall we offer our good Lord."—*God's Husbandry.*—TUNE, Evesham, 1761.

This is John Wesley's translation from the German of Augustus G. Spangenberg, and is found in "Hymns and Sacred Poems," 1742, page 16. The original, which is in thirteen double stanzas, commences thus—

> "High on His everlasting throne."

The first ten verses are omitted. The original German was given to Count Zinzendorf, on his birth-day, in the year 1734. James Montgomery has inserted the greater part of the hymn in his "Christian Psalmist." Speaking of the hymn in his preface to that work, Mr Montgomery says : "It contains one of the most consistent allegories in verse on the manner in which it hath pleased God, by the ministry of the gospel, to redeem a world from the desolation which sin hath made." Mr La Trobe has ascribed the translation of this hymn to Bishop Gambold, but the translation used by Mr Wesley was his own.

The author, Augustus Gottlieb Spangenberg, was born of pious Lutheran parents, at Klettenberg, in Hanover, July 15, 1704. He was educated at the University of Jena, where he changed the study of law for the gospel. In 1727 he became acquainted with Count Zinzendorf, and in 1735 removed to the Moravian settlement at Herrnhut, from whence he was appointed to visit the churches of the Brethren in America, the West Indies, and England. He married one of the Sisters in 1740, and was afterwards ordained Bishop of Herrnhut. Much of his time subsequently was spent in missionary labours in America. After the death of Zinzendorf, he was considered the chief adviser of the Brethren. He died at Berthelsdorf, September 18, 1792. Knapp designates him "The Melanchthon of the Brethren."

HYMN 493.—"The people that in darkness lay."—*Giving of Thanks.*—TUNE, Norwich, 1761.

Charles Wesley's, made up of five of his "Short Scripture Hymns," vol. i., founded on Isaiah ix. 2-5, Nos. 974-978.

HYMN 494.—" Lo ! God is here ! let us adore."—*Public Worship.*—TUNE, Sheffield, 1761.

From " Hymns and Sacred Poems," 1739, page 188. It is John Wesley's translation from the German of Gerhard Tersteegen, and is based on Genesis xxviii. 16, 17. For an account of the author, see under Hymn 344.

It is a truly noble composition ; " a hymn," says Mr Love, " that I should be glad to hear sung at the opening of divine service every Sabbath morning." The late Rev. Benjamin Clough, uncle of Mr Punshon, who went to India with Dr Coke, states that being in London with him, the Doctor said, " My ,dear brother, I am dead to all but India." Mr Clough thought over this remark, and these words occurred to his mind : " They left all and followed Him." This raised Mr Clough's fainting spirits, and he began to sing the third verse of Hymn 494—

> " Gladly the toys of earth we leave,
>   Wealth, pleasure, fame, for Thee alone :
> To Thee our will, soul, flesh, we give ;
>   O take, O seal them for Thine own !
> Thou art the God, Thou art the Lord :
> Be Thou by all Thy works adored."

Dr Coke heartily joined Mr Clough in singing that hymn of self-dedication. One knows not in which most to glorify the grace of God : the veteran of the cross, about to launch out into an enterprise of great magnitude ; or the devoted youth, strong in his victorious faith, driving away from his heart the evil spirit of fear by a burst of sacred song.

Under a sermon preached by the venerable John Wesley, Mr W. Caudle, of Colchester, was induced to join the Methodist Society ; and, soon afterwards, he found peace in believing. He lived a godly and useful life, and died like a patriarch, in the full possession of his intellect, blessing and counselling his friends. A few hours before he died, he repeated, with much feeling, the couplet—

> " Lo ! God is here ! let us adore,
>   And own how dreadful is this place !"

He fell asleep in Jesus, faintly whispering to his family, " Good-bye ; God bless you ! "

HYMN 495.—" Come, let us arise, And press to the skies."—*For Christian Friends.*—TUNE, New Year's Day, 1761.

Charles Wesley's, forming No. 204 of " Hymns and Sacred Poems," 1749, vol. ii., where it is printed in double verses, single measure.

HYMN 496.—" The earth is the Lord's, And all it contains."— " *Seek ye first the kingdom of God*," &c.—TUNE, Triumph, 1761.

Charles Wesley's, being No. 178 of " Hymns and Sacred Poems," 1749, vol. ii. The fourth verse of the original is omitted : it speaks of God's bounty in supplying us with daily food.

HYMN 497.—" Come, all whoe'er have set."—*On a Journey.*— TUNE, Cardiff, 1761.

Charles Wesley's, being No. 180 of " Hymns and Sacred Poems," 1749, vol. ii.

For forty-six years, Francis Beacham, of Clutton, Bristol, was a useful member of the Methodist Society, and a local preacher for forty years. There was a freshness and power in his preaching, which always secured for him a welcome in the circuit ; this was the result of his habit of intercessory prayer. He spent one hour every morning, before the family was up, in earnest devotion, and had brief family worship four times every day. During his illness, his mind was delightfully stayed on God. Shortly before he died, he said to his son, " Christ is mine, and I am His." Finding himself near the eternal world, he whispered—

> " Nearer, and nearer still,
>   We to our country come :
> To that celestial hill,
>   The weary pilgrim's home,
> The New Jerusalem above,
> The seat of everlasting love."

His end was most peaceful. He died, breathing out—" Christ is precious !"

HYMN 498.—" Come, let us anew Our journey pursue."—*On a Journey.*—TUNE, Derby, 1781.

Charles Wesley's, forming No. 181 in "Hymns and Sacred

Poems," 1749, vol. ii. The last lines of verses seven and eight are transposed; that which was printed to the eighth verse is placed to the seventh.

When about the age of twenty, Miss Jackman (afterwards Mrs Spencer, of Slaidburn, and mother-in-law to the Rev. Adam Fletcher) sought and found salvation through Christ, and became confirmed in her choice of the Methodists, chiefly through the ministry of the Rev. William Bramwell. She was one of the first-fruits of Methodist preaching in her native place. By a course of uniform piety, and of more than ordinary devotedness to God for sixty-five years, she proved the genuineness of the change wrought in her heart. Their house was opened for many years for preaching, and many were saved through the services. When nature was fairly worn out by age, she spent much of her time in repeating portions of the Word of God and verses of hymns; and just before her death, she sung part of the hymn—

> " Come, let us anew Our journey pursue;
>   With vigour arise,
> And press to our permanent place in the skies;"

after which, peacefully and imperceptibly, she passed away to her "Father's house above."

For several years, Mrs M. M. Fison, of Barningham, Suffolk, was exercised with doubts as to her acceptance with God; but soon after her last illness commenced, the Lord so powerfully manifested Himself, after she had agonised in prayer for the blessing, that from that period her joy was unbounded, and her delight was in telling every one how happy she was, and in urging them to seek the Lord. Her confidence in God was unshaken to the last, and just before the final struggle, after great agony of pain, she said, with sweet composure—

> " The fiercer the blast, The sooner 'tis past."

Her last message, to her Thetford friends, was, " Tell them Jesus is precious."

A life of only thirty years was allotted to Matilda Smedley, of Sandiacre, and during twenty of them she faithfully served the Lord. As a Sunday-school teacher and a collector for missions and the Bible Society, she was most diligent and successful. Two years of affliction were appointed to her; but

patience had its perfect work. On the day of her death, referring to the difficulty of breathing, she said, "It is hard work;
but—

> ' The fiercer the blast, The sooner 'tis past :
> The troubles that come
> Shall come to our rescue, and hurry us home.'"

Her dying prayer was, "Bless me, even me, O my Father."

HYMN 499.—"Come, let us ascend, My companion and
friend."—*For Christian Friends.*—TUNE, Builth, 1761.

This appears in Charles Wesley's "Hymns and Sacred
Poems," 1749, vol. ii., No. 231, and is printed in single measure. The poet embodies in this vigorous hymn the apostle's
climax, "The greatest of these is charity." Writing of this
hymn, the seraphic Fletcher, of Madeley, says, "When the
triumphal chariot of perfect love gloriously carries you to the
top of perfection's hill ; when you are raised far above the common heights of the perfect ; when you are almost translated
into glory, like Elijah, then you may sing the 499th Hymn."

One of the many converts to God, through the ministry of that
blessed man of God, Joseph Sutcliffe, was Richard Buttle, of
Hull. At the age of sixteen, he gave his heart to the Lord. In
after life, he served in the office of class-leader and local
preacher, with acceptance and profit to those who heard him.
On the Sunday on which he died, his confidence in God was
strong, and his prospect of heaven bright. He repeated the
lines to a friend sitting by him—

> " Come, let us ascend, My companion and friend,
> To a taste of the banquet above ;
> If thy heart be as mine, If for Jesus it pine,
> Come up into the chariot of love ;"

and added, "Oh for a gust of praise !" After urging his
daughter to live to God, he peacefully entered into rest.

The reading of Baxter's " Saints' Rest," was blessed to the
conversion of Miss Nancy Holland, of Kerridge, Macclesfield,
when she was nineteen. Soon afterwards, she joined the
Methodist Society, and maintained a consistency of conduct
through life. A sudden and unexpected illness closed her
earthly career ; but though fever prostrated her strength, her

mind was kept in peace. Shortly before her departure she desired that Hymn 499 should be read to her. After the sixth verse was read—

> " Hallelujah, they cry, To the King of the sky,
> . To the great everlasting I AM ;
> To the Lamb that was slain, And liveth again,
> Hallelujah to God and the Lamb ! "

she was enraptured, and seemed ready to mingle with the celestial throng of the redeemed before the throne, whither her happy spirit soon fled, her last words being, " Jesus is precious."

A miller and baker in a country village has many temptations to Sabbath-breaking ; but in the case of Thomas Palmer, of Eye, Peterborough, the temptation was invariably resisted. For more than thirty years he was a consistent Methodist, and later in life a useful class-leader and circuit steward. In his last illness he was reduced to such extreme debility, that he could scarcely speak ; but just previous to his death, to the surprise of all his friends, he broke out, and sang most delightfully—

> " A day without night We feast in His sight,
> And eternity seems as a day ! "

He continued to sing at intervals some of his favourite hymns till within an hour of his peaceful departure to heaven.

HYMN 500.*—" All praise to our redeeming Lord."—*At Meeting of Friends.*—TUNE, Birstal, 1761.

Charles Wesley's, from Hymns for those that seek Redemption, 1747, page 63. It was added after Mr Wesley's death.

The lengthened widowhood of Mrs Isabella Day, of Bere-Heath, Dorchester, was spent in helping forward the work of God. When severely afflicted, she did not absent herself from the means of grace. On the eve of her last day on earth, the usual weekly prayer meeting was held at her house, when she prayed with great energy, and, at its close, gave out and sung—

> " And if our fellowship below
> In Jesus be so sweet,
> What heights of rapture shall we know
> When round His throne we meet ! "

On the following morning her happy spirit went to realise those raptures.

HYMN 501.—"Jesus, great Shepherd of the sheep."—*For Believers.*—TUNE, Wednesbury, 1761.

Charles Wesley's, from "Hymns and Sacred Poems," 1749, vol. i., No. 136. The seventh verse of the original is left out.

Many chapel-keepers have had to thank God for enabling them to realise the truth of the Psalmist's declaration, that it is better to be a door-keeper in the Lord's house than to dwell in the tents of wickedness. Such an one was Samuel Simpson, of Chapeltown, Leeds. He had been a useful Methodist from the age of twenty. One day, while he was at work in one of the stone-quarries near Leeds, both his legs were accidentally broken, and from the first all hope of recovery was gone. He exultingly endured his acute sufferings, saying, "Jesus is mine, and I am His." Among his last words to his friends, who visited him in the Infirmary, were these—

> " Together let us sweetly live,
>   Together let us die ;
> And each a starry crown receive,
>   And reign above the sky."

Shortly afterwards, his released spirit escaped to heaven.

Another instance of the value of Wesley's Hymns, almost at the hour of death, is recorded in the *Wesleyan Magazine* in connection with the sudden death of Mr Charles Copland, of Etruria. The writer of the notice alludes to the last service for social worship which he attended, when he expressed his delight that eleven new members were added to the Society, and after he had received his ticket of membership, part of Hymn 501 was sung. Mr Copland set the tune, and sang heartily the lines :—

> " Together let us sweetly live,
>   Together let us die ;
> And each a starry crown receive,
>   And reign above the sky."

He walked home, joining in religious conversation ; on arriving at his residence, he became suddenly unconscious, and in an hour he passed from the singing of hymns on earth to join in the everlasting song above.

HYMN 502.—" Come, Thou omniscient Son of Man."—*For any who think they have already attained (full redemption).*— TUNE, Fetter-lane, 1761.

Charles Wesley's, from " Hymns and Sacred Poems," 1749, vol. ii., No. 124. Three verses of the original are left out.

HYMN 503.—"Try us, O God, and search the ground."—*A Prayer for Persons joined in Fellowship.*—TUNE, Brooks, 1761.

Charles Wesley's, from " Hymns and Sacred Poems," 1742, page 83. The original is a long hymn in four parts, of which this is the first.

No hymn in the collection has been more frequently used in social worship. Objectors are occasionally found to the couplet :—

> " When to the right or left we stray,
> Leave us not comfortless "—

implying that even out of the narrow path that leads to heaven wanderers might hope for the Holy Spirit's comforting presence. The poet rather prays that prodigals may not be abandoned when in the broad way that leads to destruction. This hymn has afforded consolation and encouragement to followers of Jesus in various conditions of experience. In the *Local Preacher's Magazine* for 1852, there is an account of the last days of George Machin, of Stockport, who, in early life, had been bandmaster to a volunteer corps. When he became a Methodist he gave up his military pursuits. His last illness was severe, but in the midst of much suffering he would point towards heaven and sing—

> "There all the ship's company meet,
> Who sailed with the Saviour beneath," &c.

On the Monday he raised himself up in bed, and gave out in a firm voice part of Hymn 503, affixing a favourite tune, and, joined by those friends who surrounded him, sang with surprising influence and power the verse—

> " Then, when the mighty work is wrought,
> Receive thy ready bride ;
> Give us in heaven a happy lot
> With all the sanctified."

The last two lines were repeated again and again, the dying pilgrim concluding his song with a fervent Amen. The next day he exchanged mortality for life.

As far back as 1762, John Middleton, of Hartlepool, saw in Methodism that which led him to leave the communion of the Church of England in which he had been brought up. He opened his house for preaching, and a society has been continued there up to the present time. From the time of his joining the Society, he maintained a uniform cleaving to God in Christ as his all in all; and a peaceful end closed a holy life. During his last illness he repeated a favourite verse which he had often sung at family worship—

> " Then, when the mighty work is wrought,
>   Receive thy ready bride ;
>   Give us in heaven a happy lot
>   With all the sanctified."

In this state of peaceful tranquillity he remained till his death.

In the year 1800, a young man named John Wilkinson came to London from York, and being a Methodist, went to the Bookroom to buy some paper on which to write to his mother. Mr George Whitfield, the book steward, invited the young man to his class, which met at City Road every Sunday morning at six o'clock. He continued a member of that class for sixty years: one of the other members was the late venerable Dr Leifchild. Soon after joining Mr Whitfield's class, Mr Wilkinson joined the Community, and in this self-denying service laboured hard and long to benefit the sick and poor in destitute localities. He loved his Bible, was attached to all the means of grace, and was a cheerful happy Christian. He commemorated the dying love of the Saviour in City Road Chapel on the first Sabbath of March 1862 ; and on the last Sabbath of that month he was drinking the wine new with Christ in His kingdom above. In allusion to his own expected removal, during his last few days, he often sang—

> "Then, when the mighty work is wrought,
>   Receive thy ready bride ;
>   Give us in heaven a happy lot
>   With all the sanctified."

He enjoyed robust health for nearly eighty-seven years ; and as the weary wheels of life were standing still, he faintly whispered, " My Saviour ! my Saviour !"

HYMN 504.—"Jesus, united by thy grace."—*A Prayer for Persons joined in Fellowship.*—TUNE, Aldrich, 1761.

Charles Wesley's, forming the fourth part of a long hymn, of which No. 503 is the first part.

HYMN 505.—"Unchangeable, Almighty Lord."—"*He that believeth shall not make haste.*"—TUNE, Zoar, 1761.

Charles Wesley's, from "Hymns and Sacred Poems," 1742, page 173, founded on Isaiah xxxvii. 16. The original is in four parts, of which this forms the third, and Hymn 280 the fourth part. The soft and easy flow of the language accords admirably with the gentle spirit which pervades the hymn.

HYMN 506.—"Father of our dying Lord."—*For the Day of Pentecost.*—TUNE, Amsterdam, 1761.

Charles Wesley's, from "Hymns and Sacred Poems," 1742, page 166, founded on John xiv. 16, 17.

HYMN 507.—"Saviour of all, to thee we bow."—"*Unto the angel of the Church of Làodicea,*" &c.—TUNE, Invitation, 1761.

Charles Wesley's, from "Hymns and Sacred Poems," 1742, page 300, founded on Rev. iii. 14, &c. The original is a long hymn in three parts; this forms the first portion of the third part, with some verses omitted. Hymn 454 is part of the same. A writer in the *Southern Methodist Quarterly*, vol. ii. (American), remarking on this hymn, says, "As faith is a receiving and appropriating, not a bestowing nor imparting grace, there have been objections to the line, 'The heavenly manna faith imparts.'"

HYMN 508.—"God of love, that hear'st the prayer."—*For those that have found Redemption.*—TUNE, Foundery, 1761.

Charles Wesley's, from "Hymns for those that seek Redemption," 1747, page 19. Portions of four of the verses are omitted.

HYMN 509.—"Jesus, Lord, we look to thee."—*For a Family.*—TUNE, Hotham, 1761.

Charles Wesley's, from "Hymns and Sacred Poems," 1749, vol. i., No. 146.

HYMN 510.—"Thou God of truth and love."—*For Christian Friends.*—TUNE, Fonmon, 1761.

Charles Wesley's, from "Hymns and Sacred Poems," 1749, vol. ii., No. 203. The original has seven verses, the last of which is omitted. The sixth verse commences thus, " O might the Spirit seal,"—" might " is changed for "may." The hymn contains a graceful expression of sympathy and unity between married souls.

The work of a Methodist preacher was never what a worldly man would envy, and up to the close of the last century, and for some twenty years in the present century, a Sabbath-day's toil for an earnest preacher would have been a "weariness of the flesh" indeed, had not the heart been engaged. With a burning love for souls, Jabez Bunting, D.D., once said, " Many attribute their conversion to their having attended a love-feast; I owe mine to having been shut out of one." Excluded from that means of grace by the firm discipline of Mr Alexander Mather, he went home to pray; "and he is now in paradise, praising God for the transactions of that hour." He was born May 1779, and commenced to travel in 1799. In 1803 he was located in London, where he was stationed when he was married, and resided near Long Lane, Southwark.

An entry in his journal at this period furnishes an illustration of the use of this hymn, which will be read with interest. He proceeds as follows:—" Sunday evening, September 11 [1803]. —At half-past ten I read prayers at Snowsfields Chapel, in the Borough, and preached from 1 John i. 9. I begin to feel a little more at home in the pulpits of the metropolis and its vicinity, than I did when I first came. . . . At three o'clock I began to give tickets at Rotherhithe ; at six, I preached there from Luke xv. 2, and was enabled, as Mr Wesley used to phrase it, ' to speak some strong, rough words.' After finishing the renewal of tickets, I walked home. Mr Taylor (superintendent of the circuit) came a little after me, and says this has been the hardest day's work he has ever performed since he left Cornwall, many years ago. We tried to rouse each other by singing—

> 'O may Thy Spirit seal
>   Our souls unto that day,
> With all Thy fulness fill,
>   And then transport away !

Away to our eternal rest,
Away to our Redeemer's breast !'—

but we had not strength enough to finish the verse ; so we gave
it up, and began to talk about Macclesfield,"—from which place
he had married Miss Maclardie only a short time previously.

HYMN 511.—"Forgive us, for Thy mercy's sake."—*For a Preacher
of the Gospel—Moses' Wish.*—TUNE, Canterbury, 1761.

Charles Wesley's, from " Hymns and Sacred Poems," 1749,
vol. i., No. 181, the first verse of the original being omitted.
Founded on Exodus xxxiii. 12 to xxxiv. 9.

HYMN 512.—" Centre of our hopes Thou art."—*For Christian
Friends.*—TUNE, Dedication, 1761.

Charles Wesley's, from " Hymns and Sacred Poems," 1749,
vol. ii., No. 236, the first verse being left out.

HYMN 513.—" Jesus, with kindest pity see."—*For Christian
Friends.*—TUNE, Marienburn, 1761.

Charles Wesley's, from " Hymns and Sacred Poems," 1749,
vol. ii., No. 199. There is an unwonted ambiguity in some of the
phraseology used by the poet in this hymn.

HYMN 514.—" Father, at Thy footstool see."—*For Christian
Friends.*—TUNE, Plymouth, 1761.

Charles Wesley's, from "Hymns and Sacred Poems," 1749,
vol. ii., No. 194. The two last verses of the original are left out.
The first verse is an address to God the Creator ; the second to
Jesus the Saviour; the third to the Heavenly Comforter ; the
fourth to the United Trinity. The petitions are distinct and
appropriate. The hymn is also remarkable for the rhyme being
between first and second, and third and fourth verses, instead
of between alternate lines.

HYMN 515.—" Father, Son, and Spirit, hear."
    „   516.—" Other ground can no man lay."
    „   517.—" Christ, our Head, gone up on high."
    „   518.—" Christ, from whom all blessings flow."
The Communion of Saints.—TUNES, Love-feast, Salisbury, and
Ascension, 1761.

Charles Wesley's, being four parts of a long hymn from

" Hymns and Sacred Poems," 1740, page 188. Portions of some
verses of the original, and the whole of others, are left out.
When the Church of Christ realises in its members' experience
the conditions which are stated in the concluding stanza, we
shall rejoice in the blessings of millennial glory.

HYMN 519.—" Come, and let us sweetly join."
„   520.—" Come, thou high and lofty Lord !"
„   521.—" Let us join ('tis God commands)."
„   522.—" Partners of a glorious hope."

The Love-Feast.—TUNES, Love-feast, Cookham, Foundery, 1761.

Charles Wesley's, from " Hymns and Sacred Poems," 1740,
page 181. This hymn, which is in five parts, and includes, in
the whole, twenty-two double stanzas, immediately precedes, in
the original, the four which it here follows. The whole of the
fifth part is omitted. The last lines of this hymn were inserted
by Hogarth on one of his caricatures.

HYMN 523.—" O Thou, our Husband, Brother, Friend."—*Hymn
of Intercession.*—TUNE, Purcell, 1761.

Charles Wesley's, from " Hymns and Sacred Poems," 1749,
vol. ii., No. 62. The two last verses of the original are left out.

HYMN 524.—" Our friendship sanctify and guide."—*For
Christian Friends.*—TUNE, 113th Psalm, 1761.

Charles Wesley's, from " Hymns and Sacred Poems," 1749,
vol. ii., No. 195, commencing with the second verse of the
original. This hymn was specially written by the poet for himself and his brother, which will at once account for the personal
character of the phraseology.

HYMN 525.—" Jesu, thou great redeeming Lord."—"*The Grace
of our Lord Jesus Christ,*" &c.—TUNE, 112th Psalm, 1761.

Forms the last of Charles Wesley's "Short Scripture Hymns,"
vol. ii., No. 807 ; founded on the benediction in Rev. xxii. 21.

HYMN 526.—" Except the Lord conduct the plan."—*For a
Family of Believers.*—TUNE, Musicians, 1761.

Charles Wesley's, from " Family Hymns," page 37. A hymn
full of earnest devotional feeling.

It has been used on tens of thousands of occasions, in asking for divine guidance, in private, social, and public services, especially at the opening of all deliberative assemblies for promoting the spread of the work of God.

In the early part of his life, Richard Harwood, of Darwen, Blackburn, entered the army, and whilst abroad was afflicted in his eyes, and ultimately lost his sight. For thirty years after leaving the army, he was a zealous Methodist, and for eighteen years a class-leader. He was remarkable for punctuality and early attendance at the class and prayer meetings, and the public ministry of the Word. His death was sudden. He had been at the six o'clock Sunday morning prayer meeting, and at nine attended to open the Sunday-school by singing and prayer. Having given out, and joined in singing, the verse—

> "Except the Lord conduct the plan,
> The best-concerted schemes are vain,
>   And never can succeed :
> We spend our wretched strength for nought :
> But if our works in Thee be wrought,
>   They shall be blest indeed ; "

immediately, without a groan, "he ceased at once to work and live."

HYMN 527.—" Come, Wisdom, Power, and Grace Divine."—*For a Family of Believers.*—TUNE, Snowsfields, 1761.

Charles Wesley's, from " Family Hymns," page 39.

HYMN 528.—"O Saviour, cast a gracious smile."—*For a Family of Believers.*—TUNE, Chapel, 1761.

Charles Wesley's, from " Family Hymns," 1757, page 40.

HYMN 529.—" Holy Lamb, who Thee confess."—*For a Family of Believers.*—TUNE, Hotham, 1761.

Charles Wesley's, from " Family Hymns," 1757, page 41. The original is printed in four-line stanzas.

Some have taken objection to the closing couplet of the hymn.

> "Till we, on the sacred tree,
>   Bow the head, and die like Thee."

It is manifest that the poet did not mean in any way to countenance Romish practices.

HYMN 530.—"Come, Thou all-inspiring Spirit."—*For a Family of Believers.*—TUNE, Westminster, 1761.

Charles Wesley's, from "Family Hymns," 1757, page 42.

HYMN 531.—"Christ, whose glory fills the skies."—*A Plant of Renown :* Ezekiel xxxiv. 29, 30.—TUNE, Kingswood, 1761.

Charles Wesley's, being No. 1267 of "Scripture Hymns" (1762), vol. i., based on Ezekiel xxxiv. 29, 30. The editor of Toplady's Works has, in error, given the authorship of this hymn to that clergyman. James Montgomery has selected the first verse of this and two verses of Hymn 156 to make a hymn for his "Christian Psalmist."

HYMN 532.—"Come, let us use the grace divine."—"*Join ourselves to the Lord in a covenant.*"—TUNE, Brockmer, 1761.

This forms No. 1242 of Charles Wesley's "Scripture Hymns" (1762), vol. ii., and is based on Jeremiah l. 5. The original was written in three double stanzas. This hymn is frequently used, both in England and America, at the renewing of the Covenant by the Methodist societies. The appropriateness of the language and sentiment are remarkable, the more so as the hymn was not designed for any such service ; although the words of the prophet indicate such a dedication : "Come let us join ourselves to the Lord in a perpetual covenant, that shall not be forgotten."

HYMN 533.—"Lord, we Thy will obey."—*At Parting.*—TUNE, Trumpet, 1781.

Charles Wesley's, from "Hymns and Sacred Poems," 1749, vol. ii., No. 209. This hymn commences the fourth section, with the title, "For the Society at Parting." The poet, with his usual skill, has wrested from infidels a sentiment which has at times been frequently quoted by them : as Christians, Mr Wesley writes :—

> "We, only we, can say,
>   'Whatever is, is best.'"

HYMN 534.—"Blest be the dear uniting love."—*At Parting of Christian Friends.*—TUNE, Aldrich, 1761.

From Charles Wesley's "Hymns and Sacred Poems," 1742, page 159. The fifth and sixth verses of the original are left out, and the others altered. This hymn is inserted in the New Congregational Hymn-book, and erroneously ascribed to Cennick.

HYMN 535.—" And let our bodies part."—*At Parting.*—TUNE, Lampe's, 1746.

From Charles Wesley's "Hymns and Sacred Poems," 1749, vol. ii., No. 233. The original is in two parts, the second of which is entirely omitted. When the Rev. Robert Newton was last leaving New York to return home, his American friends, standing on a separate steamer alongside, joined very heartily in singing this hymn. (See "Life of Rev. R. Newton," page 222.)

HYMN 536.—" Jesus, accept the praise."—*At the Parting of Friends.*—TUNE, Trumpet, 1781.

Charles Wesley's, forming No. 48 of "Redemption Hymns," 1747. There are some sublime thoughts in this hymn; the sixth verse is especially worthy of notice.

HYMN 537.—" God of all consolation, take."—*At Parting of Friends.*—TUNE, Liverpool, 1761.

Charles Wesley's, forming part of a paraphrase of Revelation vii. 9, in "Hymns on Redemption," 1747, page 68. The original is printed in double stanzas; parts of the first and second are omitted.

It was the privilege of John C. Clendinnen, formerly a preacher in the Irish Conference, to be brought to a knowledge of the truth through the ministrations of the early Methodist preachers, and whilst a youth he heard a sermon by the venerable John Wesley, who, according to his custom, laid his hands on his head, and invoked a blessing on him. In 1796 he commenced his itinerant labours, and suffered much from persecution during the Irish rebellion. In those troublesome times, whilst holding a love-feast, he was seized and sent to prison, and on his way thither reproved the officer in command for profane swearing, an act which converted an enemy into a friend. After a pilgrimage over the greater part of Ireland, extending to more than fourscore years, he delighted as much as ever in the Word of God and in Wesley's hymns. His wife, shortly before he died, quoting—

> " Our souls are in His mighty hand,
> And He shall keep them still,"

he took up with much energy and joy the remainder of the verse—

> \   "And you and I shall surely stand,
>   With Him on Zion's hill;"

adding, "Sing it! sing it!"   Shortly afterwards he tried to say, "Hallelujah," but the unfinished word died on his lips as he escaped to paradise.

· In the morning of her days, Elizabeth Jackson, wife of the Rev. Robert Jackson, received the evidence of her acceptance with God, and through much painful suffering she held fast her confidence to the end of her life.   During her later years she made the Bible and Wesley's Hymns her constant companions; and when eternity was in full view she said of her troubles, "The Lord hath gently cleared my way : I can still praise Him; I shall find it all right soon :—

> 'Him eye to eye we there shall see,
>   Our face like His shall shine;
> O what a glorious company,
>   When saints and angels join!'"

Half-an-hour before her mortal sickness she was working for a missionary basket, and remarked, as she laid her work down, "I love the mission cause."   In peaceful serenity she entered her "Father's house on high."

The parents of Mary Worth, mother of the Rev. W. Worth, were amongst the first Methodist converts in Tiverton.   When Mr Wesley first formed the Society there, he invited all who felt a desire to "flee from the wrath to come" to meet him at his lodgings after preaching.   Amongst those who went were John and Sarah Tipper.   They went in different parties; neither knew what the other had done till they met at home.   "I have joined the society," said one; "So have I," said the other; and they were both faithful till death.   Mary, their eldest daughter, received the evidence of pardon whilst communing at the Lord's Supper, in her twenty-third year.   She suffered much during life, but endured with patience the Lord's will.   When death was at hand, she said, "The Lord does comfort and support me; He is my portion for ever."   On another occasion she said, "Sing glory, glory!"   Speaking of heaven, clapping her hands, and looking upward, she added—

> " 'Palms in our hands we all shall bear,
>   And crowns upon our head.'

The Lord is my portion." Within a few minutes of her death she repeated—

> " To patient faith the prize is sure," &c. ;

and in that peaceful frame passed into the skies.

It was under the ministry of the Rev. Walter Griffith, in London, that Mrs Bywater, of Temple-Newsam, was convinced of sin, and led to give her heart to the Lord. Henceforth the desire of her life was to bring others to Jesus. She watched for souls ; she wept for souls ; she agonised in prayer for souls ; and in her sphere she laboured for souls ; and God crowned her efforts by using her in plucking " brands from the burning." She had a seventy years' pilgrimage on earth without much sickness ; her last illness was short ; the feebleness of age crept upon her, and when near the end of life's journey she found comfort by her friends reading to her verses of Charles Wesley's hymns. When a friend had ceased, on the last occasion, she herself gave out, with all the emphasis she could—

> " Then let us lawfully contend,
>   And fight our passage through ;
> Bear in our faithful minds the end,
>   And keep the prize in view."

In this happy state she continued for a short time, when she entered into rest.

Michael Ward, of Greenheys, Manchester, was converted to God in his youth, and throughout life he faltered not in his fidelity to the truth and in his attachment to the cause of God. He loved the sanctuary, and took special delight in the services. The last three times he met his class he gave out the verse :—

> " Then let us hasten to the day
>   When all shall be brought home !
> Come, O Redeemer ! come away,
>   O Jesus, quickly come !"

A few hours before his death, he solemnly commended his wife and family to the guardian care of his heavenly Father. He was hurriedly caught up to his rest in heaven.

HYMN 538.—"Jesus, soft, harmonious Name."—*At parting of Christian Friends.*—TUNE, Hotham, 1761.

Charles Wesley's, from "Hymns and Sacred Poems," 1749, vol. ii., No. 243.

HYMN 539.—"Lift up your hearts to things above."—*At parting of Christian Friends.*—TUNE, Wednesbury, 1761.

Charles Wesley's, from "Hymns and Sacred Poems," 1749, vol. ii., page 331, No. 244. The original is in twelve four-line stanzas, the third and eighth being omitted, and the ninth and tenth transposed.

This hymn forms the last in the collection as it was published by John Wesley in 1780, and it is there No. 525. All the hymns which follow have been added as supplements at various periods. Other Methodist bodies which have adopted these hymns have added to this portion the short hymn commencing—" Lord, dismiss us with thy blessing."

THE ADDITIONAL HYMNS.

SOME years after Mr Wesley's death, the Hymn-Book underwent very considerable revision and alteration, and in this form it appeared in 1797. A copy of the book, with the alterations marked, is now before us. How that book was received by the Conference and by the people may be gathered by the answer to Question 27 in the "Minutes" of 1798. It reads thus : "Dr Coke, and Brothers Storey, Moore, and Clarke, are appointed to reduce the large Hymn-Book to its primitive simplicity, as published in the second edition [in 1781], with liberty to add a word now and then, in the way of notes, to explain a difficult passage, for the sake of the unlearned ; and a discretionary power is given them in respect to the additional hymns." The sale of the 1797 edition was stopped, and the unsold copies destroyed.

The annotated edition of the Hymn-Book provided by authority of this resolution did not give much more satisfaction than its predecessor, so far as the notes were concerned. These were afterwards left out, so that the edition with the notes is scarce. We have a copy before us, and venture to think that it was wisely determined to print the book as Mr Wesley prepared it,

with the addition of some twenty-two hymns, commencing with
Hymn 540 and ending with Hymn 560. As, however, amongst
these additional hymns there were none which gave the Conference a copyright in the collection, other parties continued to
publish the book, and the people in the provinces bought
largely of these unofficial editions, partly because they were a
little cheaper, and sometimes they had the attraction of a little
brighter binding. As at this time there appears to have been
only three editions of the Hymn-Book issued by the Conference,
we learn by the " Minutes " of 1801, Question 13, that the prices
of these were as follows:—The Small Pocket Hymn-Book, 1s. 3d.,
with clasp, 1s. 6d. ; The Large Pocket Hymn-Book (18mo), 3s. 6d.,
with clasp, 4s. ; The Large Hymn-Book (12mo), 4s. 6d. A
Nota Bene was added, very wisely, urging the societies not to
purchase any but the Book-room editions. In this form the
book continued to be published till 1830, when the Supplement
was added.

HYMN 540.—" Before Jehovah's awful throne."—*Paraphrase of
Psalm C.*—TUNE, 100th Psalm.

Dr Watts' version of the Hundredth Psalm, second metre
(1719). It was altered by Mr Wesley, and inserted by him in
his Collection of Psalms and Hymns, third edition, enlarged,
1744. The first verse of the original is left out ; the second
verse, as published by Dr Watts, commences as follows :—

> " Nations attend before His throne
> With solemn fear, with sacred joy."

These lines John Wesley has substituted by two others, which
give increased solemnity and grandeur to the whole hymn.
They are as follows :—

> " Before Jehovah's awful throne,
> Ye nations bow with sacred joy."

Never was a transformation more complete than the one made
by this alteration. From being a hymn comparatively unnoticed and unnoticeable, it has been made one of solemnity,
power, and sublimity. Many of the great celebrations of religious ordinances both in England and in America have, for
more than a century, been commenced by the singing of this
commanding poetical address to the Deity.

The late Dr Dempster, while senior professor in the Garrett

Biblical Institute, America, related substantially the following facts. He and his wife, while on their way to South America, with two other missionaries and their wives bound for other fields, were pursued three days by a pirate vessel. As their disguised enemy, refusing to exchange salutations, came near, all went on deck and united in singing to the tune of Old Hundred, the hymn commencing—

> " Before Jehovah's awful throne,
> Ye nations bow with sacred joy ;
> Know that the Lord is God alone,
> He can create and He destroy."

Kneeling in prayer they awaited what appeared to be their certain doom, unless God especially interfered to save them. The Lord delivered them from the mouths of cannon and the wrath of men, who waited a time near the side of the missionary ship, then turned and left. Are we pursued by enemies, let us resort to true, earnest prayer, and living faith. We give this incident from the *North-Western Christian Advocate ;* and at the time we write we are privileged with the personal friendship, in London, of the Rev. Dr Bannister, the contemporary of Dr Dempster, and his successor in the professorship.

Possessing an athletic frame, a mind of great energy, and a natural fearless daring, John Marris, of Stallingborough, Grimsby, was distinguished amongst his worldly companions for folly and dissipation. In 1785 he was convinced of sin through a sermon preached by the Rev. L. Harrison, and soon afterwards found peace in believing under a sermon by the Rev. George Holder. His clear perception of divine truth made him a great blessing to many dwelling in the darkness which surrounded him ; and as a class-leader and local preacher he was earnest, affectionate, firm, and stimulating. He was a good man, and carried the power of his goodness about with him. God spared his useful life for eighty-three years, and when death was at hand he maintained his confidence in God unshaken. With great strength of voice and fervour of spirit, just before he died, he repeated—

> " Wide as the world is Thy command ;
> Vast as eternity Thy love ;
> Firm as a rock Thy truth shall stand,
> When rolling years shall cease to move."

S

And shortly afterwards he faintly breathed out, " I am bound
for the Kingdom : go to glory with me ; " and so he entered into
rest.

HYMN 541.—" Lord of the worlds above."—*Longing for the
House of God.*

Dr Watts' paraphrase of Psalm lxxxiv. This was inserted in
Mr Wesley's " Collection of Psalms and Hymns," 1738 ; and
also in the same work enlarged, in 1744, with the second and
fifth verses of the original omitted.

In the year 1788, Thomas Kiddear, of Ashby-de-la-Zouch, was
awakened to a sense of his lost condition as a sinner, under the
ministry of the Rev. George Gibbon, and soon after obtained
the remission of sins. As a class-leader from 1809, a leader in
singing and in prayer-meetings, a trustee, and Society steward, he
served God and Methodism faithfully for fifty-two years. In his
last illness, during one of his nights of pain, he was praising
God ; and amongst other hymns in which the privileges of
Christian believers are described, he repeated the whole of the
one commencing—

> " Lord of the worlds above !
>   How pleasant and how fair
> The dwellings of Thy love,
>   Thy earthly temples, are !
> To Thine abode my heart aspires,
> With warm desires to see my God."

He found Christ precious, till his released spirit departed to be
where He reigns alone.

The name of Agar stands honourably connected with Methodism in York for nearly a hundred years. Benjamin Agar, the
elder, heard both John and Charles Wesley preach in London,
and when he returned to York he had the honour of entertaining
J. Wesley at his house, on the occasion of his last visit to that
city. During that visit, both his children had Mr Wesley's
hands laid on their heads, and received the good man's blessing.
Joseph became a preacher among the Methodists, and his
brother Benjamin found pardon in early life, whilst at prayer in
a poor but godly man's cottage. He gave up much of party
politics and worldly influence to devote his time to the interests
of religion. He served the office of class-leader well, and gave

liberally of his substance to promote Methodism. When laid
aside by illness, he was graciously sustained, saying, " The
everlasting arms are around me. The Lord is very good ; He
supports me." He frequently repeated this verse—

" The Lord His people loves ;
His hand no good withholds
From those His heart approves,
From holy, humble souls :
Thrice happy he, O Lord of hosts,
Whose spirit trusts alone in Thee."

As the end of life drew nigh, he said, " Lord, save me ! On
Thee, my Lord, on Thee, I depend." And just as life was
ebbing out, he whispered to Mrs Agar, " My dear, I am going
to claim—to claim "—— when his voice faltered, and she added,
" Your mansion in the skies." He replied, " Oh yes." Thus did
he sleep in Jesus, and go to be " for ever with the Lord."

HYMN 542.—" Lord and God of heavenly powers."—" *Therefore
with angels, and archangel,*" &c.

Charles Wesley's paraphrase of that part of the communion
service of the Church of England commencing, " Therefore
with angels and archangel," &c. It appears in " Hymns and
Sacred Poems," 1739. The word archangel, both in the title
and text of this hymn, should be printed in the singular number,
as we read of but one archangel, Michael, in heaven. This
error is also perpetuated in the Book of Common Prayer.

HYMN 543.—" Being of Beings, God of Love !"—*Grace after
Meat.*

Charles Wesley's, from " Hymns and Sacred Poems," 1739,
page 35. It breathes a spirit of grateful adoring love, but some
of its expressions are not suited for indiscriminate use.

HYMN 544.—" The Lord of Sabbath let us praise."—*On the
Sabbath-Day.*

Was written by Samuel Wesley, jun., and appears in his
" Poems on Several Occasions," 1735 ; also in John Wesley's
" Collection of Sacred Poems," vol. iii., page 178. It will be
found in the author's works, 1862, page 364. It is a hymn of
great excellence : the energy of the thoughts and expressions is

equal to that found in the hymns of his two brothers. The
concluding couplet is particularly comprehensive and fine—

> " 'Twas great to speak a world from nought ;
> 'Twas greater to redeem !"

The mother of Dr Jobson received the first convictions of sin
in her own heart by examining the ten commandments, with
her father, as a preparation for her first communion at the
Lord's Supper, in the cathedral, Lincoln. Attending that service, with a heart softened by self-examination, and especially
whilst partaking of the memorials of the Lord's passion, she
experienced that bruisedness of spirit which can only be appre-
hended by a sincere penitent. From the table of the Lord she
went home with a broken and contrite heart to her closet ; and
there, whilst repeating the hymn commencing—

> " Behold the Saviour of mankind,
> Nailed to the shameful tree ;
> How vast the love that Him inclined
> To bleed and die for thee !"

she was enabled to appropriate by faith to her own case the
merits of the death of Christ, and her soul rose into the light
and liberty of the children of God. When she became
acquainted with the nature and design of Methodist class-
meetings, she at once became a member of Society, and soon
after the leader of a class. The joyous nature of her religion
led many to court her company and counsel ; and with rich and
poor alike she was faithful in discharging her duty towards their
souls and towards her Saviour. When she visited London, the
prevailing wickedness almost overpowered her sensitive spirit :
she yearned over perishing sinners, and prayed earnestly for
their salvation. She spent much time in faithful pleading with
God, and her life was one of great peace, usefulness, and activity
in all its duties. Several months' illness preceded her death,
but her acceptance with God, and her hope of heaven, were
clear and firm. On Friday, the day on which she exchanged
mortality for life, which she thought was the Sabbath, she
exclaimed, " What a beautiful Sunday morning is this !" and
immediately commenced singing—

> " The Lord of Sabbath let us praise,
> In concert with the blest,
> Who, joyful, in harmonious lays
> Employ an endless rest."

Shortly her speech failed, and her spirit left the tenement of clay to mingle with those around the throne of God.

HYMN 545.—" O Thou eternal Victim, slain."—*A Memorial of the Death of Christ.*

This forms No. 5 of Charles Wesley's " Hymns on the Lord's Supper," 1745. The full title is, " The Lord's Supper as it is a memorial of the sufferings and death of Christ." The sacramental hymns of Charles Wesley are, to a large extent, based on the sentiments recorded by Dr Brevint in his treatise on that subject, which is usually prefixed to the hymns. A thoughtful reader of both will readily discover the sentiments both of Dr Brevint and Thomas à Kempis ; but these are embellished by Charles Wesley with all the charm of sacred poetry.

HYMN 546.—" Come, all who truly bear."—*A Memorial of the Death of Christ.*

Charles Wesley's, forming No. 13 of " Hymns on the Lord's Supper," 1745.

HYMN 547.—" Come, Thou everlasting Spirit."—*A Memorial of the Death of Christ.*

Charles Wesley's, forming No. 16 of " Hymns on the Lord's Supper."

HYMN 548.—" Lamb of God, whose bleeding Love."—*A Memo- rial of the Death of Christ.*

Charles Wesley's, forming No. 20 of " Hymns on the Lord's Supper."

HYMN 549.—" Jesu, at whose supreme command.—*Before the Sacrament.*

Charles Wesley's, from " Hymns and Sacred Poems," 1742, page 28. Line 3 of the second verse is altered from " Affix the sacramental seal." The original is printed in eight four-line stanzas. It also forms No. 30 in the same author's " Hymns on the Lord's Supper," 1745.

HYMN 550.—" Come, Holy Ghost, Thine influence shed."—*The Sacrament as it is a sign and means of grace.*

Charles Wesley's, forming No. 72 of " Hymns on the Lord's Supper."

HYMN 551.—"Victim Divine, Thy grace we claim."—*The holy Eucharist as it implies a Sacrifice.*

Charles Wesley's, forming No. 116 of "Hymns on the Lord's Supper." Dr Brevint's remarks on page 15 of his essay, furnish the thoughts on which this hymn is founded.

HYMN 552.—"Jesus drinks the bitter cup."—*A Memorial of the Death of Christ.*

Charles Wesley's, forming No. 21 of "Hymns on the Lord's Supper," 1745. The original has nine stanzas, the first three of which are left out. The omitted verses form Hymn 621, commencing, "God of unexampled grace." In this hymn, the poet notices, in bold and striking language, the signs and wonders accompanying the death of Christ : the phraseology is comprehensive, solemn, and sublime. In the second verse of this hymn the poet alludes to a rumour recorded by Plutarch, that in the reign of Tiberius, who was Emperor of Rome at the time of the crucifixion of Jesus, an extraordinary voice was heard near some islands in the Ionian Sea, which exclaimed, "The great Pan is dead." The augurs were consulted by the Emperor, but they could not explain the meaning of the supernatural voice. The fact of the rumour being on record is remarkable. The heathens regarded the god Pan as the source of fecundity, and as the principle or origin of all things. What they in ignorance attributed to Pan belonged really and truly to the Lord Jesus Christ. Hence our Christian poet sings, in verse two—

> " Dies the glorious cause of all !
> The true eternal Pan
> Falls, to raise us from our fall,
> To ransom sinful man."

What is here applied by the poet from heathendom to the death of the Saviour is by Milton applied to his birth in his " Hymn for the Morning of Christ's Nativity," where the poet says—

> " The shepherds on the lawn,
> Or e'er the point of dawn,
> Sat simply chatting in a rustic row ;
> Full little thought they then
> That the mighty Pan
> Was kindly come to live with them below."

The Rev. Samuel Wesley, rector of Epworth, in his exquisite
devotional piece, entitled, "Eupolis' Hymn to the Creator," published in several of the Wesley volumes, alludes in like manner
to the name and power of this great heathen deity, thus—

> " Thy herbage, O great Pan, sustains
> The flocks that graze our Attic plains. "

HYMN 553.—" He dies ! the Friend of sinners dies ! "—*Christ's
dying, rising, and reigning.*

Dr Watts', from " Horæ Lyricæ, 1705.
This hymn is as much improved by John Wesley's judicious
alterations as is the same author's version of the Hundredth
Psalm.   Dr Watts wrote thus—

> " He dies ! The heavenly Lover dies !
> The tidings strike a doleful sound
> On my poor heart-strings : deep he lies
> In the cold caverns of the ground."

We need not stay to point out the weakness of this ; let John
Wesley's amended lines make their own appeal—

> " He dies ! the Friend of sinners dies !
> Lo ! Salem's daughters weep around !
> A solemn darkness veils the skies,
> A sudden trembling shakes the ground."

In Mr Wesley's " Select Hymns for the Use of Christians of all
Denominations," he has printed this hymn in its unaltered form ;
thus showing that he took special pains in preparing the Hymn-
book designed " For the Use of the People called Methodists."

HYMN 554.—" Our Lord is risen from the dead."—*On the Ascension of Christ.*

Charles Wesley's version of Psalm xxiv. 7–10, found in the
enlarged edition of " Psalms and Hymns," 1743.

HYMN 555.—" Come, Desire of nations, come ! "—*Written on
the Earthquake in London,* 1750.

Charles Wesley's, from " Hymns occasioned by the Earthquake, March 8, 1750," Part II., No. 13.
When all London was in a state of violent consternation, the

inhabitants fleeing into the open country, foolishly thinking the earthquake might not there reach them, and supposing that the apparent threatenings of the Almighty were against the buildings and not against the citizens of London, multitudes giving up everything from fear, and crowding round the Wesleys and Whitefield in their homes, at the Foundery, and in Hyde Park, Moorfields, and Kennington, then, and under such exciting circumstances, the faith of Charles Wesley was manifested by his writing and printing immediately such hymns as this—

> " Come, Desire of nations, come !
> Hasten, Lord, the general doom ! "

Thus the faith of the Christian poet enabled him to pray for that which the affrighted unbelieving worldlings so much dreaded ! This hymn is also printed in Mr Wesley's " Select Hymns, with Tunes annext," 1761 ; and in the " Sacred Melody" it has the tune " Plymouth " affixed.

HYMN 556.—" To the hills I lift mine eyes."—*Psalm* cxxi.

Charles Wesley's paraphrase of Psalm cxxi., &c., found in the enlarged edition of " Psalms and Hymns," 1743. This is placed under the title, " On Miscellaneous Subjects."

Methodism has flourished in Yorkshire with scarcely any exception or interruption. Against much opposition Hugh Gill, of Weeton, Otley, joined the Methodist Society, through the preaching of Richard Burdsall and his contemporaries, and soon afterwards he became a local preacher and often travelled long journeys, to proclaim the salvation which he himself had found. He and his son, who also was a local preacher, so thoroughly canvassed the village on behalf of the mission cause, that they collected nearly two shillings annually for every resident therein ; and the greatest delight of Mr Gill's family was to have the house full of guests at the missionary anniversary, and to give each a thoroughly Yorkshire welcome. When seventy-four summers had passed over his head, during fifty of which he had acted as a local preacher, he was as much attached to the means of grace as ever. On Good Friday, 1827, he attended a prayer-meeting, and poured out his soul before God with much earnestness and power. On Easter Sunday he met his class in the morning, and gave out the hymn—

> " To the hills I lift mine eyes,
>   The everlasting hills ;
>   Streaming thence, in fresh supplies,
>   My soul the Spirit feels."

He was taken ill while singing, yet he afterwards tried to pray. His voice began to falter, articulation became difficult, and in a few days his happy spirit escaped to the land of rest, as he whispered, " I feel Jesus precious—very precious."

Sarah Haldom feared the Lord from her youth ; and after being more than fifty years a consistent member of the Methodist Society, she died in great peace at Newington Green, London, with an unshaken reliance on the Saviour. During her long and severe illness, she often repeated the verse—

> " To the hills I lift mine eyes,
>   The everlasting hills ;
>   Streaming thence, in fresh supplies,
>   My soul the Spirit feels :
>   Will He not His help afford ?
>   Help, while yet I ask, is given !"

HYMN 557.—" Ye servants of God, Your Master proclaim."—*To be Sung in a Tumult.*

Charles Wesley's, from " Hymns for the Times of Trouble and Persecution," 1744, page 43. The third verse of the original is left out, and the last verse is taken from Charles Wesley's " Funeral Hymns," page 24, where it is the fifth.

HYMN 558.—" Come, Lord, from above, The mountains remove." —*For those that seek Redemption.*

Charles Wesley's, from " Hymns for those that seek Redemption," 1747. It contains a lively and instructive presentation of the plan of salvation. The marrow of the gospel scheme is embodied in this couplet—

> " Who on Jesus believes, Without money or price,
>   The pearl of forgiveness and holiness buys."

HYMN 559.—" God moves in a mysterious way."—*Light Shining in Darkness.*

William Cowper's, from " Olney Hymns," No. 15, Book III., 1779.

In instances innumerable this hymn has been a source of encouragement and consolation to the tried, afflicted, and distressed followers of the Redeemer. The title is "Light Shining out of Darkness." What that darkness was, a brief glance at the history of the author and the hymn will sufficiently explain. Partly from pecuniary difficulty, and partly from deep remorse on account of sin, Cowper had to be placed under the care of Dr Cotton as a lunatic. Ultimately he so far recovered as to be removed from the asylum, and allowed the liberty of free action. Even then he was occasionally so much depressed as to be a source of anxiety to those around him. In one of these attacks of mental derangement he unhappily believed that the divine will was that he should drown himself in a particular part of the River Thames at London. He one evening, in his thirty-second year, called for a post-chaise, and ordered the driver to take him to the Tower Wharf, intending, as he records, "to throw myself into the river from the Custom-house Quay. I left the coach upon the Tower Wharf, intending never to return to it. But I found the water low, and a porter seated on some goods as if on purpose to prevent me. This passage to the bottomless pit being mercifully shut against me, I returned to the coach, and ordered the man to drive me back to the Temple." Thus the snare was broken. Cowper escaped the temptation, and immediately he sat down and wrote the hymn, which indeed speaks of "light shining out of darkness," which has ministered comfort to thousands, and will yet afford consolation to thousands of others for many generations to come. James Montgomery says of this hymn that it "is a lyric of high tone and character, and rendered awfully interesting by the circumstances under which it was written—in the twilight of returning reason."

The late Rev. Hugh Stowell, of Manchester, at a public meeting, related an incident which very touchingly illustrates this hymn of Cowper's. One of the Lancashire mill-owners, who had struggled long to keep his hands employed during the cotton famine arising from the American war, 1865, at last found it impossible to proceed, and, calling his workpeople together, told them that he should be compelled, after the usual notice, to close his mills. The news was received with sadness and sympathy; to them it meant privation and suffering, to him it might be ruin None cared to speak in reply; when suddenly arose the voice of song from one of the girls, who was a Sunday-school teacher, and who, feeling it to be an occasion requiring divine help and guidance, gave out the verse of Cowper's hymn—

> "Ye fearful saints, fresh courage take,
>   The clouds ye so much dread
> Are big with mercy, and shall break
>   In blessings on your head."

All the mill-hands joined in singing the verse amidst deep emotion.

Few persons have had a better parentage, a better training, better companions, or a better end of life than the Rev. Joseph Entwisle the second. When a scholar at Kingswood School, at the age of ten, he became the subject of saving grace, and maintained his piety throughout a long life. At the age of twenty-five he was received into the Wesleyan ministry, having been preceded by a father, of the same name, one of the most handsome, holy, useful, and venerable of men. The son, like his sire, carried his religion into everything, and lived as one who had habitual communion with God. In 1864 he was travelling in the Yeadon circuit, and one Thursday evening he was preaching at Moorside. He had just given out the second two lines of the first hymn for the service—

> "God moves in a mysterious way," &c.,

and whilst the congregation was singing the fourth line of the verse—

> " And rides upon the storm,"

the preacher quietly sank down in the pulpit, and in a few moments his meek and quiet spirit passed away, to be for ever with Him "who rides upon the storm," who is " His own interpreter," and who will in His own good time make all such dispensations " plain."

HYMN 560.—"Lord, dismiss us with Thy blessing."—*A Benediction.*

This is believed to have been written (1793) by the Rev. Edwin Smythe, formerly of Dublin, afterwards of Bath and Bristol, and who was associated with the Wesleys in their labours at the close of the last century. Mr Smythe was nephew to the Archbishop of Dublin in 1777. The widow of Mr Smythe was known to several Methodists during the present

century. A sister of the Archbishop had twenty-seven children, and one of her grandchildren was the wife of the Rev.
Dr Morison, of China.   This hymn must not be confused with
another which commences with the same first line, which was
written by the Rev. Walter Shirley in 1774, but which is in three
stanzas.

THE SUPPLEMENT.

THOSE to whom the affairs of Methodism were intrusted—
namely, the " Legal Hundred"—during the quarter of a century
following the death of its founder, found sufficient occupation
in carrying on, consolidating, and extending the work of preaching the gospel, and the duties resulting therefrom ; hence
several minor matters, as they were then thought to be, which
have since occupied a large share of the attention of the Connexion, were left in abeyance for "a more convenient season."
One of these matters was the extension of the Collection of
Hymns used by the body.   When the Hymn-book proper, with
the twenty-one additional hymns, was finally agreed upon,
selfish, and sometimes merciless printers in the country invaded
the rights of the Book Committee, by bringing and pushing
into the market cheap, unauthorised, and often very inaccurate
editions of that work, to the injury of the funds of Methodism,
and not much to the credit of any one else.   This question
often came before the Book Committee in London ; and ultimately, in 1829, or thereabouts, the desire for an increased
variety of hymns was urged with so much reason and force by
many of the preachers and Societies, that it was resolved to add
a Supplement to the Collection, and the preparation of that
work was intrusted to the editor (at that time the Rev. Thomas
Jackson), the Rev. Richard Watson, and the Rev. W. M.
Bunting.   This addition of 209 hymns was published at the end
of the year 1830, at first in a separate form, so as to place it
within easy reach of the members of the Society and congregations, and after a year or two it was regularly bound up as part
of the authorised Collection, in which form alone it has since
been sold.   The frequency with which the hymns in this part
of the book have been given out from that time to the pre-

sent, is the best possible evidence that the addition thus made was required by the Societies, and really appreciated by them.

The following short preface will explain what further may be required to be known as the reason for making such an addition.

"The following Supplement is designed to furnish a greater number of hymns suitable for public worship, for festivals, and for occasional services, than are found in that invaluable Collection, in common use, which the piety and genius of the Wesleys bequeathed to the societies raised up by their ministry. It is compiled chiefly from the festival and other hymns which Mr Charles Wesley published in separate pamphlets, and from his unpublished poetry, which, by purchase from his heir, along with other papers, has lately become the property of the Connexion. To these some hymns have been added from other authors, chiefly from Dr Watts ; and a few which, though they sink below the rank of the Wesley poetry, are inserted because of some excellence which will be found in the sentiment, and the greater choice of subjects which they afford. Most of the hymns of this class, however, were inserted in the 'Morning Hymn-Book,' prepared by Mr Wesley for the London congregations, or in a smaller Collection published by him ; and so had his sanction. A few others have been introduced because of their popular character, and their being favourites with many of our people. Limited as this Supplement is, it will render our congregations more familiar than they have ever been with some noble hymns of Mr Charles Wesley, only to be found in Collections which are in the hands of comparatively few persons ; whilst it brings into use, for the first time, a number of his compositions not inferior to those which he himself published. The Preachers will here find hymns adapted to various subjects on which they address the people ; and our fine occasional hymns, which were seldom used, because not in the hands of the congregations generally, will be ready for festival occasions ; and will be found in many instances adapted also, at least in some of their stanzas, to general use. As several of the hymns in this Collection are selected from the papers of Mr Charles Wesley above referred to, and have not before been published, a copyright is established in this Supplement, and all pirated editions are rendered liable to legal process. To guard against such attempts to turn to private profit what is sacredly applied to the support of the work of God, this Collection has been regularly entered at Stationers'-Hall.—LONDON, _Nov._ 9, 1830."

HYMN 561.—" Hail, Father, whose creating call."—_A Hymn to God the Father._

This was written by Samuel Wesley, jun., and forms the first hymn in his volume of "Poems on Several Occasions," 1736, second edition 1743, and reprinted in 1862, page 365.

There are three of these hymns, the second being addressed to God the Son, which commences the second section of the Supplement, No. 601 ; and the third addressed to God the Holy Spirit, which commences the third section, Hymn 649. These were not printed in the original quarto edition of Mr Samuel Wesley's poems, published in 1736, but in the second and enlarged edition, 12mo, 1743, with a portrait, the finest which has ever appeared of the author. Samuel Wesley, the elder brother of John and Charles, was born in London, February 10, 1690. As a child he showed a taste for poetry. He was educated at Westminster School and Christ Church, Oxford, whence he returned, after he had taken his M.A. degree, to become one of the ushers of Westminster School, where he had his brothers for some time under his care. Whilst residing there he became one of the founders and principal promoters of the Westminster Hospital, a work of charity and benevolence in which he took special pleasure. After residing in Westminster cloisters for twenty years, he was appointed head-master of the Grammar School, Tiverton, in 1732. He there issued the first edition of his poems in 1736, and died in 1739, at the early age of forty-nine. He was not friendly to the religious views of his brothers, but died before the Methodist Societies were really founded. There are six of his hymns in the Collection. The following lines originally formed the fourth verse of this hymn—

> "Pleased to behold Thine image bright
> With rays co-equal shine ;
> Begotten, uncreated Light,
> As infinite as Thine."

HYMN 562.—"Hail, co-essential Three."—*The Trinity in Unity.*
Charles Wesley's, from "Hymns on the Trinity," 1767, page 107.

HYMN 563.—"Great is our redeeming Lord."—*The Holy Church throughout all the world doth acknowledge Thee.*

Charles Wesley's version of Psalm xlviii., published by Henry Fish, A.M., 1854.

HYMNS 564.—" Infinite God, to Thee we raise."
,,   565.—" Messiah, joy of every heart."
,,   566.—" Saviour, we now rejoice in hope."
Te Deum laudamus.

Charles Wesley's, forming the first portion of his elegant poetical paraphrase of that sublime devotional hymn known as the " TE DEUM." It is found in that poet's " Hymns for those that seek Redemption," 1747. It there appears in fourteen stanzas ; but in the Hymn-book it is divided so as to make three hymns. There is a sublimity in the language and character of the *Te Deum,* which the poet has admirably caught and embodied in his masterly rendering of the same. Who, for instance, can repeat the solemn truth, " We believe that Thou shalt come to be our Judge," without deep emotion, or sing the same in the strain of the Methodist poet—

> " And Thou, with judgment clad, shalt come,
> To seal our everlasting doom."

This paraphrase has been very generally ascribed to the poet Dryden, but erroneously. He has published a version of this fine hymn ; but it is much inferior to this one by Charles Wesley. His is in the decasyllabic verse, and commences thus—

> " Thee, sovereign God, our grateful accents praise,
> We own Thee Lord, and bless Thy wondrous ways."

HYMN 567.—" The spacious firmament on high."—" *The heavens declare the glory of God,*" &c.

Joseph Addison's, being one of his five hymns, and thought to be the best of them. It is a version of the first four verses of Psalm xix., and was published in 1712. It is found in the *Spectator,* No. 465, Saturday, August 23, 1712. It is a sublime composition ; but it is remarkable that, whilst it exhibits the works of God in exalted strains, the name of God or of Jesus Christ does not once occur in the hymn. There has been much controversy concerning its authorship. Partisans have been found to claim it for Watts, Tickell, and Marvel; but though the evidence of actual authorship is not so clear as it might be, the claim of Addison is supreme.

Joseph Addison was born May 1, 1672, and was the son of

the rector of Milston, in Wiltshire. He was educated at Ames-
bury, Salisbury, and the Charterhouse, where he became acquainted with Richard Steele. He afterwards graduated at
Queen's College, Oxford, and at the age of twenty-two addressed
some elegant verses to the veteran poet, Dryden. When only
twenty-five, he obtained a crown pension of £300 per annum to
enable him to travel, for a complimentary poem on the king.
He afterwards contributed liberally to the *Tatler*, *Spectator*,
and *Guardian*, and his Saturday papers in the *Spectator* contained his hymns. In 1716 he married the Countess-Dowager
of Warwick, and in 1717 he became Secretary of State, This
office he soon relinquished on a pension of £1500 a-year, and
died at Holland House, Kensington, June 17, 1719. His works
are numerous, and possess high moral excellence as well as distinguished literary merit. Hence there is a proverbial saying,
"Whoever would attain to an elegant English style, must give
his days and nights to the study of Addison."

HYMN 568.—"God is a name my soul adores."—*The Creator
and Creatures*,

Dr Watts', from "Horæ Lyricæ," 1705. This was inserted in
John Wesley's "Collection of Psalms and Hymns," 1738. The
second verse of the original is left out, and several alterations
are made in those which are adopted. Mr Bunting has suggested as a tune for this hymn, "Webb's—very slow."

HYMN 569.—"The Lord Jehovah reigns."—*The Divine
Perfections.*

Dr Watts' version of Psalm cxlviii. It is found in John Wesley's "Psalms and Hymns," 1738, and considerably improved
by John Wesley's alterations.

HYMN 570.—"High in the heavens, eternal God."—*The
Perfections and Providence of God.*

Dr Watts' version of Psalm xxxii. 5, 6. The fifth verse is
omitted.

HYMN 571.—"With glory clad, with strength array'd."—
"*Holiness becometh Thine house, O Lord, for ever.*"

Tate and Brady's version of Psalm cxiii., licensed in 1696.

HYMN 572.—"The earth and all her fulness owns."—"*The earth
          is the Lord's,*" &c.

Charles Wesley's version of Psalm xxiv. 1–5.   It is printed in
John Wesley's "Psalms and Hymns," enlarged, 1741, with
verses 6–13 omitted.

HYMN 573.—" Come, sound His praise abroad."—*A Psalm
          before a Sermon.*

Dr Watts' version of the ninety-fifth Psalm, with two verses
left out.

HYMN 574.—" How lovely are thy tents, O Lord!"—
          Psalm lxxxiv.

Charles Wesley's version of Psalm lxxxiv., first printed
in the *Arminian Magazine*, and also included in Mr Fish's
collection of Charles Wesley's Psalms.   The second and fifth
verses are left out.

HYMN 575.—" Who Jesus our Example know."—"*Peter and
          John went up into the temple at the hour of prayer.*"

Charles Wesley's paraphrase of Acts iii. 1.

HYMN 576.—" My soul, inspired with sacred love."—
          Psalm cxlvi.

Charles Wesley's paraphrase of Psalm cxlvi., with two verses
omitted.   It was printed first in the *Arminian Magazine*, and
is also inserted in Mr Fish's collection of Charles Wesley's
Psalms.   There is a similarity in some of the lines to portions
of Addison's hymn commencing "When all Thy mercies, O my
God" (Hymn 592).

Under the ministry of the Rev. Joseph Hollingworth, at Bar-
wick and Yarm, John Mowbray Pearson was convinced of sin;
and whilst attending a prayer-meeting in the Wesleyan Chapel,
Yarm, he believed on Christ, and obtained the blessing of pardon
and the spirit of adoption, when in his seventeenth year.   He
soon became a prayer-leader and local preacher, and in 1832
was received into the itinerant ministry, covenanting with God
to use every opportunity for improvement in the Church and in
bringing glory to God.   Illness set in, which cut short his
career of usefulness; but at the commencement of it he had the

T

clearest assurance of his acceptance with God. A short time before his death, he requested a friend to read to him Hymn 576, commencing—

> " My soul, inspired with sacred love,
>   The Lord thy God delight to praise ;
> His gifts I will for Him improve,
>   To Him devote my happy days ;
> To Him my thanks and praises give,
> And only for His glory live."

Clasping his hands, he exclaimed, "Thank God, this hymn contains my experience, my principles, and my determination." When the sweat of death was on his brow, waving his hand in token of victory, he said, with his expiring breath, " Come, Lord Jesus, come quickly ;" and he fell asleep in Jesus.

HYMN 577.—" Great God, attend, while Sion sings."—*God and His Church ; or, Grace and Glory.*

Dr Watts' version of the eighty-fourth Psalm, 1719.

HYMN 578.—" Sweet is the work, my God, my King."—*A Psalm for the Lord's Day.*

Dr Watts' version of the ninety-first Psalm, Part I., 1719, the sixth verse left out.

In early life, Mr George Nott, brother of General Sir W. Nott, G.C.B., had a strong bias towards the Christian ministry, but circumstances did not favour his object ; yet his highly cultivated mind and powerful intellect were occasionally exercised as a local preacher in Methodism, to which Society he belonged for nearly fifty years. As a class-leader, he greatly excelled, owing to his deep spiritual experience, his accurate acquaintance with Scripture, and his remarkably retentive memory. He loved prayer, and was regular at the weekly prayer-meeting. In retirement, during his last illness, when laid aside by paralysis, he delighted to converse on the heavenly state ; and the mention of its nearness and blessedness would at once awaken strong feelings of attachment to the better land, which he would give expression to in some favourite stanza. Often did he break out in this strain—

> " Then shall I see, and hear, and know,
>   All I desired and wished below ;

And every power find sweet employ
In that eternal world of joy."

Full of such expectations, he passed away from his earthly home
at Carmarthen to his everlasting one in heaven.

HYMN 579.—" Great is the Lord our God."—*The Church is the
Honour and Safety of a Nation.*

Dr Watts' version of Psalm xlviii., verses 1-8, Part I., with
three verses of the original left out.

In one of the omitted stanzas the poet has shown most con-
vincingly how the power of the Almighty is the defence of any
nation that trusts in Him—

" When navies, tall and proud,
    Attempt to spoil our peace,
    He sends His tempests, roaring loud,
    And sinks them in the seas."

Similar in sentiment is that line of Charles Wesley's in which
he prays for the defeat of the French navy : when that nation
was seeking to invade England, Charles Wesley's prayer for the
intruding invaders was very pointed—

" Sink them in the Channel, Lord."

HYMN 580.—" Great God, this hallow'd day of Thine."—*Hymn
for the Lord's Day Morning.*

Written by Miss Ann Steele, under the signature of " Theodosia." It appears in the third volume of her " Miscellaneous
Pieces, in Verse and Prose," 1760, page 138. The third and
fourth verses are left out.

She was the daughter of the Rev. William Steele, Baptist
minister, Broughton, Hants, and was born in 1716. She was a
member of her father's church ; and wrote a number of hymns
and poems, full of scriptural teaching, breathing a pious spirit.
They have a wide and deservedly high reputation. A few hours
before the time fixed for her marriage, the young man was
drowned, and this sad accident, and her own delicate frame,
made her a great sufferer through life. She died at Broughton
in 1778, aged sixty-one, and was buried in the churchyard there.

The original hymn has four verses, the first and second only
being given. In the first line, " sacred " is changed for " hal-

lowed" day of Thine; and the fourth line reads, "These solemn,
these devoted hours." Neither of these alterations are improvements. The Rev. W. M. Bunting has added the following verse
to his copy of this hymn, under date of "May 7, '65, 8 A.M."

> "And let Thy mercy lighten, Lord,
>   On all who thus look up to Thee;
> Distil the comfort of Thy Word
>   Like dew from heaven, my God, on ME.
> So be both sanctified and blest
> To me, to all, this day of rest."

HYMN 581.—"Welcome, sweet day of rest."—*The Lord's Day.*

Dr Watts', from Book II., Hymn 14, 1709.

In conversion and on death-beds this hymn has been made a
blessing to many. John Watson, of Baildon, Yorkshire, was
apprenticed to a cloth-worker at the age of nine years, to remain
till he was twenty. During that time he was allowed one shil-
ling per year for pocket-money. This sum he preserved for five
years, and, after much reasoning, he purchased a Bible and Dr
Watts' Hymn-Book with his five shillings. He was much elated
with his bargain, although he could not read them. He had
regularly attended the Baptist Chapel at Rawdon, but had
realised nothing beyond serious impressions. It was the practice of the family with whom he resided often to read the Scriptures, and to sing hymns; and on one of these occasions, whilst
repeating the verse—

> "One day amidst the place
>   Where my dear Lord has been,
> Is better than ten thousand days
>   Of pleasurable sin,"

he felt unutterable joy. He withdrew, and took a walk into the
fields, where his peace in communing with God was overflowing.
He was impressed to go and hear the Methodists, which he did
on the following Sunday: he joined the Society, and remained
a faithful and consistent member for sixty years, a class-leader
for fifty years, and, at the age of eighty, died in great peace, saying, "Christ is precious; He is precious indeed."

So few were the privileges of the Gospel in some parts of
England seventy years ago, that in order to attend the preaching of the Methodists, in which his soul felt comfort and satisfaction, John Dixon, of Bassingham, had to go to Newark, nine

miles, to hear a sermon on the Sabbath morning, and to Retford, twenty miles, to hear another sermon on the Sabbath evening. In 1801, the Rev. John Hickling was invited to preach in Mr Dixon's house, and from that time a society was formed in the village, which has been made a blessing to many souls. He had a delicate frame, and suffered much during his short life, but he found constant consolation in religion. When the last summons came, he was asked what he thought of religion and of Methodism. He spoke in the most exalted terms of religion, and added, in reply to the other question, " Defend Methodism, for it is of God ; particularly the great doctrines of the witness of the Spirit, and Christian perfection." He thought highly of Watts' Hymns, and often quoted from them.   His last utterances were—
" Precious, precious Jesus,"

> " My willing soul would stay
>   In such a frame as this,
> And sit and sing herself away
>   To everlasting bliss."

Almost immediately his released spirit entered the port of heaven in the triumph of faith.

HYMN 582.—" Lord of the Sabbath, hear our vows."—*The Eternal Sabbath.*

This is Dr Doddridge's hymn, written to illustrate the text, Heb. iv. 9, with the date January 2, 1736-7, in the author's MS.

Dr Doddridge wrote his hymns to be sung after the sermons which he preached, and adapted them specially to the texts which he selected.   He died in Lisbon in 1751, aged forty-nine years. His hymns were published in 1755 by his friend Job Orton.

Philip Doddridge, born in London in 1702, was the son of an oilman.   He received a good education, one of his tutors being the excellent Samuel Clark, author of "Scripture Promises."   He joined the Dissenters, and became one of their ministers, although the Duchess of Bedford offered to maintain him at Cambridge if he remained in the Church.   At the early age of twenty-seven, entreated by his friend Dr Watts, he opened an academy —a school of the prophets—for the education of young men for the ministry.   In 1730, he removed to Northampton, where his theological college was carried on to the time of his death (from consumption) in 1751.   Some two hundred students were educated by him, one hundred and fifty of whom entered the ministry. Here he wrote his numerous works, was the minister at the Castle Hill Meeting-house, and became one of the founders of the Book Society for providing good and cheap books for the poor. Lady Frances Gardiner, wife of Colonel Gardiner, urged Doddridge to publish his hymns, but he had been dead four years before they appeared. They are three hundred and sixty-four in number, to which some others were added in another volume of hymns, published in 1838, by John Doddridge Humphryes. Montgomery says of Doddridge's Hymns :—"They shine in the beauty of holiness ; and, like the saints, they are lovely and acceptable for fervid, unaffected love to God, His service, and His people."

The words of Hagar, " Thou, God, seest me," so rested upon the mind of Anne Hamer in early life, that she was constrained to forsake worldly pleasures ; and at the age of sixteen, during the progress of a revival in Shropshire, she found the Lord, to the joy of her heart. Her life ever afterwards was devoted to the service of God ; in the Sabbath-school, and as a missionary collector, she was remarkably useful. Her last illness was brief, but her peace and joy were unshaken. When the midnight preceding her departure was passed, she was reminded that the Sabbath had commenced. She immediately replied—

> " Thine earthly Sabbaths, Lord, we love ;
> But there's a nobler rest above ;
> To that our lab'ring souls aspire,
> With ardent pangs of strong desire."

Adding, " I shall soon be before the throne of God and the Lamb : I shall hunger no more, neither thirst any more : the Lamb shall lead me to fountains of living waters, and God shall wipe away all tears from my eyes." In this ecstasy of joy and praise she continued for some time ; then, turning to her husband, repeated, " Farewell ! and let me languish into life ;" and so she passed away.

Dr Doddridge's description of heaven in this hymn would scarcely be appreciated by Christians dwelling in an Eastern clime, where the " sun-cloud" and " midnight-shade" are the very paradise of life's enjoyment. A noble missionary, who spent thirty years in Jamaica and Old Calabar, remarks :—" One who knows what it is to be exposed to the sun of the torrid zone shudders to read the dreadful lines in a hymn by Dr Doddridge, describing heaven :—

'No midnight shade, no clouded sun,
But sacred, high, eternal noon.'

The idea is intolerable. It terrifies one to think of it. The man who wrote that line must have lived far north, where a glimpse of the sun was a rare favour, and his highest enjoyment to bask in its rays a live-long summer's day. I met once in Jamaica with a black boy, under the shade of some cocoa-nut trees, where we both had taken shelter from the glare of the meridian sun and the dazzle of the sea-side sandy road. I said, 'Well, my boy, did you ever hear of heaven?' 'Me hear, massa.' 'And what sort of place do you think it will be?' 'Massa, it must be very cool place.' That boy knows more of the Bible on that subject than some hymn-writers."

HYMN 583.—"Again our weekly labours end."—*On the Sabbath.*

This is part of a hymn of fourteen stanzas, originally written by Joseph Stennett, and published in 1732. It has been so altered by some one, that, as it appears in the Methodist collection, only the last five lines are copied in their integrity. Stennett's hymn has many admirers, and is found in other collections unaltered. The first verse reads thus :—

" Another six days' work is done,
Another Sabbath is begun ;
Return, my soul, unto thy rest :
Revere the day thy God has blest."

The Rev. W.-M. Bunting has added this note : " For other good Sabbath-morning hymns, see 647, 652, 654, 664, and 698."

The author of this hymn, the Rev. Joseph Stennett, D.D., was born at Abingdon, Berks, in 1663, and under his father's ministry was converted in early life. His education embraced every branch of knowledge then taught. After he became the pastor at Devonshire Square Chapel, he ministered to a congregation of Seventh-day Baptists ; but he also preached to other congregations on the first day. He also trained young men for the ministry. He was the author of " Hymns for the Lord's Supper," 1697 ; "A Version of Solomon's Song," 1700, and twelve " Hymns on Believers' Baptism," 1712. He also published a commendatory poem on the Rev. Samuel Wesley's " Ingenious Poem entitled The Life of Christ," &c., 1693. He died in 1713. His collected works, hymns, poems, sermons, letters, and life, appeared, in four volumes, in 1732. This hymn is found in a dozen collections.

HYMN 584.—" O render thanks to God above."—*"His mercy endureth for ever."*

Tate or Brady's version of Psalm cvi. 1–6. The original is in forty-eight stanzas, five only of which are selected. The last line is altered from

"Sing loud amens, praise ye the Lord."

HYMN 585.—" Far as creation's bounds extend."—*The Goodness of God Acknowledged.*

James Merrick's paraphrase of part of Psalm cxlv., and first published in 1765. Only a small portion of the original is given.

James Merrick, A.M., was born in 1720, and was educated for the ministry at Trinity College, Oxford ; but his health failing him, he was not ordained. He translated or paraphrased the Psalms in English verse, and published the work in 1765, but it failed to secure royal favour, so rests simply on its intrinsic merits. Dr W. B. Collyer thought so highly of Merrick's version, that he included over fifty of his psalms and hymns in his collection. He died at Reading, in January 1769, aged fifty years.

HYMN 586.—" Eternal depth of love divine."—*" God with us."*

John Wesley's translation from the German of Count Zinzendorf. It is found in " Hymns and Sacred Poems," 1739, page 195. The original is in four double stanzas, the last of which is omitted.

HYMN 587.—" Let every tongue Thy goodness speak."—*Mercy to Sufferers.*

Dr Watts' version of Psalm cxlv. 14–17. The fourth verse is left out, and the third altered.

HYMN 588.—" This, this is the God we adore."—*God our Trust.*

Joseph Hart's, from " Hymns Composed on Various Occasions," 1759. The original consists of seven stanzas, the last only of which is here given. It forms No. 73 in the author's own book, the first line being—

"No prophet or dreamer of dreams."

Joseph Hart was born in London in 1712. In early life he

attended Whitefield's Tabernacle, Moorfields.   He was a sound
classical scholar, and became a teacher of languages.   He was
converted under the preaching of Whitefield, and himself became a preacher.   The Rev. J. Towers, of Barbican Chapel,
describes his preaching and hymns as "a treasury of practical,
doctrinal, and experimental divinity."   He died in London,
May 24, 1768, and is interred in Bunhill Fields.   One of his
sons became a barrister and Lord High Chancellor of Ireland,
although the father left his family in destitute circumstances
when he died.   There is scarcely a verse in the Hymn-book
which has met with more acceptance, or which has been more
frequently repeated on death-beds, than this one of Mr Hart's.
We have only space for three brief notices.

The mother of the Rev. Samuel Lucas was first convinced of
sin under the ministry of the Rev. J. A. James, and found peace
through believing on Jesus from attending the preaching of the
Methodists in Birmingham.   For twenty years she held fast
her faith in God.   During a long affliction she was preserved in
patience and resignation.   Nearly her last words were expressive of her confidence and thankfulness, and were in the lines
of Hart's hymn, which she had often sung in health—

> " 'Tis Jesus, the first and the last,
>   Whose Spirit shall guide me safe home ;
> I 'll praise Him for all that is past,
>   And trust Him for all that 's to come."

Soon afterwards she fell asleep in Jesus.

In early life the Rev. Daniel West was brought to a saving
knowledge of the truth mainly through the instrumentality of the
Rev. John M'Lean.   He soon became a useful local preacher, was
admitted into the Methodist ministry, and left blessed fruit of
his labours in the circuits in which he travelled.   At the request
of Conference, he went to visit the mission-stations on the Gold
Coast of Africa, and there his work was cut short in righteousness.   He was taken suddenly ill at the Gambia.   The night
before he died he said to a missionary, " I have never forsaken
God, and He has not forsaken me."   With his fast-departing
breath he repeated the lines—

> " 'Tis Jesus, the first and the last,
>   Whose Spirit shall guide me safe home ;"

and then entered on his eternal rest.

The mother of the Rev. Dr Jobson was made instrumental in bringing her brother, Mr James Caborn, of Beverley, to a knowledge of the truth through faith in Jesus Christ.   He was fortynine when this happy change took place, and for thirty-six years afterwards he adorned the doctrine which he so ardently believed, devoting his mind, his energies, and his substance to the furtherance of the gospel, and in helping the neglected and poor. His testimony to the inward witness of the Spirit was clear, and his joy in the Holy Ghost often abounded.   In his last illness he was staying with Dr Jobson at Bradford.   He expressed his confidence in God in numerous verses from the Scriptures and the Hymn-book, at intervals of his severe sufferings, and up to the end of his earthly pilgrimage of eighty-five years, he spoke to himself in psalms and hymns and spiritual songs.   His last quotation was from Hymn 588 :—

> " This, this is the God we adore,
>   Our faithful unchangeable friend ;
> Whose love is as great as His power,
>   And neither knows measure nor end.

> " 'Tis Jesus, the first and the last,
>   Whose Spirit shall guide us safe home ;
> We 'll praise Him for all that is past,
>   And trust Him for all that 's to come."

In this tranquil, resigned, and peaceful frame of mind he entered the Heavenly Jerusalem.

HYMN 589.—" Sweet is the memory of Thy grace."—*The Goodness of God.*

Dr Watts' version of Psalm cxlv. 7, &c.   This is a continuation of Hymn 587, and should not be separated from it.   Hart's one verse would come in best after Hymn 590.

Early conversion to God, and devotion to His service was the privilege of William Naylor.   Commencing his career of religious usefulness soon after the death of Mr Wesley, he was acceptable as a local preacher, and at the age of twenty he commenced to travel as a Methodist preacher.   For sixty years he laboured with zeal and diligence in the arduous and responsible duties of the ministry, filling posts of honour, and occupying the more important circuits of the connexion.   He was a painstaking and earnest preacher of the doctrine of universal redemption, and a

diligent pastor.   He was a man of prayer, and his ministry was
one of power.   He took part in founding the Wesleyan Missionary Society, and was privileged to preach one of the jubilee
celebration sermons.   For six years he was diligently helping
forward the work of God as a supernumerary; and in his eighty-
fifth year, being then the oldest minister in the connexion, he
calmly entered into rest.   During a short illness which preceded
his death it was his custom to sing through, before retiring to
rest, Hymn 227, commencing—

> " How do Thy mercies close me round."

Those privileged to hear him will never forget the fulness of
feeling with which he sang it.   Words fail to convey the depth
of humility, the clinging trustfulness and utter reliance of faith,
that were expressed in the tones of his voice as he sang, with
a power as of early days—

> " Thou never, never wilt forsake
> A helpless worm that trusts in Thee."

When at last confined to bed, he would delight in singing "Rock
of Ages," and " Jesu, lover of my soul," both of which have so
often thrown the radiancy of heaven into the opening tomb.   The
last interviews he had with Mr and Mrs Mills and Mrs H. Banks
were closed by his singing through the last-named hymn.   Thus
the very footsteps of death beat time to the songs of triumphant
joy.   There was in his last days a depth of humility, and a marvellous sweetness of spirit shining forth, which indicated in him
" heaven begun below."   He also delighted, at the last, in singing
Hymn 589—

> " Sweet is the memory of Thy grace,
> My God, my heavenly King," &c. ;

and particularly the closing lines—

> " But we, who taste Thy richer grace,
> Delight to bless Thy name."

His happy spirit scarcely touched the rolling flood, for the
heavenly chariot flashed suddenly through that sacred room,
and conveyed him to the mansions on high.

HYMN 590.—" In all my vast concerns with Thee."— *God is
everywhere.*

Dr Watts' version of Psalm cxxxix., Part I.   The original has
ten verses, the last five being omitted.

HYMN 591.—" O that I could, in every place."—"*I have set the Lord always before me.*"

Charles Wesley's version of Psalm xvi. 8.

HYMN 592.—"When all Thy mercies, O my God."—*Thanksgiving for a Particular Providence.*

Joseph Addison's, from No. 453 of the *Spectator.* This was inserted by Mr Wesley in his collection of "Psalms and Hymns," enlarged edition, 1743. The original has thirteen stanzas, five of which are omitted. Mr Wesley chose the title.

In connexion with this hymn, the author observes, in the *Spectator* : "If gratitude is due from man to man, how much more from man to his Maker ? The Supreme Being does not only confer upon us those bounties which proceed more immediately from his hand, but even those benefits which are conveyed to us by others. Any blessing we enjoy, by what means soever derived, is the gift of Him who is the great Author of good, and the Father of mercies."

First, as the teacher of the preachers' sons in Old Kingwood School, and finally as the classical tutor of the "Sons of the Prophets," at Didsbury, as well as during a useful intermediate ministry in Methodism, in both England and India, the Rev. Jonathan Crowther served his generation with energy and fidelity. In his life he was a bright example of Christian piety and simplicity, of sanctified learning, and of untiring diligence in the discharge of his duties. During a visit to his friend, the Rev. W. Willan, at Leeds, he was seized with the illness which soon afterwards closed his earthly career. Just before consciousness departed a friend repeated, "Who shall separate us from the love of Christ ?" He took up the passage and continued it to the end of the verse ; and then, with peculiar emphasis, said—

> "When all Thy mercies, O my God,
>   My rising soul surveys,
>   Transported with the view, I'm lost
>   In wonder, love, and praise."

He then repeated, "He maketh me to lie down in green pastures. He leadeth me beside the still waters." His last utterance was, "I am thankful."

For more than fifty years William Stephens, of Duncannon,

Wexford, Ireland, maintained an unblemished Christian character as a member of the Methodist Society.   During many years
he provided, rent free, a preaching-place for his neighbours to
hear the Word of God.   His character was marked by faithfulness, truth, and integrity.   He bore a long and painful illness
with patience, and just before closing his earthly career he
repeated the verse—

> " Through all eternity to Thee
>   A grateful song I 'll raise ;
> But O eternity 's too short
>   To utter all Thy praise ! "

Addison uses a poet's license when he limits the extent of the
word eternity.   His meaning is plain, but it is incorrectly expressed.   As the rhyme is not preserved in the verse, perhaps
the following couplet will more correctly express the poet's
meaning—

> " Eternity will but suffice
>   To utter all Thy praise."

HYMN 593.—" The Lord, how wondrous are His ways!"—*God's
Gentle Chastisements.*

Dr Watts' version of Psalm ciii. 8.   Three verses are omitted.

HYMN 594.—" Father of earth and sky."—*The Lord's Prayer.*

Charles Wesley's, made up of seven of his " Short Scripture
Hymns," Vol. II., Nos. 60–66, founded on Matt. vi. 9–13.

HYMN 595.—" Plunged in a gulf of dark despair."—*Praise to the
Redeemer.*

Dr Watts' hymn, Book II., No. 79, with three verses omitted.
In early life Lancelot Thurlow entered into the liberty of the
children of God, and was for thirty-five years an earnest
and faithful Methodist local preacher.   The last days of his pilgrimage were cheerful and bright, from the indwelling presence
of God.   The night preceding his death he was greatly comforted
by meditating on passages of Scripture, and portions of hymns,
and several times he repeated the verse, referring to the great
love of God :—

> " O for this love let rocks and hills
> Their lasting silence break,
> And all harmonious human tongues
> The Saviour's praises speak ! "

He was exceedingly happy; and just as his freed spirit fled, as if he heard the music of heaven, he shouted, " Hark ! " and he went to join in the anthem he doubtless heard.

HYMN 596.—" Who can describe the joys that rise."—*Joy in Heaven for a Repenting Sinner.*

Dr Watts', Hymn 101, Book I., founded on Luke xv. 7.

HYMN 597.—" Great God, indulge my humble claim."—*Longing after God.*

Dr Watts' version of Psalm lxiii., with four verses omitted, one altered, and one supplied.

HYMN 598.—" My heart is fix'd, O God, my heart."—*Praise.*

Charles Wesley's version of Psalm lxvii., verses 7–11, and appears in the " Collection of Psalms and Hymns," second edition, 1743, page 81. The first six verses are left out.

HYMN 599.—" Begin, my soul, some heavenly theme."—*The Faithfulness of God in the Promises.*

Dr Watts', Hymn 69, Book II. Several lines are altered.
Ann, the wife of William Walkington, Esq., of Grantham, feared the Lord from her youth, and in early life united herself with the Methodist Society. Her life was one of cheerful, consistent piety, and her benevolence greatly benefited the poor and the cause of God. Through much severe suffering her confidence in God was unshaken. One of the ministers visiting her repeated that the Lord would " never leave nor forsake " her ; to which she meekly replied, " No ; He never will ; " and added—

> " I trust the all-creating voice,
> And faith desires no more."

She soon afterwards peacefully breathed her spirit into the hands of God.

HYMN 600.—"Jesus, Thou everlasting King."—*The Coronation of Christ and Espousals of the Church.*

Dr Watts', Hymn 72, Book I., founded on Solomon's Song, iii. 2.

HYMN 601.—"Hail, God the Son, in glory crown'd."—*A Hymn to God the Son.*

Samuel Wesley, jun., from "Poems on Several Occasions," second edition, 1743; also in the enlarged edition, 1862, page 366. The fourth verse is omitted. See Hymns 561 and 649. This is the first hymn in the second section of the Supplement, with the title, "On the Incarnation, Sufferings, Glory, and Work of Christ."

HYMN 602.—Hark! the herald-angels sing."—*For Christmas-Day.*

This is one of the most popular hymns in the English language. It was written by Charles Wesley, and published in "Hymns and Sacred Poems," 1739, page 206. The original has ten verses. The first and second lines read thus :—

> " Hark how all the welkin rings,
> Glory to the King of kings."

One remarkable circumstance in the history of this hymn, and one which has contributed much to its being so widely known, is the fact that it is printed at the end of the metrical psalms in the Book of Common Prayer for the use of the Church of England. How it came there, and to be printed by authority, by the printer to the University, is a puzzle to many ; but the fact is indisputable. The only reasonable way of accounting for the remarkable circumstance is, that on one occasion the University printer, having a blank page in the Prayer-book, put in the hymn without either knowing its author, or asking any one's authority for so doing ; and once having a place there, it is almost impossible to displace it, an act which has been contemplated by some Churchmen since its author has become generally known. The hymn is now included in many church hymnals, and is universally sung at Christmas time.

HYMN 603.—"Celebrate Immanuel's name."—*The Incarnation of Christ.*

Charles Wesley's, made up of parts of several of the poet's "Short Scripture Hymns." Verse 1 forms No. 6 in vol. ii., founded on Matthew i. 23; the second and third verses are from the *Arminian Magazine*, 1789, page 390.

HYMN 604.—"Sing, all in heaven, at Jesu's birth."—*The Incarnation of Christ.*

Charles Wesley's. The first and second lines are from No. 324, vol. ii., of "Short Scripture Hymns," Luke ii. 14. The other portion is from the amended form of the hymn, as left by the author in manuscript.

HYMN 605.—"To us a Child of royal birth."—*The Incarnation of Christ.*

Charles Wesley's, founded on Luke ii. 11, and left in manuscript for publication after his death.

HYMN 606.—"Light of those whose dreary dwelling."—*Christ the Light of the Gentiles.*

Charles Wesley's, forming No. 11 of his "Hymns for the Nativity of our Lord."

HYMN 607.—"Glory be to God on High."—"*Immanuel, God with us.*"

Charles Wesley's, being No. 4 of his "Nativity Hymns."

HYMN 608.—"Stupendous height of heavenly love."—*Christ the Light of the world.*

Charles Wesley's, being one of his "Scripture Hymns," left in manuscript, to be published after his death.

HYMN 609.—"Let earth and heaven combine."—"*God with us.*"

Charles Wesley's, being No. 5 of his "Nativity Hymns," the third and fifth verses being left out.

HYMN 610.—"O God of gods, in whom combine."—*Supplication for Grace.*

John Wesley's translation from the German of Count Zinzendorf, and printed in "Hymns and Sacred Poems," 1739, page 182.

HYMN 611.—"Jesus, Thee Thy works proclaim."—*The Miracles of Christ.*

Charles Wesley's, left in manuscript at his death, and printed in the *Arminian Magazine,* 1790, page 277, founded on Matt. iv. 23.

HYMN 612.—"Behold, the blind their sight receive."—*Miracles of Christ.*

Dr Watts', Hymn 137, Book II.

HYMN 613.—"From whence these dire portents around?"—*On the Passion of our Saviour.*

Samuel Wesley, jun., found in his "Poems on Several Occasions," second edition, 1743, and in Nichol's edition, 1862, page 360. Charles Wesley commences the fifth of his "Earthquake Hymns" in very similar words—

> "From whence these dire portents around,
> That strike us with unwonted fear?
> Why do these earthquakes rock the ground,
> And threaten our destruction near?"

HYMN 614.—"'Tis finish'd! The Messias dies."—*"It is finished."*

Charles Wesley's, forming one of his "Scripture Hymns," enlarged, and left in manuscript. The first verse only forms part of No. 387 of his "Short Scripture Hymns," vol. ii., founded on John xix. 30; but it is placed amongst the hymns under the heading "St Luke."

HYMN 615.—"Not all the blood of beasts."—*Faith in Christ, our Sacrifice.*

Dr Watts', Hymn 142, Book II., the third and fourth verses of the original being left out.

One of those omitted verses is very characteristic of the doubting faith of its author, when contrasted with the bold confiding faith of Charles Wesley—

> "My soul looks back to see
> The burdens Thou didst bear,
> When hanging on the cursed tree,
> And hopes her guilt was there."

Some have doubted whether the teaching contained in the first

verse is in accordance with that of Holy Scripture. (See Matt.
vii. 28; ix. 13; and Lev. xvi. 15, &c.) The Jew, when he had
offered his sacrifice, and fulfilled the ceremonial law, certainly
must have felt his guilty conscience at peace, and his sins
washed away, although the sacrifices in themselves had no in-
herent value; yet they were of divine appointment to accomplish that end. The Jewish sacrifices, no doubt, received their
value in association with the death of Christ.

There are several instances on record of the value of this particular hymn. One of the Bible Society's colporteurs was one
day offering Bibles for sale in the Jews' quarter, at the east end
of London, when a Jewess informed him, if any of their people
bought a Bible, read it, and became converts to Christianity,
they would certainly return to their former belief, and die in the
faith of Abraham. The Bible-man replied that when he was a
city missionary he had been induced to call upon a dying Jewess.
" She had been brought from affluence to abject poverty for the
faith of Christ: at one time she had kept her own carriage.
One day her eye rested on the leaf of a hymn-book, which had
come into the house covering some butter, and she read upon
it these words—

> ' Not all the blood of beasts,
>   On Jewish altars slain,
> Could give the guilty conscience peace,
>   Or wash away the stain.'

The verse haunted her; she could not dismiss it nor forget it.
After a time she went to a box where she remembered she had
a copy of the Bible, and, induced by that verse, she began to read
it, and she read on till she found Christ Jesus, 'the Lamb slain
from before the foundation of the world.' She became openly a
convert to Christianity. This caused her Jewish husband to
divorce her. He went to India, where he married again, and
died. She lived in much poverty with two of her nation, Jewish
sisters, who had also become Christians. All this," said the
Bible man, "I knew; and as I stood by her bedside, she did not
renounce her faith in her crucified Lord, but died triumphing in
Him as her rock, her shield, and her exceeding great reward."

The religious course of Mrs Harriet Hirst, of Bedford Place,
Leeds, commenced in early life, and her membership as a Methodist continued nearly sixty years. She ever took delight in the
means of grace, especially in the class-meeting and love-feasts.

During the trials of a long widowhood, as well as in old age, her reliance on Christ was unshaken. Again and again she expressed her confidence in God in the words of Dr Watts—

> "; But Christ, the heavenly Lamb,
>   Takes all our sins away ;
>   A sacrifice of nobler name,
>   And richer blood, than they. "

In great peace she fell asleep in Jesus, aged seventy-eight.

A chequered course was the lot of John Henry Cassell. At the early age of nine years the godly instructions of his good Moravian mother led him to the Saviour, and he rejoiced in the knowledge of sins forgiven. But the severe trials arising from the evils of the wars with France deprived him of his religion, and his parents of all their earthly substance. Coming to London, they had to commence life again without money or friends. A seafaring life for both father and son, for some years, revealed to them such a condition of wickedness and profanity, that they relinquished it for fear of impending judgments. The son, of whom we write, settled down at Poplar, sought again the favour of God, realised afresh his adoption into His family, joined the Community, in which he was for nearly a quarter of a century a preacher, and as a class-leader greatly aided a rising Methodist Society at Poplar. He opened his house for preaching, and rejoiced to see many sinners there brought to know their sins forgiven. His love of prayer and of the means of grace were marked characteristics of his life. The Rev. John Farrar gave him and his family the sacrament of the Lord's Supper, and a more solemn celebration has seldom been held. Shortly after, on another visit of Mr Farrar's, the dying man said, "I feel my account is made up : I know whom I have trusted : I know the power of Jesus ; I feel His love. I am the Lord's and He is mine. Yesterday" (during the sacrament) "I seemed to be in heaven : surely I could not be happier if there. How much the hymn we sang at the sacrament has been on my mind. Read it." It was read ; and taking up the last verse with energy of voice, he exclaimed—

> " ' Believing, I rejoice
>   To feel the curse remove ;
>   I bless the Lamb with cheerful voice,
>   And trust His bleeding love.'

That is my experience," he added ; "the curse is gone ; His

blood cleanses me from sin ; Christ is all in all." Thus triumphantly died this tried but faithful follower of Jesus.

HYMN 616.—"All ye that pass by."—*Invitation to Sinners.*

Charles Wesley's, forming No. 42 of "Hymns and Sacred
Poems," 1749, vol. i.

A copy of Wesley's Hymns was lent to the father of the
late Lord Derby, and when it was returned the word
"anger" in the second verse was altered to "mercy," thus :—
"The Lord, in the day of His mercy, did lay," &c. The alteration is an improvement. Mr Bunting has made other improvements in this hymn. In line 3, verse 4, for "your work he hath
done," read "your burden 's undone" (Isa. lviii. 6), and in line
5, verse 7, for "Acquitted I was," read "For ransomed I was."

The father of Mrs Hatton, of Birmingham, was descended
from the old Puritans, and preserved the principles of their stern
and primitive piety. He was a strong Churchman, not free from
bigotry, and was induced to ride over from Ilkestone to Nottingham to hear Mr Whitefield preach at the market-cross. As
he drew near the outer circle of the crowd, the preacher was
giving out with much earnestness Mr Wesley's lines—

> " All ye that pass by,
> To Jesus draw nigh ;
> To you is it nothing that Jesus should die ? "

The words deeply impressed his mind, the last line in particular, which he received as a direct appeal to himself. From
that hour his heart and manner of life were both changed ; he
became a new creature in Christ Jesus, and all his family commenced soon afterwards to follow in his footsteps.

The guardian care of an elder sister produced those deep
religious impressions on the mind of Betsy Surr, which led to her
ultimately finding pardon through faith in Christ, whilst reading
the "Life of Carvosso." Her after-life was a clear testimony to
the change Divine grace had wrought. She cheerfully gave up
home and friends to leave England for Jamaica as the wife of
the Rev. Wilson Lofthouse. Here, during her brief sojourn, her
piety was matured by earnest and almost incessant prayer, but
her feebleness of body greatly hindered her joy. Sometimes she
would become plaintive in her supplications for more of the
mind of Christ ; and she would arouse herself from a sorrowful
tone by singing the verse—

" For you and for me
He died on the tree :
His death was accepted, the sinner is free !
That sinner am I,
Who on Jesus rely,
And come for the pardon God cannot deny."

This was her last testimony for God.   She bore much suffering
with extreme submission, and peacefully entered into rest.   The
evening of the day on which she died her remains were deposited,
with those of her infant, in a grave beside those of the Rev.
Valentine Ward, at Spanish Town.

In the *Wesleyan Magazine* we read of the death of Holrody
Walker, of Leeds, who in his eighteenth year was dangerously
ill, was very anxious about his soul, and earnestly sought salvation.   After suffering much distress of mind, he obtained a
sense of God's pardoning mercy while thinking over the sixth
verse of Hymn 616, so adapted to his state—

" My pardon I claim ;
For a sinner I am :
A sinner believing in Jesus's name.
He purchased the grace
Which now I embrace :
O Father, Thou know'st He hath died in my place."

He believed in the finished work of Christ, and rejoiced in God
as his reconciled Father.   He lived two years afterwards ; but
just before he died he said, " I have a sweet assurance that my
sins are forgiven, and that I am accepted in the Beloved."

HYMN 617.—" Thou very Paschal Lamb."—*The Lord's Supper
as a Sign and Means of Grace.*—TUNE, Brentford, 1761.

Charles Wesley's, being No. 51 of " Hymns on the Lord's
Supper."   It also forms No. 11 in John Wesley's " Select
Hymns, with Tunes Annext," 1761, with the tune Brentford.

HYMN 618.—" This, this is He that came."—*The Lord's Supper
as a Sign and Means of Grace.*

Charles Wesley's, forming No. 74 of " Hymns on the Lord's
Supper."

HYMN 619.—" O Thou, whose offering on the tree."—*The Holy
Eucharist as it implies a Sacrifice.*

Charles Wesley's, forming No. 123 of " Hymns on the Lord's

Supper. The original has four double verses; the last eight lines are omitted.

HYMN 620.—"Behold the sure foundation-stone."—*Christ the sure Foundation of His Church.*

Dr Watts' version of Psalm cxviii. 22, 23.

HYMN 621.—"God of unexampled grace."—*The Lord's Supper a Memorial of the Death of Christ.*

Charles Wesley's, being No. 21 in "Hymns on the Lord's Supper." The original has nine verses; those omitted here form Hymn 552.

HYMN 622.—"Whom Jesu's blood doth sanctify."—*Confidence in Christ.*

Charles Wesley's, being one of his "Scripture Hymns" left unpublished at the time of his death, and founded on Deut. xxxiii. 3.

HYMN 623.—"When I survey the wondrous cross."—*Cucifixion to the World by the Cross of Christ.*

Dr Watts', from Book III., No. 7; a very popular hymn, founded on Gal. vi. 14. The fourth verse is left out.

Mr J. Cramp, a local preacher at Longford, Staffordshire, had preached three times on the Sabbath, and at the close of the evening he observed, "It is all over with me; my work is done." This was his last Sabbath; he lingered on for a few days, and on July 9 he tranquilly resigned his spirit into the hands of his Saviour, nearly his last words being—

> " When I survey the wondrous cross
> On which the Prince of glory died,
> My richest gain I count but loss,
> And pour contempt on all my pride."

From very tender years the mind of Miss Jordan, of Norwich, was impressed with divine things, and whilst yet a child, during a thunderstorm, she earnestly entreated the Lord to pardon her sins. These impressions wore away for a time, under the teachings of a Calvinistic minister. In 1790, the Rev. John Hickling was appointed to the Norwich circuit, and as Miss Jordan had commenced to attend the ministry of the Methodists, she soon discovered the errors she had been taught;

under the preaching of Mr Hickling she learned the way of salvation, and at a prayer-meeting in the chapel she found peace in
believing on Jesus.   Two years afterwards she was married to
Mr Hickling, and for twenty years they were helps-meet for
each other. She was a true Methodist, and a sincere Christian,
taking especial interest in those young preachers who were from
time to time located with them.   Her last illness was short, but
severe ; she had gone to visit some friends at Beverley, was
suddenly seized with fatal symptoms, and in a few days exchanged mortality for life.   The last time she attended her
class, her leader asked her to give out a verse and pray. She
gave out—

> " Were the whole realm of nature mine,
>   That were a present far too small ;
>   Love, so amazing, so divine,
>   Demands my soul, my life, my all."

This verse gave her comfort in her latest hours ; she repeated it
with her dying breath, and in great peace her happy spirit fled
to the realms of glory.

HYMN 624.—"Rock of Ages, cleft for me."—*A Living and Dying
    Prayer for the Holiest Believer in the World.*

Augustus Montague Toplady's, and first published in the *Gospel
Magazine* for March 1776, of which he was then the editor.

It is printed at the end of an article in prose, signed J. F.
The allusion in the title to the " Holiest Believer in the World,"
is believed to refer to the Rev. John Wesley, who had a short
time previously published a tract entitled " Predestination Calmly
Considered," which is thought to have been a reply to the opinions
published by Mr Toplady on that much-disputed doctrine.
The term "holiest believer" can only have been designed
by Mr Toplady as a sneer at the doctrine of entire holiness,
which both the Wesleys so strongly enforced in their preaching
and hymns. The original is in four stanzas, and it was uni-
formly so printed till Mr Montgomery and the Rev. T. Cotterill
prepared the Sheffield Hymn-book in 1810.   In that collection
Toplady's hymn was printed with considerable alteration, and
abridged so as to make only three stanzas instead of four.   In
the altered form there published, the hymn has been copied into
the Methodist and some other collections.   As altered, it is
manifestly an injustice to the author ; hence, in most modern

hymnals, it is given in its original integrity. From the importance which now attaches to this hymn throughout the world, it
may be desirable to give the exact reprint of it. This hymn
gave consolation to the late Prince Consort in his dying hours ;
and Dr Pomeroy relates, that when he was visiting an Armenian
church in Constantinople, he saw many in tears whilst they were
offering praise, and on inquiry, found that they were singing a
translation of this hymn of Toplady's—

> " Rock of Ages, cleft for me,
> Let me hide myself in Thee ;
> Let the water and the blood,
> From Thy riven side which flow'd,
> Be of sin the double cure,
> Cleanse me from its guilt and power.

> " Not the labours of my hands,
> Can fulfil Thy law's demands ;
> Could my zeal no respite know,
> Could my tears for ever flow,
> All for sin could not atone ;
> Thou must save, and Thou alone.

> " Nothing in my hand I bring,
> Simply to Thy cross I cling ;
> Naked, come to Thee for dress ;
> Helpless, look to Thee for grace ;
> Foul, I to the Fountain fly ;
> Wash me, Saviour, or I die !

> " While I draw this fleeting breath,
> When my eyestrings break in death,
> When I soar through tracts unknown,
> See Thee on Thy judgment-throne ;
> Rock of Ages, cleft for me,
> Let me hide myself in Thee !"

Its first appearance in the Wesleyan collection was in the
supplement issued in 1830; and in 1832 the Rev. Richard
Watson, in a letter to the *Wesleyan Magazine*, erroneously
attributes its authorship to the Rev. Charles Wesley. If the
reader will turn to the preface on the "Christian Sacrament and
Sacrifice," by Dr Brevint, which usually precedes the editions of
Charles Wesley's " Hymns on the Lord's Supper," on page 8
of that preface he will find all the thoughts which are with so
much force and elegance embodied in the hymn by the poet.

This hymn was translated into elegant Latin verse by the Right Hon. W. E. Gladstone, M.P., in which form it was copied into many of the newspapers of England, the Continent, and America, and so became a subject of general inquiry and remark. The Premier has since translated the same hymn into Greek.

General Stuart, of the Confederate army of America, died at Richmond of wounds received in a cavalry charge. Just before he died, he turned to the Rev. Mr Peterkin, of the Episcopal Church, of which the General was an exemplary member, and asked him to sing the hymn commencing—

> " Rock of Ages, cleft for me,
> Let me hide myself in Thee "—

the General joining with all the voice and strength he could command. He then joined in a prayer with the minister. To the doctor, who was standing by, he said, "I am going fast, now : I am resigned : God's will be done ;" and then he died.

The incidents which cluster around this hymn are sufficiently numerous and interesting to make a lengthy chapter. A few only can be noticed.

The Rev. Theophilus Lessey was converted to God at the age of seventeen, and dedicated to His service in baptism by the venerable John Wesley. In early life his delicate constitution made it very doubtful whether he would reach manhood ; but his education and training at Kingswood School prepared him for the distinguished sphere in which he afterwards moved. First as a local preacher, and then as one of the foremost preachers in the Wesleyan ministry, and as president of the Conference in the Centenary year, he was "a burning and a shining light." Soon after the close of his Conference year, he was seized with that illness which, after two years' suffering, closed his career of great public usefulness. When he was nearing the eternal shore, he was reminded of the prevalent intercession of Christ, and of His sympathy with our sufferings and infirmities, when he replied with affecting emotion, "Yes, Christ is my only hope; on His atonement I rest, His precious atonement ;" and, in the words of Toplady, he added—

> " In my hand no price I bring,
> Simply to Thy cross I cling."

Several portions of this expressive hymn were often on his lips, and he tried to sing the hymn through, his family joining ; when unequal to that effort, he would repeat a line, and raise

his hand as an act of devotion.   He died suddenly at last, from
the rupture of a blood-vessel, and was buried in the graveyard
behind City Road Chapel.

Under the ministry of the Rev. Robert Gover, Jane, the
beloved wife of the Rev. Samuel H. Wardley, was convinced of
sin in early life, and at a prayer-meeting soon afterwards she
obtained peace in believing on Jesus Christ.   She retained the
evidence of her acceptance with God through life, and manifested
its possession by her love to the people of God, and to the
means of grace.   Consumption cut short her earthly course, but
shortly before she died she found much comfort in the hymn
"Rock of Ages," which was so expressive of her inmost feelings.
Her last words were, "Jesus is gloriously precious."

At the early age of sixteen, the Rev. David Edgar found peace
through believing in Jesus, and soon afterwards began to call
sinners to repentance.   For fourteen years he laboured with
fidelity and success in the Wesleyan ministry.   He suffered
much affliction for several years previous to his death, but his
soul was kept in peace.   A few days before he died, he repeated
the hymn commencing—

> "Rock of Ages, cleft for me,
> Let me hide myself in Thee!"

and on ending it he said, "It is there I am resting: None but
Christ! none but Christ!"   He died in great peace.

The parents of the Rev. John Nesbett were Irish Presbyte-
rians, and he was by them designed for the ministry of that
body; but his conversion to God through the Methodists in
that country determined his future course; and for fifty-seven
years he laboured with untiring zeal and energy in the Methodist
ministry, and had the satisfaction of seeing hundreds of his
countrymen converted to God as the fruit of his hallowed and
successful toil.   During the four years' illness which preceded his death, he read the Bible four times through, with
Mr Wesley's, Mr Sutcliffe's, and Dr Adam Clarke's comments
thereon.   A few days before he died, he sent £50 to the mission
fund, and £50 to the Preachers' Annuitant Society, as a token
of his love and gratitude to Methodism.   On his last Sabbath
on earth, after the usual reading of the Scriptures, and of some
hymns, coming to the lines in Hymn 624—

> "In my hand no price I bring,
> Simply to Thy cross I cling,"—

he cried out, "That is my experience! my feet are upon the Rock: that Rock is Christ: Christ is all in all!" In this frame of mind he breathed out his soul into the hands of God.

HYMN 625.—"Sinners, rejoice: your peace is made."—*Christ seen of Angels.*—TUNE, Sheffield, 1761.

Charles Wesley's, being one of his "Hymns for Ascension-Day," 1746.

It is a masterly composition. There is a bold and striking passage in the fifth verse—

> "The wounds, the blood! they heard the voice,
> And heighten'd all their highest joys."

For ascribing a voice to the blood of Christ, the poet has the authority of the apostle Paul in Heb. xii. 24. The fine hyperbole in the next line may remind the reader of some noble lines in Milton, who represents Satan as saying—

> "And in the lowest deep, a lower deep,
> Still threatening to devour me, opens wide."

At the close of this admirable lay, the poet, after speaking of "the unutterable happiness" of heaven and the angels, adds—

> "But all your heaven, ye glorious powers,
> And all your God, is doubly ours."

Part of this lay forms one of the "Select Hymns, with Tunes Annext;" and in the "Sacred Melody," 1761, the tune is Sheffield. The sixth verse of the original is omitted.

HYMN 626.—"Jesus, to Thee we fly."—*The Living Way Opened.*

Charles Wesley's, being No. 7 of "Hymns for Ascension-Day," 1746.

The title of this hymn was literally realised by one of the most zealous, loving, and laborious ministers in the Wesleyan body. To thousands, especially amongst the young in Methodism, the name of Nehemiah Curnock is cherished as a household treasure, as "the children's preacher;" and with apt and abundant illustrations, and extraordinary vigour, conducted services for their benefit. Born at Bristol, in 1810, he made religion his choice in early life, and at the age of thirteen he gave his heart to the Lord, and joined the Methodist Society. Immediately he started on that career of untiring usefulness in the service of God which terminated only with his life. As a Sunday-school teacher, prayer-leader, exhorter, and local preacher, he was distinguished for his activity whilst yet a mere youth. He entered the Wesleyan ministry in 1834; and his whole pastoral career was eminently practical, faithful, and earnest, and attended with many blessed evidences of the Divine favour in leading sinners to Jesus. In February 1869, through visiting a bereaved family at Bayswater, he took the illness which ended in his death. He suffered much, but endured all with patience. Up to within a week of his departure, he anticipated becoming a supernumerary; but on Monday, July 26, he found "the living way opened" to paradise, and entered the rest we toil to find, with almost his last breath, altering the first word from "our" to "my," and repeating—

> "My anchor sure and fast
> Within the veil is cast."

HYMN 627.—" Enter'd the holy place above."—*Priesthood of Christ.*

Charles Wesley's, being No. 701 of " Short Scripture Hymns," vol. ii., founded on Heb. ix. 24.

HYMN 628.—" Ye humble souls, that seek the Lord."—*The Resurrection of Christ.*

Dr Doddridge's, being No. 196 in his Hymns, founded on Matt. xxviii. 5, 6. The third verse is left out.

HYMN 629.—" Christ, the Lord, is risen to-day."—*For Easter-Day.*—TUNE, Georgia.

From Charles Wesley's " Hymns and Sacred Poems," 1739, page 209. The original has eleven verses, five of which are omitted. This hymn is universally adopted in the psalmody of the Church of England, a tune called Georgia being used to it, being an adaptation of the one by Handel, " See the Conquering Hero."

When about twenty-five years of age, Thomas Lacy was brought to the enjoyment of a conscious sense of God's pardoning love, under the ministry of the Rev. Charles Atmore. He had previously been favoured by attending the ministry of the Rev. John Crosse, vicar of Bradford. He joined the Methodist

Society, and ever afterwards was one of its brightest ornaments. He filled the office of leader and steward with satisfaction to his brethren, and was a liberal giver to church funds. He was ill for some time before his death. On Easter-Day he repeated to his sister, with a faltering voice—

> "Christ, the Lord, is risen to-day,
>   Sons of men and angels say ;
>   Raise your joys and triumphs high ;
>   Sing, ye heavens ; thou earth, reply."

When his medical man announced his end was near, he said, "I have a pleasant prospect before me," and after a few words of the like nature, he gently fell asleep in Jesus.

HYMN 630.—" Hail the day that sees Him rise."—*For Ascension-Day.*

Charles Wesley's, from " Hymns and Sacred Poems," 1739, page 211.

The poet had a great liking to the word " pomp," if we may judge from the frequency of its occurrence in his hymns. He takes care, however, not to use it in a loose, indiscriminate manner ; but seems ever to have his eye upon the original import. It was a religious word among the Greeks, and was used by them to denote a religious procession. Accordingly the poet, in verse 2 of this hymn, says, " There the pompous triumph waits ;" and in other places, " And lead the pompous triumph on," " By the pomp of thine ascending," &c. The word is not peculiar to Charles Wesley, as it is found in all the best English writers.

HYMN 631.—" Sons of God, triumphant rise."—*After the Sacrament.*

Charles Wesley's, from " Hymns and Sacred Poems," 1739, page 190. Four verses of the original are omitted, and the eighth is altered. It also forms No. 144 of the same author's " Hymns on the Lord's Supper," 1745, where the whole of the verses are given.

HYMN 632.—" Father, God, we glorify."—*On the Resurrection of our Lord.*

Charles Wesley's, forming No. 9 of his " Hymns for our Lord's Resurrection," 1746.

Hymn 633.—"Hail, Thou once despised Jesus."—*Our Lord's Resurrection.*

This hymn was written by John Bakewell, one of the earliest of Mr Wesley's lay preachers. There is much that is interesting belonging to this hymn and its venerable author, which Mr Stelfox, of Belfast, has embodied in a short article in the *Wesleyan Magazine.* The author was born in 1721, and died March 18, 1819. He was a lay preacher among the Methodists from 1749 to the end of his life. He composed many hymns. The one commencing, "Hail, Thou once despised Jesus," appeared in part in "A Collection of Hymns addressed to the Holy, Holy, Holy Triune God, in the person of Jesus Christ, our Mediator and Advocate," 1757. It is also found in Madan's Collection, 1760, and in Toplady's "Psalms and Hymns," 1776, with an additional verse. In its altered form it was added to the Methodist Collection as revised in 1797, as Hymn 103*, but was omitted again in 1808. When the Supplement was added in 1830, it was again inserted, Toplady's version being adopted in the first, second, and fourth verses, and Madan's version in the third verse. The fifth verse is omitted. The author was on intimate terms with John and Charles Wesley, Toplady, Madan, and other good men. He was present at the ordination of the Rev. John Fletcher, in 1757. He resided successively in Derbyshire, London, Bedford, Kent, and Staffordshire, closing his career at Lewisham, in 1819. He introduced Methodism into Greenwich. The first regular class met in his house, and there the Rev. Thomas Rutherford died. At an earlier date Mr Bakewell resided at Westminster, where Thomas Olivers spent some time on a visit, and in whose house he wrote his grand hymn, "To the God of Abraham." The Rev. William Moulton and the Rev. James Rosser married two of his grand-daughters. His remains are interred near to those of John Wesley, behind City Road Chapel, where a stone marks his resting-place, on which is the following inscription :—"Sacred to the memory of John Bakewell, of Greenwich, who departed this life March 18, 1819, aged ninety-eight. He adorned the doctrine of God our Saviour eighty years, and preached His glorious Gospel about seventy years." The Rev. James Creighton buried his old friend, and a few days afterwards Mr Creighton finished his own earthly course. He was an eminent, benevolent, intelligent, pious, humble man of God.

HYMN 634.—" What equal honours shall we bring."—*Christ's Humiliation and Exaltation.*

Dr Watts', Hymn 63, Book I., with the fourth verse left out.

HYMN 635.—" God is gone up on high."—*Christ Glorified.*

Charles Wesley's, being the second of his " Hymns for Ascension-Day," 1746.

HYMN 636.—" Great God, whose universal sway."—*The Kingdom of Christ.*

Dr Watts' version of Psalm lxxii., Part I.

HYMN 637.—" My heart and voice I raise."
    „   638.—" Jerusalem divine."
        The Kingdom of Christ.

Written by Benjn. Rhodes, one of the second generation of Methodist preachers, who began to travel in 1766. These two hymns form the first and second of four parts of a poem on the Messiah. Mr Rhodes was born in 1743, and died at Margate in 1815, aged seventy-two years. His portrait appears in the *Arminian Magazine* for 1779 and 1797. Others of Mr Rhodes' hymns will be found in a volume of " Hymns for Children and Young Persons," issued by the Rev. Joseph Benson, in 1806.

HYMN 639.—" My heart is full of Christ, and longs."—*The Kingdom of Christ.*

Charles Wesley's version of Psalm xlv. The original has twenty-one verses. The poet has admirably embodied the sacred fire of the Hebrew poet in his verses.

HYMN 640.—" Come, let us join our cheerful songs."—*Christ Jesus, the Lamb of God, Worshipped by all the Creation.*

Dr Watts', from Book II., No. 62.

The child of many prayers and religious advantages, Miss Hannah Sophia Corderoy, of Lambeth, at the early age of thirteen, was convinced of sin, and soon afterwards obtained pardon, under a sermon preached by the Rev. Richard Felvus. The peace which she then received remained with her during

her brief earthly pilgrimage.   In the Sunday-school, and in
visiting the sick poor, she became very useful.   Illness, short
and severe, resulted in her early death ; but she was quite
happy, and her mind was sweetly stayed on Jesus.   Once, after
a severe attack of pain, she exhorted her sister and others to
give their hearts fully to God, and she began to sing—

> " Come, let us join our cheerful songs
> With angels round the throne ;
> Ten thousand thousand are their tongues,'
> But all their joys are one."

Urged to try and get some sleep, she said, "How can I sleep?
I must praise God with my latest breath."   Again she tried to
sing, but was not able.   As the end drew nigh, she had intercourse with the heavenly world.   She said, " I see Jesus!
Blessed Jesus ! He has come for me.   Oh, what music is that?
it is heavenly music ! What light is that I see ? How bright !
My Saviour, my Saviour ! what a mercy that such a sinner as I
have been should enter heaven ! I am not fit for heaven ; but
Jesus, my blessed Saviour, died for me."   In this truly happy
frame, in the quietness of sleep, she entered the gates of the
New Jerusalem.

A sailor at the approach of death was aroused at the prospect
before him.   He was ill, had no Bible, nor even the power
to read one.   He thought of the Sunday-school, but its lessons
seemed lost upon him.   In this mental darkness he remembered
two verses of Watts' hymn commencing—

> "Come, let us join our cheerful songs,"

and—

> "Worthy the Lamb that died, they cry."

On completing the second verse, the words "slain for us," rung
in his ears, and he repeated them over and over till light broke
in on his mind.   He caught a glimpse of the plan of salvation ;
the verse brought to his mind a teacher's instruction, and, believing in Christ's finished work, he found pardon and peace, and
died happy.

Susannah Harrison, a very poor orphan girl of Ipswich, was
called to lead a desolate and suffering life.   She solaced herself
by writing " Songs in the Night," in which are manifest a reverent
cheerfulness and a placid resignation.   In her last hours she
sung softly with her friends one of Dr Watts' hymns, then, after
a pause, she added, " Let us sing again—

'Come, let us join our cheerful songs.' "

The scene was affecting ; no one seemed able to sing with her.
Her voice for the time seemed more than human, and she waved
her hand exultingly as she sang. "You do not sing with me,"
she said ; "I cannot forbear." She continued through the night,
warbling softly the lines of this hymn. Her last night was full
of song, and as she took her upward flight she pointed heavenward, and said, "I cannot talk, but I shall soon sing THERE."

At a very early period of life, the Rev. Walter Oke Croggon
became the subject of deep religious impressions ; and at the
age of nineteen he found redemption in the blood of Jesus, the
forgiveness of sins. "I felt," he said, "as if I received heaven
into my heart." He retained his confidence in God, and, throughout a happy and useful course as a Wesleyan minister, walked
in the light of God's countenance. He travelled and preached
in France, Greece, Ireland, and England, with blessed results,
and with his pen he delighted the young in the pages of the
"Youth's Instructor." His life and its end were one uniform
testimony to the power of Divine grace. Standing on the verge
of eternity, he anticipated the songs of the blessed by quoting
the lines—

> "The whole creation join in one,
>   To bless the sacred name
> Of Him that sits upon the throne,
>   And to adore the Lamb."

HYMN 641.—"Join all the glorious names."—*The Offices of
Christ.*

Dr Watts' Hymn, Book I., No. 150. It is founded on several
passages of Scripture. The seventh and ninth verses are left
out, and three others are a little altered.

Thomas Holmes, of Bilston, Leeds, had the advantage of
godly Methodist parents. He began to meet in class whilst a
teacher in Mr Sigston's school, Leeds ; and at the prayer-meeting held on the Methodist quarterly fast-day, his convictions
of sin were so deepened, that he rested not till he found peace.
Removing to Bradford, under the direction of the Rev. John
Gaulter, he, with his young friend the Rev. Joseph Fowler,
established the first Methodist Sunday-school in that town. At
the age of twenty he was made a class-leader, and at twenty-one

X

he was received as a local preacher. During a life of more than seventy years, he devoted his best energies to the furtherance of religion in his family and neighbourhood. When illness set in he had no fear of death. He found much consolation in reading hymns, and especially the verse—

> "Jesus, my great High Priest,
>   Offer'd His blood and died;
> My guilty conscience seeks
>   No sacrifice besides;
> His powerful blood did once atone,
> And now it pleads before the throne."

The last words he was heard to utter were, "Precious promises."

HYMN 642.—"Christ, the true anointed Seer."—*The Offices of Christ.*

This is one of Charles Wesley's "Scripture Hymns," left in MS. at his death. It is based on Matt. i. 16. Soon after the poet's death, John Wesley obtained his brother's MS. "Scripture Hymns," and he announced their publication in the *Arminian Magazine*, for May 1789, the first of which now forms Hymn 642.

Mr Bunting has suggested two corrections in this hymn. In line 2, for "the Most High," read "God Most High;" and in line 6, for "that unction," read "the unction."

HYMN 643.—"Come, O Thou Prophet of the Lord."—*Christ a Prophet.*

Charles Wesley's, forming No. 6 of "Hymns for our Lord's Resurrection," 1746, with four verses omitted.

HYMN 644.—"Coming through our great High Priest."—*Christ's Intercession.*

Charles Wesley's, being No. 697 of "Short Scripture Hymns," vol. ii., founded on Heb. vii. 25. The sentiment expressed in the second verse, "He ever lives for us to pray," will be found also in Hymns 127 and 202.

HYMN 645.—"Blow ye the trumpet, blow."—*The Year of Jubilee.*

This bold and characteristic composition is No. 3 of Charles Wesley's "Hymns for the New Year," 1750. It is inserted also in Toplady's Collection, 1776.

This fine hymn is founded on the year of jubilee, as appointed by the Levitical law.   It presents an attractive contrast between the law and the redemption wrought out for mankind by the shedding of the Saviour's blood.   The fifth verse is almost a paraphrase of the law which enjoins the return of all alienated property to its original owner.   The fact of this hymn appearing at so early a date in Toplady's Collection, although altered, has led many to attribute its authorship to him ; but the further fact that it is found in Charles Wesley's tract of " Hymns for the New Year," twenty-six years before Toplady's Collection was published, and when Toplady himself was only ten years old, determines the authorship beyond dispute. This hymn was sung at Leeds in 1863, at the jubilee celebration of the Wesleyan Missionary Society.

HYMN 646.—" With joy we meditate the grace."—*Christ's Compassion to the Weak and Tempted.*

Dr Watts', forming No. 125, Book I.   The third verse is left out.   It is founded on three various passages of Scripture, and was first selected by John Wesley for the enlarged edition of his " Psalms and Hymns," 1743.   In the second line, verse 3, Mr Bunting suggests changing " His cries " to " strong cries."

The parents of the Rev. John Aikenhead were members of the Scotch Church, and he often attributed to his mother's fervent prayers his conversion in early life.   The Rev. William Atherton records the fact that the ministry of the Rev. Robert Johnson and the Rev. John Doncaster was made useful to him at the time of his conversion.   His piety was of the most decided character, and his diligence in his holy vocation great.   He was made a leader and local-preacher in early life, and when twenty-eight he was admitted into the Methodist ministry, in which he laboured with fidelity, zeal, and success, for nearly forty years. On the Sabbath before he died, he had read to him St John xi., after which he slept ; and on awaking, said, "Sleep in Jesus ! I have been thinking on that expression ; as if He were the repository of even the bodies of the saints."   During the night, he said, " It will soon be over ;" and repeated the hymn—

> " With joy we meditate the grace
> Of our High Priest above ;
> His heart is made of tenderness,
> His bowels yearn with love."

On the two last lines he laid particular emphasis—

> "I shall obtain delivering grace,
> In the distressing hour."

He found God faithful to His promises. His last utterance was, "Lord, still smile upon me, and take me to heaven." He composed himself for sleep, and quietly breathed his last.

HYMN 647.—" O Sun of Righteousness, arise."—*A Prayer for the Light of Life.*

This hymn has been attributed to both John and Charles Wesley; its defective rhyme may show that it is John's composition; for although he had marvellous skill in transforming and improving the hymns of others, yet he had to depend on his brother Charles to polish his own original poetical efforts. This will be found in his " Collection of Psalms and Hymns," enlarged edition, 1743, page 43. Mr Bunting suggests changing the word " pride," in the fifth line, to either " guilt," or " doubt." He also suggests that it would make a very suitable Sabbath morning hymn.

HYMN 648.—" Let everlasting glories crown."—*The Excellency of the Christian Religion.*

Dr Watts', Hymn 131, Book II., two verses left out.

HYMN 649.—" Hail, Holy Ghost, Jehovah, Third."—*A Hymn to God the Holy Ghost.*

By Samuel Wesley, jun., being one of his three hymns to the Trinity, and published in his " Poems on Several Occasions," 1743. It also appears in the enlarged edition of John Wesley's " Collection of Psalms and Hymns," 1743 ; in the " Moral and Sacred Poems," 3 vols., 1744 ; and in " Nichol's Revised Edition of Samuel Wesley's Poems," 1862, page 367. This hymn is the first in the third section of the Supplement, with the title, " On the Divinity and Operations of the Holy Spirit." The other two hymns of the series are Nos. 561 and 601.

HYMN 650.—" Branch of Jesse's stem, arise."—*Prayer for the Holy Spirit.*

Charles Wesley's, forming Nos. 983, 984, and 985 of " Short Scripture Hymns," vol. i., based on Isa. xi. 1-3.

HYMN 651.—" Sovereign of all the worlds on high."—*A Filial Temper the Work of the Spirit, and a Proof of Adoption.*

Dr Doddridge's, forming No. 281 of his " Hymns," founded on Gal. iv. 6.   Every verse is altered, and the fifth verse is omitted.

HYMN 652.—" Come, Holy Spirit, heavenly Dove."—*Breathing after the Holy Spirit.*

Dr Watts', No. 34, Book II. The second verse is left out. Mr Wesley printed it in his " Collection of Psalms and Hymns," enlarged edition, 1743, page 44.

Another instance of the value and influence of hymns is furnished by the following incident :—" A young man who had been the leader of gaiety amongst the middle ranks of the place in which he dwelt, went to a Scripture-reading at the persuasion of a friend ; and the Word of God went like an arrow to his heart. To stifle his convictions, he went to a neighbouring public-house, where several young men spent their evenings in revelry. His talent for singing made him doubly welcome amongst them. In the midst of singing a song, the words vanished from his mind ; he tried in vain to recall them ; the only lines he could remember were these, by Dr Watts—

> ' Come, Holy Spirit, heavenly Dove,
>   With all Thy quickening powers ;
> Come, shed abroad a Saviour's love,
>   And that shall kindle ours.'

He left the house deeply wounded in spirit, his pride humbled, and, seeking earnestly for pardon till he found it, he spent the rest of his life in the service of God."

HYMN 653.—" Come, Holy Spirit, raise our songs."—*For the Day of Pentecost.*

This hymn is made up from two sources. The first, second, and third verses were written by Robert Carr Brackenbury ; the remaining portion of the hymn is from Charles Wesley's " Hymns and Sacred Poems," 1742, page 165. Mr Brackenbury was one of the most useful men in Methodism for about half a century. He was born in Lincolnshire in 1752, and began to itinerate, as an endeared friend of both John and Charles Wesley, in 1782.

He founded Methodism in the Channel Islands, at Weymouth, and Portland. To divert his mind, on the death of Mr Wesley, he wrote, collected, and published a small volume of " Sacred Poems and Hymns," 1792. Mr Brackenbury died in August 1818. A most interesting record of his life was lately published by Mrs Smith, daughter of Dr Adam Clarke, under the title of " Raithby Hall." This estimable man felt a strong objection to anything being said to his praise after his death. The writer of these notes has secured a copy of a private portrait of him, which exhibits the dignity of the gentleman, and the meekness and gentleness of the Christian.

Mr Bunting describes the first three words in the third and fourth lines as helping to make two clumsy lines ; whilst the third verse is so bad, he has supplied the verse in an amended form, with the date of 1859 written to it.

> " By this the blest disciples knew
>   Their risen Lord had reach'd His throne ;
>   Obtain'd the grace by promise due,
>   And shower'd its fulness on His own."

The word " promise " in the third verse, by Mr Brackenbury, and the same word in the fourth verse, by Mr Wesley, is used in two different senses. In the latter instance, Mr Bunting suggests, instead of " The apostolic promise given," to read, " The evangelistic promise given ; "—as the promise alluded to in that line was given to the apostles, not by them.

HYMN 654.—" Creator, Spirit, by whose aid.—*Veni Creator Spiritus.*

The renown of this hymn extends over some fifteen hundred years. It has been generally attributed to Charlemagne, but some scholars object, and give their reasons ; others affix the name of Ambrose, Bishop of Milan in the fourth century, as the writer of the original Latin hymn. It is of very early date ; and the Church has recognised its claim to superiority over all others, by retaining it in the offices for the ordering of priests, the consecration of bishops, the coronation of kings, the celebration of synods, the creation of popes, and on other like great occasions. The translation at present in use was made from the Latin by John Dryden, a celebrated English poet, towards the end of his life, and after he had joined the Church of Rome, to try, by such religious duties as that Church appointed, to amend some of the errors of his former life. Dryden was born in 1631, and educated at Westminster, and Trinity College, Cambridge. He was a man of letters from his youth, and is one of the most distinguished of England's poets. He died in 1700, and is buried in Westminster Abbey. The translation from which this hymn is selected, consists of thirty-nine lines, nine of which are omitted. Mr Wesley first inserted this hymn in his collection of " Psalms and Hymns," 1738, and it was also included in subsequent editions.

HYMN 655.—"Jesus, we on the words depend."—*For Whit-Sunday.*

Charles Wesley's, forming No. 12 of " Hymns of Petition and Thanksgiving for the Promise of the Father," 1746, founded on John xiv. 25-27. Mr Bunting suggests these alterations :—In line 3, verse 4, " His legacy " to " Thy legacy :" in the next line, "our Lord's " to " Thine own :" and the last line,

> " And change, and make us all like Thee,"

altered to

> " And make us all, O Christ, like Thee."

HYMN 656.—" Why should the children of a king."—*The Witnessing and Sealing Spirit.*

Dr Watts', being No. 144, Book I.

It will be found in John Wesley's " Collection of Psalms and Hymns," second edition, 1741.

One hundred years ago, on one of Mr Wesley's visits to Chesterfield, he had commenced an out-door service in the market-place. During the first prayer the constable came and demanded his presence before a magistrate. The prayer ended, the man with authority marched off with the preacher; but before doing so, the man of prayer showed his faith by saying to his hearers, " Friends, sing a hymn whilst I am gone,—I shall soon be back ;" and he gave out the couplet—

> " Why should the children of a king
> Go mourning all their days?"

Mr Wesley returned and preached before the hymn had been sung through a second time.

HYMN 657.—"*Eternal Spirit, come.*"—*For Whit-Sunday.*

Charles Wesley's, being No. 3 of "Hymns of Petition and Thanksgiving," &c. The third verse is left out.

HYMN 658.—"Father, glorify Thy Son."—*For Whit-Sunday.*

Charles Wesley's, being No. 9 of "Hymns of Petition and Thanksgiving," &c., founded on John xiv. 16, 17. The second and fourth verses are omitted, and several lines are altered. The last line reads thus—

> " Jesus said, it shall be so."

HYMN 659.—"O Thou that hear'st when sinners cry."—*The Backslider Restored.*

Dr Watts', being his version of Psalm li., Part III. ; one line is altered, and the fifth verse is left out. This commences the fourth section of the Supplement, with the title " Penitential Hymns."

HYMN 660.—"How sad our state by nature is!"—*Faith in Christ for Pardon and Sanctification.*

Dr Watts', Hymn 90, Book II. The fifth verse is omitted.

Methodism in York had true and sincere friends in Robert Spence and his wife. Mrs Spence was convinced of sin under the preaching of two godly clergymen ; but by their teaching she proceeded no further in the spiritual life. Under deep convictions for sin, she went to hear the Methodists in Yorkshire, when it was thought to be a reproach to be even associated with them. She was led to cast in her lot amongst them, and her decision soon led to her finding pardon. Her usefulness in the Church commenced at once. Not content with the blessings she had received, she read what books she could obtain on entire sanctification, and gave herself no rest till that great blessing was her own happy experience ; and in its enjoyment she lived to the end of her life. When on the threshold of eternity, she acknowledged her indebtedness to grace alone for salvation. "This," she said, "will never fail"—

> " To the blest fountain of Thy blood,
>   Incarnate God, I fly."

She continued to praise God till her happy spirit escaped to paradise.

A godly ancestry was the happy privilege of Mary Elizabeth
Rowe, wife of the Rev. Thomas Rowe. Her maternal grandfather was Dr James Hamilton, who was so long and continuously associated with Mr Wesley, who once preached before
the Conference by his desire, and whose portrait, with that
of Mr Cole, form a trio, so often engraved, representing Mr
Wesley walking with his two friends in Edinburgh. The sudden
death of a sister induced Mrs Rowe to join the Methodist
Society, and soon afterwards she was made a partaker of the
pardoning love of God. Her after-life was in accordance with
this godly beginning ; and when laid aside by illness, she had
an impression on her mind that her end was near, but retained
her unshaken trust in Christ. A few hours before she expired,
she exclaimed with great fervour—

> " A guilty, weak, and helpless worm,
>   Into Thy hands I fall ;
> Be Thou my strength and righteousness,
>   My Saviour, and my all."

In this resigned, happy frame she soon afterwards entered into
rest.

The Rev. George Marsden records of one of his interviews
with the Rev. Richard Watson, during his last illness, with what
pleasure the suffering divine spoke on the subject of Christ
crucified. He dwelt for some time on its infinite importance,
as the only foundation on which to rest for pardon, acceptance
with God, and eternal life. He then spoke of his own unworthiness, and of his firm reliance on the atonement, and repeated
with solemn and deep feeling the last verse of Hymn 660—

> " A guilty, weak, and helpless worm,
>   Into Thy hands I fall ;
> Be Thou my strength and righteousness,
>   My Saviour, and my all."

For more than fifty years, Walker B. Benson, of Liverpool,
was a useful member and officer of the Methodist Church.
After a short seafaring life, he settled down to business in Leeds,
where, at the age of twenty, a dangerous illness was blessed to
his conversion. A consistent and holy walk marked his future
life. As a class-leader he was useful and diligent, in Leeds, in
Canada, and at Mount Pleasant, Liverpool. His last illness was

brief, but his confidence in God was unshaken, and his dying
testimony was expressed with peculiar emphasis in the words—

> " A guilty, weak, and helpless worm,
>   Into Thy hands I fall ;
> Be Thou my strength and righteousness,
>   My Saviour, and my all."

As early in life as her eleventh year, Eliza Neilson, third
daughter of the Rev. William Burt, was truly converted to God,
and she left the marks of her godlikeness on the society in which
she moved ever afterwards, and enjoyed for some years before
her death the inestimable blessing of perfect love.   Her last illness was brief and unexpected, but every word of her conversation "had respect to her love to Christ, her happy state, and her
hope of heaven."   When dying, Mr Neilson asked, " Are you
going to leave us ?"   She exclaimed, in reply—

> " A guilty, weak, and helpless worm,
>   Into Thy hands I fall ;
> Be Thou my strength and righteousness,
>   My Saviour, and my all."

And after adding, " All is well !" she entered the heavenly Jerusalem.

HYMN 661.—"O Thou who hast redeem'd of old."—*Desiring to*
Love.

Charles Wesley's, being No. 24 in " Hymns and Sacred
Poems," 1749, vol. i, with four verses omitted.

HYMN 662.—" Regardless now of things below."—*Looking unto*
Jesus.

Charles Wesley's, from " Hymns and Sacred Poems," 1740,
page 21.

HYMN 663.—"O for a closer walk with God."—*Walking with*
God.

William Cowper's, forming No. 3 in the " Olney Collection,"
written in 1779, and founded on Gen. v. 24.
Considering the depressing circumstances under which
Cowper wrote many of his hymns, there are few which indicate
more spiritual hopefulness from under a cloud than this earnestly-expressed hymn of supplication, desire, and self-sacrifice.

Those of his hymns are the most pathetic which give expression
to his own inward fears and conflicts.

Mrs Mathison and the Rev. John Anderson were children
together in the same school, and they remained friends of each
other, and friends of Methodism, during life. In 1812 the first
Methodist sermon heard by Mrs Mathison was preached by the
Rev. Joseph Benson in Great Queen Street Chapel. The word
came with power to her heart ; she joined the Society, and
received her note of admission at the hands of the Rev. John
Barber, and her first ticket from the Rev. Dr Adam Clarke.
She became a useful class-leader both in London and Liverpool. She was called to pass through both prosperous and
adverse circumstances, but her faith and piety changed not.
When the end drew nigh she said, " I have given all into the
hands of Jesus, and repeated the lines—

> " O for a closer walk with God,
>   A calm and heavenly frame ;
>   A light to guide me on the road
>   . That leads me to the Lamb !"

and in a few minutes life gently ebbed out, and the redeemed
and sanctified spirit entered the paradise of God.

Many men have commenced a long career of prosperity in
London with but small beginnings. Mr Robert Middleton came
from Durham to the metropolis in the last century an entire
stranger. Divine providence guided his steps ; at the age of
thirty he heard a sermon by a Methodist preacher, believed
to have been the Rev. John Pawson, under which he became
thoroughly convinced of sin, and in the solitude of his closet
that night he found that peace which passeth understanding,
and which for sixty years afterwards enabled him to render
important and cheerful service to the cause of Methodism in
London. For half a century the principal preachers of the
body found a welcome home under his roof, and the funds of
the connexion were greatly aided by his munificence. Nor
were the poor of the Lord's people less noticed, or less benefited by his benevolence. Up to the age of ninety he had witnessed a good confession : his last days found him enfeebled
and speechless, yet his desire for a closer communion with God
was expressed, just before he lost the power of speech, in the
lines of Cowper's hymn—

" O for a closer walk with God,
    A calm and heavenly frame," &c.

He was soon afterwards gratified by being permitted to " walk
with Him in white " in the better land above.

HYMN 664.—" Infinite Power, eternal Lord."—*The Comparison
                    and Complaint.*

Dr Watts', from " Horæ Lyricæ," 1705. The fifth and tenth
verses are left out. It is published in John Wesley's " Psalms
and Hymns," second edition, 1743.

HYMN 665.—" Long have I sat beneath the sound."—*Unfruit-
    fulness, Ignorance, and Unsanctified Affections.*

Dr Watts', No. 165, Book II. The second verse is omitted,
and the fifth line is altered from " My dear Almighty and my
God," and improved by the change.

HYMN 666.—" Father, I stretch my hands to Thee."—*Prayer
                    for Faith.*

Charles Wesley's, from " Psalms and Hymns," second edition,
1743. Two of the verses are altered.

HYMN 667.—" By secret influence from above."—" *Thou triest
                man every moment.*"

Charles Wesley's, a " Scripture Hymn," founded on Job vii.
17, 18, and left in manuscript when the author died.

HYMN 668.—" Long have I waited, Lord."—" *I have waited for
                Thy salvation, O Lord.*"

Charles Wesley's, a " Scripture Hymn," founded on Gen. xlix.
18, and left in manuscript at the author's death.

HYMN 669.—" The God of Abraham praise."
    „   670.—" Though nature's strength decay."
    „   671.—" Before the great Three-One."
        To the God of Abraham.

This hymn was written by Thomas Olivers, and published by
him in 1772. Whilst the author was on a friendly visit to John
Bakewell, of Westminster (one of the very early Methodist lay
preachers), he visited the Jews' Synagogue, where he heard a
celebrated air sung by the priest, Signior Leoni. Olivers was

so captivated with the singing and the air, that he resolved at
once to write a Christian hymn to suit the air, so that the Methodists might sing it, and in Mr Bakewell's hospitable dwelling
that truly magnificent hymn was written. It was received with
such enthusiasm by the Methodists, that in the second year
eight editions had been demanded. The original is in three
parts; it is based on several passages in the Old Testament.
Olivers was a remarkable man. Born in 1725, he led a very
profligate life as a shoemaker, till converted under the ministry
of Mr Whitefield; and in 1753 Mr Wesley accepted him as a
preacher of the gospel, and in his later years he was employed as corrector of the press. He died in March 1799,
and is interred in the same vault with Mr Wesley, in City
Road Chapel Yard. Olivers wrote two or three other hymns of
considerable merit, and some fierce controversial works. James
Montgomery says of this hymn, "The God of Abraham:"—
"There is not in our language a lyric of more majestic style,
more elevated thought, or more glorious imagery. Its structure,
indeed, is unattractive on account of the short lines, but like a
stately pile of architecture, severe and simple in design, it
strikes less on the first view than after deliberative examination."
This hymn commences the fifth section of the Supplement, with
the title, "The Experience and Privileges of Believers." The
only portrait of Mr Olivers is in the *Arminian Magazine* for 1779.

In the *Wesleyan Magazine* several instances of the usefulness
of this hymn have been recorded. Mrs Booth, of Huddersfield,
who died September 17, 1856, a few days before her death
asked that the hymn to "The God of Abraham" might be read
to her. After listening to the third verse—

> " He calls a worm His friend,
> He calls Himself my God ;
> And He shall save me to the end,
> Through Jesu's blood "—

she exclaimed, "It will be so, and that very soon: read it again
and the whole hymn ; it is just my experience at present. Oh,
how I long to be with Jesus !"

The uncertainty of life was marked by a sentence written by
the Rev. J. Relph in reference to one of his college friends :—
"Of the candidates for the ministry who entered the Wesleyan
Theological Institution at Hoxton in 1837, nearly one-half have
already died !" The name of the Rev. John Smart was then

added to the number. In early life he was converted to God,
and whilst yet a youth, was appointed the leader of a class, and
was found a diligent labourer in the Sunday-school, the Benevolent Society, the Tract Society, and in other spheres of
usefulness. He had a short but glorious career as a Methodist
preacher. When illness prostrated his body, his faith continued strong. The day but one before he died he exclaimed,
with holy joy and triumphant faith, "Christ is mine! heaven is
mine!" During the following night he repeated—

> " He by Himself hath sworn,
> I on His oath depend ;
> I shall, on eagles' wings upborne,
> To heaven ascend.' "

A friend, standing by, repeated the remainder of the verse—

> "I shall behold His face," &c.,

to which he immediately referred, observing to his wife what
a happy effect had been produced on his mind nearly two years
before by the appropriate quotation of that verse by a lady in a
love-feast at Barnsley. After urging his daughter to begin to
love God, he peacefully entered into rest.

The ministrations of the Rev. L. Hargreaves and the Rev. R.
Needham were, through the blessing of God, instrumental in
bringing several members of the Fishwick family to a knowledge
of sins forgiven. Mr William Fishwick, of Longholme, seeing
the good work in the family, went himself to hear the Methodists,
and his prejudices against them at once gave way. The Rev.
Jabez Bunting's sermon on "Justification by Faith," which he
read, pointed out to him the way of salvation, and at the age of
twenty-two he received his first ticket of membership from the
Rev. Isaac Keeling, and soon afterwards found the Lord, to the
joy of his heart. He retained to the end of his life a clear
assurance of his acceptance with God. As the employer of
several hundreds of persons, he exemplified the character of "a
master," as set forth by Charles Wesley in the 470th Hymn in
the collection. He was a friend to those he employed, to the
poor around him, and to the cause of God generally. He laid
the foundation-stone of the large Wesleyan Chapel at Burnley
in 1839, and contributed liberally to its funds. His last illness was short and severe; but he enjoyed the presence of
his Master. His last strength was spent in a prayer for his

children ; and being exhausted, he lay still for a time, and then
said—

> " I shall behold His face ;
> I shall His power adore."

As he seemed unable to proceed, Miss Kaye, his sister, repeated
the next line—

> "And sing the wonders of His grace."

He instantly took it up, and added, " For evermore, for evermore, for evermore ! " repeating these words as long as his
strength lasted ; and with a parting prayer for God's blessing,
he peacefully fell asleep in Jesus.

The ministry and holy conversation of the Rev. Dr Adam Clarke
were the means of the conversion, in early life, of Elizabeth
Geake, of Frogwell, Cornwall. As Miss Lingmaid, she frequently rode on her pony to various Methodist preaching-places,
for she was a good singer, and she had special pleasure in aiding
the psalmody. When upwards of eighty years of age she said,
" My voice is weak, but I can still sing ; I sing here," pointing
to her heart. A friend asked her to give her a morning-song.
" I think I can," she replied, and with a thin, tremulous voice
she chanted some sweet lines, which, she said, Dr Adam Clarke
taught her when a girl, when he used to preach in her father's
parlour. The lines were Olivers' hymn, "The God of Abraham,"
sung to Leoni. She could repeat the whole hymn verbatim.
Shortly before her death she observed to a friend, " I can look
at the mattock, the shovel, and the grave without dread." She
closed her lengthened earthly pilgrimage by repeating this fine
hymn.

The Rev. William Worth, Wesleyan minister, when closing
his earthly course, said, "Yes, precious Saviour ! Thou art mine !—

> ' I shall behold His face,
> I shall His power adore ;
> And sing the wonders of His grace
> For evermore.' "

The eminently pious Richard Watson, when near the end of
his last illness, one night, moved by a sudden impulse, as he lay
in bed, exclaimed, with tears flowing down his languid countenance, " I am a worm, a poor, vile worm, not worthy to lift its
head ; but then the worm is permitted to crawl out of the earth
into the garden of the Lord, and there, among the flowers and

fruits, if it can, to speculate on the palace and ivory throne of Solomon—

> ' I shall behold His face,
> I shall His power adore ;
> And sing the wonders of His grace
> For evermore.'"

It was remarked, " No doubt you will see His face." " Yes," he rejoined, " there is doubt of everything, but the great, deep, infinite mercy of God ; that is sure." And again, just before final unconsciousness set in, he said, " I long to quit this little abode, gain the wide expanse of the skies, rise to nobler joys, and see God." He closed this last conversation by repeating this favourite stanza of Olivers'—

> " I shall behold His face," &c.

Good Richard Pattison, after a ministry of nearly fifty years in Methodism, when nearing the harbour of refuge above, speaking of the confidence we ought to place in the faithfulness of God, said, " Many times, in storms on the ocean, or crossing from one island to another in small vessels "—during his seven years of missionary life in the West Indies—" I have held by a rope, and sang—

> ' The watery deep I pass,
> With Jesus in my view ;
> And through the howling wilderness
> My way pursue ; '

and I have felt my faith in God wonderfully strengthened." He was greatly attached to the Hymn-book, and found great comfort in the frequent repetition of some of the hymns in all the circumstances of life, and even with his latest breath.

In his twentieth year, Joseph Simpson, at a Methodist watch-night service in 1844, gave his heart to the Lord, and entered into the liberty of the children of God in the February following. He made considerable progress in classical and other studies in youth, and afterwards became one of the tutors in Kingswood School. In 1849 he was sent as a supply to the Gwennap circuit, and from thence he was appointed to the Ely circuit, in both which he laboured with untiring zeal for the salvation of sinners. Consumption cut short his work in righteousness, but his peace with God was unshaken, and when all hope of recovery was gone, he expressed his confidence in God in some of the hymns he loved so much. Once his sister

proposed to read a few verses, when he selected Olivers' hymn
to the God of Abraham.   When the first part was finished, he
repeated the lines—

> "I shall behold His face,
> I shall His power adore ;
> And sing the wonders of His grace
> For evermore."

His sister then proceeded with the reading of the second and
third parts, and at the close he replied again, with deep feeling—

> "Hail, Abraham's God, and mine !
> (I join the heavenly lays,)
> All might and majesty are Thine,
> And endless praise."

In this happy spirit he found the dark valley of death illumined
from heaven, and in this glorious light he entered the realms of
the blessed.

HYMN 672.—"Awake, our souls ! away, our fears !"—*The
Christian Race.*

Dr Watts', No. 48, Book I., founded on Isaiah xlviii. 28, &c.,
and was inserted by Mr Wesley in "Psalms and Hymns," enlarged
edition, 1743.

HYMN 673.—"Commit thou all thy griefs."
    „   674.—"Give to the winds thy fears."—
            Trust in Providence.

John Wesley's translation from the German by Paul Gerhard,
founded on Psalm xxvii. 5, 6.   There are twenty-four of John
Wesley's translations inserted in the collection, all of which are
named together on another page ; the first, Hymn 23, was
written by Gerhard, and this, which is the last of the series, is
by the same author.   The sixth verse of the original is left out.
There is not a hymn in the book which has afforded more
comfort and encouragement than this one to the Lord's tried
people.   In a village near Warsaw there lived a pious German
peasant named Dobry.   Without remedy, he had fallen into
arrears of rent, and his landlord threatened to evict him.   It
was winter.   Thrice he appealed for a respite, but in vain.   It
was evening, and the next day his family were to be turned out
into the snow.   The church bell called to evening prayer, when
Dobry kneeled down in the midst of his family.   They sang—

" Commit thou all thy griefs
And ways into His hands."

As they came to the last verse, in German, of Part I.—

" When Thou would'st all our need supply,
Who, who shall stay Thy hand?"

there was a knock at the window close by where he knelt, and
opening it Dobry found a raven, one which his grandfather
had tamed and set at liberty. In its bill was a ring, set with
precious stones. This he took to his minister, who said at once
that it belonged to the King Stanislaus, to whom he took it, and
related the story. The king sent for Dobry, and rewarded him,
so that he had no need, and the next year built him a new
house, and gave him cattle from his own stall. Over the house
door, on an iron tablet, there is carved a raven with a ring in its
beak, and underneath this address to Divine Providence—

" Thou everywhere hast sway,
And all things serve Thy might;
Thy every act pure blessing is,
Thy path unsullied light."

The origin of this hymn is itself such a remarkable proof of the
blessing of trusting in Providence that it cannot be omitted in
this place. Paul Gerhard was a preacher in Brandenburg, 1659,
and he loved to preach from his heart what he believed. The
Great Elector admonished him, and threatened his banishment
if he did not preach as the Elector desired. Gerhard returned
a message to his sovereign that it would be hard to leave his
home, his people, his country, and his livelihood; but he would
only preach what he found in the Word of God. So into banishment he went with his wife and children. At the end of the
first day's journey they rested at a little inn for the night. The
little ones were crying and clinging to their mother, and she
also, overcome with fatigue, could not restrain her tears. The
sad sight gave Gerhard a very heavy heart, so he went alone
into the dark wood to commend the whole to God. Whilst
there his mind was comforted with the text : "Commit thy way
unto the Lord: trust also in Him, and He shall bring it to pass."
"Yes," he said, "though banished from house and home, and
not knowing where to take my wife and children on the morrow,
yet God sees me in the dark wood; now is the time to trust Him."
He was so happy that he had remembered the text, and so

thankful to God, that he made the text, in connection with his saddening lot, into a hymn, as he paced to and fro amongst the trees. Every verse begins with a word or two from the text, so that if you read the first words of each verse in the German, you just read the text. When he returned into the house, he told his wife about the text, and repeated to her his hymn. She soon dried up her tears (the children having gone to sleep), and became as hopeful and trustful in God as her husband. They had scarcely retired to rest when a loud knocking was heard at the door. The landlord, on opening the door, found a messenger on horseback, who said aloud, " I come from Duke Christian of Meresburg, and am in search of Paul Gerhard ; has he passed this way?"   "Yes," said the landlord, "he is in my house."   "Let me see him instantly," said the Duke's messenger. A large sealed letter was at once handed to the banished pastor from the good Duke Christian, who said in it, "Come into my country, Paul Gerhard, and you shall have church, people, house, home, and livelihood, and liberty to preach the Gospel as your heart may prompt you."

William Dawson, of Barnbow, near Leeds, the farmer Methodist preacher, after a useful career of sixty-eight years, was suddenly seized with fatal illness. His last words were the closing lines of Paul Gerhard's hymn on Providence—

> " Let us in life, in death,
>   Thy steadfast truth declare."

In attempting to repeat the concluding lines—

> " And publish with our latest breath
>   Thy love and guardian care,"

utterance failed him, he crossed his hands upon his breast, and expired, in July 1841. On another occasion this hymn had afforded hope and encouragement to the same man of God. Worldly troubles and anxieties about his farm had disturbed his peace for some time, and one day, whilst working in the fields on the brow of some rising ground leading to the farm-house, he paused, and to divert his mind took from his pocket sundry notices which had accumulated there, which had from time to time been sent up to him in the pulpit to read. After reading them, to awaken more cheering thoughts in his mind, he tore them up into small pieces, and threw the handful of frag-ments up into the air, the wind carrying them about like so

many butterflies. Instantly the verse came to his mind, and he
repeated it with emphasis—

> " Give to the winds thy fears ;
> Hope, and be undismay'd :
> God hears thy sighs, and counts thy tears ;
> God shall lift up thy head."

Mrs Chadwick, of Halifax, was mother of Mrs Atmore, wife
of the Rev. Charles Atmore. For more than forty years she
was a member of the Methodist Society, during which time she
had to endure many hardships, privations, and much suffering,
but her faith in God failed not ; when more than four-score
years old, she was attacked by cholera, from which she did not
recover. In the midst of much pain, she said to Mrs Atmore,
" My dear, I feel my mind very low and much depressed, but
that verse is just come with much sweetness to my soul—

> " Give to the winds thy fears ;
> Hope, and be undismay'd :
> God hears thy sighs, and counts thy tears ;
> God shall lift up thy head."

Then she added, " He will lift up my head for ever !" This
seemed to be her last conflict, and shortly afterwards she peacefully passed away, like a shock of corn ready for the garner.

In accordance with Mr Wesley's advice and custom, Henry
Ridley, although a member of the Methodist Society, regularly
attended the Sunday-morning service in the Church of England.
For nearly sixty years, Wesleyan ministers were welcomed under
his roof for their Master's sake, and for thirty years he faithfully
served the office of class-leader. He was greatly attached to
the means of grace, and in his later years was a most diligent
reader of the Word of God. He was seized with illness on
leaving the house of God on the Sabbath, and though called to
pass through a short but severe illness, he murmured not. He
knew that he was dying, and shortly before the end came, after
one of his painful attacks, he exclaimed, " Jesus is my Rock,
and He is a sure foundation." Several times he repeated—

> " Let us in life, in death,
> Thy steadfast truth declare,
> And publish with our latest breath
> Thy love and guardian care."

His ransomed spirit escaped to paradise, shortly after he had breathed the prayer, "Lord Jesus, into Thy hands I commend my spirit, soul, body."

HYMN 675.—"Away, my needless fears."—*In Danger of Losing his Friends.*

Charles Wesley's, being No. 225 in "Hymns and Sacred Poems," 1749, vol. ii. The original is in ten double stanzas, of which seven are left out.

HYMN 676.—"Bless'd are the humble souls that see."—*The Beatitudes.*

Dr Watts', Hymn 102, Book I., founded on Matt. v. 2–12. Three of the verses are left out.

HYMN 677.—"Who in the Lord confide."—*Psalm* cxxv.

Charles Wesley's version of the one hundred and twenty-fifth Psalm, verses 1, 2, and 4. It is printed in John Wesley's "Psalms and Hymns," second edition, 1741. Three of the verses are omitted.

HYMN 678.—"God is the refuge of His saints."—*The Church's Safety and Triumph among National Desolations.*

Dr Watts' paraphrase of Psalm xlvi. The last line is altered from "Built on His truth, and armed with power."

HYMN 679.—"My Shepherd will supply my need."—*God our Shepherd.*

Dr Watts' version of the twenty-third Psalm, with the last verse omitted.

HYMN 680.—"Happy the heart where graces reign."—*Love to God.*—TUNE, Oatlands.

Dr Watts', Hymn 38, Book II.

This fine hymn was probably never more appropriately or impressively used than after a sermon preached by Dr Hannah, in Brunswick Wesleyan Chapel, Sheffield, one Sunday evening during the Conference of 1835. The writer had listened in a crowded audience, bathed with perspiration, to a discourse of masterly power, from the words, "And now abideth faith, hope, charity; these three, but the greatest of these is charity." The sermon was long, the attention fixed; but much beyond the usual time for closing, that devout man of God said he had dwelt at considerable length on "faith and hope;" he must leave it to eternity to reveal the extent of the meaning of "charity;" and then in a solemn manner announced this hymn—

> "Happy the heart where graces reign," &c.

The effect was very happy and very successful, and it was felt to be a plain, pointed, and powerful application of the whole discourse. The singing was solemn and hearty, thoroughly characteristic of Yorkshire, and the hallowed effect of it, and even the tune, is fresh on the mind after a lapse of thirty-four years. The tune was "Oatlands."

HYMN 681.—"Vain, delusive world, adieu."—"*I am determined to know nothing save Jesus Christ and Him crucified.*"

Charles Wesley's, from "Hymns and Sacred Poems," 1742, page 257 ; five verses omitted. This hymn has been a source of encouragement to hundreds of new-born souls, who, having experienced the blessedness of those who have passed from death unto life, and have discovered the vanity of all earthly things, have joyfully sung—

> "Vain, delusive world, adieu,
>   With all of creature-good !
> Only Jesus I pursue,
>   Who bought me with His blood :
> All thy pleasures I forego,
> I trample on thy wealth and pride :
>   Only Jesus will I know,
>   And Jesus crucified."

This volume bears ample testimony to the wisdom of the choice thus made by such persons.

HYMN 682.—"O Jesus, full of truth and grace."—*Waiting for the Promise.*

Charles Wesley's, from "Hymns and Sacred Poems," 1742, page 238. Five verses are omitted, and several lines altered. The third line in verse 5 is altered from "sinless sinner" to "helpless creature."

HYMN 683.—"Author of faith, appear."—"*Look unto me, and be ye saved, all the ends of the earth.*"

Charles Wesley's, from "Hymns and Sacred Poems," 1740,

page 166, founded on Isa. xlv. 22. The first five verses of the original are left out.

HYMN 684.—"God of Daniel, hear my prayer."—*Daniel in the Den of Lions.*

Charles Wesley's, from "Hymns and Sacred Poems," 1742, page 211. Two verses are left out. This is an admirable gospel rendering of a popular Old Testament incident.

HYMN 685.—"To God the only wise."—*Persevering Grace.*

Dr Watts', Hymn 51, Book I., founded on Jude, verses 24, 25.

HYMN 686.—"In every time and place."—"*Get thee out of thy country,*" &c.

Charles Wesley's, one of his manuscript hymns, founded on Acts vii. 3, and sets forth the cheerful, obedient faith of Abraham as a pattern for the Christian.

HYMN 687.—"O that now the church were blest."—"*Then had the churches rest, and were edified,*" &c.

Charles Wesley's, being one of his manuscript "Scripture Hymns," founded on Acts ix. 31.

HYMN 688.—"Blessed are the pure in heart."—"*Blessed are the pure in heart.*"

Charles Wesley's, one of his manuscript "Scripture Hymns," founded on Matt. v. 8. This hymn urges all to pray for spotless purity and perfect love, a leading doctrine of the founders of Methodism.

HYMN 689.—"Jesu, my God and King."—*Hymn to Christ the King.*

Charles Wesley's, from "Hymns and Sacred Poems," 1739, page 171. The original has eleven verses, the last four of which are omitted. In the ninth verse, the poet describes the expulsion of Lucifer from heaven in these emphatic words :—

> "Lucifer as lightning fell,
>   Far from heaven, from glory far,
>   Headlong hurl'd to deepest hell!"

This hymn commences the sixth section of the Supplement, with the title, "On the Establishment and Extension of Christ's Kingdom."

HYMN 690.—"Earth, rejoice, our Lord is King!"—*To be sung in a Tumult.*

Charles Wesley's, from "Hymns and Sacred Poems," 1740, page 115. The original has fourteen verses, eight of which are omitted.

This hymn is a joyous triumph of Christ's kingdom over that of the kingdom of darkness. Twice the poet boldly apostrophises Satan and the infernal hosts, defying them in the name of the Lord, and bidding them fear and tremble in the presence of Christ.

> "Every knee to Him shall bow ;
> Satan, hear, and tremble now."

And again—

> "God with us, we cannot fear ;
> Fear, ye fiends, for Christ is here !"

What a sublime and dignified attitude is thus claimed for the Christian believer ! The security of the child of God is stated in forcible language in another couplet—

> "Hell is nigh, but God is nigher,
> Circling us with hosts of fire."

HYMN 691.—"Come, Thou Conqueror of the nations."—"*King of kings, and Lord of lords.*"

Charles Wesley's, being the eighth of his "Hymns for the Expected Invasion" [of England by the French], 1759, founded on Rev. xix. 11. The fifth verse is omitted.

HYMN 692.—"Father of boundless grace."—"*Thy kingdom come.*"

Charles Wesley's, being No. 1156 of his "Short Scripture Hymns," vol. i., founded on Isa. lxvi. 18. The second verse is omitted. This hymn is well adapted for missionary services : one couplet is worthy of note—

> "And new-discover'd worlds arise,
> To sing their Saviour's praise."

HYMN 693.—" Head of Thy Church, whose Spirit fills."—
Hymn of Intercession.

Charles Wesley's, from " Hymns and Sacred Poems," 1749,
vol. ii., No. 61.   Three verses of the original are left out.

HYMN 694.—" Eternal Lord of earth and skies."—"*For the
mouth of the Lord hath spoken it.*"

Charles Wesley's, being made up of parts of three "Short
Scripture Hymns," vol. i., No. 1059, Isa. xlv. 21 ; No. 1060,
Isa. xlv. 23 ; and 1043, Isa. xlii. 4.   The last line is altered
from, " And fill the universe with God."

HYMN 695.—" Let Sion in her King rejoice."—*God fights for
His Church.*

Dr Watts' paraphrase of Psalm xlvi.   In the second line the
word " tyrants " is changed to " Satan."

HYMN 696.—" Arm of the Lord, awake, awake."—" *Be Thou
exalted in the whole earth.*"

Charles Wesley's, being made up from three of the poet's
" Hymns of Petition and Thanksgiving for the Promise of the
Father," 1746.   Verse 1 is from Hymn 18 ; verse 2 from Hymn
21 ; and verses 3 and 4 from Hymn 22.   Mr Montgomery has
inserted this hymn in his "Christian Psalmist."

HYMN 697.—" Jesus shall reign where'er the sun."—*Christ's
Kingdom amongst the Gentiles.*

Dr Watts' paraphrase of Psalm lxxii.   The second and third
verses of the original are left out.

The fulness and completeness of the redemption by Christ is
clearly stated in the fourth verse—

" In Him the tribes of Adam boast
More blessings than their father lost."

Perhaps one of the most interesting occasions on which this
hymn was used is that on which King George of Tonga, of
blessed memory, gave a new constitution to his people, ex-
changing a heathen for a Christian form of government.   Under
the spreading branches of the banyan trees sat some five
thousand natives from Tonga, Fiji, and Samoa, on Whit-Sunday 1862, assembled for divine worship.   Foremost amongst

them all sat King George himself. Around him were seated
old chiefs and warriors who had shared with him the dangers
and fortunes of many a battle,—men whose eyes were dim, and
whose powerful frames were bowed down with the weight of
years. But old and young alike rejoiced together in the joys
of that day, their faces most of them radiant with Christian joy,
love, and hope. It would be impossible to describe the deep
feeling manifested when the solemn service began, by the entire
audience singing Dr Watts' hymn—

> "Jesus shall reign where'er the sun
>   Doth his successive journeys run ;
>   His kingdom stretch from shore to shore,
> ·   Till suns shall rise and set no more."

Who, so much as they, could realise the full meaning of the
poet's words ? for they had been rescued from the darkness of
heathenism and cannibalism ; and they were that day met for
the first time under a Christian constitution, under a Christian
king, and with Christ himself reigning in the hearts of most of
those present ! That was indeed Christ's kingdom set up in the
earth. Still more recently, Madagascar has thrown off the yoke
of heathenism and idolatry, and established a Christian government and constitution. How would those godly, prophetical
poets, Watts and Wesley, have rejoiced to see the realisation of
such earnestly-expressed prayers as are contained in this and
other of their missionary hymns !

HYMN 698.—"The heavens declare Thy glory, Lord."—*The
Books of Nature and Scripture compared.*

Dr Watts' paraphrase of the nineteenth Psalm. The last
verse of the original is left out.

HYMN 699.—" From all that dwell below the skies."—*Praise to
God from all People.*

Dr Watts' paraphrase of Psalm cxvii., the shortest in the
Bible ; the third verse is taken from some author unknown, and
the fourth is Bishop Ken's doxology.

There is a charm in poetry and music which has never been fully
realised. An instance of this was witnessed recently in a large
school of poor children in London. The day's work was done, the
usual singing and prayer were over, and three hundred boys were
expecting in a moment to be free from authority and at play.

This psalm by Dr Watts had just been sung to the tune of the Portuguese Hymn. The master made a few remarks about the pleasure music produced, and asked the children to try and sing the hymn again. They did so : it was done with care and much feeling. Again the request was preferred,—would they like to sing it again? The reply from hundreds of voices was a simultaneous "Yes." It was repeated, if possible with increased delight to the boys. Then followed a few remarks about the music of heaven, and how sweet it must be there ; and the boys were asked if they had not felt more happy by that singing than if they had been at play. Another unanimous "Yes" was the response ; and again they were asked to sing. "Oh yes," was the instant reply ; and thus half an hour of their playtime was occupied by singing praise to God by three hundred poor children, immediately under the shadow of the palace of the Archbishop of Canterbury, at Lambeth, and the children thanked the teacher for the pleasure their own voices had afforded to themselves. The hymn and tune were fixed in their memories for life.

For thirty-six years, John Severs, of Ripon, lived with the form of godliness in the Church of England, but did not know its saving power, till, through the ministry of the Rev. John Phillips, in 1798, who so plainly set forth the condition of unregenerate man as "stung by the scorpion, sin," that the Holy Spirit carried the truth home to his conscience, and he was enabled to believe at once on the Lord Jesus Christ for forgiveness. After two years he was made a class-leader, and he lived to see his family of five children useful and active members and officers in the Methodist Society. At the ripe age of seventy-seven his usual good health gave way, and he suffered much in his last illness, but he was constantly giving thanks and singing praises to God. A few hours before he died, he repeated with feebleness the couplet—

> " From all that dwell below the skies,
>   Let the Creator's praise arise ; "

and, after a few minutes, he faintly breathed his last testimony, " My ever blessed Father !"

HYMN 700.—" Lord of the harvest, hear."—*A Prayer for Labourers.*

Charles Wesley's, from " Hymns and Sacred Poems," 1742 page 282.

HYMN 701.—" How beauteous are their feet."—*The Blessedness of Gospel Times.*

Dr Watts', Hymn 10, Book I., founded on Isa. lii. 7, and Matt. xiii. 16, 17.　In the second verse, " charming " is changed for " cheering."

HYMN 702.—" Salvation !　O the joyful sound !"—*Salvation.*

Dr Watts', Hymn 88, Book II.　The third verse of this popular hymn is found in Lady Huntingdon's Collection, but its author is unknown ; so also is the author of the chorus of this hymn. The Rev. Walter Shirley, one of the chaplains to the Countess, is the probable author of both.

The ministry of the Rev. John de Quetteville, of Guernsey, was the means of bringing Mrs Elizabeth Arrivé to a knowledge of the truth, when Methodism was in its infancy in the Channel Islands ; and shortly afterwards the ministry of Dr Adam Clarke, then a very young man, was made the means of the conversion of her husband.　Mrs Arrivé derived much good from the conversation of Mr Wesley and Dr Coke during their visit to the island in 1787.　From that time onward she was the leader of three classes, and devoted her best energies to promote the kingdom of God in the world.　For many years she proved the mainstay and support of Methodism in Guernsey, and a great comfort to the ministers during their repeated and severe trials and persecutions.　In her last illness she was very happy, and often broke out in exalted strains of praise and adoration. On one occasion she exclaimed—

" 'Salvation !　O the joyful sound !
　What pleasure to our ears !
　A sovereign balm for every wound,
　A cordial for our fears.'

This," she said, " is my experience now ;" and added, " All fear is gone from me : I am so weak I cannot say much ; but all fear is gone."　In this peaceful frame of mind she continued till the weary wheels of life stood still, and she entered into rest.

Early in life, Charlotte Whittingham, wife of the Rev. J. B. Whittingham, entered into the liberty of the children of God, and, during life, adorned her profession of godliness.　A short time before her death, she exclaimed with much energy and pathos—

> " Glory, honour, praise, and power,
>   Be unto the Lamb for ever."

Her death was somewhat sudden, but it was a peaceful entry into
the " Father's house above."

HYMN 703.—" Saviour, whom our hearts adore."—*For the
Nation.*

Charles Wesley's, being No. 11 in " Hymns for the Nation,"
1782. It was written at the time of the war between England
and America, the latter country being then an English colony.
The second verse is left out.

HYMN 704.—" Jesu, Thy wandering sheep behold !"—*A Prayer
for Labourers.*

Charles Wesley's, from " Hymns and Sacred Poems," 1742,
page 283, and is a continuation of Hymn 700, with five verses
omitted.

HYMN 705.—" The Law and Prophets all foretold."—*Christ a
Light to the Gentiles.*

Charles Wesley's, one of his manuscript " Scripture Hymns,"
founded on Acts xxvi. 23.

HYMN 706.—" Jesus, the word bestow."—" *So mightily grew the
word of God, and prevailed.*"

Charles Wesley's, one of his manuscript " Scripture Hymns,"
founded on Acts xix. 20.

HYMN 707.—" Saviour, we know Thou art."—" *The Lord added
to the Church daily,*" &c.

Charles Wesley's, one of his manuscript " Scripture Hymns,"
founded on Acts ii. 47.

HYMN 708.—" Lord, if at Thy command."—" *And the hand of
the Lord was with them.*"

Charles Wesley's, one of his manuscript " Scripture Hymns,"
founded on Acts xi. 21. These manuscript hymns, the property of the Wesleyan Conference, are now being printed with
the uniform edition of the " Poetical Works of John and Charles
Wesley," in twelve volumes.

HYMN 709.—" The Lord of earth and sky."—*For New Year's Day.*

Charles Wesley's, being No. 148 in "Hymns and Sacred Poems," 1749, vol. i. It is also inserted in the same author's "Hymns for New Year's Day," 1750, No. 6. It is a fine paraphrase of our Lord's parable of the barren fig-tree (Luke xiii. 6). It forms the first hymn in the seventh section of the Supplement, with the title, "Time, Death, Judgment, and the Future State."

HYMN 710.—" Let me alone another year."—*A Hymn of Preparation for Death.*

Charles Wesley's, one of his manuscript hymns, and on the same subject as Hymn 709.

HYMN 711.—" Eternal Source of every joy."—*The Year crowned with the Divine Goodness.*

Dr Doddridge's hymn for New Year's Day, founded on Psalm lxv. 11. The second verse is omitted.

HYMN 712.—" Sing to the Great Jehovah's praise!"—*For New Year's Day.*

Charles Wesley's, being No. 7 of "Hymns for New Year's Day," 1750.

HYMN 713.—" Wisdom ascribe, and might, and praise."—*For New Year's Day.*

Charles Wesley's, forming No. 1 of "Hymns for New Year's Day," 1750. Three verses are omitted. There are few more beautifully sublime passages in Charles Wesley's hymns than the fourth stanza of this one, which is omitted. The idea of the poet is that of a sinner weighed in the "balance" of the gospel, and found wanting : the beam begins to preponderate, a soul begins to topple into hell ; but hark ! the "remnant" (Rom. ix. 27) are praying, the Holy Ghost is groaning, the Son interceding, the Father becomes propitious, and the swift-winged angel of mercy executes his commission by touching the quivering scale, and lo ! that soul is saved—

> "Still in the doubtful balance weigh'd
> We trembled, while the remnant pray'd ;
> The Father heard His SPIRIT groan,
> And answer'd mild,—It is my Son !

> He let the prayer of faith prevail,
> And mercy turn'd the lab'ring scale ! "

Those who remember the sermons of the late William Dawson, of Barnbow, Leeds, will recognise in the above verse, and the previous description, the outline of one of that eminent man's most powerful and impressive discourses, " The Windlass."

HYMN 714.—" God of my life, through all my days."—*Praising God through the whole of our Existence.*

Dr Doddridge's, being No. 71 of his hymns, founded on Psalm cxlvi. 2. Like some few other special favourites, this hymn has had so many admirers that nearly every line of it has been used in connexion with the experience of some of the Lord's people. A dozen of these are referred to in the index. Only two or three can be noticed here.

It was the privilege of John Jeffs, and his estimable father, to introduce Methodism into Stoke Newington, in the year 1814. In early life the son was converted to God; and from the commencement to the close of his religious course was extensively useful and deservedly esteemed. For many years he was a useful leader, and conducted the singing in the chapel to the satisfaction of the whole church. The last time he conducted his class, he gave out the whole of the 714th Hymn, and he read and sung the hymn, deeply impressing all present. The same feeling was again manifested at the leaders' meeting the same evening. He closed the meeting with a very earnest prayer, the last amongst his brethren.

Early in life Mrs Laws, of Sunderland, was favoured with many godly advantages. Her father, the Rev. William Sanderson, placed her at school under the paternal care of the Rev. Joseph Benson, who placed her as a member of Society in Miss Ritchie's class. She afterwards resided some years with the Rev. Joseph Sanderson, her uncle, most of whose gifts and excellences she inherited. For fifty-seven years she was an attached and useful member of the Methodist Society. She kept up close and constant intercourse with God, and for some time prior to her decease she triumphed gloriously over the fear of death. Some of her last words were—

> " But O when that last conflict's o'er,
> And I am chain'd to earth no more,

> With what glad accents shall I rise
> To join the music of the skies?"

When the Rev. John Kemp entered the Wesleyan ministry, the salary of a preacher would not enable him to ride to his appointments, and he also found it needful to walk from Wales to Aberdeen to save costs to his circuit. His love for the work and for perishing souls enabled him to endure hardship and privation, such as is unknown at the present time. He suffered much in his eyes for some years, but he murmured not. When more than fourscore winters had passed over him, he was favoured with a beatific view of the heavenly Jerusalem ; and though his pains were intense, his joy was transporting, and a heavenly smile lighted up his face : this rapture lasted two days : he declared his joy to be so great he could not describe it. One evening just before he died he cried out—

> "But O when that last conflict's o'er,
> And I am chain'd to earth no more,
> With what glad accents shall I rise
> To join the music of the skies ! "

He gradually sank, till his released spirit fled to the paradise of God.

Miss Jane Gill, of Modbury, Kingsbridge, was converted to God at the age of seventeen, and five years afterwards she exchanged mortality for life. Three years of suffering through which she passed proved only to be the process of her ripening for glory. As her bodily strength decayed, her spiritual joy increased, and often she repeated the lines—

> "Soon shall I learn the exalted strains
> Which echo through the heavenly plains ;
> And emulate, with joy unknown,
> The glowing seraphs round the throne."

In this state of blessed resignation she fell asleep in Jesus.

Mrs Poles, of Masborough, Rotherham, on the Sabbath preceding her death, requested her husband to read her a hymn. He selected No. 714, by Dr Watts, and having read the first and second verses, was proceeding to read the third, when she began it herself—

> "When death o'er nature shall prevail,
> And all the powers of language fail,
> Joy through my swimming eyes shall break,
> And mean the thanks I cannot speak."

She died in great peace in March 1861 ; her last words being, "I am going to heaven ; I am very happy."

HYMN 715.—"Jesus, was ever love like Thine?"—"*He yielded up the Ghost*" (*Dismissed His Spirit*—Greek).

Charles Wesley's, being No. 270 of "Short Scripture Hymns", 1762, vol. ii., founded on Matthew xxvii. 50. The author of the second and third verses is unknown.

In early life the mind of Miss Eliza Hoole, daughter of Mr Holland Hoole of Manchester, and sister of the Rev. Elijah Hoole, D.D., was seriously impressed with the necessity of religion, and at the age of sixteen became a member of the Methodist Society, having, through faith in Jesus Christ, entered into the liberty of the children of God. She never wavered afterwards in her religious course. During a long affliction she suffered much, but she derived comfort from the blessed promises of God and the beautiful hymns in the Wesleyan collection. For many years she had been a constant and happy believer in Jesus Christ, but her illness had caused her to seek improved health at Douglas, Isle of Man. Whilst there she observed her usual custom of reading portions in the Hymn-book and in the Word of God. On the morning of her death, she had read the 715th hymn, every line of which is so admirably suited to the condition of a person on the very verge of heaven. She had marked the hymn by a bit of Berlin wool. In the New Testament her mark was at the chapter commencing, "There remaineth, therefore, a rest for the people of God." This hymn and this chapter were probably the last she ever read. She went out for a walk, and on her return was seized with violent hæmorrhage from the lungs, and in less than five minutes her spirit had escaped to mansions of heavenly blessedness, at the age of forty-one years. For such a glorious exit, what could be a better preparation than these lines?—

"Thy death supports the dying saint :
    Thy death my sovereign comfort be ;
While feeble flesh and nature faint,
    Arm with Thy mortal agony ;
And fill, while soul and body part,
    With life, immortal life, my heart.

"O let Thy death's mysterious power,
    With all its sacred weight, descend,

Z

> To consecrate my final hour,
> To bless me with Thy peaceful end :
> And, breathed into Thy hands divine,
> My spirit be received with Thine ! "

When, after the death of Miss Hoole, the Rev. W. M. Bunting called at her late residence, the books were shown to him with the marks in them. He was much delighted, and said, " I cannot think of anything more glorious than such a death." His own happy departure from earth was also glorious and triumphant.

HYMN 716.—" Hear what the voice from heaven proclaims."— " *Blessed are the dead which die in the Lord.*"

Dr Watts', No. 18, Book I., first and second verses only, founded on Rev. xiv. 13 ; the third and fourth verses have no author's name yet affixed to them.

HYMN 717.—" Tremendous God, with humble fear."—*A Hymn of Preparation for Death.*

Charles Wesley's, printed first in the *Arminian Magazine*, vol. iii., page 679. Is it true, as the poet says in the second verse, line 2, that man is born " only to lament and die ?" Surely this must have been one of the poet's very early, or one of his unrevised hymns.

Blessed with a truly godly mother, the Rev. John James had his mind fixed on heavenly things as early as his tenth year, and when he was fifteen he could rejoice in God as his reconciled Father, a blessing realised under the preaching of the Rev. William Jenkins. A small company of God-fearing young men was formed in Liverpool, where he resided, to cultivate their minds, and the graces of the Spirit. Of this band Mr James writes some time afterwards, in a letter to one of his band-mates, the Rev. E. Grindrod : " One is gone to glory, another appointed a class-leader, and three of us have been thrust out into the ministry." At the age of twenty-one he entered the Wesleyan ministry, and laboured with a zeal and success which distinctly marked the attendant power of the Holy Spirit to bless the Word. His mind was solemnly impressed by that terrible coach accident on his way to the Sheffield Conference, when two of his brethren, Messrs Sargent and Lloyd, were fatally injured, whilst he was spared. In 1822, he came to London ; and, in the following year, was made one of the General Missionary Secre-

taries ; his fitness for which office was manifested by the happy
results. In 1831, symptoms of apoplexy appeared ; and, in the
following year, the repetition of these symptoms cut short his
work. On the last Sabbath he spent on earth, he commenced
the devotions of the family by singing Hymn 717, little thinking that it was to be his closing act of domestic worship on earth.
The third and fourth verses are as follows—

> " Submissive to Thy just decree,
>   We all shall soon from earth remove ;
> But when Thou sendest, Lord, for me,
>   Oh, let the messenger be love !
> Whisper Thy love into my heart,
>   Warn me of my approaching end,
> And then I joyfully depart,
>   And then I to Thy arms ascend."

He preached that evening at City Road Chapel, but was unable
to walk home after service, and by the time the coach had conveyed him home, he found the hour of death was approaching,
and his happy spirit escaped to heaven on the following
Tuesday.

HYMN 718.—" I call the world's Redeemer mine."—"*I know
that my Redeemer liveth,*" &c.

Charles Wesley's, being No. 750 of " Short Scripture Hymns,"
vol. i., and also in *Arminian Magazine*, vol. iii., 1780, founded
on Job xix. 25–27.

By adopting the erroneous translation of the passage put
forth in what is called the authorised version of the Scriptures,
Mr Wesley has fallen into the generally-received error,
" Though after my skin worms destroy this body," &c. The
poet says—

> " And though the worms this skin devour;"

And again, in the fourth verse—

> " Then let the worms demand their prey.".

Dr Watts has the same idea in Hymn 721, *post ;* and Hart, in
one of his hymns, embodies the same opinion. In Hymn 726
the same idea is found ; but the opinion is not found in the
original Scriptures, nor is it a recognised physical fact that
worms destroy the bodies of the dead.

HYMN 719.—" May not a creating God."—" *Why should it be thought a thing incredible with you that God should raise the dead ?*"

Charles Wesley's ; left in manuscript at his death, founded on Acts xxvi. 8. Mr Bunting suggests altering the seventh line of verse 2, to—

" Call them out of nature's tomb."

HYMN 720.—" Why do we mourn departing friends ?"—*The Death and Burial of a Saint.*

Dr Watts', Hymn 3, Book II. The second and third verses left out.

HYMN 721.—" And must this body die ?"—*Triumph over Death in Hope of a Resurrection.*

Dr Watts', Hymn 100, Book II. A hymn of much sweetness and encouragement to Christians.

HYMN 722.—" Almighty Maker of my frame."—*The Shortness of Time, and Frailty of Man.*

Miss Ann Steele, from " Poems by Theodosia," vol. ii., page 168. A fine hymn, founded on Psalm xxxix. 4-7. The original has thirteen verses, nine of which, including the first, are left out. For diction, comprehensiveness, fidelity, and power, this hymn will compare favourably with many of far greater pretensions.

HYMN 723.—" Happy who in Jesus live."—*A Funeral Hymn.*

Charles Wesley's, being No. 16 of his " Funeral Hymns," 1744.

In early life, William Allwood, of Mansfield, Woodburn, served his country in the militia. On returning home, the godly conversation of a local preacher, and the conversion of his eldest daughter, led to his own conversion. From that time, the whole course of his life was changed. He was made a class-leader, and laboured with exemplary patience in the Sabbath-school. After the death of his wife, with whom he had lived happily for fifty years, his mellowing experience showed the ripening of his own spirit for glory. After this bereavement, he commenced his first class-meeting by singing the hymn—

> " Happy who in Jesus live ;
>   But happier still are they
> Who to God their spirits give,
>   And 'scape from earth away.
> Lord, Thou read'st the panting heart,
>   Lord, Thou hear'st the praying sigh ;
> Oh, 'tis better to depart,
>   'Tis better far to die."

It was a solemn meeting, remembered by all his members, and not very long afterwards he was himself called to rejoin his late partner in the skies.

HYMN 724.—" Hosanna to God."—*A Funeral Hymn.*

Charles Wesley's, being No. 15 of " Funeral Hymns," 1744. The original has eight verses, the second and each alternate verse being left out.

Under the ministry of Robert Carr Brackenbury, Esq., William Barnett, of Horncastle, was convinced of his sinful condition, and brought to a knowledge of the truth, whilst yet young in years. For thirty-five years he was acceptably and usefully employed as a class-leader and local preacher, and was instrumental in rescuing many souls from sin, and leading them to Christ. He loved the class-meeting, believing it to be essential to the spirituality and effectiveness of Methodism, and established a Society himself in a neighbouring village. He suffered much in his last illness, but was kept in perfect peace. When his end drew nigh, he solemnly blessed each of his children ; and having done so, he shouted with triumph—

> " For us is prepared
>   The angelical guard ;
>   The convoy attends,
> A minist'ring host of invisible friends :
>   Ready winged for their flight
>   To the mansions of light,
>   The horses are come,
> The chariots of Israel to carry us home."

His last words were, " There is light in the valley," and then his spirit fled away to the skies.

HYMN 725.—"Happy soul, thy days are ended."—*For one departing.*

Charles Wesley's, being No. 55 in "Hymns and Sacred Poems," 1749, vol. ii.

It has been sung in the death-chamber of many a departing saint amongst the Methodists, and not a few have entered "Jerusalem the Golden" with the music of

> "Go, by angel-guards attended,
> To the sight of Jesus go!"

sounding in their ears, commingled with that other song, "Worthy is the Lamb," sung by the redeemed.

Mrs Smith, daughter of the Rev. Wm. Sanderson, and mother of Mrs Hindson, of Gainsbro', and Mrs Simon, of Southport, was fifty years a member of Society. The testimony of her friends is, that few have done so much or so well in the Church and in the world for the glory of God. When near death, she sweetly sang the hymn commencing—

> "Happy soul, thy days are ended,
> All thy mourning days below;
> Go, by angel-guards attended,
> To the sight of Jesus go!
>
> Waiting to receive thy spirit,
> Lo! the Saviour stands above;
> Shows the purchase of His merit,
> Reaches out the crown of love."

When her spirit was departing, she said, "The frail bark is nearing the shore, and the haven of glory is full in view."

HYMN 726.—"I know that my Redeemer lives."—*Job* xix. 25.

Charles Wesley's, from "Hymns and Sacred Poems," 1742, page 126.

HYMN 727.—"O when shall we sweetly remove."—*Funeral Hymn.*

Charles Wesley's, being No. 7 of "Funeral Hymns," 1744, with two verses omitted.

HYMN 728.—"There is a land of pure delight."—*A Prospect of Heaven makes death easy.*

Dr Watts', Hymn 66, Book II. Watts wrote this delightful

hymn in early life, at his native home in Southampton, while
sitting at the window of a parlour which overlooked the river
Itchen, and in full view of the Isle of Wight. The landscape
there is very beautiful, and forms an enchanting model for a
poet when describing the paradise above. Tradition points out
the place where, just across the channel, that charming island
presents itself to the enraptured vision. The waters before him
suggested to the mind of the poet the final passage of the Christian over the dark river, so gloriously imaged by Bunyan, as
described in his " Pilgrim's Progress "—

> " Death, like a narrow sea, divides
>   That heavenly land from ours."

The second and third verses especially are descriptive of the
prospect presented to the eye of the poet. Dr Samuel Stennett
probably had the verse commencing, " But timorous mortals " in
his mind when he wrote the following stanza :—

> " Fill'd with delight, my raptured soul
>   Would here no longer stay ;
>   Though Jordan's waves around me roll,
>   Fearless I 'd launch away."

The attraction of this hymn for the suffering and dying has
centred chiefly in the opening stanza, connected with which are
many sacred memories of departed friends.

The Rev. Joseph Wilson was taken, at the age of thirteen, to
a Methodist prayer-meeting at the almshouses in his native
village, and there that love of religion was awakened which
resulted in a career of godliness extending over sixty years.
The Rev. William Bramwell admitted him to membership, and
for fifty-six years he laboured with acceptance and success as a
Methodist preacher. His illness was short, and his last act of
worship was to join as best he could in singing the hymn commencing—

> "There is a land of pure delight," &c.

At its close, he whispered, " I cannot sing ; I cannot pray with
you ; but the Lord knows my mind." His end was peaceful as
a child's slumbers.

A most singular coincidence is recorded in the *Wesleyan
Methodist Magazine* for 1841. In the October and December
numbers are recorded the deaths of Miss Harriet Keith and
Miss Harriet Reid, both of whom were converted to God in

early life, both lost sisters at the age of seventeen, both died in
the town of Leicester on the same day, June 20, 1841, both were
aged twenty years, and both died repeating—

> " There is a land of pure delight,
>   Where saints immortal reign ;
> Infinite day excludes the night,
>   And pleasures banish pain."

In her eighteenth year, Mrs Stanley, wife of the Rev. Thomas
Stanley, was convinced of sin, under a sermon she heard
preached by her uncle, the Rev. Joseph Entwisle ; and she
obtained peace through believing shortly afterwards, whilst at
the sacramental table. It was her privilege to have delightful
Christian fellowship with such pious women as Mrs Pawson
and Mrs Mather. After the death of Mr Stanley, she removed
to Deptford, where she conducted a class for some years. She
died at Derby, in great peace. On the last Sabbath she spent
on earth, she sang the hymn through, commencing

> " There is a land of pure delight,
>   Where saints immortal reign," &c.

Her family, knowing her extreme weakness, wished her to
repeat, and not sing the hymn ; but she continued it to the end,
and then said, " I 'll praise Him while He lends me breath."
Her last testimony was, " Precious Jesus, His blood was shed
for me !"

During thirty years, Ellen Nelson was the exemplary wife of
the Rev. John Nelson, Wesleyan minister, herself filling the
office of class-leader in many of the circuits in which they travelled, and manifesting a hallowed and fervent joy when
sinners were converted and joined to the Church of Christ.
During her last illness, she seemed to hold special communion with happy spirits, and on one occasion mentioned
Mr H. Longden of Sheffield, Mr Bramwell, and Mr Levick,
as amongst those " ministering spirits" surrounding her bed.
After she had made the remark, " I shall soon be with you,"
a friend asked to whom she spoke. She replied, " It is
my dear husband." Filled with triumphant joy, she exclaimed—

> " Could I but climb where Moses stood,
>   And view the landscape o'er,
> Not Jordan's stream, nor death's cold flood,
>   Should fright me from the shore."

Next day she was reminded of her happiness, when she replied, " How could I be otherwise? There was a legion of happy spirits in the room." With that glorious convoy, she passed in triumph to the skies, aged eighty-one.

HYMN 729.—" Lift your heads, ye friends of Jesus."—*Thy Kingdom come.*

Charles Wesley's, being the last of his Hymns of Intercession for all Mankind, 1758. The original has eight verses, two of which are left out.

HYMN 730—" Give me the wings of faith to rise."—*The Examples of Christ and his Saints.*

Dr Watts', Hymn 140, Book II., 1707.

At the age of sixteen, Ann Sanderson gave her heart fully to God, and obtained a clear sense of her acceptance with God as His child. Though often assailed with doubts, even in her last illness, on the morning of her last Sabbath on earth, while a friend and the family were engaged in prayer on her behalf, she seemed inspired with the full assurance of faith, and requested them to sing her favourite hymn—

> " Give me the wings of faith to rise
>   Within the veil, and see
> The saints above, how great their joys,
>   How bright their glories be."

She had a desire to depart, and to be with Christ. Her last words were, " All is right—all is well."

The parents of William Pike had the joy of seeing all their children filling useful stations in society, and also walking in the law of the Lord. William, when a boy, joined the Methodist Society at Oldham Street, Manchester, and was for forty-five years a teacher in the Sunday-school in that circuit. In youth he joined other young men (some of whom afterwards became " merchant-princes") in religious and mental improvement meetings held at each other's houses ; and many delightful memories still gather round those times of happy reunion. His mental and spiritual gifts he devoted to the service of the young in the Sabbath-school ; and to this department he remained faithful, when urged to devote his energies to the duties of the ministry of the Word. Some of his addresses are still remembered for their beauty, simplicity, earnestness, and power.   A few days before his death, he pointed to the Bible as the only book in which he could trust, and Jesus as his only refuge.   To the friend who was then with him, alluding to those members of his family who had gone to heaven before him, pointing to their portraits, he added—

> " I ask them whence their victory came ;
>   They, with united breath,
> Ascribe their conquest to the Lamb,
>   Their triumph to His death."

All around was holy quiet, and he peacefully resigned his spirit to God who gave it.

HYMN 731.—" Where shall true believers go ?"—*Of Heaven.*

Charles Wesley's, being No. 8 of Hymns for Children.
The third and fourth verses are very similar in sentiment to a verse by Dr Watts.

> " There we shall see His face,
>   And never, never sin ;
> There, from the rivers of His grace,
>   Drink endless pleasures in."

In the village of Middleton, Cromford, Francis Buckley was led to choose a religious life through the death of his brother. He became earnest in the service of God as a teacher in the Sunday-school as a class leader, and local preacher.   In these duties he was blessed himself, and made a blessing to others. His custom was to rise early in the morning, and spend nearly an hour in devotion with God.   In his last illness, he said he had a bright prospect of heaven, and, shortly before his death, he desired his friends to sing the hymn commencing—

> " Where shall true believers go,
>   When from the flesh they fly?
> Glorious joys ordain'd to know,
>   They mount above the sky," &c.

During the singing he was enraptured with thoughts of heaven, and shouted "Hallelujah !"   His last testimony was, "God is love."

HYMN 732.—"The saints who die of Christ possest."—"*They rest from their labours,*" &c.   .

Charles Wesley's, being No. 857 of "Short Scripture Hymns," vol. ii., founded on Revelation xiv. 13.

HYMN 733.—" How happy every child of grace!"—*A Funeral Hymn.* .

Charles Wesley's, being the second of his Funeral Hymns, 1759, and was considered by John Wesley to be one of his brother's finest compositions.

In the account of Susanna Spencer, in John Wesley's Journal, vol. iv., page 32, an instance is recorded of the value of this hymn. One of the most remarkable incidents on record of the effective power there is in a hymn is the recital of this one in open court in Exeter Castle during the trial of a prisoner. A good young woman had been set upon by a ruffian, on her way from Sunday-school, and was left for dead by the roadside. On being discovered, she was restored to consciousness so far as to identify her murderer, and then she died, lost to her intense bodily suffering in the sublime joy she had in commending her spirit to God in the words of Charles Wesley's hymn—

> " How happy every child of grace,
>   Who knows his sins forgiven !
> This earth, he cries, is not my place,
>   I seek my place in heaven :
> A country far from mortal sight ;—
>   Yet, O ! by faith I see
> The land of rest, the saints' delight,
>   The heaven prepared for me."

The counsel for the prosecution, in his appeal to the jury, described the death-scene, and rehearsed the hymn, a part of which the dying girl had sung in her last moments. The judge, the jury, all but the prisoner, wept. Who could help it ? To hear in that solemn court, just before passing sentence of death on the murderer, the youthful martyr's dying song of glory ! And such a song !

That captivating piece of biography entitled " The Successful Merchant," from the pen of the Rev. William Arthur, has made the name and memory of Mr Samuel Budgett of Kingswood known and esteemed in thousands of homes throughout the land. From the closing scene of his life we gather these particulars :—" After the sacramental elements had been administered to him, he asked for a hymn to be sung, but his friends fearing the effort would be too much for him, he exclaimed, ' Sing, sing.' The Rev. C. Clay then gave out part of the hymn, ' Behold the Saviour of mankind,' which was sung, whilst Mr Budgett, his countenance beaming with joy, his eyes streaming, his lips quivering, and his hands uplifted, joined heartily in the song of praise. He appeared quite in an ecstacy as they sang—

> ' O Lamb of God ! was ever pain,
>   Was ever love, like Thine !' .

After a short pause he asked for another hymn, on which Edwin's favourite was chosen—

> ' How happy every child of grace,
>   Who knows his sins forgiven !
> This earth, he cries, is not my place,
>   I seek my place in heaven,' &c.

He joined heartily in the singing of that song of triumph. Shortly afterwards he tried to repeat another hymn, ' With glorious clouds encompassed round ;' but his work was done, and his happy spirit passed away to the skies."

Mr Baker Banks was convinced of sin under a sermon preached by the Rev. John Byron in Cornwall, and eleven years afterwards he by faith entered into the liberty of the children of God. Having tasted that the Lord is gracious, he devoted himself to the service of God. As a class-leader he was most watchful over the spiritual state of his members, himself living in the full enjoyment of the direct witness of the Spirit to his adoption, and of entire sanctification. He was a true friend to the poor and afflicted, and a generous supporter of Methodism. During his last trying affliction he bore much suffering with resignation, and desired that the hymns 733, 734, and 735 might be read to him. He spoke in strong terms of the beauty of those hymns, and of their suitability to his experience. After a pause he said, with a look indescribable, and an emphasis that touched every heart,

> " The heaven prepared for me ;"

and having the 733d hymn again repeated to him, when he came to these words —

> " But O, the bliss to which I tend
>   Eternally shall last !"

he lifted up his eyes and hands, and exclaimed aloud, "Eternally, eternally! Bless the Lord!" In this happy frame he continued till his sufferings ceased, and his joys became eternal.

From childhood the Rev. George Prior Heston sat under the Wesleyan ministry, and in early life he realised a sense of sins forgiven. In the Sabbath-school, and as a local preacher, he was a punctual and diligent toiler. Passing through the Theological Institution at Didsbury into the ministry, he devoted the remainder of his short life to God's service. His health failed him whilst yet young, but in his sufferings he found Christ precious. So remarkably was the love of God manifested towards him that he was delivered from all fear of death, and became almost impatient to depart. As if in soliloquy, he repeated—

> "What is there here to court my stay,
>   Or hold me back from home,
> While angels beckon me away,
>   And Jesus bids me come?"

Then suddenly turning to his wife he said, "Yes, there are you and the dear children, but you will be taken care of, I know; and, if permitted, I shall watch you with holy interest till we meet in the skies." With the exclamation, "Glory, glory! praise God!" he "found the rest we toil to find."

During a ministry of thirty-eight years in Methodism, the Rev. William Vevers faithfully and lovingly performed the duties of his high calling. Whilst located at the Collegiate Institution, Taunton, his earthly course was terminated, but in all his sufferings his mind was kept in calm submission to the will of God, and in joyful anticipation of seeing Him face to face. The night before he died he said, "The Lord will be the strength of my heart, and my portion for ever," and then he repeated—

> "What is there here to court my stay,
>   Or hold me back from home,
> While angels beckon me away,
>   And Jesus bids me come?"

His last words were, "Come, Lord Jesus, and come quickly," and soon afterwards he sweetly slept in Jesus.

The biographies in the Methodist Magazines were made a great blessing to Elizabeth Batty in early life. A sermon, preached by the Rev. William Warrener in 1804, led her to decide to cast in her lot with the people of God, and at a love-feast held the same day she was enabled to believe on Christ for pardon. Some years afterwards, she entered in her diary, "I am longing for holiness more than my necessary food." In this frame of mind she tried to live during her earthly pilgrimage, and at its close, when eternity was near, and just as the preacher who was visiting her was leaving the room, she whispered—

> "Oh would He more of heaven bestow,
>   And let the vessel break,
>   And let my ransom'd spirit go
>   To grasp the God we seek."

A few minutes afterwards she said, "Jesus is precious ; my confidence increases; I am dying ;" and immediately her spirit returned to God who gave it.

At the age of twenty-one, the Rev. William M'Cornock was called out to preach the gospel in connection with Methodism ; and he continued his labours for thirty-five years. When by illness and age his strength had decayed, no cloud overshadowed his mind ; he was happy and resigned. He longed for his release, and frequently said,

> "O would He more of heaven bestow,
>   And let the vessel break,
>   And let my ransom'd spirit go
>   To grasp the God we seek."

In this state of calm resignation his redeemed spirit fled to heaven.

HYMN 734.—"And let this feeble body fail."— ### *A Funeral Hymn.*

Charles Wesley's, being the third of his "Funeral Hymns," 1759, founded on Romans viii. 18. The original has nine verses, two of which are left out.

Thousands of pious souls have been cheered while passing through the dark valley by the words of this hymn. There is not a verse of it but has been made a blessing to some pilgrim just closing life's journey.

From the age of seventeen, when he entered into the liberty of the children of God, the path of the Rev. John Lesson was "as the shining light, that shineth more and more unto the perfect day." As a Methodist preacher, he was instant in season and out of season, in the chapel and in the open air. On one

occasion, he commenced preaching in a village where tractarian
clergymen were supreme. The constable was ordered to stop
the preaching, and tried to do so ; but, as there was no breach
of the peace, the man of assumed authority yielded to the decision of character shown by the preacher, listened attentively
to the sermon, and retired from the service convinced that he
had best done his duty by letting the preacher alone. Disease
of the heart put a sudden termination to his ministerial career ;
but his submission to the divine will made his sufferings
welcome. At one time, with unutterable feeling, he exclaimed :

> " And let this feeble body fail,
>   And let it droop and die ;
> My soul shall quit the mournful vale,
>   And soar to worlds on high."

Sometimes, when thought to have been asleep, he would suddenly exclaim, " Bless God ! I feel his presence. How good
the Lord is ! how kind to me ! " In this blessed state of resignation he exchanged mortality for life.

Mary, relict of the Rev. Peter Prescott, senior, yielded her
heart to God at the age of fourteen, and at once became a
member of the Methodist Society. From that period to the
close of her life, her decided piety was manifest in the devotedness of her spirit and the consistency of her conduct. Having
been insensible for two days, she recovered consciousness for a
few hours, and during that time she sang, with remarkable
energy and clearness, the whole of the verse :

> " I see a world of spirits bright,
>   Who reap the pleasures there ;
> They all are robed in purest white,
>   And conquering palms they bear :
> Adorn'd by their Redeemer's grace,
>   They close pursue the Lamb ;
> And every shining front displays
>   Th' unutterable name."

In this happy and exulting frame she passed away to join her
husband in the skies.

The Rev. Corbett Cook, after serving God in the Methodist
ministry for half-a-century, retired from active work to Guernsey,
where, blind, but happy, he diligently attended to the duties of
the sanctuary, till called to his reward in the land of the

blessed. In his last hours he rejoiced in singing the fourth verse of hymn 734—

> "O! what hath Jesus bought for me!
>   Before my ravish'd eyes
>   Rivers of life divine I see,
>   And trees of Paradise!"

He died rejoicing in the hope of heaven.

More than forty years ago, a pious young lady in ill-health was resting on her couch, and by her side sat a beloved brother, himself scarcely well, and utterly without a feeling of love to God. His sister, as descriptive of the emotions of her soul, repeated to him, with remarkable emphasis, the fourth verse of hymn 734—

> "O what hath Jesus bought for me!
>   Before my ravish'd eyes
>   Rivers of life divine I see,
>   And trees of paradise:
>   They flourish in perpetual bloom,
>   Fruit every month they give;
>   And to the healing leaves who come
>   Eternally shall live."

Scarcely had she uttered these words before he began to think seriously on the state of his soul, and asked himself, "Has Jesus bought nothing for me?" He sought and found pardon, and both brother and sister, with another brother, not long after that happy change, departed for missionary labour in Ceylon.

Mrs Stevens, wife of the Rev. John Stevens, in early life had to endure many hardships and privations; but after her conversion to God, she always laid by in store for the Lord's cause and people some portion of their weekly income; and as a principal agent in founding the Benevolent Society, Kingswood, was thereby the means of doing very much good. During her last illness, she often engaged in singing the praises of God. A few hours before dying, she said with a glow of pleasure, "Jesus Christ and a convoy! O what delight! The thought of being for ever with Him whom my heart loveth, how delightful!" and then she exclaimed—

> "O what are all my sufferings here,
>   If, Lord, thou count me meet
>   With that enraptured host t' appear,
>   And worship at thy feet!"

She then attempted to sing, but her voice failed her ; she added, " Well, never mind, I shall soon sing more loud, more sweet, and Christ shall be my song ;" and soon afterwards her spirit fled to the realms of the blessed.

The same verse was a source of comfort also to Mrs Mary F. West, wife of the Rev. Francis West, and mother of the Rev. F. A. West. She would sometimes exclaim, " What a miracle of grace if I reach heaven !" After much suffering she gained the haven of rest.

Two of the most excellent and most loved women of Methodism were two sisters—one was the second wife of the Rev. Henry Moore, the other the wife of the estimable and venerable Joseph Entwisle. Mrs Entwisle was eminently holy in her life : her delicate frame often deprived her of the joy she always experienced in the worship of the sanctuary, but her privations were sources of spiritual joy to her at home. Her simple reliance on God was expressed in the words of the last verse of Hymn 734 ; and, without a struggle or even a sigh, she entered into the rest prepared for the people of God.

More than ordinary interest attaches to the memory of the aged and venerable Sarah Snowden, of Hull, who was for eighty-four years an exemplary and worthy member of the Methodist Society. She joined it soon after the first was formed in Hull, in 1746, and continued steadfast in the faith till she had counted nearly the circle of a century of years. She was converted to God at the age of sixteen, under the ministry of Mr Hetherington, the first local preacher in Hull. The record of her life, though brief comparatively, is one of the most instructive articles in the *Wesleyan Methodist Magazine* for 1837. For many years she had the privilege of entertaining under her roof Mr Wesley, John Nelson, Mr Fletcher, Messrs Pawson, Mather, Benson, Griffith, and most of the eminent ministers of the connexion, and this she esteemed to be much more of a blessing conferred upon her than any obligation on those whom she so heartily welcomed to her hospitable home. Her regard for Mr Wesley was truly filial. In her last lingering affliction, her recollections of his kindness and urbanity, as well as of his luminous sermons, appeared to survive all intervening events, and often in her allusions to the recognition of friends in heaven, she pictured to her fancy the peculiar gratification of finding most prominent amongst the beatified millions that man of God,

2 A

whom she revered as her most honoured friend and spiritual sire. Her son Benjamin, who lived with his mother for seventy years, says of her, " She did not say great things ; but she lived them." Amid painful suffering and languor, she had strong consolation ; but her pain subsided as eternity approached ; and on Good-Friday 1835, she expressed her confidence in God in the verse she had so often quoted—

> " O what are all my sufferings here,
>   If, Lord, Thou count me meet
> With that enraptured host t' appear,
>   And worship at Thy feet ! "

and a few hours afterwards the mortal strife terminated, in the hundredth year of her pilgrimage.

Mrs Mary Moulton, eldest daughter of the venerable Thomas H. Squance, was born at Point de Galle, Ceylon, in 1819, her father being then a missionary. She feared the Lord all her life. In 1848 she was married to Mr Joseph Moulton, who has a father and two brothers in the Wesleyan ministry. Serving God in every sphere of life in which she moved, her last home was at Castle Donington, where her literary and religious efforts were crowned with success, whilst imparting instruction to young ladies intrusted to her care. In her last illness, she was often repeating passages of Scripture and verses of hymns. The night before she died, she said, " I am on the Rock." She was reminded of the joys of paradise, when she replied—

> " O what are all my sufferings here,
>   If, Lord,"——

but she was unable to complete the verse. A few minutes before she expired, she said, " Come, Lord Jesus, come quickly ; " she immediately added, " Not my will, but Thine be done," and her spirit entered heaven.

The godly faithfulness and loving heart of Mr Charles Post, a bridge-master of Hull, were the means of bringing the late Mr John Lidgett to a knowledge of the truth. He had often spoken kindly to the young man, and at length secured his attendance at a class-meeting ; but the ordeal was too searching, and he fled from the room. His faithful monitor followed him, remonstrated, and they returned together. From that night his connexion with the Methodist Society was uninterrupted till he went to join the church of the redeemed. That same man of God was the means of obtaining for Mr Lidgett his release from a ship, just on the point of sailing,—and that ship was never heard of again! At twenty-seven he suffered shipwreck, and his crew, in Russia : they were all spared, whilst other ships' companies in that storm were all lost. These providences awakened in Mr Lidgett's mind a deep sense of gratitude to God, and an earnestness in His service which knew no abatement whilst health allowed him to be occupied. The poor, the neglected, and the sailors were his especial care. When apprised that he could not live long, he cheerfully gave up the world, and expressed a hope that he might enter the haven in full sail. He had sweet foretastes of heaven before he died, and heard some of its glories. He watched the sun setting on his last day on earth, and then joined his family in singing—

> " O what are all my sufferings here,
> If, Lord, Thou count me meet
> With that enraptured host t' appear,
> And worship at Thy feet !"

He then said, " I want to go." He spoke no more, and in full triumph he entered paradise.

HYMN 735.—" Come, let us join our friends above."—*A Funeral Hymn.*

Charles Wesley's, being No. 1 of " Funeral Hymns," 1759.

This and the two preceding hymns are sublime compositions, and first appeared in the poet's second and much enlarged tract of " Funeral Hymns." They embody almost every legitimate idea which the human mind can form as to the state, employment, and happiness of departed saints, and they are clothed in language glorious yet chaste, elegant yet simple, impassioned yet correct. This hymn expands the idea that saints above and saints below, the church militant on earth and the church triumphant in heaven, are all one—one family, one army ; that even now the intercourse is not totally suspended, but by faith we hold communion with those who are gone before. Had Charles Wesley composed only these three incomparable hymns, he would have conferred a great and enduring benefit on the Church of God, and would have immortalised his name as a Christian poet.

A few years ago, a *long* procession passed down the church path from the town of Redruth, pressing round a bier, as if they would affectionately guard it in the front, flank, and rear, and singing as they moved. They were keeping up the custom of their Cornish fathers of an evening funeral, and the singing of a burial-hymn from the house to the grave. The hymn was—

> " Rejoice for a brother deceased."

After the solemn service in the church and at the grave, as the benediction was pronounced, the devout multitude once more lifted up its full and mighty voice, and pressing round the open grave, uttered in impressive tone that glowing and impassioned hymn, No. 735—

> " Come, let us join our friends above
> That have obtain'd the prize,
> And on the eagle wings of love
> To joys celestial rise."

The swell of the closing appeal of the hymn was thrilling Among the singers was one young man, who appeared to be rapt while he sang. It seemed as if his music were that of a pure spirit. How his face kindled as he poured forth the closing notes! One who saw him there under the calm light of the evening sun saw indications of his approaching end. Soon afterwards he was found on his death-bed; but he had not lost the spirit of that triumphant hymn. To the friend who had seen him at the grave, he said, "I am going; I am going early; but God has brightened my short life into a full one! Oh! those hymns! they have taught me to live in the light of the future! They have been my songs in the house of my pilgrimage. How often when I have sung them down in the deep mine has the darkness been light around me! Never since I learnt to praise God from my heart have I begun to work in the rock for blasting without stopping to ask, If the hole should go off unawares, am I ready for heaven? Sometimes, sir, there has been a shrinking and a doubt, but I have dropped on my knees and asked God to bless me before I gave another stroke; and never did I pray in vain; my prayer has always passed in praise. Those blessed hymns have gone bursting from my heart and lips as I have toiled at the very point of death! O sir, do you remember our singing at the last funeral?" "Yes," was the reply; "and some thought then that you would never sing again on such an occasion!" "Never sing again, sir! Why, I shall sing for ever! Oh! that glorious hymn! let us sing it now." And he began at the last verse—

> '" O that we now might grasp our Guide !
> O that the word were given !
> Come, Lord of hosts, the waves divide,
> And land us—land—ME—now in " ——

" Heaven !" he would have sang, but ere he could do so he was there—he had joined another choir !

The conversion of a relative was made the means of awakening Thomas Bateson, of Stockport, to a sense of his condition as a sinner. The ministry of the Rev. H. S. Hopwood was made useful in directing his mind to the Saviour. His Christian course after his conversion was steady, consistent, and enduring. As a class-leader he walked worthy of his high vocation. His last sickness was protracted, but the language of his heart was continually, "Thy will be done." Perceiving that the parting scene was near, his wife said—

> " Part of the host have cross'd the flood,
> And part are crossing now."

He tried to finish the hymn, but his strength failed ; he fell into sleep, and in that sleep he passed from a suffering to a triumphant church.

HYMN 736.—" Great God, Thy watchful care we bless."—*The Church the Birthplace of the Saints, and God's care of it.*

Dr Doddridge's, being No. 49 of his hymns, founded on Psalm lxxxvii. 5. The first and second verses of the original are left out, and the third is altered from " Our Father's watchful care we bless." This hymn commences the eighth section of the Supplement, with the title " Miscellaneous Hymns."

HYMN 737.—" Thou, who hast in Sion laid."—*On Laying the Foundation of a Chapel.*

Agnes Bulmer's, written in 1825.

Mrs Bulmer was the wife of Mr Joseph Bulmer, of Watling Street, London. The hymn was written whilst the author was on a journey in a coach, and at the special request of the late James Wood, Esq., of Manchester, with whose family this " elect lady of Methodism " had been on a visit. It was first sung at the laying of the foundation-stone of the Wesleyan Chapel in Oxford Road and Ancoat's Lane, Manchester, on July 11, 1825 ; and since that period it has been used on many similar occasions. Mrs Bulmer (Miss Collinson before marriage) was

born in London, in the month of August 1775. In early life she
was admitted into the Society by Mr Wesley, who gave her her
first ticket. She was a member of Mrs Hester Ann Roger's
class, was married in 1793. In 1795 she became acquainted
with Dr and Mrs Adam Clarke, which friendship ripened into
love for life. In 1815 Mrs Bulmer began to write sacred poetry,
and for twenty years the *Wesleyan Magazine* and the
Youth's Instructor abound with her charming contributions.
These were afterwards collected, and, with a life of her by the
late Rev. W. M. Bunting, were published, and for some years
were in great demand. She died in the Isle of Wight, August
30, 1836, and was buried in the catacombs underneath City
Road Chapel, London.

HYMN 738.—"How pleasant, how divinely fair."—*The Pleasures
of Public Worship.*

Dr Watts' version of Psalm lxxxiv., Part I. Two verses of the
original are left out.

HYMN 739.—"Father of all, Thy care we bless."—*God's Gracious
Approbation of the Religious Care of our Families.*

Dr Doddridge, being No. 2 of his Hymns, founded on Gen.
xviii. 19. Several alterations are made in it.

HYMN 740.—"God of eternal truth and love."—*At the Baptism
of a Child.*

Charles Wesley's, being one of his "Hymns for a Family,"
page 63. The second verse is left out. It is open to question
how far we are justified in asking for such blessings on an infant
as are expressed in the third verse. Can a child realise on
earth "pardon, and holiness, and heaven?" "Praise" is perfected out of the mouths of "babes and sucklings."

HYMN 741.—"How large the promise, how divine."—*Abraham's
Blessing on the Gentiles.*

Dr Watts', Hymn 113, Book I., founded on three texts—
Gen. xxii. 2 ; Rom. xv. 8 ; Mark x. 14.

HYMN 742.—"Lord of all, with pure intent."—*The Presentation
of Jesus in the Temple.*

Charles Wesley's, left in manuscript at his death, founded on
Luke ii. 22.

HYMN 743.—"See Israel's gentle Shepherd stand."—*Christ's Condescending Regard to Little Children.*

Dr Doddridge's, No. 198 of his Hymns, founded on Mark x. 24, with two verses left out.

HYMN 744.—"The Saviour, when to heaven He rose."—*The Institution of a Gospel Ministry from Christ.*

Dr Doddridge's, written for an ordination service, and forms No. 289 of his Hymns, founded on Eph. iv. 11, 12. The first verse of the original is left out, and the hymn is otherwise altered.

HYMN 745.—"Father, live, by all things fear'd."—*To the Trinity.*

Charles Wesley's, from "Hymns and Sacred Poems," 1740, page 101. It is also in the same author's hymns entitled "Gloria Patri," 1746.

HYMN 746.—"Father of mercies, in Thy word."—*The Excellence of the Holy Scriptures.*

Miss Ann Steele. The original has twelve stanzas, of which seven are left out.

HYMN 747.—"Jesus, Thy servants bless."—*Preaching the Kingdom of God.*

Charles Wesley's, being one of his "Scripture Hymns" left in manuscript, founded on Acts xviii. 31.

HYMN 748.—"O God! how often hath Thine ear."—*The Covenant with God Renewed.*

William Maclardie Bunting's. It was written when the author was a youth of only fifteen years, and was first published in the *Methodist Magazine* for January 1824, page 72, with the signature of "Juvenis." This is the only one of many hymns of great excellence from the pen of the same author which is found in the "Methodist Hymn-Book," and this was inserted by the desire of the Rev. Dr Bunting, and almost against the wishes of his son, who, as he informed the writer in person, thought it not worthy of a place in such a collection. About forty of Mr Bunting's hymns will be found in the late Rev. Dr Leifchild's

collection of "Original Hymns," and amongst them a revised
copy of this Covenant Hymn. A copy of that revision of the
hymn will also be found in the *Local Preachers' Magazine*
for January 1869, page 23. In the year 1859, a few years before
the author's death, he revised it again, and the alterations,
though not numerous, are important ; this being the final
revision, we are permitted to give the hymn as last corrected by
its accomplished, devout, and scholarly author. The first word
in the first verse is changed ; a comma is added in the third
line ; the third word in the third verse is changed from " of " to
" to ;" and in the fourth and fifth verses several important
emendations will be found—

> "My God ! how often hath Thine ear
>   To me in willing mercy bow'd !
> While, worshipping Thine altar near,
>   Lowly I wept, and strongly vow'd :
> But ah ! the feebleness of man !
> Have I not vow'd and wept in vain ?
>
> "Return, O Lord of hosts, return !
>   Behold Thy servant in distress ;
> My faithlessness again I mourn ;
>   Again forgive my faithlessness ;
> And in Thine arms my spirit take,
> And bless me for the Saviour's sake.
>
> "In pity to the soul Thou lov'st,
>   Now bid the sin Thou hat'st expire ;
> Let me desire what Thou approv'st,—
>   Thou dost approve what I desire ;
> And Thou wilt deign to call me Thine,
> And I will dare to call Thee mine.
>
> "This day Thy covenant I sign,
>   The bond of mercy, grace, and peace ;
> Nor can I doubt its truth divine,
>   Since seal'd with Jesu's blood it is :
> That blood I plead, that blood alone,
> And make the cov'nant peace mine own.
>
> "Oh that my love no more may know
>   Or change, or interval, or end,—
> Help me in all Thy paths to go,
>   And evermore my voice attend,
> And gladden me with answers mild,
> And commune, Father, with Thy child !"

Every alteration will be its own commendation. We may, however, give an extract from a letter of the author's respecting this hymn from the *Local Preachers' Magazine*, just quoted, which is interesting. Writing to Mr Parker, Mr Bunting says : —" I wrote the hymn out of the fulness of personal feeling, while yet a youth at school ; and I was so ashamed of it as a literary production, that I could not yield it up to my father for publication in the *Magazine* under my then recognised sobriquet [ALEC], but disguised the authorship under the apologetic signature of JUVENIS. When Mr Watson, with whom I lived, did me the honour to consult me about the selection of hymns for the Supplement, and decided to introduce this hymn, it was entirely on his own responsibility, and against *my* strong sense of its unworthiness. When dear Dr Leifchild asked me for a hymn on dedication to God, I took this to save time and trouble, and from *sheer dissatisfaction* with what I thought feebleness in one place, obscurity in another, and so on, reconstructed it as it appears in his collection."

This pleasant sketch of the history of the hymn will have prepared the way for a few particulars respecting its author. William M. Bunting was the eldest son of the Rev. Jabez Bunting, D.D., and Sarah Maclardie Bunting. He was born in Manchester, in November 1805, and was specially dedicated to God from his birth. He was educated at Woodhouse Grove School, at Kingswood, and finally at St Saviour's Grammar School, Southwark. His conversion is traced to his meditations on the words, " Him that cometh unto me I will in no wise cast out," whilst passing over Old London Bridge, in his seventeenth year. In his nineteenth year he entered the Wesleyan ministry, and for a quarter of a century he occupied a most distinguished place in the body. For many years he was the last surviving author of those whose hymns appear in the Methodist Hymn-book. Between the years 1820 and 1840, many of his poetical compositions appeared in the *Wesleyan Magazine.* He was a man of high intellectual and moral worth, of deep, sincere, and unassuming piety, and of fine catholic spirit. We had the privilege of his personal friendship, and knew, from delightful intercourse, something of his high moral and spiritual worth. He died somewhat suddenly, at Highgate Rise, November 13, 1866, aged sixty-one years, and is interred in Highgate Cemetery. We are glad to know that

his poetical works, with a sketch of his life, may be expected
shortly to appear, written by one who knew and loved him.

HYMN 749.—"O how shall a sinner perform."—*In Temptation.*

Charles Wesley's, being No. 111 in "Hymns and Sacred
Poems," 1749, vol. i. Two lines are altered.

HYMN 750.—"O happy day that fix'd my choice."—*Rejoicing
in our Covenant Engagements to God.*

Dr Doddridge's, being No. 23 in his Hymns, founded on
1 Chron. xv. 15, with one verse altered. It is a hymn often used
to close the social means of grace, especially class and band
meetings. Mr Montgomery has written concerning it, "Blessed
is the man who can take the words of this hymn and make
them his own from similar experience."

In very early life Hugh Browne, of Donaghadee, Ireland,
was the subject of deep religious impressions; but it was
during a revival in Belfast, after he came of age, that he
found peace through believing in Jesus. The death of his
father seemed to hasten his own; and during his short illness
he found that Christ was the Rock of his salvation. Whilst
exulting in a clearly-manifested pardon, he exclaimed—

> " O happy day that fix'd my choice
> On Thee, my Saviour and my God !
> Well may this glowing heart rejoice,
> And tell its raptures all abroad."

His last words were in testimony of his triumph over sin by the
blood of Jesus.

Under the preaching of Thomas Riley, sergeant-major in the
7th Dragoon Guards, at Colchester, in 1811, William Balls was
enabled to believe for salvation. The witness of the spirit of
his adoption he retained through life, and his name was in the
first place as a local preacher in the Colchester circuit. Subsequently he was appointed a class-leader and circuit-steward.
His piety was sincere, enlightened, and elevated, and he was an
unwearied labourer in the Lord's vineyard. His favourite
hymn through life was No. 346, " For ever here my rest shall
be," &c. During the night before his death, he said, " Behold,

God is my salvation! Praise, praise, talk of Jesus!"   On the
day he died, he repeated, with deep feeling—

> " He drew me, and I follow'd on,
>   Charm'd to confess the voice divine."

His last testimony was, "Thanks be to God, who giveth me
the victory."

HYMN 751.—"The promise of my Father's love."—*The New
Testament in the Blood of Christ is the New Covenant sealed.*

Dr Watts', Hymn 3, Book III., 1707.

In early life Charlotte Cullen (afterwards Mrs Slater, of
Sheffield, and sister-in-law of the Rev. Barnard Slater) found
her chief pleasure in the ball-room and at the card-table ; but
under a sermon preached by the Rev. Robert Bryant, at Mildenhall, from "Prepare to meet thy God, O Israel," she was so
deeply convinced of her sinful condition, that she had no rest
till she found it in sins forgiven ; and in her seventeenth year
she joined the Methodist Society. As governess in the family
of the Rev. Thomas Padman, she had many spiritual advantages. Afterwards, it was the intense joy and delight of her
heart to learn that her mother, sister, and other members of the
family had obtained the blessing of justification by faith in Jesus
Christ. She herself strove long till she obtained the blessing
of entire sanctification. In the enjoyment of this happy experience she lived, till, at the age of forty, she exchanged mortality
for life eternal. During her last affliction, which was painfully
severe, her confidence in God was unwavering. When the end
drew nigh, the Rev. John Burton administered to her the sacrament of the Lord's Supper, after which she desired her family
to sing what had long been her favourite hymn, commencing—

> ' The promise of my Father's love
>   Shall stand for ever good,'
> He said ; and gave His soul to death,
>   And seal'd the grace with blood."

With peculiar ardour and delight, she joined in singing the
whole hymn. During the service, she was filled with the presence of God, and her latest moments were tranquil and
happy.

HYMN 752.—"From Jesu's sacrifice."—*The Lord's Supper.*

Charles Wesley's, being one of his hymns left in manuscript.

HYMN 753.—" Let all who truly bear."—*The Lord's Supper, as it is a Memorial of the Sufferings and Death of Christ.*

Charles Wesley's, being No. 4 of his " Hymns on the Lord's Supper." The original is in four stanzas of eight lines each, the half of each verse being left out.

The Rev. Charles Wesley has been charged recently by the Ritualistic party in the Church of England with holding and teaching in many of his Hymns on the Lord's Supper the doctrine of the Real Presence, and they claim him as one of their best advocates. To make good this charge, one of the publishers for the Ritualists has reproduced some of Mr Wesley's " Hymns on the Lord's Supper." It should be remembered that these hymns were written in the very early part of the poet's life, and near to the time when he was an avowed High Churchman ; a legal Christian without Christ, a Ritualist without spiritual life, living in the letter only of the law, not having known the Spirit which giveth life. Charles Wesley's after-life, teaching, preaching, and poetry, demonstrate the opposite of all this, from and after the year 1745. The Rev. Dr Rigg, in an article in the *London Quarterly*, July 1868, has demonstrated that the teaching, preaching, and poetry of both John and Charles Wesley were thoroughly Presbyterian, evangelical, and spiritual from 1745 to the end of their lives.

HYMN 754.—" Prostrate, with eyes of faith I see."—*For the Lord's Supper.*

Charles Wesley's, one of his hymns left in manuscript. It is copied into Russell's Collection.

HYMN 755.—" Lord, Thou hast bid-Thy people pray."—*For the King and Royal Family.*

Charles Wesley's, being one of his " Hymns written for Times of Trouble and Persecution," published in 1744. The original has six verses, two of which are left out. The time of trouble alluded to was A.D. 1743.

HYMN 756.—" Brethren in Christ, and well-beloved."—*On the Admission of any Person into Society.*

Charles Wesley's, from " Hymns and Sacred Poems," 1740, page 169 ; the second verse being left out.

HYMN 757.—"Awake, my soul, and with the sun."—*A Morning Hymn.*

Thomas Ken, D.D., Bishop of Bath and Wells. The three compositions by this eminent man of God, the Morning, Evening, and Midnight Hymns, were first published in 1675 at the end of the "Manual of Prayers," written for the use of the boys at Winchester School, in which the Bishop himself was educated. The original is in fourteen stanzas, nine of which are left out. This morning hymn has undergone many changes by many hands; some, alas! who could but little enter into the devout spirit of the pious author. Well might James Montgomery say of these three hymns, "Had the Bishop endowed three hospitals, he might have been less a benefactor to posterity."

Dr Ken having been one of the proscribed seven bishops, but little was known of him for many years. He was born at Little Berkhampsted in July 1637. After his ordination, he was made successively chaplain to the Princess of Orange and to Charles II. He was consecrated Bishop of Bath and Wells in 1684. James II. sent him, with six other bishops, to the Tower, but popular feeling secured their release after a trial. At the Revolution he declined to swear allegiance to William III., and retired into private life, spending his remaining days in the magnificent mansion of an endeared friend, at Longleat, Wilts, where he died in March 1710, and he was buried in Frome churchyard: a neat tomb covers his remains. No single stanza of poetry ever written has attained to greater popularity than the last verse of the Morning-Hymn, which is known all the world over as THE DOXOLOGY—

"Praise God, from whom all blessings flow."

"Bishop Ken's well-known doxology," writes James Montgomery, "is a masterpiece at once of amplification and compression: amplification on the burden, 'Praise God,' repeated in each line; compression by exhibiting God as the object of praise in every view in which we can imagine praise due to Him—praise for all His blessings; yea, for all blessings, none coming from any other source; praise by every creature, specifically invoked, 'here below,' and in 'heaven above;' praise to Him in each of the characters wherein He has revealed Himself in His word—'Father, Son, and Holy Ghost.' Yet this comprehensive verse is sufficiently simple, that by it ' out of the mouth of babes and sucklings' praise might be ' perfected ;' and it appears so easy, that one is tempted to think hundreds of the sort might be made without trouble. The reader has only to try, and he will be quickly undeceived ; though the longer he tries the more difficult he will find the task to be."

This glorious doxology has afforded comfort to many departing saints, as well as it has fittingly expressed the joy of the Lord's people in ten thousand instances when a new-born soul has entered into the liberty of the children of God. One instance, of which we have a distinct personal recollection, is worthy of note. Bridgehouses Wesleyan Chapel had been opened, and at night the preacher was William Dawson. The seed sown during the day had been accompanied by many earnest and faithful prayers : and after the evening service the body of the chapel and the side galleries had each its separate prayer-meeting. These were continued till near ten o'clock at night, when the praying souls and the seeking sinners adjourned to the school-room under the chapel, and there sat William Dawson, wrapped in his drab greatcoat, for it was winter-time, counting and recording the trophies of that day's spiritual warfare. Before eleven o'clock that Sabbath evening, the doxology had been repeated in earnest joyful song thirty-five times. A twelve miles' walk, through the midnight hours, and in the snows of a cold February, did not dissipate the blessedness of the memories of that day, and they are fresh and fragrant on the mind of the writer after the lapse of more than thirty years.

An early religious training was followed, in the experience of Phillis Downes, of Salford, by her conversion to God at the age of seventeen. From that day, and for forty years, she had not a doubt of her acceptance with God. In 1811 she experienced a deeper work of grace, and to the end of life testified to the entire sanctification of her nature. On the morning of her last day on earth, she said, whilst struggling for breath, "This is the last struggle. I have often sung, and now it is the language of my heart—

> ' Let it not my Lord displease,
>   That I would die to be His guest ;
> Jesus, Master, seal my peace,
>   And take me to Thy breast.' "

Shortly afterwards, she exclaimed—

" Praise God, from whom all blessings flow."

These were the last words she uttered distinctly; but "praise" was upon her lips when the power of utterance had failed.

Where the Spirit of the Lord is there is liberty. The mind of Elizabeth Hudson, of Hitchin, was awakened to a sense of its condition before God at the age of sixteen, but it was not till she was twenty years old that she found the Lord. The Methodists worshipped in a barn; she longed to join them, for she was seeking the Lord with all her heart. Her friends forbade her; so out of her window she looked at the lights in the rude barn where the people of God were gathered for worship. She wept and prayed, and the Lord showed her His mercy. That night her burden was removed, and she was able to rejoice in the liberty of the children of God. Her heart was filled with love to God and to all around her. Soon afterwards she heard the Methodist preacher at another village, and in the fulness of her joy invited the preacher to tea at her father's house. She made it a matter of earnest prayer that her opposing parents might receive the man of God. He came and was kindly welcomed. After tea, the parents were invited to the preaching. The service ended, the parents invited the preacher to stay all night. From that day that house was the home of the Methodist preachers at Baldock, and from that day Methodism began to flourish there. A Society was formed, and from that Society several have gone forth to preach the unsearchable riches of Christ in the ranks of the Methodist ministry. Mrs Hudson became a class-leader, and her husband a useful local preacher. For twenty years they were the chief support of Methodism at Baldock. They removed to Hitchin; here also Mrs Hudson was the principal instrument in the establishment of Methodism, and a prosperous Society has since sprung up there also. Thus one devoted godly woman founded two Societies of Methodists, and lived to see them enjoying considerable prosperity. This work accomplished, a preacher's house built, and a Wesleyan minister resident in the town, she said to her Christian friends, "Lord, now lettest Thou Thy servant depart in peace, for mine eyes have seen Thy salvation." Her work was done. Shortly afterwards typhus fever set in, and when she found out the fatal nature of her disease, she rejoiced that she was so near the "fair haven." To a friend who inquired if she was happy, she said, " Oh, yes ! I feel more than I can express ;" and in

the evening, waving her hand in an ecstasy of joy, she exclaimed—

> " Praise God, from whom all blessings flow ;
> Praise Him, all creatures here below ;
> Praise Him above, ye heavenly host ;
> Praise Father, Son, and Holy Ghost."

Her last words were, "Christ is precious, and I long to be
with Him ;" and in her sixtieth year she joined the church
triumphant.

When persecution was a sure consequence of becoming a
Methodist, John West, of Mark, Banwell, was converted, and at
once joined the Society. His heart was right, and no fear of
man intimidated him. For several years his attendance at the
means of grace was so regular, that it was a common saying in
the village, "If there is no one else at the chapel, Mr West will
be there." He attended the house of God till, in the seventy-
eighth year of his age, he received a peaceful summons
to his Father's house above. Some of his last words were,
"Glory be to God, I am come to the mount! I am filled with
glory and with God." He then made an effort to sing—

> " Praise God, from whom all blessings flow ;
> Praise Him, all creatures here below," &c.,

and he added, "Tell the friends, Jesus is a precious Saviour."
In this happy frame he continued till his voice was lost in
death.

For more than thirty years, Letitia Oakes, of Brompton,
Rochester, adorned her Christian profession by exemplary love
to the means of grace, and to the ambassadors of Christ, and
also by her blameless life and great liberality. For several
years she was confined to her room by extreme feebleness, but
her cheerful piety testified to her submission to her heavenly
Father's will. Just before the "weary wheels of life stood still,"
she said, "Not a wave of trouble rolls across my peaceful
breast," and, without apparent suffering, she gradually sunk,
literally dying with the unfinished accents of—

> " Praise God, from whom all blessings flow,"

lingering on her lips, at the advanced age of eighty-five.

HYMN 758.—"Glory to Thee, my God, this night."—*An Evening
Hymn.*

Thomas Ken, D.D., Bishop of Bath and Wells ; forms part of

his "Evening Hymn," 1675. The original has twelve verses, seven of which are left out, and the first and third are altered.

Endeared to multitudes of Christians, this hymn was the dying song of Roger Miller, once a drunken copperplate printer of London, afterwards a city missionary in Broadwall, Lambeth where he laboured long and usefully amongst the profligate and destitute. On the death of his mother, in 1847, Mr Miller left London for Manchester, to attend her funeral. It was near midnight, when, as the train approached Wolverton, an accident occurred : the train ran off the lines, and several were killed. Mr Miller had a few moments before united with the other passengers in singing the "Evening Hymn," that they might close the day with a devotional song. The praises of the passengers arose amidst the noise of the rushing train, but most seemed heartily to join. How appropriate the words—

> " Teach me to live, that I may dread
> The grave as little as my bed ;
> Teach me to die, that so I may
> Rise glorious at the awful day."

The music of their voices became, with one, at the least, in that company, blended with the hallelujahs of the redeemed, for Roger Miller was hurried in an instant to glory.

> Hymn 759.—" O Thou that hangedst on the tree."
>   „   760.—" Canst Thou reject our dying prayer ? "
> *Hymns for Condemned Malefactors.*

Charles Wesley's, forming together No. 100 in " Hymns and Sacred Poems," 1749, vol. i. ; founded on Psalm lxxix. 11. The original is in fourteen stanzas ; the second and third are left out in the first part ; the second part commences with the eighth verse, and the three last are left out. The unceasing labour of the brothers Wesley in trying to benefit the wretched beings in our prisons is manifested in the hymns and prayers which the poet of Methodism wrote for those outcasts of men. Yet of these even he has left evidence of the rescue of many ; and in this hymn the great cardinal doctrine of our holy religion, FAITH, is clearly stated and strongly enforced.

Mr Bunting has appended several notes to this hymn, first part. Note 1.—" Mr Frankland at K[entish] T[own], after we had administered at the Lord's Table, December 3, 1865. He had preached from 1 John ii. 2." This service seems to have called

2 B

attention to this hymn. Note 2.—Line 1, verse 2, to the word "outward" this note is appended,—" Even—not, even the pretence or appearance of righteousness." Note 3.—The third verse is emended as follows—the italics mark the corrections :—

" Save us by grace, through faith alone,
 A faith Thou *wilt* Thyself impart ;
 The faith that *by its fruit is known,*
 The faith that purifies the heart."

The fourth verse is entirely marked out, as marring the harmony of the hymn.

HYMN 761.—" Lord of the wide, extensive main."
   „   762.—" Infinite God, Thy greatness spann'd."
         To be Sung at Sea.

Charles Wesley's, from "Hymns and Sacred Poems," 1740, page 31. The original is in ten verses, and not divided. It was probably written in 1735, previously to the poet and his brother John sailing to America with General Oglethorpe and the Moravian settlers. The language of the second verse indicates with tolerable plainness what was the occasion of the hymn being written.

HYMN 763.—" Lord, whom winds and seas obey."—*On Going on Shipboard.*

Charles Wesley's, being one of his hymns left in manuscript, and probably written on one of the occasions when the poet was leaving Bristol for Wales, or London, or Cornwall.

HYMN 764.—" Lord of earth, and air, and sea."—*On Going on Shipboard.*

Charles Wesley's, being one of his hymns left in manuscript, and probably written at the same time as the preceding.

HYMN 765.—" How are Thy servants blest, O Lord !"—*A Thanksgiving for Deliverance from Imminent Danger.*

Joseph Addison's, and originally published in No. 489 of the *Spectator*. Its admission into the Methodist Collection when the Supplement was made was by a special favour, as the limping of the rhyme had almost caused its exclusion. It is sometimes called " The Traveller's Hymn." It was originally written in the first person singular, and is described as made " by a gentleman at the conclusion of his travels." It consists of ten stanzas, the third, fourth, fifth, and sixth being left out. The hymn is fine in sentiment, and elegant in language, but defective in Christianity: in it no reference is made, directly or indirectly, to the Redeemer of mankind, man's only hope for salvation, and the source of all our deliverances from danger and harm. In this respect it forms a strong contrast to the three hymns preceding it, which are by Charles Wesley.

HYMN 766.—" How many pass the guilty night."—*A Midnight Hymn.*

Charles Wesley's, being the first of his " Hymns for the Watchnight," 1742. As such it appears in " Hymns and Sacred Poems," 1742, page 135 ; where the first line reads thus : " Oft have we pass'd the guilty night." The fourth verse is left out.

HYMN 767.—".Join, all ye ransom'd sons of grace."—*For the Watchnight.*

Charles Wesley's, being the last of his eleven hymns for the Watchnight. The fourth verse is left out.

HYMN 768.—" Out of the depth of self-despair."—*Psalm* cxxx.

Charles Wesley's, being his version of Psalm cxxx. It appears in " Psalms and Hymns," enlarged edition, 1743.

HYMN 769.—" I give immortal praise."—*A Song of Praise to the Blessed Trinity.*

Dr Watts', Hymn 28, Book III., 1707.

This ends the Notes on the " Collection of Hymns for the Use of the People called Methodists."

There are two other hymns which have been so extensively used on death-beds by Wesleyans, that a work of this nature would be incomplete without some notice being taken of them. For more than fifty years, they will both be found quoted frequently in the biographical department of the *Wesleyan Magazine*, from which source they have both become so widely known, that not a few believe that they form part of the Collection of Hymns. The first of these is known by the following lines—

> " Not a cloud doth arise
> To darken the skies,
> Or hide for a moment my Lord from my eyes."

The original has the title " Hymns for Believers," and forms No. 130 in Charles Wesley's "Hymns and Sacred Poems," 1749, vol. i. It contains eighteen verses, the first five of which are as follows :

> 1. " All praise to the Lamb !
> Accepted I am,
> I am bold to believe on my Jesus's name.

> 2. "Strength and righteousness,
> And pardon and peace,
> In the Lord, my Redeemer, I surely possess.

> 3. " In Thee I confide,
> Thy blood is applied ;
> For me Thou hast suffer'd, for me Thou hast died,

> 4. " My peace it is made,
> My ransom is paid,
> My soul on Thy [perfect] atonement is stay'd.

> 5. " Not a doubt can arise
> To darken the skies,
> Or hide for a moment my Lord from my eyes."

The fifth is the only verse which is generally known ; and the first line of that usually appears in an altered form, as indicated above.

For twenty-two years, Mrs Nelson shared the toils of her husband, the Rev. John Nelson, in the itinerancy of Methodism, nearly half of which were spent in the West Indies, where she laboured to be useful by meeting classes, teaching in the schools, visiting the sick, and by other works of mercy. During the last few months of her life, the increased spirituality of her mind was an indication of the deeper fervour of her devotion, and her growing fitness for the rest which remaineth for the people of God. At Huddersfield, she was suddenly seized with paralysis, and survived the attack but twelve days ; but her mind was at peace, and she manifested unhesitating reliance on Christ, waiting the Lord's pleasure with calm fortitude, and with a joyful hope

of glory. No doubt or temptation disturbed her last hours :
more than once she exclaimed—

> " Not a cloud doth arise
> To darken the skies,
> Or hide for a moment my Lord from my eyes."

Thus she died in the full triumph of joyful faith and hope.

At the age of sixteen, Mrs Horton, the wife of the Rev.
William Horton, experienced the saving grace of God, and
became a member of the Methodist Society. In 1820, she was
married to a Wesleyan minister, and with her husband devoted
all her energies to the service of God in the missionary field.
In Van Diemen's land, and also in New South Wales, her
talents and influence were consecrated to the service of Christ.
To the female inmates of the jail and hospital at Hobart Town,
she regularly imparted religious instruction. As a class-leader,
she was useful and beloved ; and as a visitor of the sick and
dying, she was pre-eminently successful in promoting the good
of souls. Her health, always delicate, failed her in the foreign
service. After her return home she rallied a little, but
her strength was again much reduced, and for a time her
spiritual enjoyments were dimmed, and she was beginning to
doubt her acceptance with God, when, after an evening of
prayer with the Rev. W. H. Clarkson, she recovered her sense
of the divine favour, and the joy which followed was ecstatic.
At one time she expressed her feelings in these words, " I am
so unspeakably happy : Oh, help me to praise the Lord ! I must
praise Him : Oh, how good the Lord is to me, who am so unworthy ! Yes, precious Jesus, I can say—

> ' Not a cloud doth arise
> To darken the skies,
> Or hide for a moment my Lord from my eyes.'

Oh, the blessedness of the saints ! I shall be with Jesus to
all eternity." She had always valued Wesley's hymns as a
rich treasury of devotional sentiment ; and now she found in
them words which exactly expressed her religious feelings. She
died saying, " I have now nothing to do but to praise God to all
eternity."

Amongst the members forming the first Methodist class at
Kingston, Jamaica, was William Harris, a native of Charles-
town, who came from America about the time of the war, 1780.

Soon as Dr Coke arrived in the West Indies, Mr Harris and his wife waited on the Doctor, and offered their assistance to him, and thus became the first Methodists in the island. Having found peace in believing, Harris became the first leader ; and before Dr Coke left the island, eight members had joined the class. This humble coloured Christian lived to see Methodism extend in the colony, until there were nearly eight hundred leaders, and twenty thousand members in Society there. For years he travelled with the missionaries on their preaching-excursions, and twice he accompanied Dr Coke through the country. For more than fifty years he held fast his confidence in God, and laboured without ceasing to bring souls to a knowledge of sins forgiven. During seven years of fierce persecution, when the chapels were shut up, and they were prohibited from meeting for divine worship, he continued to hold private meetings on his premises, at night, and in the dark, to prevent detection ; thus was the Society kept together, and many converts were added to them. He continued to lead a class to the end of his days ; and when honoured age and infirmity laid him aside from active service, he maintained his confidence in God unshaken. Shortly before he died, he encouraged some of the members of his class who came to see him, by exhorting them to hold on, and hold fast their confidence, exclaiming—

> " Not a cloud doth arise
> To darken the skies,
> Or hide for a moment my Lord from my eyes."

Thus happily passed away this venerable servant of the Lord, aged ninety-six years.

The age of womanhood was reached by Lois Hickson before she saw the evil of a life of worldliness. Attending the Methodist preaching at Leek, the sermon, one of great faithfulness, was as a message of God to her soul, and she gave her heart to the Lord. Becoming the wife of the Rev. Thomas Hickson, she spent ten years in the foreign mission field, and many others most usefully in the work at home. As a class-leader, she was most acceptable, watching over her members with deep solicitude. She prayed for each member daily by name in her closet, and would not allow any of them to remain in a doubtful state of mind as to their acceptance with God, without faithful admonition and prayerful promptings. She aimed to encourage the young to seek to know their sins forgiven from a conviction that this knowledge was absolutely necessary to the prosperity of the cause of God. The meetings of her class were times of refreshing from the presence of the Lord ; and she saw her members growing in grace, and in the knowledge of our Lord Jesus Christ. She sought to have a clear and full knowledge of the inspired volume, and made herself familiar with Mr Wesley's notes, and the commentaries of Mr Benson and Dr Adam Clarke. These helps contributed much to the solidity and richness of religious experience ; and she became an example of all good works. Once she was suddenly tempted to doubt her confidence in God, but by a resolute exercise of faith, the snare was broken, and she exclaimed, "Satan, I am the Lord's ! I am the Lord's !" and then with much feeling she added—

> "Not a cloud doth arise
> To darken the skies,
> Or hide for a moment my Lord from my eyes."

With these words she often baffled the tempter's power, and maintained her confidence in God. She died saying, "Lord Jesus, receive my spirit."

A career of about thirty years of sin and folly was suddenly ended one day in a very providential manner. Richard Cousins, a poor man, in the pursuit of worldly pleasure visited a relative at Tetney, Grimsby, at the time of the village fair. It became necessary for Richard to sleep at a neighbour's house with a man who was a stranger to him. Before retiring to bed, the stranger said, "Young man, I will read a chapter," and read Romans viii. Prayer followed the reading, and the spirit of conviction followed the prayer ; so that Richard said to himself, "If this man is right, I am wrong." He sought earnestly for pardon, and found peace at a village prayer-meeting. For seventy-one years he continued a faithful and consistent member of the Methodist Society, and a diligent class-leader. He lived to enter on his one-hundredth year. Two days before his death, a friend visiting him found him seated in the corner of his room, his body bent with pain, till his head rested on his knees. To the question, "Richard, I want to know from yourself if there is any cloud on your sky ?" lifting up his hands, worn with a century of hard toil, and with a most benignant smile, he answered by repeating the verse—

> " Not a cloud doth arise
> To darken the skies,
> Or hide for a moment my Lord from my eyes."

He died, as he had lived, in favour with God and man.

A class-leader in Ireland took his two daughters with him to his Sunday-class; but, as they were young, he passed the children by without any remark. On the second Sunday, one of the girls, feeling deeply that she was passed by, burst into tears, and sobbed out, in the depth of her sorrow, the conviction she felt of her sinfulness. That work of grace was carried on till Ann Hardy realised a sense of sins forgiven, and joined the Methodist Society. She was afterwards married to the Rev. James Horne, and went out with him to Jamaica. She very soon fell a victim to the climate, but lived long enough to show forth the blessedness of that grace by which she had been saved. On being asked the state of her mind, after the physician had said recovery was hopeless, she said, " I hope He will finish the work He has begun ;" and after a little pause, she added—

> " Not a cloud doth arise
> To darken the skies,
> Or hide for a moment my Lord from my eyes."

She died very happy ; and her memory was so precious to the coloured people amongst whom she had lived, that they collected £43 to obtain from England a tombstone to be erected over her grave.

After an itinerant ministry of thirty-one years, the Rev. William Nother retired as a supernumerary ; but he continued to labour till his strength entirely failed. During his last affliction, which was long and heavy, his mind was kept in perfect peace. As the end drew nigh, in reply to the question, What was the state of his mind ? he said—

> " Not a cloud doth arise
> To darken the skies," &c.

and added—

> " My God is reconciled,
> His pardoning voice I hear."

Here he stopped, his breath failed him. Thus peacefully he entered into rest.

Early in life Richard R. Mole, Wesleyan minister, experienced the converting power of divine grace, becoming soon afterwards a local preacher ; and in 1818 he began to itinerate. He laboured with much acceptance and success, till his health failed, in 1839. He preached his last sermon on the day the Centenary of Methodism was celebrated. His health rapidly decayed, and, as his end drew nigh, he was peaceful and happy, giving his experience, in reply to a friend, in the language of Charles Wesley's hymn—

> "Not a cloud doth arise
> To darken the skies,
> Or hide for a moment my Lord from my eyes."

His last testimony was, that he felt that the blood of Jesus Christ cleansed him from all sin, and that he rested on the Rock of Ages.

At the age of seventeen, Elizabeth, daughter of the Rev. Thomas Staton, Wesleyan minister, gave her heart to the Lord ; and during the ten years of her life which followed, she served the Lord with full purpose of heart. A long and painful illness tried her severely ; but her confidence in God was unwavering. As the end of life drew nigh, amidst much suffering, she said, "All is clear; I have no doubt, no uncertainty. I cling to the cross ; I am sure I am going to heaven." Immediately afterwards, she added—

> "Not a cloud doth arise
> To darken the skies,"

and then peacefully entered into the better land.

At the age of thirteen, Mrs Brayshay, of Hull, received her first ticket of membership as a Methodist from the Rev. Joseph Benson, and for fifty-six years she continued a member of that Society, and walked continuously in the light of God's countenance. During much suffering, her mind was kept in peace ; and when told that all hope of recovery was gone, her cheerful reply was, " Is not that blessed news ?" Almost her last words were—

> " Not a cloud doth arise
> To darken the skies,
> Or hide for a moment the Lord from my eyes."

A pious parentage is the gift of God. Of all the blessings of life, this is one of the most prominent. It was the privilege of Maria Ann Vickers (who afterwards became the wife of the Rev. William M. Punshon) to share in early life in this rich inheritance. Her early days were marked by the bloom of health, a lively disposition, and all that makes childhood happy. Her early religious life was marked by doubt and want of spiritual

comfort ; but at the age of twenty-three she accompanied her
mother to a Christian fellowship-meeting, when, with a trembling spirit, she confessed her sinfulness, and entreated the
prayers of the Lord's people. The Saviour appeared to her in
mercy.   She saw Jesus Christ evidently set forth crucified
before her eyes, and resting on His atonement, she lost the burden of sin, she believed on Christ, and was made unspeakably
happy. She remained on her knees four hours wrestling for
liberty, and resolved not to rise till she realised the blessing,
which God vouchsafed to her a few minutes after midnight.
The change was instantaneous and glorious, and was at once
manifest in her countenance, her conversation, and her life ;
and from that time to the end of her pilgrimage, the class-meeting became to her a welcome and blessed means of grace. For
three years her labours in the Sabbath-school, and in other
spheres of Christian service, bore testimony to the intensity of
her love and gratitude to God, and her desire to benefit the
souls of those around her. For about ten years, as the wife
of the estimable minister whose work she so worthily shared,
she found fields of usefulness in the Church, in which she
manifested how thoroughly the Holy Spirit had fitted her
to be a help-meet in watching for and tending the souls
committed to her care. Members of the Sabbath-school and
Bible-class, at both Newcastle and Sheffield, will long treasure
hallowed recollections of their intercourse with her. The illness of her husband, and the loss of her children, were borne
with holy submission to the Divine will ; and in her own
painful illness she proved the sufficiency of Divine grace to
keep her, even in the severest trials. On the last day on which
she was able to leave her room, she conversed freely with the
members of her family, expressed her strong confidence in
Christ, and cheerfully added—

> " Not a cloud doth arise
>   To darken the skies,
> Or hide for a moment my Lord from my eyes."

Her stricken husband then administered to her the emblems of
the death of Christ, after which her happy spirit was released,
whilst she said, " I am going ; going to glory."

One of those stanzas which stand pre-eminently above others
is the one which last proceeded from the mind of Charles Wesley.

Having sketched the lives of other writers of the hymns, we add a brief notice of that one writer, who, through the Divine blessing, has been especially made the honoured instrument of comforting thousands of the Lord's people when passing through the dark valley and the shadow of death. The stanza to which reference has been made is as follows—

> " In age and feebleness extreme,
>   Who shall a sinful worm redeem ?
>   Jesus, my only hope Thou art,
>   Strength of my failing flesh and heart ;
>   Oh could I catch a smile from Thee,
>   And drop into eternity ! "

Charles Wesley was born at Epworth, December 18, 1708, being sixteen years younger than his brother Samuel, and five years younger than his brother John. From his birth to the termination of his long life of fourscore years he was never strong. He was educated, first at home by his mother, then by his brother Samuel at Westminster, and thence he went to Christ-Church College, Oxford. Here it was that he joined his brother and others in those works of piety and self-sacrifice which caused them to be called Methodists. He went with his brother to America as a missionary in 1735, and both brothers returned to England after a brief sojourn in Georgia. Charles and John were both converted to God in the month of May 1738, and Charles, who had begun to distinguish himself for his religious poetry even before that period, more diligently than ever devoted his mind and energies to preaching the gospel and writing hymns, and in this blessed work he ceased not for about half a century. His attainments as a scholar were worthy of the advantages which he enjoyed in his early life, when he acquired an efficient knowledge of the Latin, Greek, Hebrew, and French languages, and a proficiency in writing Byrom's shorthand. His exact and critical knowledge of the Holy Scriptures was strikingly manifested in his hymns and in his preaching. As a writer of devotional poetry, Charles Wesley will be permanently remembered, and his name will live in the annals of the Church. " In the composition of hymns adapted to Christian worship, he has no equal in the English language, and is perhaps superior," says Mr Jackson, "to every other uninspired man that ever lived." No man has ever written so many hymns, or hymns of such surpassing excellence. The natural weakness of his constitution caused him to differ often with his brother John, with whom he was associated during the whole of his public life. The points of difference between the two brothers are thus stated by Charles: "With my brother it was first the Methodists, then the Church; with me it was first the Church, then the Methodists. My brother is all hope; I am all fear." Yet Charles Wesley loved the Methodists with a much deeper and intenser passion than he ever loved the Church. The trials which he endured throughout his whole life of nearly fourscore years were something marvellous, until at times, in the intensity of his sorrow and trial, he prayed from the depth of his heart that the Lord would take him to heaven to get away from his troubles. In the complete edition of his poetry, this desire for death occurs frequently, and the anxieties of his family, as well as the care of the Societies which fell to his lot, would have overwhelmed thousands with less faith in God. Although his income seldom exceeded £100 per annum, yet when he was offered a living in the Church of the value of £500 a year, he chose, as Mr Moore informs us, Methodism with poverty to strict churchmanship and wealth. No two brothers ever worked more harmoniously or effectively together for so long a period than did John and Charles Wesley. When the latter was within a few days of the end of life, he received this laconic note from John, "Dear brother, you must go out every day, or die. Do not die to save charges. You certainly need not want anything as long as I live." Dr Whitehead attended him in his last days, but as there was no disease to cure, the only medicine he could give was sympathy and prayer, and the doctor says he always found him influenced by "unaffected humility and holy resignation to the will of God; his mind was kept in perfect peace." His body was reduced to the most extreme state of weakness. Mr Bardsley, one of the London preachers, who sat up with him during the last night but one of his life, says of him, "He had no disorder but old age; he had very little pain; his mind was as calm as a summer evening. Some months before his departure he said he should die in March, and so he did." While he remained in the state of extreme feebleness, having been silent for some time, he called Mrs Wesley to him, and requested her to write, at his dictation, the lines given above. "Thus, for fifty years, Christ, as the Redeemer of men, had been the subject of his effective ministry and of his loftiest songs; and he may be said to have died with a hymn of praise upon his lips. On the last morning of his life he was unable to speak. Mrs Wesley desired him to press her hand if he knew her, which he did. His last audible breathings were, " Lord—my heart—MY GOD !" He then drew his breath short, and at last so gently, that the exact moment on which his happy spirit fled was unknown. The postscript of a letter to Henry Moore, in the handwriting of John Wesley, now before us, reads thus : " My brother fell asleep so quietly, that they who sat by him did not know when he died." He departed March 29, 1788, aged seventy-nine years and three months. He was interred in the graveyard of Old Marylebone Church, which has long been closed to the public.

At the early age of eight years, William Jones was impressed with views of the dying love of Jesus ; but it was not till he was twenty that he gave his heart to the Lord. After several years' usefulness as a local preacher, he gave himself to the work of the Methodist itinerancy, and for twenty years he was an acceptable preacher ; and when the infirmities of age overtook him, he still laboured whilst he had strength. A short but severe affliction found him ready both to suffer and to die. Some of his last words were—

> " In age and feebleness extreme,
> Who shall a sinful worm redeem ? " &c.

His last recorded words were, " I have strong consolation ; my anchor is cast within the veil."

The conversion of a school-fellow was the chief means, in the hands of God, in the conversion of Charles Atmore. Not having before heard of the people called Methodists, when he became acquainted with them, he soon formed the resolution —" This people shall be my people, and their God my God." Under a sermon by the Rev. Joseph Pilmoor, his convictions for sin were so deepened that he sought earnestly and continuously for pardon ; and whilst he was following the plough, like Elisha, and meditating on the sermon he had heard, the verse of the hymn commencing—

> " Oh that in me the sacred fire
> Might now begin to glow," &c.,

was so impressed on his mind, he urged his plea for pardon with so much earnestness, the love of God was instantly shed abroad in his heart, his joy and grace were boundless, and when twenty years old, he joined the despised Methodists. He began to exhort and to preach in the villages around; and with so much acceptance, that on being introduced to Mr Wesley at Loddon, in Norfolk, in February 1781, that venerable man at once appointed him the fourth preacher in the Norwich circuit. The variety, extent, and value of his labours as a Methodist preacher are recorded in a most interesting memoir of his life in the *Wesleyan Magazine* for 1845. For forty-five years he preached with great acceptance in many parts of England; his last service was to preach and meet classes at Stoke-Newington in December 1825. An illness of several months followed, in which he suffered much from the inability to lie down, but although his strength failed, his inward man was renewed day by day. As the end approached, Jesus and glory were his only themes, and he frequently repeated the memorable lines of Mr Wesley, as applicable to his own case—

> "In age and feebleness extreme,
> Who shall a sinful worm redeem?" &c.

Shortly before midnight of June 30, 1826, he fell into a soft slumber, to which he had been an entire stranger for many months; and in that slumber, at ten minutes past midnight, July 1, he peacefully entered the paradise of God. For many years, it is believed that more than five hundred conversions per annum resulted from Mr Atmore's labours as a Methodist preacher.

"A mother in Israel" was Mrs Elizabeth Gillings (mother of the Rev. James Gillings) whom we remember with pleasure about the time when her son entered the itinerancy. At about the age of twenty-five, she was converted under the ministry of the Rev. Corbett Cooke. For many years she was a much esteemed class-leader, an office for which she was, by her rich' and clear experience, well qualified. During a severe affliction she rejoiced greatly that she had consented to her son becoming a missionary to the heathen. Her heart was filled with gratitude to God, and all she spoke was praise. When dying, she said with much energy, "I know that my Redeemer liveth," and repeated Charles Wesley's lines—

> "O let me catch one smile from Thee,
> And drop into eternity!"

Her last words were, "I shall soon be with my Saviour: all is well!"

The mother of the Rev. William Pennington Burgess, A.M., Wesleyan minister, was born in 1766, at one of the homes of the early Methodist preachers, in Aldermanbury, London. As the daughter of a Methodist preacher, she was acquainted with religion from childhood. At the age of fourteen she was converted to God, and began to meet in class; at the age of seventeen she heard Mr Wesley preach in Dublin, and was much blessed by his ministry. For several years she accompanied her husband to his various stations whilst he followed a military profession. This he afterwards abandoned, and became a preacher of the gospel, and during an itinerancy of forty-two years his wife was really a help-meet to the faithful servant of God. At the advanced age of more than fourscore years, and when death was at hand, in the last letter she wrote, addressed to her son, she concluded thus, " I often find Charles Wesley's dying hymn—

> 'In age and feebleness extreme,
> Who shall a helpless worm redeem?' &c.,

very sweet to me : only I want to dwell *now* under a constant sense of my Saviour's smile, and then to catch a brighter one at the last." In her eighty-second year she died, leaving as her dying motto, " Love! thanks! blessing !"

Under the powerful and heart-searching ministry of the Rev. Joseph Benson, in Oldham Street Chapel, Manchester, the excellent James Wood was convinced of sin, sought and found pardon, and in 1794 joined the Methodist Society there. His character throughout a long career of godliness was marked by every Christian virtue, and his public services, philanthropic and religious, were worthy of the vocation wherewith he was called. In the Sunday-school, prayer-meetings, as a visitor of the Strangers' Friend Society, he exercised those talents which made him afterwards an acceptable and useful class-leader and local preacher. His high moral rectitude in business, his large-hearted catholicity, his judicious counsels and seasonable liberality in connexion with Methodism, made his name and memory precious in the Society where he worshipped. He was accustomed, when a youth, to accompany Dr Coke to solicit contributions in Manchester for the missions, and one of the last acts of his public life was to send his annual subscription of £100 to the Wesleyan missions, some months before it was due, to lessen the necessity for borrowing. In his last illness he endured much suffering without a murmur. As the end approached he desired one of his daughters to copy for him the last lines composed by Charles Wesley, which, for several days, were continually upon his lips—

> "In age and feebleness extreme,
> Who shall a sinful worm redeem?" &c.

His last words were those of triumph, "Glory! glory!" and after a pause, "Hallelujah!"

Respect for the Sabbath-day was inculcated on Joseph Meek from early childhood. At the age of fifteen, under a sermon by the Rev. Joseph Pilmoor, he was convinced of sin, but he did not realise a sense of sins forgiven for more than a year. During a great revival in Yorkshire, in 1793, after hearing the Rev. William Perceval preach at Easingwold, the word came with power to his heart; he yielded a cheerful obedience to the Divine call, and obtained a sense of pardon. Soon after his conversion he was made the leader of a class, composed principally of recent converts, which, in a few months, numbered forty members. On Sunday morning, it was his custom to accompany his religious friends four miles to Easingwold, to attend the six o'clock prayer-meeting, and to enjoy the other ordinances of God's house. After this preaching was commenced in his native village, and in 1800 he was called into the Methodist itinerancy by the Rev. James Wood; and for fifty years he laboured with diligence and acceptance, winning many souls for Jesus. In 1839 he retired from the full ministry, and for ten years spent himself and his time in doing all the good he could, especially to the young. He bore affliction uncomplainingly; asked the prayers of the Lord's people; and shortly before he died, he frequently repeated the verse commencing—

> "In age and feebleness extreme,
> Who shall a sinful worm redeem?" &c.

His last prayer to God was, "I resign my soul, my body, my family, my all, into the arms of Thy mercy."

When only eleven years of age, Miss Butterfield, who afterwards became the wife of the Rev. Thomas Raston, began to meet in class, but she did not realise a sense of pardon till death a second time visited her family. She embarked for Sierra Leone in 1847 as the wife of a missionary—a life, the trials, privations, and afflictions of which experience only can make known. She at once became the leader of a class of twenty-five females, who greatly benefited by her instructions. Severe affliction soon prostrated her strength, and baffled all the medical skill of the colony. She had to return home to England, where, after lingering a few months, she became fully resigned to the will of God. For eighteen months health, strength, and voice were all but gone, so that she spoke but in faint whispers; but just at the close, she was so filled with Divine love, her strength returned, and she exclaimed, "O the glory! I am going! Jesus is here! O praise God! O the goodness of God!" From this time a heavenly smile sat upon her countenance. She lingered in pain but in patience, oft repeating—

> " O let me catch a smile from Thee,
> And drop into eternity !"

Her last words to her husband, on his leaving her bedside to attend a missionary-meeting at Manchester, were, "Tell the people they will never repent of what they do for the perishing heathen." She breathed out her happy spirit with the words quivering on her lips—

> " O let me catch a smile from Thee !"

One of the converts at the glorious revival in Cornwall, in 1795, during that remarkable preaching-tour of the Rev. Joseph Benson, was Miss Mary Garland, who afterwards became the wife of the Rev. James Odgers. At an early period of her religious life, she sought earnestly and found the blessing of entire sanctification, and she long bore a faithful testimony to the efficacy of the blood which cleanseth from all sin. The Bible was her daily companion, and prayer her delight. The Lord honoured her by giving her fulness of happy days, and a triumphant death. Shortly before she escaped to paradise, she said—

> " O let me catch a smile from Thee,
> And drop into eternity !"

Then, lying composedly, she added, "Farewell! I am near home," and peacefully expired.

Hannah Lacy lived till she was twenty-one years old without any knowledge of saving religion. In 1785, a great revival broke out at Todmorden, under the preaching of the Rev. Charles Atmore and his colleagues, and more than eight hundred members were added to the Church in two years, one of whom was Han-

2 C

nah Lacy. In those days carriages were unknown in that part of England; Mr Grimshaw, Mr Crosse, Mr Fletcher, and Mr Wesley all rode there on horseback. David Lacy, Hannah's father, was the leader of a class at Todmorden, in the early days of Methodism; at his death, his son, Henry, became its leader; and at his death, his sister undertook the duty. Thus was one class kept in the charge of one family for nearly eighty years, and in that class she had continuously met for nearly seventy years. There was spiritual life in that Methodist class; there were many such at that period; would there were many more now! The religion of Hannah Lacy was " Glory begun below;" she was cheerful, happy, and always doing something for God. When more than eighty years of age, she continued to meet her class, starting the tunes, and adding life to the service. Even at that age, she would attend the service at the chapel three times on the Sabbath. Her last illness was short; but as in health, so in sickness, the cause of God lay near her heart : all her glorying was in Christ. To nearly all inquirers about her health, she replied in Charles Wesley's words, which she had uttered almost daily for many years—

> " In age and feebleness extreme,
> Who shall a sinful worm redeem?
>
> .   .   .   .
>
> O let me catch a smile from Thee,
> And drop into eternity ! "

She spoke with great confidence of the future glory of Methodism, and in her eighty-ninth year, died in peace, and entered heaven in triumph.

At the age of seventeen, Sarah Gibbs gave her heart to the Lord, after hearing Mr Brackenbury preach in the Isle of Portland, in 1793. She became an esteemed class-leader in 1810, welcomed all Methodist preachers to her cottage and hospitality, and was a fine specimen of primitive godliness, an Israelite indeed. When eighty-five years were passed, and the weary wheels of life were standing still, she raised her head, and whispered—

> " O let me catch a smile from Thee,
> And drop into eternity ! "

In early life, Mrs Wightman, of Belfield House, Sheffield, gave her heart to the Lord, and her support to Methodism. She attended the services at Carver Street Chapel, from the time of its opening to the end of her life. She was a member of Society for fifty-seven years, and during that time had an unwavering trust in God. The influence of her godly example was impressed upon all around her ; her last long affliction was borne with exemplary patience, and she spoke constantly in the language of praise and prayer. She repeated with much emphasis, when in great weakness of body, Charles Wesley's verse commencing—

“ In age and feebleness extreme," &c. ;

and, at the age of eighty-five, she calmly entered into rest.

When the whole county of Kent formed but one circuit in Methodism, with only two preachers to work it, under a sermon, preached at five o'clock in the morning by the Rev. John Wesley, Mr H. Hilliard was convinced of sin, sought and found pardon, and joined the Society, at Chatham, in June 1783. He had the privilege of hearing John Wesley preach nine times, and his brother, the Rev. Charles Wesley, he heard once. He was a member of Society more than eighty years, and a class-leader more than seventy years. He walked before his family and the world with a perfect heart. When death was plainly before him, he peacefully said, " I am going home to meet all my friends who have gone before me." His dying testimony was in these words : "My meditation of Christ and of His atonement is sweet, and I will thank Him. And now I have but one desire—

‘ In age and feebleness extreme,
  Who shall a sinful worm redeem ?
  Jesus, my only hope Thou art,
  Strength of my failing flesh and heart ;
  O could I catch a smile from Thee,
  And drop into eternity !’ "

His desire was granted ; a few hours later he breathed out his life, as gently as a summer wave dies on the shore, in his ninety-sixth year.

INDEX

To the incidents given in the volume, in the order of the Hymns. Those marked * are named only in the index.

The names in capitals are those of Methodist Preachers or members of their families.

Full biographical sketches will be found in the volumes of the Wesleyan Methodist Magazine named in the fifth and sixth columns.

HYMN—"In Age and Feebleness extreme," &c.

Hymns translated by John Wesley, viz. :—From the German, Hymns 23, 26, 133, 189, 190, 196, 210, 240, 241, 279, 338, 339, 344, 350, 353, 373, 341, 492, 494, 586, 610, 673, 674 ; from the French, Hymn 285 ; from the Spanish, Hymn 437.

Hymns inserted in the Collection after Mr Wesley's death, and before the Supplement was added, viz. :—Hymns 38, 39, 66, 90, 97, 107, 111, 119, 120, 143, 149, 162, 169, 213, 228, 253, 257, 263, 276, 490, 500.

THE POETICAL WORKS OF JOHN AND CHARLES WESLEY.

Date of first Publication.	TITLE.	No. of pages.	Size.	No. of Hymns.
1738	Collection of Psalms and Hymns, by John Wesley,	84	12mo	70
1739	Hymns and Sacred Poems, by John and Charles Wesley,	223	12mo	139
1740	Hymns and Sacred Poems, by John and Charles Wesley,	209	12mo	96
1741	Collection of Psalms and Hymns, by John and Charles Wesley,	126	12mo	165
1741	Hymns on God's Everlasting Love, two parts, by Charles Wesley,	84	12mo	38
1742	Hymns and Sacred Poems, by John and Charles Wesley,	304	12mo	155
1742	Collection of German Hymns, by John Wesley,	36	12mo	24
1742	A Collection of Thirty-six Tunes, set to music, as they are sung at the Foundery,	36	12mo	
1743	Collection of Psalms and Hymns, enlarged, by John and Charles Wesley,	138	12mo	138
1743	Poems on several occasions, 2d edit., by Samuel Wesley,	332	12mo	104
1744	Hymns for Times of Trouble and Persecution, by John and Charles Wesley,	47	12mo	33
1744	A Collection of Moral and Sacred Poems, 3 vols., by John Wesley,	1008	12mo	213
1744	Hymns for the Nativity of our Lord, by Charles Wesley,	24	12mo	18
1744	Hymns for the Watch-night, by Charles Wesley,	12	12mo	11
1744	Funeral Hymns, by Charles Wesley,	24	12mo	16
1745	Hymns for Times of Trouble, for the year 1745, by Charles Wesley,	69	12mo	15
1745	A Short View of the Differences between the Moravian Brethren and John and Charles Wesley,	24	12mo	6
1745	Hymns on the Lord's Supper, by Charles Wesley,	141	12mo	166
1745	A Word in Season, &c., by John Wesley,	8	12mo	2
1745	Hymns for Times of Trouble, &c., 2d edit., additional, by Charles Wesley,	22	12mo	15
1746	Hymns for Times of Trouble, by Charles Wesley,	12	12mo	6
1746	Hymns (9) and Prayers (4) for Children, [John and Charles Wesley],	12	12mo	9
1746	Gloria Patri, &c., Hymns to the Trinity, by Charles Wesley,	12	12mo	24
1746	Hymns on the great Festivals and other occasions, by Charles Wesley, with music by Lampe [2d edit., 1753],	64	4to	24
1746	Hymns of Petition and Thanksgiving for the Promise of the Father, Whit-sunday, by John and Charles Wesley,	36	12mo	32
1746	Hymns for Ascension Day, by Charles Wesley,	12	12mo	7
1746	Hymns for our Lord's Resurrection, by Charles Wesley,	20	12mo	16
1746	Graces before and after Meat, by Charles Wesley,	12	12mo	26
1746	Hymns for the Public Thanksgiving, October 9, 1746, by Charles Wesley,	12	12mo	7
1747	Hymns for those that seek and those that have Redemption in the Blood of Jesus Christ, by Charles Wesley,	72	12mo	52
1748	Hymns on his Marriage, unpublished, by Charles Wesley,			17

Date of first Publication.	TITLE.	No. of pages.	Size.	No. of Hymns.
1749	Hymns on occasion of his being prosecuted in Ireland as a Vagabond, unpublished, by Charles Wesley.			
1749	Hymns and Sacred Poems, 2 vols., by Charles Wesley,	668	12mo	455
1749	Hymns extracted from the Brethren's Book, by John Wesley,	12	12mo	20
1750	Hymns for New Year's Day, 1751, by Charles Wesley,	11	12mo	7
1750	Hymns occasioned by the Earthquake, March 8,	24	12mo	19
1753	Select Hymns for the use of Christians of all Denominations, by John Wesley,	157	12mo	149
1753	Hymns and Spiritual Songs intended for the use of real Christians, &c.,	132	12mo	116
1755	An Epistle to the Rev. Mr John Wesley, by Charles Wesley,	16	12mo	1
1755	An Epistle to the Rev. Mr George Whitefield, by Charles Wesley [first published in 1771],	16	12mo	1
1756	Hymns occasioned by the Earthquake, 2d edit.,	36	12mo	22
1756	Hymns for the Year 1756, particularly for the Fast Day, February 6, by Charles Wesley,	24	12mo	17
1758	Hymns of Intercession for all Mankind, by Charles Wesley,	34	12mo	40
1758	Hymns for the use of Methodist Preachers, by Charles Wesley,	12	12mo	10
1759	Funeral Hymns, enlarged, by Charles Wesley,	70	12mo	43
1759	Hymns on the expected Invasion, by Charles Wesley,	12	12mo	8
1759	Hymns to be used on the Thanksgiving Day, November 29, and after it, by Charles Wesley,	24	12mo	15
1761	Hymns for those to whom Christ is all in all, by Charles Wesley,	144	12mo	134
1761	Select Hymns, with Tunes annext,	318	12mo	132
1762	Short Hymns on select Passages of Holy Scripture, 2 vols., by Charles Wesley,	824	12mo	2,030
1763	Hymns for Children, by Charles Wesley,	84	12mo	100
1765	Hymns on the Gospels in MS., by Charles Wesley,			
1767	Hymns for the use of Families, and on various occasions, by Charles Wesley,	176	12mo	188
1767	Hymns on the Trinity (including Hymns and Prayers to the Trinity), by Charles Wesley,	132	12mo	182
1772	Preparation for Death, in several Hymns, by Charles Wesley,	46	12mo	40
177.	A Hymn praying for his Brother's long life, by Charles Wesley.			
1780	Collection of Hymns for the use of the People called Methodists,	504	12mo	525
1780	Hymns written in the time of the Tumults, June 1780, by Charles Wesley,	19	12mo	13
1781	Protestant Association, written in the midst of the Tumults, June 1780,	24	12mo	
1782	Hymns for the Nation, and Hymns for the National Fast Day, February 8, 1782, by Charles Wesley,	47	12mo	32
1785	Prayers for condemned Malefactors, by Charles Wesley,	12	12mo	10

By ISAAC WATTS, D.D.

1705	Horæ Lyricæ: Poems of the Lyric kind, in three Books,	299	12mo	136
1707	Hymns and Spiritual Songs, in three Books,		12mo	697
1719	New Version of the Psalms,		12mo	150

INCIDENTS NOT IN THE PREVIOUS INDEX.

PRINTED BY BALLANTYNE AND COMPANY
EDINBURGH AND LONDON

www.ingramcontent.com/pod-product-compliance
Lightning Source LLC
Chambersburg PA
CBHW032304280326
41932CB00009B/688